CGI
Programming
with
Visual Basic 5

Ofer LaOr

McGraw-Hill

New York   San Francisco   Washington, D.C
Auckland   Bogotá   Caracas   Lisbon   London
Madrid   Mexico City   Milan   Montreal   New Delhi
San Juan   Singapore   Sydney   Tokyo   Toronto

Library of Congress Cataloging-in-Publication Data

LaOr, Ofer
   CGI Programming with Visual Basic 5 / Ofer LaOr.
      p.   cm.
   Includes index.
   ISBN 0-07-913688-05
    1. Microsoft Visual BASIC.   2. CGI (Computer network protocol).
3. Internet programming.

QA76,73.B3L365   1997
005.2˙762 — dc21

McGraw-Hill

A Division of The McGraw-Hill Companies

The views expressed in this book are solely those of the author, and do not represent the views of any other party or parties.

1 2 3 4 5 6 7 8 9 0 DOC/DOC   9 0 2 1 0 9 8 7

ISBN   0-07-913688-5

The sponsoring editor for this book was Judy Brief. It was set in New Century Schoolbook by Marjorie Campolongo, freelance designer for McGraw-Hill's Professional Book Group composition unit.

Printed and bound by R.R. Donnelley & Sons Company.

McGraw-Hill books are available at special quantity discounts to use as premiums and sales promotions, or for use in corporate training programs. For more information, please write to the Director of Special Sales, McGraw-Hill, 11 West 19th Street, New York, NY 10011. Or contact your local bookstore.

Dedication

This book is dedicated to my beautiful daughter, Jordan.

This book would never be possible were it not for my wife, Orit LaOr. Being such an understanding wife, tolerating the innumerable hours that I worked on this book and the other various projects I was involved with. I love you and thank you for it.

Special thanks to Aric Levin for asking the right questions and inspiring me to write a significant amount of the code in this book.

I would also like to thank Mo Klein and Bill Parducci.

Table of Contents

Part III – oCGI and Client Side Constructs/Advanced Issues

About the Author

Introduction

This book is intended for intermediate and expert programming professionals interested in programming Internet/Intranet applications. While oriented towards Visual Basic, the lessons in this book can be quite easily adapted to work with any other development language capable of 32-bit Windows programming and access to the Win32 API.

This book assumes a good working knowledge of HTML and a good grasp of Visual Basic and database basics. Simply put, most database-oriented examples in this book will use some form of SQL statements. This book was primarily designed to generate ideas and inspire Webmasters and other web programmers as well as to demonstrate the most advanced features of Visual Basic 5.0.

In addition, this book can be used a "cook-book" or a tutorial for web application development. Several topics will be discussed that can be easily adapted to work elsewhere (e.g., client/server development and regular Visual Basic development, the live image capture, HTML parsing and more).

The oCGI Library

The oCGI library provides an extra layer above the standard CGI interface. This simplifies some of the aspects of CGI while maintaining full support for CGI. The full source code for oCGI is included and can be used *directly* instead of using the oCGI2.DLL. In addition, the oCGI library/code-samples can be easily modified to communicate with other types of servers utilizing other communication methods such as OLEISAPI2.

In most cases, however, it would be better to "dismember" the oCGI portion that manages virtual cookies and utilize it in place of adapting oCGI to work with ASP or OLEISAPI2. This is because these systems were designed to work independently of other development tools and their overall design concepts may not be completely interchangeable.

The source codes have only been fully checked for compatibility with Microsoft Web servers (IIS and PWS). Please note that IIS version 1.0 provides support for CGI/1.0 and so does not support cookies.

Software Requirements

The source code requires a working Microsoft Internet Server, preferably version 2.0 or higher. The code has been used and tested on Windows 95 using the Personal Web Server (PWS) that comes with FrontPage 97 (as well as in OSR2, or downloadable from the Internet).

The code in this book requires Visual Basic 5.0 professional edition or better. Most of the code examples will work without any modification with 32-bit Visual Basic version 4.0. In some of the advanced chapters, some VB 5.0 features have been utilized. In such places, incompatibility with Visual Basic 4.0 will be noted.

Microsoft Access 97 (or higher) should be used to access the database files. Alternatively, the Data Manager utility, which comes with Visual Basic, can be used to browse and modify the database as needed.

For the browser, this book primarily focuses on advanced browsers such as Microsoft Internet Explorer 3.0 or Netscape 3.0. Most of the code is directly applicable towards less able browsers such as Netscape 2.0. Some code-segments, primarily JavaScript code, had only been tested with IE 3.0 and Navigator 3.0 and are not guaranteed to work using other browser types.

Following is a brief look at each chapter, along with the topics presented.

Part I - Introduction to CGI programming

Chapter 1 - What is CGI? An Introduction to Web Programming

This chapter describes the purpose of CGI and its history. It includes a discussion of CGI's capabilities and current alternatives, and describes the basics of HTML programming.

Chapter 2 - CGI Programming Fundamentals

Chapter 2 introduces CGI programming to the reader without overly complex HTML information, using line drawings to show how the web server interfaces with the CGI application. It describes why PERL and C++ are currently the prime development platforms for CGI programming, and presents the oCGI library. Readers will create a simple "Hello world!" application.

Chapter 3 - Learning CGI with the oCGI Library

This chapter describes the oCGI library, its usability, alternatives and how it can be used as generic layer for communicating with the web server. This library is totally independent of any web server and greatly eases the most annoying aspects of web development. This chapter introduces the library of functions and shows the reader how to write simple web applications using the oCGI library.

Chapter 4 - Cookies and Parameters in oCGI

Chapter 4 explains how parameters and cookies are handled in oCGI, offering several alternatives for the user to access the parameter and cookie information. It explains when and how cookies can be used. This chapter develops a user-security application in an incremental manner to include parameters and cookies.

Chapter 5 - Error Handling

How should a program handle errors without causing the user or server to wait forever for the application to end? In Chapter 5, simple techniques are provided to resolve potential Visual Basic errors that may halt the user or server.

Part II - Using CGI for Real World Applications

Chapter 6 - Search Engine

This chapter focuses on creating a database independent Visual Basic search engine that can easily be inserted into any CGI application in any context. It explains how position can be retained between pages and how to implement the "Next # of records" button.

Chapter 7 - Advanced HTML and Additional Server Side Constructs

The reader learns about additional information that can be retrieved from the client and how to utilize that information for the application. Chapter 7 also discusses sending e-mail from the server and other advanced techniques, as well as using frames with a CGI application.

Chapter 8 - Shopping Bag

This explains how to implement shopping bags using client-based cookies. The design process and development process is also described. The programmer learns to implement complex CGI constructs and to harness the power of oCGI to create advanced web applications.

Chapter 9 - Security and CGI Applications

This chapter explains how to secure the shopping bag using SSL technology.

Chapter 10 - Shopping Bag, Improved

This chapter improves on the shopping bag, adding more constructs and more ways to access and order the information.

Chapter 11 - The Debugging Process

This chapter shows several techniques for debugging a web application and how to determine where a problem may lie in the application. Potential incompatibilities are described among the leading browser implementations.

Part III: oCGI and Client Side Constructs / Advanced Issues

Chapter 12 - Adding JavaScript to the Mix

This chapter shows how JavaScript can be used in conjunction with CGI to provide validation and similar uses to create a complete Internet client/server application.

Chapter 13 - Localized VB Components

This chapter shows how Visual Basic 5.0 can be used to create a client/server application using a standard web server application to interact with.

Chapter 14 - Advanced Issues

This chapter shows how to implement dynamic server pages and how the server can interact with the client. It also discusses using SQL server as the database engine, and distributing the system and load balancing for better user performance.

Chapter 15 – Active Server Pages

This chapter demonstrates writing advanced Visual Basic applications using Microsoft ASP.

Chapter 16 – What's Next?

This chapter goes over upcoming technologies.

Appendixes

Appendix A - oCGI Reference

Each function and feature of oCGI is covered, along with full documentation on the function's source code.

Appendix B - Performance Tuning CGI Applications.

Appendix B offers some tips and tricks for optimizing CGI applications, and things that slow down the application. It also covers optimizing performance using SQL server and ODBC.

Appendix C - Sending Out E-Mail

Appendix C covers encapsulating the SMTP protocol. Full source code for a VB SMTP control is included.

Appendix D - Files and libraries required by Visual Basic

Appendix B includes a listing of all dependencies required by VB CGI applications.

Appendix E - Resources

Appendix E lists resources about CGI and VB programming.

PART I

AN INTRODUCTION TO CGI PROGRAMMING

AN INTRODUCTION TO WEB PROGRAMMING

- Historical background on the Web and CGI
- Thin clients vs. "thick" clients
- Introduction of IIS, ASP, HTTP, IE4
- Web applications: how they are used and how they are created
- CGI applications vs. CGI scripts
- "Push" technology vs. "pull" technology
- CGI and the standard UNIX console streams (STDIN/STDOUT)
- CGI submission methods
- HTML forms
- Languages that can be used with CGI
- Cookies: who and what are they good for
- Web server operating systems (most prominently, Windows NT)
- Visual Basic as a CGI compatible language
- Overview of the oCGI2 library: benefits, functions and abilities
- Other techniques of interfacing between VB and web servers: a working comparison
- Other techniques of writing web applications
- Server/application interaction

Some Historical Background

Web programming is a relatively new science. Web servers showed up at a time when the bulk of servers on the Internet were UNIX servers. The first web servers were designed with easy UNIX interoperability in mind — rather than ease of use.

As the need for more dynamic and smarter content on the web grew, several forms of scripting for these web servers were required. Whereas Client/Server programming requires both the client and the server to have significant computing power, Web programming uses a thin client initiating requests to a "smart server" using "client pull" (i.e., the client must initiate all requests to the server).

The Thin Client Paradigm

The thin client paradigm took the computing world by storm, causing an explosion of activity and a worldwide rush to the web. The issues that many Information System (IS) shops were facing concerning operating system compatibility and support were easily resolved using a thin, portable client that could really work on any operating system. On the server end, IS was typically impressed by the thin client's ease of installation, and the complete lack of dependence on any one operating system or vendor (as was the case with the older Client/Server systems).

When this author was first introduced to Microsoft's new web server (IIS) 1.0, the Microsoft technical salesman had boasted that anyone could install IIS in less than 5 minutes. Selecting a user at random, he had actually demonstrated this as part of his presentation. The latest release of IIS doesn't change this concept, and it can still be installed in the same time range by a user who has no previous experience with web servers. Figure 1.1 shows a snapshot from an IIS installation.

Figure 1.1
Installing IIS

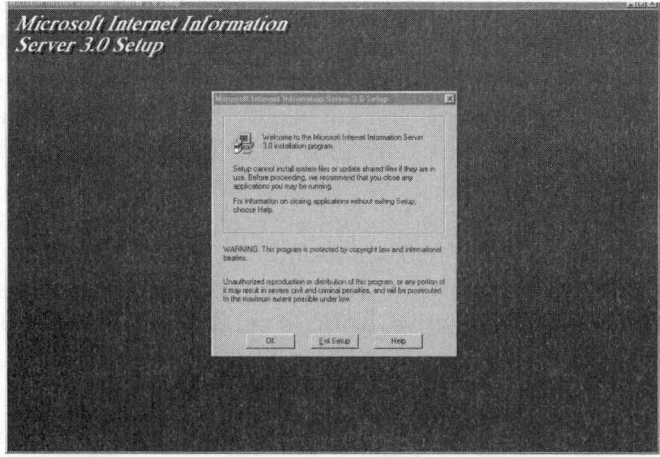

Currently there are various attempts underway to modify the thin client paradigm somewhat. There were several reasons why thin clients became so popular, interoperability being the most important. Additionally, the ease with which a thin client can run with the most confining platforms (palmtops — or, in the future, toasters…) enables applications and documents created in this fashion to work transparently, regardless of the platform they may be running on.

The thin client paradigm is ideal for a network like the Internet. (The Internet, to be politically correct about it, is unbelievably slow at times… and unbearably slow at other times!) Even users with high-speed connections often find themselves waiting impatiently for something or other to stop downloading.

Thin clients are oriented towards minimal interaction with the server, and often achieve good performance with minimal bandwidths.

Changing this paradigm is usually attempted by bringing these types of systems closer to the Client/Server methodology. These are attempts at making thin clients more interactive and closer to the other applications that users have become used to on Windows, Macintoshes and UNIX platforms. Thin clients are harder to operate, and provide minimal interaction. This often proves frustrating to the more technically aware users (which Internet browsing users often are).

Unfortunately, some of this problematic behavior is embedded quite deeply in the HTTP/1.0 protocol; and it will require substantial changes before any type of wide acceptance by the industry can take place. HTTP/1.1 makes significant strides towards improved interactivity and tackles some of the deficiencies that were inherent in HTTP/1.0. It should be noted, however, that concepts such as the connectionless session are here to stay for a while yet...

In the Interim, several techniques can be utilized in order to allow the client to become smarter or "less thin." By fusing thin techniques with traditional "thick" approaches, an application can simultaneously be interactive, utilize a small bandwidth... and work on a vacuum cleaner!

Typically, most of the popular techniques are not as efficient on the network, or client, as native Client/Server (C/S) systems. A Visual Basic C/S application typically runs significantly faster than an equivalent Java application, while requiring less CPU for the task. Similarly, JavaScript is less interactive than a native VB application. These techniques, however, allow these clients to run where Visual Basic applications cannot, and where C++ applications require a significant rewrite in order to operate. (Or, in the best case scenario — for non-graphical applications — where they require a recompilation for any particular machine.) Web-oriented applications will work transparently on any system.

Stronger attempts to create a much thicker interface usually result in making the browser sort of an "operating system within an operating system." Both Netscape and Microsoft are integrating thick components into their browsers, making them much thicker than ever before. Of course, they still support the thinner interfaces, allowing the programmer to pick and choose components along the way.

Modern browsers allow true, classic Client/Server interaction to take place — resulting in compatibility, portability and fair performance. Thicker interfaces/browsers, however, are never as portable as the older, thin browsers — since they are incredibly hard to port to low-end platforms such as palmtops, smart cellular phones and other ideal Internet platforms.

The major trend in the newer web browsers, such as Microsoft Internet Explorer 4.0 (IE4), is to merge the operating system and web browser into one generic entity. This makes it hard for a person to determine where the machine ends and the Internet begins. Integration with the operating system also allows the user to run some Internet-style components locally, further blurring the borderline between operating system and browser.

As it has become necessary to retrieve smarter, more complex information from web servers, the industry has demanded that an open technology be utilized to permit web applications to be both portable *and* easy to manage. The technology for writing such applications should allow the server to interact with a diverse group of languages and tools.

Other recent trends in browsers include "push" technology. The original idea behind standard thin clients is connectionless "pull" technology, in which the browser requests and posts information to servers. The browser, in this type of connection, is the driving force in the connection. Push technology is initiated from the web; so the information shows up on the browser.

This causes the browser to become a low-end TV set (unlike a normal TV set, which is able to show high-quality Video and stereo sound in real-time!). It is this author's opinion that users are much more interested in looking around for information they might be interested in viewing, rather than seeing what the server is interested in advertising to them... (It seems that web fans are divided on this point — some view push technology as the most significant improvement on the Internet since the invention of HTML.)

Most modern browsers utilize "scheduled pull" rather than true server push for most tasks.

The Common Gateway Interface

Because of the great variety of tools and languages found in UNIX, browser technology had to be simple, flexible and, most predominately, portable. Enter the *Common Gateway Interface* ("CGI").

CGI relies on the lowest common denominator in UNIX applications: STDIN and STDOUT. These are simple file streams which most C programmers learn in their first working program. The STDIN stream allows simple console applications to read key strokes. The STDOUT stream allows the application to print text back out to the console. Traditional console applications for operating systems such as DOS, UNIX and Windows 95/NT support STDIN and STDOUT as file streams, allowing simple programs to interact with the console (keyboard + monitor).

In UNIX, most tools and languages interact with the user through these two streams. To the programmer, these streams are easily accessible in any standard language (Pascal, C, C++, etc.). Console applications and batch files are the primary focus of these streams. Most Graphical User Interface (GUI) applications, however, do not need to interface with these streams. They utilize graphical methods instead, which are more advanced and complex than the old console interfaces (STDIN/STDOUT).

The major goal behind creating applications on the web was to make minimal changes to the existing web protocols, browsers. At the same time, portability was a key issue. CGI applications had to be able to move effortlessly between servers and UNIX platforms.

The Common Gateway Interface (CGI) was born of this need. Before this technology had become popular, true interaction with a web-based application required rewriting of the web server. Several early search engines were, in fact, modified web servers. Most of the existing commercial search engines still operate in this manner, in order to optimize the system. Since not everyone was capable of modifying the server's source code, CGI became popular in a relatively short period of time.

The concept behind CGI emulates the standard way that standard document web pages are retrieved. The idea is both simple and elegant: the remote client (usually a browser) requests the server to execute a CGI script or CGI application.

Notes

At the beginning, web programmers typically utilized C/C++ to generate the CGI applications. Since this requires a recompilation of the application in order to port it from one system to another, programmers versed in UNIX typically turned to PERL to generate CGI applications. Since PERL is an interpreted language (using PERL "scripts"), programmers called web applications written in PERL "CGI scripts." The other option, of course, was to use a conventional language (e.g., C++), in which case the application was written as a "CGI application."

When the server determines that the request references a CGI application (assuming that the server security allows this application to be accessed), the server would launch the application.

Conceptually, this is identical to the way the server would handle any web document and send it back to the browser. In this case, an intermediate application would assist the server in producing the HTML sent back, by the server, to the end-user.

Parameters are passed to the client in one of a few predefined communication methods. The browser, upon receiving the CGI application request submission, specifies this communication method through the standard request technique. The application parses and "deciphers" the parameters, based on the information sent to it by the server. The application then has access to files, databases and a host of other external resources. Using these resources, the application returns information to the server, to be ultimately transferred back to the browser that made the request.

For reasons of compatibility, only a limited set of characters can be sent between the browser and server. Because of this, shortcuts were invented that allowed any character to be sent between the web browser and the web server. These shortcuts need to be deciphered by the application, in order to work correctly. Spaces, for example, are not allowed as parameters; so spaces are converted into plus signs (+). Other characters are sent, via their ASCII code, using the percent sign.

The application returns information to the server via the STDOUT stream. This, in fact, allows the server to retrieve this information as if it were an HTML file. Applications can send back HTML tags, producing information that would show up on the browser. This information could, in turn, produce additional HTML forms which could advance the user one more step. This allows the user to proceed through screens based on input and other parameters, producing a real, web-hosted application.

The application can then create a viable flow, allowing real Intranet-style applications to be created. The application can also return any information the server will recognize — for example, sending the user an image, or other types of binary information.

Submission Methods for CGI

The CGI standard includes three distinct ways for the server to send information to the application, and one standard way to receive information back. These include GET (also known as PUT), ISINDEX and POST. Figure 1.2 demonstrates Microsoft FrontPage's form properties dialog box, which allows the form designer to select the form submission method.

Figure 1.2
Frontpage 97's form properties dialog box

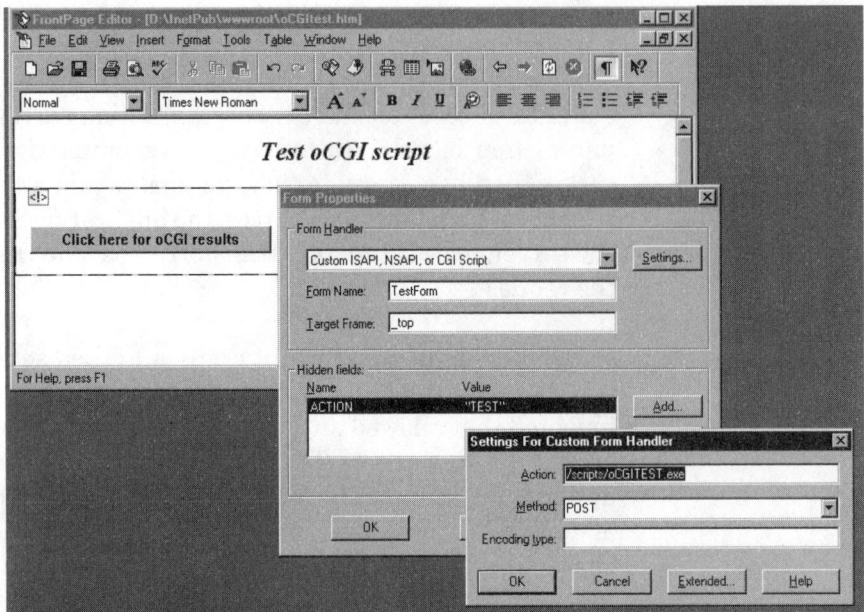

When a server interacts with a CGI application using the GET method (which is the default submission method used for standard HTML documents requested by the browser), the parameter information is passed to the client via an environment variable.

Table 1.1
Comparison of web submission techniques

Submission Method	Parameters	Additional Info
GET	Environment	Typically used to retrieve documents and initial web application page.
PUT	Environment	Typically used when submitting pages.
ISINDEX	Environment	Keeps the parameters on the browser's URL line (great when saving location to bookmarks, or when debugging an application).
POST	Command line	Most popular submission method. Less inclined to fail due to lack of environment memory space.
HEAD	None	Used to retrieve the information about a document — not the document itself.

Environment variables were, and still are, an easy-to-use method of setting system-wide parameters for applications. There are, of course, better ways to interface with system-wide information today, but environment variables are easily accessible with any language, tool and operating system. Since interoperability was a prime goal for the designers of the Common Gateway Interface, environment variables are ideal.

An alternative submission technique, which is significantly rarer, is the ISINDEX method. When using this submission method, the server sends the parameter list as command-line parameters to the CGI applications. An intended side effect of the ISINDEX posting technique allows the browser to actually view (and modify, if need be) the parameters posted to the application. This "side effect" is very beneficial in many situations (for instance, debugging, and allowing bookmarks to maintain positions or sessions in complicated application sequences).

The most popular method for transferring parameters from the server to the client is the POST method. When submitting information using the POST submission method, the server sends the information to the CGI application via the standard input stream (STDIN).

Information is always transferred back from the CGI application onto the web server utilizing the standard output stream (STDOUT).

Before any actual information is transferred between the application and the end user, the HTTP/CGI specification dictates that the application must send control information to the server. This information is used to identify the information type that will follow. For instance: is this CGI application transferring HTML, the contents of a dynamically created image, or other types of binary data to the server?

The control information can include several extended tags, including tags notifying the web client/web browser of the expiration date of the information that follows. Still other tags cause the browser to be forwarded to another web site, or set "cookie" information. For example, since weather information is only valid for a single day (it gets updated daily), a weather-reporting web site may choose to specify an expiration date on the page for tomorrow. So long as the browser is looking at the page throughout the day, the browser maintains a local copy (cached copy) of the page. When the user browses the same location the next day, however, the browser expires the cached copy of the page and retrieves an updated weather report.

When receiving this control information, the browser can prepare for incoming information and decide how it should be handled. Some types of information (e.g., HTML scripts, graphical image information) are handled natively by the browser. Other types may have "helper applications" that the server can interface with to display correctly to the user. In other situations, the user may simply want to save the file to a local disk drive.

HTML Forms

In the beginning, real applications were sorely needed on the web — which still consisted primarily of research groups and contained mostly raw, unprocessed, information. These applications ranged from simple search engines to complex information-processing systems.

To implement these applications, the old mainframe concept of "screens" was resurrected in the shape of forms. These are an integral part of the CGI concept. The concept fits perfectly, in terms of both performance gains *and* the non-interactive nature of the web (sessionless connections).

The user fills out a form with information and submits it. Once submitted, the browser connects to the server where the application is being hosted. The information contained in the form is then sent, in encoded format (allowing all ASCII characters to be sent onto the web server).

The server routes this information to the appropriate CGI application, which in turn sends the client a new form to be filled out, or produces result information. Some of these forms have information embedded in them, while others may require some user interaction (utilizing more advanced technologies). At the end of this program flow, the system presents some kind of end result. The flow is often continuous and loops through a list of different forms, always producing intermediate information.

Languages and Tools for Use with CGI

When the Internet went mainstream, more and more applications became necessary. These applications were simple, and ranged from simple hit counters and rotating ads to guest books.

Such applications do not require much intelligence. They do, however, require a great deal of flexibility. Because of the fact that non-UNIX web-servers were scarce in the beginning, flexible, native, UNIX tools were needed.

Such flexible development tools had to be able to produce portable applications. The tools had to be utilized transparently, regardless of the particular UNIX flavor or server type being used. Such tools were scarce.

The viable options included C, C++ and PERL.

- C and C++, utilizing the POSIX standard, were used to create web applications that could be recompiled for each brand of UNIX, regardless of machine type. This level of portability was not very flexible, and required a re compilation of the source code each time the CGI application needed to be changed or ported. Due to the fact that HTML was (and still is) a moving target, changes in the CGI applications were very frequent. This made C and C++ less than ideal tools for the job.

- PERL was primarily used as a high level scripting tool and batch file tool for the UNIX operating system. This was an interpreted language, and provided fairly easy access to files and STDIN/STDOUT streams. It was an ideal tool, at the time, for these web applications. Web masters were usually UNIX experts, and used PERL for their daily operations. Because of its high level of familiarity in the user community, PERL was widely adopted as the *de-facto* standard CGI scripting tool. For many people on the web, CGI is almost synonymous with PERL.

The Ominous Cookies

"Cookies" were introduced into the HTTP/CGI standards in order to overcome some of the inherent problems in the existing, CGI/1.0 standard. Cookies are small pieces of potentially persistent information located on the client's machine, easily accessible by the client's browser. They are transmitted back to the application that saved them, as it needs them, and can be used to retain client information, bookmarks, preferences, passwords, identifications, and even shopping carts. Figure 1.3 demonstrates the cookie verification dialog box in Netscape's browser.

Figure 1.3

Netscape's cookie dialog box

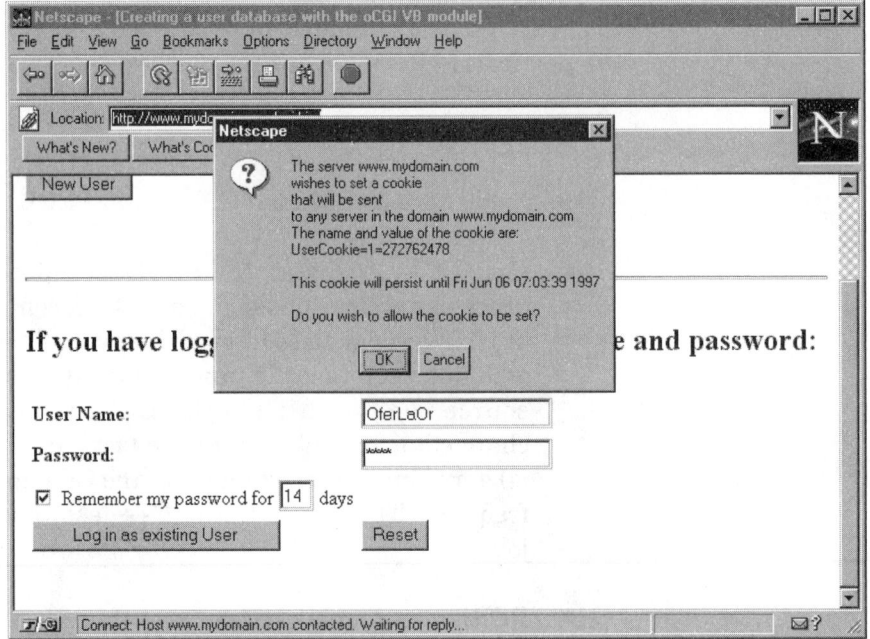

Security dictated that cookies saved by one server would *not* be accessible by another. (The specification does allow this to a degree, but only in situations where the original application saving these cookies allows for it.) Cookies are generally transmitted *just* to the original application that created them, on the server where they were originally created.

With the advent of cookies and several other improvements, the CGI/1.1 specification was born.

Web Server Operating Systems

As other operating systems were slowly adopted on the Internet, more and more web server companies ported their software to these different operating systems. Windows NT was such a system. It was designed as an application platform, thus making the web service one more application that could execute on the server.

Figure 1.4
Windows NT
start menu

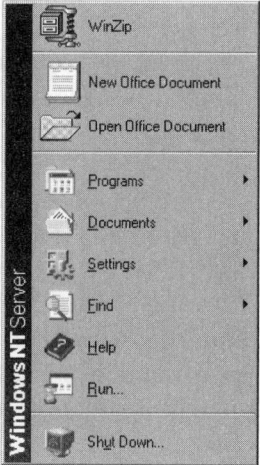

Many corporations quickly adopted Windows NT for Internet and Intranet (local corporate wide "Internet" compatible solution) servers.

Programming tools and other utilities for Windows NT were far more standardized, widely used, and popular than their UNIX counterparts. As web servers were ported to Windows NT, many web applications had to be ported over as well. Since most such applications were already written in PERL, PERL itself was ported over to Windows NT.

As the demand for web applications grew exponentially, web applications had to keep up with the times and become ever smarter. As such, PERL was much improved by companies such as Microsoft. PERL was given full access to the host of Windows NT facilities and Application Program Interfaces (APIs).

These PERL libraries, though, made PERL less and less compatible with its UNIX origins. Since the PERL language was never really meant for prime-time application development, it lacked several high-level programming facilities — such as relational database access, object orientation, and good performance.

Several web server vendors tried, at this point, to create a viable alternative to CGI. These were primarily proprietary interfaces with the server, attempting to tie an application down to a particular server or solution. But this attempt to force programmers into a closed, proprietary path was largely unsuccessful.

As web-server technology matured, Client/Server systems were gradually replaced by Intranet applications. IS shops opted for this new technology because of its reliability, stability, portability and compatibility.

The dramatic speed, however, with which this technology grew popular prevented any such alternate standard from being adopted. The alternatives to CGI were (and are) proprietary and present little or no benefit to the practical web programmer. Some of them may simplify programming to a degree — but they only cover one type of system or one type of outside access (for instance, *just* database access). Most real-life applications require a more robust, flexible development tool.

The Not-So-Near Future

The Internet community has opted for a new standard to replace some of the deficiencies in the HTTP/1.0 protocol. The HTTP/1.1 protocol will resolve issues such as multi-homing, performance of web applications, and persistence of connection (making the connection between client and server persistent, instead of requiring reconnection of the server every time a client requests more information).

Until the HTTP/1.1 protocol and its inherent modifications to the CGI specification are completely adopted by the Internet community, CGI/1.1 and HTTP/1.0 are of critical importance and will continue to serve the majority of applications on the web.

As tools grow ever smarter, the Internet community continues to search for a perfect tool to make web applications simpler and easier to program.

One very flexible, robust language is Visual Basic. This language was the catalyst in the PC's component revolution and, with the advent of Visual Basic 5, it is one of the most powerful development tools in use for the Windows operating systems today.

Visual Basic as a CGI-Compatible Language

The current Visual Basic implementation is both flexible and efficient. Visual Basic can be extended to do practically any task — from interactions with the Internet, database access, file and image processing and more. Visual Basic 4 introduced object-oriented programming to the language, as well as complete support for OLE automation. This allowed Visual Basic to create reusable components and to interact with other OLE components.

Visual Basic version 5.0 further extends this versatility in its ability to produce full-blown ActiveX controls that can be embedded in web pages and client-side web applications. In addition, VB5 presents Visual Basic ActiveX documents that allow the programmer to create and run client applications within Internet Explorer 4 web browser, an Office binder or (with the aid of Microsoft Internet Explorer) directly *in* the Windows explorer.

Due to the fact that CGI applications are console applications, several techniques — primarily work-arounds and kludgey solutions — were employed to allow Visual Basic applications to interact with web servers. These include the now infamous WINCGI solution, as well as Microsoft's OLEISAPI.

The concept behind these tools is that Visual Basic itself was unable to interact with the server, thus requiring the involvement of a mediating entity. These entities interacted with the server on its own terms (ISAPI for the Microsoft solution and CGI for the WINCGI solution), and interacted with Visual Basic using separate terms.

- OLEISAPI interacted with Visual Basic using OLE automation functions exposed by the Visual Basic application.

- WINCGI interacted with Visual Basic through a complex system of information saved in INI files.

Both of these solutions were lacking, to say the least. They were both hard to modify, completely unreliable and incredibly difficult to port from one machine/web server to another.

The assumptions that constituted the bases of these solutions resulted from a lack of understanding of how Windows NT applications really work. Because there is an apparent separation between Console applications and Graphical User Interface (GUI) applications, it was long-assumed that Visual Basic, an intensive GUI development tool, would be unable to interact with the web server as a Console application.

This is largely untrue; there is only one type of native application in Windows NT — WIN32 applications. Both Console applications and GUI applications adhere to the same emperor — Win32.

Console applications have always been capable of utilizing the full breadth of the WIN32 APIs. This enables them to do their tasks easily. Most console applications limit their use of the Win32 API to networking, memory and similar interfaces. But console applications still have the ability to utilize the user-interface functions in the API, allowing them to create windows and perform other graphic functions. The same could easily have been true of GUI applications.

Similarly, GUI applications can utilize the STDIN/STDOUT streams. This has not traditionally been used, other than in distributed applications that require rerouting of these streams in spawned applications (one such application is the Microsoft C++ development environment, which utilizes console applications and reroutes their input and output to the development system).

The ability of GUI applications to interact with STDIN/STDOUT was not very useful. Consequently, it was largely overlooked, and presented little or no benefit prior to interaction with web servers via the Common Gateway Interface. In order for a CGI application to communicate with a web server, it had to interact with STDIN/STDOUT.

STDIN is needed for use only with the POST submission method. Any type of CGI application—either using the command line or environment strings — can easily access the input information used by the other submission methods.

STDOUT is the standard method by which CGI applications send information back to the server. The server then forwards this information directly to the target web browser.

Because both the STDIN and STDOUT streams are accessible via standard WIN32 API functions, they are also accessible to Visual Basic applications. This means that, in order for a Visual Basic application to behave like a standard CGI application, it must simply import these functions and use them correctly!

Enter oCGI2

The next step was not only to enable Visual Basic to Interact with the server, but to create a layered library. This library encapsulates the functionality of the CGI input and output mechanisms, allowing the application to focus on its primary goals.

This tool has greatly simplified the development process for CGI applications utilizing Visual Basic, one of the most popular development languages of our time.

A library should buffer between the actual server access routines and the application. The oCGI library is a Visual Basic library that greatly eases the development effort involved in creating Visual Basic CGI applications. It extends the capabilities of standard CGI 1.1, making the programmer's life easier and the programming cycle shorter. This is a crucial advantage in today's quickly moving Internet technology.

The oCGI library allows the programmer to complete tasks using several different methods. The library encapsulates the "2 R's" (reading and 'riting) of communication between the server and the application. This communication works transparently, regardless of the selected submission technique.

The oCGI library parses and decodes the parameters to the application. To access parameters, oCGI presents several ways of tracking and reading these parameters for easy access to the application.

Cookies are also encapsulated in several ways. When specified, the cookies are automatically decoded and parsed for easy access by the application. Since both number and size of each individual cookie limit the user, "virtual cookies" were introduced to circumvent these issues.

Netscape browsers set the pace with a limit of 20 distinct cookies per site/application, each containing up to 4000 bytes. Subsequent implementations of cookies in browsers (read: Microsoft) follow this lead and provide similar support.

Since the sum total of cookies consists of 80,000 bytes, this "virtual cookie" system utilizes more than one cookie to construct a less confining system *within* standard cookies, while still maintaining full support for the constrictive cookie rules.

Virtual cookies can be strung together to form a single virtual cookie consisting of more than 4000 bytes. In addition, a single "real" cookie can consist of several virtual cookies, allowing more than 20 individual pieces of information to exist on the client's machine.

Utilizing this tool, which is almost completely hidden from the programmer, an Intranet application programmer can save more data than was previously possible. The results are more complex and advanced web applications.

The library itself tends to be quite simplistic, and focuses on covering the basic interaction between the server and the application.

There are presently a few other viable alternatives for programming applications for the web.

However, these are the primary benefits of oCGI over the alternatives:

- Works with any Windows NT and Windows 95 web server including Microsoft's Personal Web Server (PWS)

- Uses standard Visual Basic, not a subset or a variation

- Enables quick and easy migration from standard Client/Server (written in Visual Basic) to the web

- Provides a "protective shell" around complex CGI constructs: such as parameter passing, cookies, form submission method and more

- Provides simple functionality for providing cookie support (functions for reading and writing cookies)

- Provides "virtual cookie" functionality, that allows more than 20 cookies to be created on the client side by compressing them into more complex standard cookies

- The CGI application is oriented towards the code rather than the HTML. This allows any CGI application to be created using Visual Basic with minimal modifications, thus capitalizing on the great amount of Visual Basic code that is currently in operation

- Due to the fact that Visual Basic is used, all OLE automation objects, OCXs and other types of libraries (DLLs, remote OLE automation objects, or even DDE compatible libraries or systems) can be easily integrated into the system. ODBC objects, RDO, ADO and other high performance database libraries can be utilized for database-centric applications. Visual Basic can interface with a host of server and mainframe systems as well as other, external resources (e.g., external sensors, stock tickers, credit card stations, etc.)

The oCGI library is especially useful for diverse web or Intranet applications. This is the type of server application that is not purely a database application or form system. It includes applications that require some "intelligence"—such as an integrated shopping cart, smart search engine and a smart ordering system. Many real-world applications demand this type of diversity and flexibility.

OLEISAPI

This tool interfaces with ISAPI to give OLE automation-enabled languages (like Visual Basic) the ability to communicate with IIS.

Version 2.0 of this unsupported tool is based on better technology, and contains a second-generation interface. ISAPI is a proprietary interface, making it useful only for IIS servers. In addition, the Visual Basic applications must run as in-process DLLs in order to be processed correctly. This means that a DLL with a few badly written instructions can effectively halt the entire web server.

Most of the code in this book can easily be made to interface with OLEISAPI 2 with little effort on the part of the programmer.

Database Oriented Solutions

At times, using dedicated database tools for dynamic web applications can be difficult as well as inefficient. This is especially true in the case of extremely complex queries, or queries with complex outer joins or several unions.

This type of database access is usually hard to implement using a pure data approach and requires at least some interaction with code to be completely efficient. The mix of code and data can be difficult or even impossible to implement in database oriented web-application products (e.g., Microsoft's dbWeb). Plain CGI with Visual Basic can dramatically simplify such systems.

The combination of scripting tools and database tools usually leads to completely proprietary solutions. This often requires learning a new scripting language that may not always scale well.

Server Scripting Solutions

Recently, several scripting solutions have been added to some web servers. This simple idea provides a good alternative to PERL and even CGI.

This type of solution, however, may ultimately prove too simplistic for more complex applications. These solutions are oriented around the HTML code, instead of around the programming language. The mix of a programming language and HTML provides an easy-to-use method for inserting a small section of code into HTML. When an application requires large amounts of code, however, this mix can be both confusing and cumbersome.

Scripting solutions often involve server-licensing issues, and are most often proprietary (like Microsoft's Active Server Pages).

Microsoft's Active Server Pages is a recent addition to IIS. It was added to IIS 3.0 and should be further improved with IIS 4.0. This tool introduces server-side scripting to the IIS web server using VB Script as the integrated scripting tool. It allows one to write fully integrated web applications without ever requiring any other tool except for the web server itself. Since this is a proprietary system (there are, however, third party "ASP compatible" products adding this functionality to some of the other popular web servers) it presents a problem when planning to port to other web servers and/or systems.

In most cases, these scripting solutions simply allow the programmer easy access to interface with a Visual Basic project. The code presented in this book can work with any such system, with minimal modification.

oCGI and the Alternatives: A Completely Subjective Comparison

The fact that oCGI is oriented around Visual Basic allows the existing accumulated Visual Basic expertise to be maintained without new learning curves. Code that was written for a standard 32-bit Visual Basic 4 program can be easily ported to work as a web application with little or no changes to the bulk of the code. Visual Basic 5 will only compile for 32-bit — all VB5 applications will work here! Bound controls and the user-interface can be ported to the client using the Visual Basic 5 ActiveX user-documents. This, however, will only work with Microsoft browsers (Microsoft Internet Exporer 3.0 or higher).

Standard oCGI applications work transparently within any operating system that sports the standard browsers (for instance, Netscape Navigator 3.0 or higher, or Microsoft Internet Explorer 3.01 or higher).

Here are the alternatives to oCGI and how they measure up:

1. **ISAPI** — ISAPI's great flaw (and benefit) is that it is proprietary. This prevents one from using it in any other context other than Microsoft Web servers (and the very few supporting web servers). While IIS makes for a good server, there are many sites that already utilize another server solution and would still require a good solution.

    ISAPI requires that the application be written in C++. In fact, writing an ISAPI application is no minor programming assignment. There aren't that many applications out there that the programmer can reference.

C++ has great performance. It does, however, come with several price tags. Debugging is extremely hard to do (especially with complex applications or access to database/ODBC resources). Run-time errors and protection faults in an application can easily cause the server to crash or stop working (CGI applications run under a different context, and so will only slow down the server, not crash it!).

Application development is difficult, and there is little support for such development. Support for database development is poor and somewhat complex.

Porting code to other servers can be a substantial chore, and porting existing Client/Server code to C++ is no minor task.

ISAPI uses in-process DLLs, which run in the same virtual machine context as the web server itself. While improving performance, this also leaves the web server vulnerable to application errors that could occur in these DLLs. One DLL can easily overwrite the server's variables, with no apparent conflict or application error! The DLLs can also interfere with one another, or cause an application error that will stop both the server and the other ISAPI applications.

Since each application consists of a single DLL, the application must keep connection-specific variables in several locations linked by the connection itself. This makes for a somewhat complex application. All other variables must be kept local, since both global and static variables will be shared by all connections.

Since all of the connections run off the same DLL, a bug can easily compromise security by transmitting information meant for one connection to another. This is quite harmful when user-specific information is involved (e.g., credit card information).

Performance may require that each connection get a dedicated thread; the application must synchronize these threads *and* make sure that all threads are closed to prevent a continuous increase in threads. These issues are presented here due to the high level of expertise programmers must have, in order to accomplish relatively simple tasks.

High costs are usually associated with C++. This is a complex language, with a relatively high (and long) learning curve. Programmers who possess a profound understanding of C++ are a rare breed, and generally require a significant amount of monetary compensation in order to show off their talents (compared to programmers for other languages, that is). For this reason, C++ is usually not cost-effective for most web applications.

ISAPI is great for writing dedicated server extensions (such as an application that filters accesses to the server, performs redirection on specific URLs, does server-side includes or tracks server access accounting).

2. **OLEISAPI** — This tool was created to allow true VB programming on the server. It calls OLE automation objects from a web application (ISAPI).

    There are many problems related to the use of OLEISAPI. Primarily, it is not a very secure solution. A hacker can potentially use any OLE automation interface on the server — opening the door for many types of attacks.

    Since ISAPI is used as a back-end tool, this type of application can easily bring down the server or cause server application errors.

    Visual Basic applications written with OLEISAPI are extremely hard to develop and debug. OLEISAPI is primarily used as a tool for providing the server with simple OLE automation support. Writing the OLE automation functions in Visual Basic requires that the client application be either:

    a) A multi-create application; 3 instances of the program would all be using the same global variables.

or

    b) A single-create application; each instance would have its own global variables.

Programming without global variables using the multi-create option (the current user name, session number, etc.) is a complex task, since all of the information must be passed via function parameters. This substantially complicates the application and may lower its performance.

Using the single-create option forces the server to create a new instance of the application for every new user-connection. While easier to program, this reduces the performance improvement of using ISAPI DLLs by incurring the cost of application initialization with each browser request.

Debugging OLE automation DLLs is hard to do. It can be done, however, when approached correctly, using the new Visual Basic debugging facility.

Even if each instance of the program is thread safe, heavy processing — usually because of endless loops and other problems — may cause IIS to choke and die (whereas CGI applications simply slow down the system without stopping anything from working).

Cookies are impossible to create using OLEISAPI 1. Parsing cookies and parameters has to be done by the application.

OLEISAPI is very version dependent; a new version of the web server (e.g., IIS version 1.0 to version 2.0) may require a code update in OLEISAPI! This is because of the close connection between ISAPI and OLEISAPI. Often, this can delay a bug fix or upgrade to the web server until a new version is distributed (since it is an unsupported tool, this may take quite a bit of time).

The advanced features and code in oCGI and the rest of the book can still be utilized with OLEISAPI applications with minimal, easy changes.

OLEISAPI version 2.0 frees itself from some of the restrictions that were inherent in version 1.0 (cookie support, multi-threaded design). Still, this component suffers from mediocre performance, minimal support, and little or no example code.

In addition, the library still does not provide some of the extended functionality of oCGI — such as Virtual Cookies.

OLEISAPI has the benefit of being able to expose several functions in one application, while not requiring a workaround such as an "ACTION" or position parameter. This is due to the fact that the OLEISAPI library can embed its own information into the query string (the complete OLE class and function name to be called). DCOM can now limit and block OLE automation calls, resulting in greater security for OLE automation under NT 4.0.

Microsoft has created a similar tool that converts CGI calls to OLE automation object function calls. This tool has been largely ignored by the industry, and is similar enough to OLEISAPI so that it is not necessary to elaborate on it.

3. **NSAPI** — Netscape's proprietary answer to ISAPI; it has minimal support in the industry. NSAPI suffers from the same inherent weaknesses as ISAPI.

    This interface's only improvement over ISAPI is that it is compatible across Netscape web servers running under different platforms. This provides for a limited form of portability among tools of the same vendor.

    NSAPI requires substantial knowledge of C++. It is as difficult to maintain, port and debug as ISAPI. There aren't many code samples nor real-world examples of this technology, since most Netscape shops utilize PERL or other CGI languages to write applications for the web.

4. **WINCGI** — This kludge of a workaround allows limited support of CGI by Visual Basic, using an INI file for communication between a generic CGI application and the target application. Microsoft created an ISAPI DLL that implements this protocol while running under IIS. The tool is unsupported, and is mentioned here only to complete the picture.

    WINCGI is extremely inefficient, and provides little or no support to advanced HTTP/CGI constructs (like HTTP tags, cookies, different content types). The library provides only the simplest functionality in interaction between application and server. By not providing the extended functionality of oCGI, the application must perform these functions by itself (e.g., parameter parsing, cookies, Virtual Cookies, etc.).

Although fairly popular (because it was the first tool allowing languages such as Visual Basic to become "CGI enabled"), this tool is neither widely supported nor sufficiently portable to be a serious contender.

5. **SSI** (Server Side Includes) — This technique is primarily used in situations where the server needs to be able to implant or interface with a standard HTML page.

Ideally, this tool might be used to insert a standard logo onto all of a server's pages, or to put a standard hit counter on a page. Adding the SSI code into the HTML is a fairly simple task.

SSI is ideal for creating plug-in components for HTML (e.g., hit counters) but does not provide an easy method for creating complete, stand-alone applications. In order to create these, another method should be used (ISAPI or CGI).

6. **PERL** — This tool is a simple scripting language for UNIX. The language was designed to create simple batch files and similar tasks for people familiar with the C language.

Because of the popularity of web servers on UNIX and the lack of any other good scripting tool, this tool was commonly used for simple web development when it was in its infancy.

More recently, PERL was ported to Windows NT in order to support the existing UNIX web applications code base. Presently, the vast majority of web applications that need to be created will not opt for PERL due to lack of public support, experienced programmers, or sufficient portable programming constructs. Overall, PERL makes for an awful web application development solution.

PERL is a hard-to-read language, being born of C (the ultimate in hard-to-read languages...). It is also hard to maintain and support.

Because of local customization and great number of variations and versions, large amounts of PERL code are no longer very portable. Although PERL 5 has become somewhat of a standard, it still lacks standard support for portable, modern constructs (OLE automation is only supported on limited versions, ODBC support, MAPI support, etc.). Existing code will not port well into PERL. In most cases, a local variation of PERL is required to gain access to system specific facilities (OLE automation, ODBC, MAPI, etc.).

The lack of advanced programming constructs (object orientation is only supported in a very limited fashion, there are no collections, no information hiding or polymorphism, etc.) makes PERL a less-than-ideal tool when considering today's advanced language market.

PERL has little or no debugging capabilities — so the programmer can only use his wits and trial and error for real-world application Quality Assurance (QA). PERL has no native database library support, and it is an interpreted language like Visual Basic 4.0 — which means they have a comparable efficiency factor. (Visual Basic 5, on the other hand, is more efficient than PERL.) Finally, PERL scripts cannot reuse a component such as a function, module or class.

7. **C++** — Using C++ to create CGI applications usually yields better results than using PERL. It has substantial debugging capabilities and is a very efficient and portable solution.

Many tools exist to verify that the application is working correctly and minimize the chance for an error or bug. The low-level nature of this language, however, results in bugs that often cause application errors and similar protection faults.

The database accessibility of C++ is difficult to program. Few frameworks exist for doing standard CGI operations (such as parameter parsing, cookies, etc.) in C++. MFC and other similar tools cannot be used, because CGI applications are console applications and do not utilize the graphical user interface for MFC.

Most of the constructs in Microsoft's development toolbox rely on MFC for functionality (including MAPI, Winsock class solutions, and database access).

In recent versions, this has been improved somewhat with the advent of the ATL library. It is the author's hope that this will finally separate MFC and the rest of the class libraries, allowing console applications to utilize these classes for shorter development cycles.

Other development platforms such as Borland C++ (C++ builder) completely separate the user interface libraries from the other classes in a truly object-oriented fashion. This allows a programmer to create very complex CGI application constructs while still being able to utilize most of the code in Borland's support libraries.

The cost of maintenance is high because of the high-level programmers/consultants needed to maintain the code.

Most existing client/server systems were not written in C++ and will not port well into C++ without undergoing a complete restructuring and design process. This can be as complex as rebuilding an entire application from scratch.

8. **Database oriented custom solutions** (e.g., IDC, dbWeb, Cold-Fusion) — This type of database scripting tool allows the user to provide an HTML interface to database queries. This can be quite useful, unless the system requires any type of programming.

These tools are powerful when accessing a single query or table. When multiple queries need to be referenced using information from external resources, however, the hard work needs to take place in transact SQL or Access code modules in order to work correctly (i.e., not within the tool itself).

For example, when displaying the content of a user's shopping bag, the application should also display some of the advanced features of each item included in that bag.

If the information for each item depends on the user security level and other factors (each in a different table in the database), this cannot be done easily utilizing a single query.

Since most of these tools require the programmer to use a single query, though, the programmer is forced to create a considerably complex query. (This query is also likely to be inefficient.) A similar application created in Visual Basic could split the query into any number of smaller, more efficient queries. This is an example of environment forcing the programmer in the wrong direction.

9. **Server side scripting—Active pages / VBScript / JavaScript—** Scripting languages lack most of the advanced features found in true development languages such as Visual Basic. These scripting languages are usually comparable in performance with standard CGI applications, but are not always portable between servers (VBScript cannot be ported to UNIX servers, for example) server side, nor can application be easily ported to them.

Additionally, this type of solution is oriented around HTML, rather than the code. As previously mentioned, this is bad for an application with a substantial code base.

ASP and other tools are both server and version dependent; they must be included in every new version of the web server. This is by no means guaranteed by the creator of the server. In addition, newer versions of this tool may not be backward-compatible with the existing version. It will most likely require an investigation on the part of the programmer every time a new version of the web server is about to be distributed.

This type of script is not reusable, since code has to be replicated between each server script file (e.g., ASP files). Functions and modules must be replicated in each script file — which makes debugging, development and support of more complex applications nearly impossible.

These solutions are mostly proprietary, tying the solution to one particular vendor and server type. The programming language is usually strong enough for simple web applications;

stronger applications would require strong interaction with an external application (e.g., Visual Basic application). Performance, in such situations, is often poor, because of the number of "middle-men" that interact in the application.

There are currently no real debugging tools out there for this type of server-scripting language (a few are in the works, though).

Development systems such as FrontPage 97 provide minimal support for server-side scripting. The only development platform for such applications is Microsoft's Visual InterDev, which is a first-generation development product and still needs some refinement. Even with Visual InterDev, a programmer still has lots of work ahead of him to create a fully functional application using pure VBScript.

These tools show significant improvements over previous attempts, however. The GLOBAL.ASA file in Active Server Pages, for example, provides the ability to reuse a component throughout a connection session. Allocating a server-side ActiveX library, whose lifetime spans that of the connection, allows this feature to work. The library can supply the user with any number of server-side functionality; of course, the library can be created using Visual Basic (in fact, this is what Microsoft had in mind when creating it). It should be noted that ASP will not operate correctly, should a cookie-disabled browser connect to it!

10. **Index servers** — This type of construct functions as search engine for files on the web server—HTML or otherwise. It does not, however, provide a good solution for searches in existing databases. By using the generic search engine, searches can easily be conducted on any database supported by Visual Basic and ODBC (i.e., any windows database and Client/Server database system).

Server/Application Interaction

The interaction between the CGI application and the server is by means of the *Hypertext Modeling Language* (HTML). This language is very simple and was designed to be easily extended and customized. Different variations of HTML can coexist and still work on different browsers. The most popular browser makers are constantly adding features to their list of supported HTML functionality (usually by adding new, proprietary HTML tags), making the programmer's job — of keeping the application compatible across all browsers — close to impossible. Figure 1.5 demonstrates HTML code in FrontPage 97, with HTML tags color-coded.

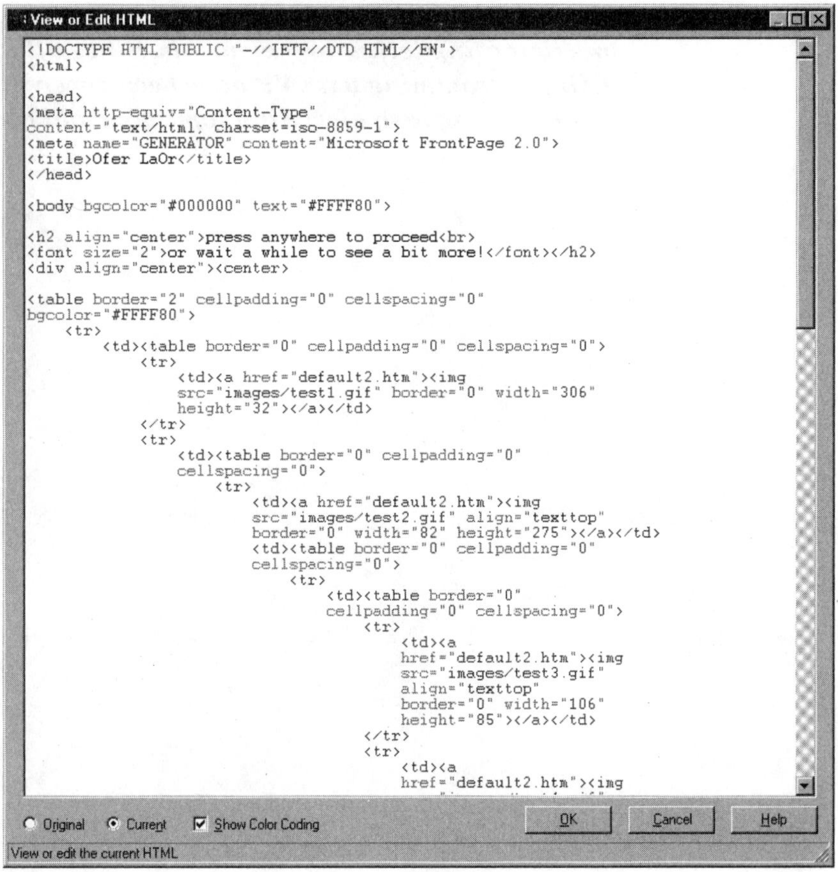

Figure 1.5
Color-coded HTML source in FrontPage 97

This book will only focus on the most popular of browsers: Microsoft Internet Explorer (version 3.0.x or higher) and Netscape Navigator (version 3.x or higher).

Most of the code in this book *will* work with other browsers, but it has only been tested with Netscape/Microsoft browsers for complete compatibility. Special care should be taken in the chapters utilizing JavaScript, due to the volatile nature of browser support for this language. JavaScript as a language currently lacks any formal standards.

Summary

In this chapter we have given a fairly broad description of how the web is structured, and described some of the major participating technology elements. Since all of the alternatives to CGI programming with VB have been covered, we can move on to the daunting task of writing some good old code.

CGI PROGRAMMING FUNDAMENTALS (CGI PRIMER)

- Communication between browser, server and application
- How URLs are parsed
- Referencing the oCGI library in a VB application
- Registering the oCGI2.dll (or other ActiveX components) on the target server
- Major differences between how VB4 and VB5 can be used for CGI applications
- A simple "hello world" VB CGI application
- Security and Execute access rights
- A simple guest-book web application
- Web form behavior
- Running CGI applications from command line

The communication between CGI applications, the web server and the CGI applications can be easily explained using Figure 2.1.

Figure 2.1
The interaction between web server, CGI application and the browser

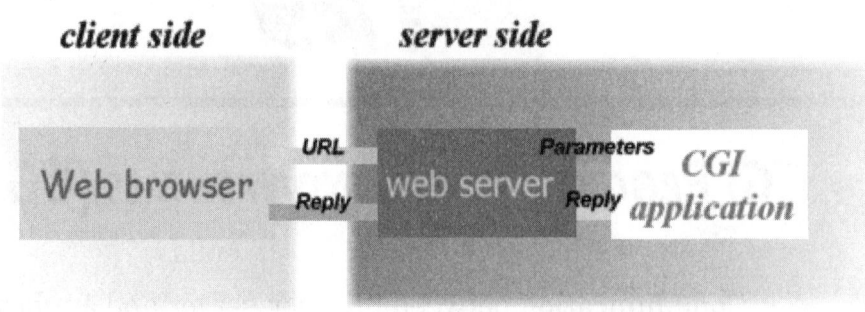

Figure 2.1 describes the flow of information from client to web server to the CGI application, and back to the client.

The client initiates contact with a request to the server. This can be a result of the user clicking on a hyperlink, pressing a button, or even specifying the exact script and parameters to the server. It is done using the Universal Resource Locator (URL). The URL is composed of the following sections:

```
http://www.someplace.com/scripts/myscript.exe?Param1=_
        value1&Param2=value2
```

`http://` — This specifies that the browser will communicate with the server using the Hypertext Transmission Protocol (HTTP). This is the standard method of communicating with the server over an unsecured channel. A secure variation on this theme, `https://` is used for communicating securely with web servers.

```
http://www.someplace.com/scripts/myscript.exe?Param1=_
        value1&Param2=value2
```

`www.someplace.com/` — This is translated into an IP address by the browser. Once the server's IP address is determined, the browser can communicate with it using TCP sockets.

```
http://www.someplace.com/scripts/myscript.exe?Param1=_
           value1&Param2=value2
```

`Scripts/myscript.exe` — This specifies what document the browser would like to see. The web server determines the type of document by the extension. The server determines that this is a CGI application by the .exe extension. Since the server determines that this is a script, it will first determine that the /scripts/ directory (sometimes called the /cgi-bin/ library) allows scripts to be executed. The question mark signals the end of the script name and the beginning of the parameter list.

```
http://www.someplace.com/scripts/myscript.exe?_
         Param1=value1&Param2=value2
```

`Param1=value1&Param2=value2` — This is the parameter list for the application. Each parameter name (e.g., Param1) is on the left of an equal sign; the value is on the right (e.g., value1). Parameters are separated with an ampersand. Symbols are "mangled" with %xx (xx is the ASCII code for the character symbolized). When the browser uses this notation, information is passed to the client via the GET method. When using the ISINDEX method, the browser is forced to actually display the parameters as part of the submission string. When using the POST and GET methods, the browser does not show the parameter string as part of the URL.

In order to create a simple web application which simply places a static text of "Hello world!", the oCGI library must first be installed. (This has traditionally been the first program taught to new programmers in conventional, console-enabled languages.)

The oCGI library was created by the author, and encapsulates most of the CGI related functionality for the Visual Basic application. It can be modified or used as is by the reader, and is included on the CD accompanying this book. The contents of the library were created using Visual Basic, and the source code for the library is also included with the book.

In order to install oCGI, some files should be copied to the directory where your application will be created. The following files should be copied there: `oCGI2.dll`, `oCGI.hlp` (`VBCrash.frm` should also be copied when developing with Visual Basic version 4.0). Once this is done, open Visual Basic with a new project. Remove the initial form that is displayed, and disable any unnecessary OCX controls (you can do this by right-clicking on any of the controls in the control bar, pressing the **Components** menu and checking off every single control in the list.)

At this point, the oCGI library can be installed by selecting the **Project | References** menu. Once there, click on the browse button and select the oCGI2.dll file, then press **OK** to exit.

If the oCGI2.dll is already registered in the system, the entry should show up as **"oCGI2 — by Ofer LaOr"** in the reference list. If not, the browse button in the references dialog box will allow the programmer to select the DLL explicitly for reference.

Referencing oCGI2 in a project allows the developed application to interact with oCGI, its functions and variables without actually linking the code statically. Rather, the application binds to the oCGI library while the application is running. The oCGI library is an in-process DLL, which means that each application has its own version of oCGI in its virtual machine context (rather than having one central library serving various applications at once). This is necessary in order to allow oCGI to interact with the web server correctly.

You may use the object browser (press **F2**) and select **oCGI** from the combo box to browse the functionality embedded in oCGI. This also allows the context-sensitive on-line help to take effect in Visual Basic.

If the oCGI library has already been registered, all that needs to be done is to select on the check box next to **oCGI2 — by Ofer LaOr** in order to assimilate the oCGI functionality into a project. Figure 2.2 demonstrates how the oCGI library can be referenced in Visual Basic.

Figure 2.2
Referencing oCGI in VB

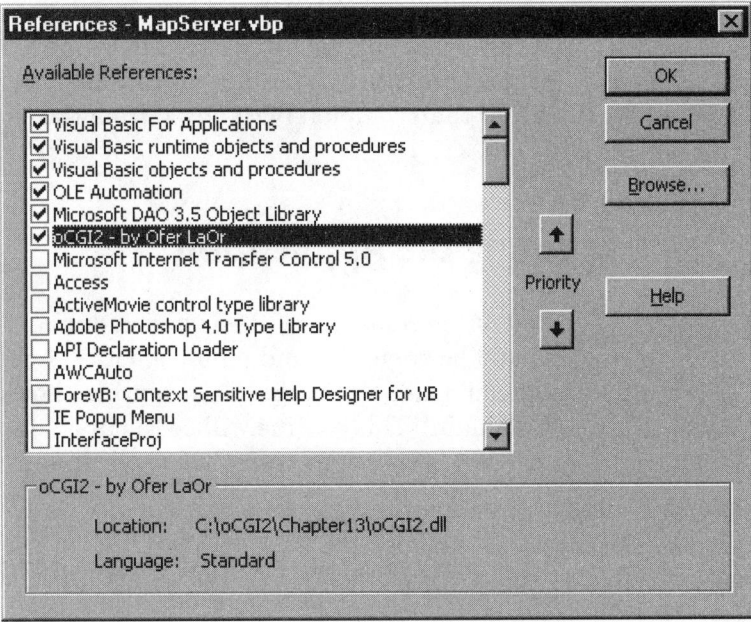

Visual Basic 4.0

Visual Basic 4.0 was never meant to be used as a console application. In fact, certain parts of Visual Basic depend on the fact that it has at least one open window handle. By creating a Visual Basic application which runs as a console application and does not even have a single form, Visual Basic tends to fault every once in a while. To prevent this, add the VBCrash form to your project.

This form should be loaded as the first thing your application does. Once the application is complete, it can be closed. Loading this form provides the application with a window handle. Having a window handle allows some of Visual Basic 4's more finicky components to work without a hitch.

Visual Basic 5.0

DAO 3.5, as well as several other components of Visual Basic that used to crash while running under the context of a web server (or even a console window), now work perfectly. For this reason, the subsequent code in this book will not load or reference the Vbcrash form. This code has been commented out in most situations in order to clarify this point, rather than completely removed from the sample applications.

Creating the Application

Any forms that Visual Basic added during the creation of the project should be removed, and a new module should be added to the project instead. Once there, the main routine should be added to the module (Sub Main). This routine will be the first subroutine executed when the web server launches your CGI application.

Due to the fact that oCGI is an OLE automation server (a.k.a., an ActiveX server application), it must be registered in order to operate correctly. If the application is developed on the target web server, Visual Basic will take care of registering the library when the project references the **oCGI.dll** file.

When dealing with a target server where the library (or any OLE enabled application, for that matter) needs to be registered, the task of registering the library can be a bit stickier.

In situations where you have full control over the web server, you can simply launch the **RegSvr32.exe** application with the full path to **oCGI.dll** as a parameter (**RegSvr32.exe** can be found in the Tools directory on the Visual Basic CD.

This is often inapplicable in situations where the programmer has only remote access to the server (e.g., FTP access, or via the FrontPage extensions).

In these situations, the application must register **oCGI2.dll** itself in order to operate correctly. This will be demonstrated in our first sample application.

It should be noted that registration is only required when **oCGI2.dll** has never been registered before, or when the library is modified and a new version installed.

When multiple versions of oCGI exist on the same server, each application may constantly try to register its own version, causing significant problems. This problem occurs for every DLL or OCX that has several working versions in the same environment. In this case, the simplest resolution is to statically link oCGI's modules (two class modules — oCGI and ParamType) by adding them to the project. Doing so causes the local copy of the classes to be used, rather than relying on the global version of oCGI.

When using OLE automation, objects contained in Executables can be easily registered by simply executing the application once. This technique, however, cannot be used with DLLs and OCXs, since they cannot be executed.

Registering ActiveX Components "On the Fly"

In the old days of 16 bits, the programmer could simply load and unload a 16-bit DLL/OCX to make it register itself. Since this carried significant overhead when no registration was needed, 32-bit libraries did away with this technique.

Most OCXs assume that they will be installed and registered by a setup program. In fact, other than copying files, this is the primary task for most setup programs. Actually, the library (OCX or DLL) registers itself, but the setup program triggers the registration process. External entities that know how to trigger the registration process, such as `RegSvr32.exe`, can register a control or library.

These libraries simply expose a standard function, named "DllRegisterServer" which is called by the registering entity (generally by `RegSvr32.exe` or an application's setup application). Once this function is called, the registration code in the library takes over and makes sure that library is correctly installed.

Development tools that create ActiveX components or OLE automation objects, such as Visual C++ and Visual Basic, automatically create this function and take care of the code behind it. The Application wizard in Visual C++ does this when creating OCXs and DLLs.

The oCGI library is an in-process DLL. This library executes within the same virtual-machine context as the application that launched it. Since oCGI requires complete access to the memory and virtual machine context of the calling application, it has to be created as such a DLL.

While Visual Basic executables verify their registration upon execution, since oCGI is a DLL, it must be registered prior to use.

Visual Basic applications can easily declare and utilize the registration function. This should be done prior to using the oCGI library, and allows the library to register itself. Once registered, the application can use all of the ActiveX functionality embedded in oCGI.

Registering oCGI

The following is the declaration statement that will register oCGI, providing that **oCGI.DLL** exists in the path or in the same directory as the application.

```
Declare Function oCGIRegister Lib "oCGI.dll" Alias _
    "DllRegisterServer" () As Long
```

The following code is the complete source code for HELLOWORLD.BAS:

```
Option Explicit

Declare Function oCGIRegister Lib "oCGI.dll" Alias _
    "DllRegisterServer" () As Long

Sub main()
On Error GoTo NormalErr
    oCGIRegister
    'Load frmVBCrash

    Dim cgi As New oCGI
    cgi.ProcessCGI Command

    cgi.WriteCGI "<HTML>"
    cgi.WriteCGI "<HEADER><TITLE>My first web_
        application</TITLE></HEADER>"
```

```
        cgi.WriteCGI "<BODY>Hello world!!!</BODY>"
        cgi.WriteCGI "</HTML>"

        Set cgi = Nothing
        End
NormalErr:
        End
End Sub
```

Please note that this is by no means the best implementation of a web application; it is simply the quickest and easiest to explain. Subsequent code will be written using stricter guidelines.

Breaking Down The Code

```
Option Explicit
```

This prevents Visual Basic from assuming that typos are actually undeclared variables. It is always a good idea to use this line, as it can prevent many silly bugs from occurring.

```
Declare Function oCGIRegister Lib "oCGI.dll" Alias _
    "DllRegisterServer" () As Long
```

This statement declares the oCGI registration function (Found in oCGI.dll under name DllRegisterServer). The function can be called from VB as oCGIRegister and returns a long return value.

```
Sub main()
```

Signifies the beginning of the main subroutine.

```
On Error GoTo NormalErr
```

This notifies Visual Basic that any subsequent errors will automatically cause VB to jump to NormalErr (which in turn, ends the application). Due to the fact that Visual Basic's default behavior is to show a message box when such an error occurs, as a console application, the server will assume that your application is still running and will subsequently keep waiting for it to end.

The web server prevents the message box from being displayed. The application, however will continue to wait for the message box to terminate (it is a modal form).

Since the web server is unable to press the **OK** button, the application will not terminate until the next system reboot. This not only takes up memory and valuable resources on the web server, it also prevents the programmer from being able to replace the executable with a new version (which hopefully fixes whatever it was that caused the error in the first place).

By placing a global Main Error Handler, the application will, at the very least, be able to terminate gracefully. In later examples, more complex error-handling techniques will allow the programmer to handle such errors more gracefully, or allow the programmer to determine what initially caused the error.

oCGIRegister

Calling this function re-registers the oCGI library every time the application is executed. This can be a bit costly, due to the large number of registry entries that the DLL needs to validate and modify in order for the ActiveX library to operate correctly.

Future examples will demonstrate how to execute this registration process only after it has been determined that the oCGI library has not been registered correctly. This ultimately lowers the application overhead.

Load frmVBCrash

As previously noted, this line is not required when using Visual Basic 5.0 or higher.

In Visual Basic 4.0, this line should be uncommented. It loads the *frmVBCrash* form. As was mentioned before, certain components of Visual Basic 4.0 require that a valid form be activated when the Visual Basic application is launched as a console application.

By launching a simple form, the Visual Basic components requiring an active window will be satisfied. DAO 3.0 running under Visual Basic is such a component. To test this, a simple Visual Basic 4.0 project containing minimal database access utilizing DAO 3.0 can be executed from the Windows NT command-line.

```
Dim cgi As New oCGI
```

This statement both declares (dim) and creates an instance (new) of the oCGI library. There should only be one concurrent, global oCGI variable in your application. This would typically be a global variable, due to the fact that most of your applications' functions require complete access to it. The creation and declaration of the cgi variable can be combined as shown, or separated using the following code:

```
Dim cgi As oCGI
Set cgi = New oCGI2
```

```
cgi.ProcessCGI Command
```

This statement causes the oCGI library to process the parameters and cookies. In this case, it is not necessary (since there are no parameters or cookies). The statement has been included for completeness.

```
cgi.WriteCGI "<HTML>"
cgi.WriteCGI "<HEADER><TITLE>My first web _
    application</TITLE></HEADER>"
cgi.WriteCGI "<BODY>Hello world!!!</BODY>"
cgi.WriteCGI "</HTML>"
```

These lines send HTML back to the server (which, in turn, transfers the HTML stream, in turn, to the client browser). It is usually more efficient to collect as much of the HTML into a variable by creating a local string variable and concatenating the HTML as needed. This minimizes unnecessary duplication of function, and provides more efficient communication with the web server.

```
Set cgi = Nothing
```

This causes the oCGI library to be freed. It should also be done at every conceivable exit point from the system (e.g., between lines 15 and 16).

```
End
```

This causes the application to terminate. In VB5, where there usually isn't an active form running, this line can be substituted with an **Exit Sub** statement. When there are forms running, the application will not terminate until those forms are explicitly (unload MyForm) or implicitly (End) removed from the system. Keeping the application running will maintain the link between client and server "forever."

In Visual Basic 4, the frmVBCrash form remains loaded as long as the application is still running. The End statement simply forces VB to terminate all running forms (e.g., frmVBCrash) and close all of the resources that haven't been explicitly closed by the application.

```
NormalErr:
    End
```

This depicts the global error handler. The handler will catch errors that have not been explicitly handled by functions called by the Main subroutine. This allows your application to handle and recover any error gracefully.

There are exceptions to this rule. For instance, not being able to connect to ODBC sources via standard DAO methods usually forces an ODBC logon form to be shown on the server — thereby stopping the application without allowing it to recover (in the same manner that *MsgBox* or an error would).

There are solutions for this type of error, too, which we will discuss in Chapter 5.

```
End Sub
```

This signifies to Visual Basic the termination of the main procedure and, incidentally, of the application.

Figure 2.3 shows the results of the "Hello World" application as it shows up on the user's browser.

Figure 2.3
Hello World results

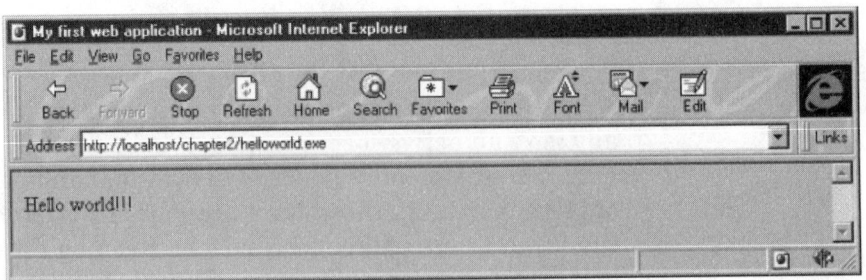

This application is extremely simple, and only shows how CGI applications send outgoing information to the web server. Most web applications must be able to both send and receive information from the web server.

Security and Execute Rights

Two levels of security rights exist on Windows NT servers when an application is created on a web server. The first is the standard NTFS file security (this does not apply in cases where the web server uses a FAT disk for web hosting) which should allow the web user *read* access to the particular file and directory being referenced.

UNIX servers — although inapplicable here (since we're dealing with VB, a Windows NT and Windows 95 only, language) — usually rely on file security only, and do not add additional levels of security on top of that. This is due to the fact that UNIX file security is more advanced, and already contains most of the security facilities required by the web server.

The user will be running under the context of the particular web server. Microsoft web server, for example, creates a new user called: IUSR_XXXX (XXXX stands for the computer name running the web server). All CGI applications will run under that user context — so the user should be allowed at least *read* access to the CGI application. Additional security rights (e.g., *write* or *delete*) should generally be handed out cautiously, in order to prevent unwanted deletions by the application.

The second set of security rights on NT web servers is provided by the web server itself. It distinguishes between directories that allow simple *read* access rights (directories containing HTML files, images, or other user data) and applications (*execute* access rights). This level of security must be changed in the management utilities provided by the web server.

In order for the "hello world" application to operate correctly, the virtual directory on the web server that `helloworld.exe` is running in must be allowed to execute.

The web server itself provides two levels of security:

- *Read* — This enables the browser to read a particular file.

- *Execute* — This allows the browser to cause an application to execute if it is in the directory in question.

When a directory is given no rights, simple HTML files cannot be read. Scripts cannot be executed on such a directory, either.

When a directory is given *just read* rights, the browser can read simple HTML files in that directory. Scripts, however, will not execute in such a directory by the server.

When a directory is given *execute* rights, scripts can execute, but simple HTML files cannot be read. This prevents the browser from downloading any code from the server. Rather, the user is only allowed to see the results that code produces.

A webmaster should avoid giving both *execute* and *read* rights to a directory. This would allow the user to download the contents of the script (or, worse yet, of the database the script may be using), possibly jeopardizing security.

Additional security measures should also be implemented to prevent users from uploading any script to an execution directory. CGI scripts running under the context of the server can often threaten the server's overall security level.

Service providers often contain a dedicated directory (e.g., cgi-bin) where such scripts can be placed. This directory usually allows only execution of scripts, and prevents the scripts themselves from being read by the client's browser.

Internet Explorer vs. Netscape Navigator on Rights

When a read-enabled directory contains an executable, the Netscape browser allows the user to download this file onto disk.

Internet Explorer, on the other hand, allows the user to "open" the file. This causes the browser to save the file in a temporary directory and execute it. This is a potentially hazardous action, which was primarily created to allow setup programs to execute directly "from the web."

Microsoft also uses this potentially dangerous feature when rolling out HTML-based help systems. HTML pages drive several recent applications (the NT4 service pack 2 is one example). When the user clicks on a "script," this causes the browser to execute the script locally, and a particular component is consequently installed.

The Netscape browser takes an especially safe path, attempting to stay clear of any unsecured client-side application that may cause the end user harm or danger.

The Guest Book Application

The next application is a simple guest book application. This requires a simple HTML form, used to contain information and to subsequently submit the form. The application will then be executed, determining the result information and displaying these results to the user's query. The HTML form is comprised of edit boxes, a combo box a check box and radio buttons.

Forms can be easily created using either a simple HTML editor (or even notepad), or more complex HTML authoring tools — such as Microsoft's FrontPage 97.

The HTML file, comprising the form, is shown below:

```
<html>
<head>
<title>Simple Guestbook application</title>
</head>
<body bgcolor="#FFFFFF">
<form method="POST" ACTION="/scripts/guestbook.exe">
<p>Enter your information, please:</p>
<table border=1>
<tr><td width=50%>Name:</td><td width=50%><input type=text _
          size=20 maxlength=256 name="Name"></td></tr>
<tr><td width=50%>How much do you like this web page?_
          </td><td width=50%><select name="LikeFactor"_
            size=1>
<option value="A whole lot ">A whole lot</option>
<option value="Alot">Alot</option>
<option value="so so">so so</option>
<option value="no comment">no comment</option>
<option value="yuck">yuck</option>
<option value="hated it">hated it</option>
</select></td></tr>
<tr><td>What's your browser?</td><td><input type=radio _
          name="BrowserType" value="IE">Internet Explorer _
            <input type=radio checked name="BrowserType" _
              value="Netscape">Netscape <input type=radio _
                name="BrowserType" value="Other">Other_
                  </td></tr>
<tr><td>Would you like for someone to contact you?</td><td>_
          <input type=checkbox name="Contact" value="ON">_
            Yes_I do!</td></tr>
<tr><td>Remarks:</td><td><textarea name="Remarks" rows=2_
          cols=20></textarea></td></tr>
</table>
<input type=submit name="Submit" value="Submit Information">
<input type=reset name="Reset" value="Reset">
</form>
<A href="/scripts/guestbook.exe">Press here to view guest book</A>
</body>
</html>
```

Figure 2.4 shows the guest-book form.

Figure 2.4

The guest-book form

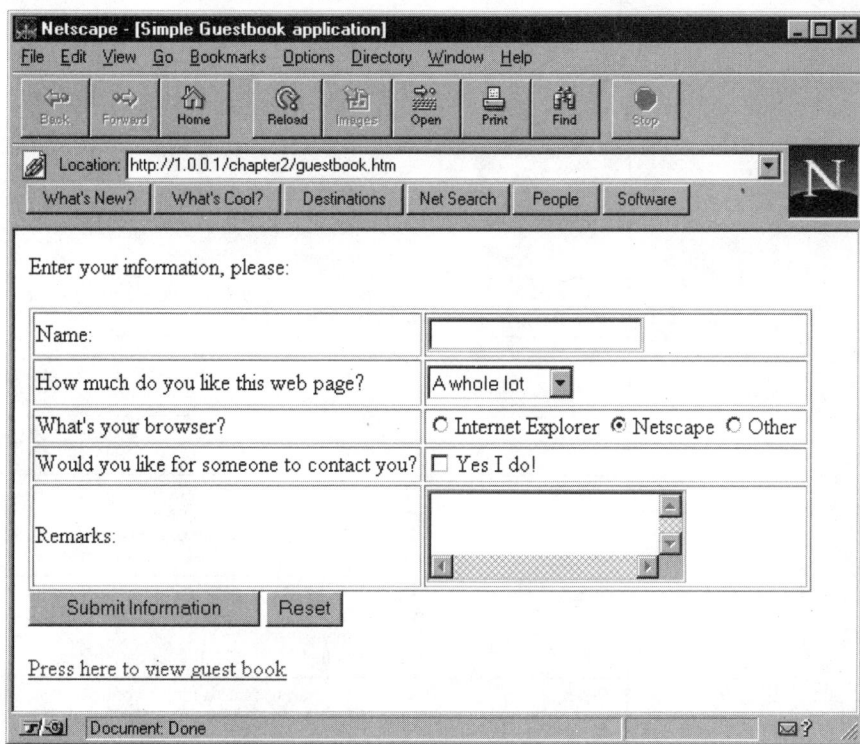

A web page can be composed of any number of autonomous forms. Each is independent and can interact with a single server application. In this case, there is only one form, taking up most of the web page and interacting with "/scripts/guestbook.exe" on the current server.

The control type is determined by the inputs type as seen in Table 2.1:

Table 2.1
Form Control types

Input type	Description
Text	A simple one-line text field.
Textarea	A multiple-line text field. The syntax for this control uses the <textarea> html tag.
Radio	A radio button. The textual description for the radio button must be added as regular text after the radio button.
Checkbox	A check box. The textual description for the radio button must be added as regular text after the radio button.
Select	A selection box. The syntax for this control uses the <select> tag. A select control can be a combo box or a list box, depending on other parameters. When used as a list box, the select control can be specified as multi-select.
Button	A simple button. This is a button that would not be used for submission. Rather, the button can be used to carry out local script code.
Submit	This control is used to create a button that can be used for submission of the form. Several such buttons can co-exist on the form, each having its own name and value. The name and value of the button used to submit the form will be submitted to the CGI application as parameters.
Image	This control is used to create a graphical object that can be used to submit the form. Several images and/or submit buttons may co-exist on the form. When submitted, the name of the image and the position where the user clicked are submitted to the CGI application as parameters.
Reset	This button is used to reset a form's controls. Information in the form's controls will revert back to the way it was when the form initially showed on the browser.

Each Input control has a name, and at least one value. When the user places **Joe** in the first (Name) edit-box, upon submission of the form the CGI application will receive **"Name=Joe"** as one of the parameters.

This applies to all of the input controls: selecting **A whole lot** in *LikeFactor* will result in the parameter: **LikeFactor=A+Whole+Lot** being passed to the CGI application.

Spaces are not supported as parameters. For this reason, spaces are converted into plus signs by the browser. Since the CGI application can receive information via the command line (when using certain submission methods), keeping spaces from appearing prevents the operating system and CGI application from becoming confused about the passed parameters.

Selecting Internet Explorer as browser type (the **BrowserType** radio button) will result in the parameter `BrowserType=IE` being passed to the server application.

If the **Contact** check box is turned off, the server will not receive any parameter with that check box's information. If it is turned on, the server application will receive `Contact=ON` as a parameter.

The **Reset** button causes the browser to revert back to the original state of the form. It does not cause any interaction between the browser and the server, or involve the CGI application in any way.

Pressing the **Submit** button results in the browser sending the updated form information to the server application for processing. The information is pre-processed by the browser, encoded, and transmitted to the web server. This encoded information is transmitted as-is to the CGI application.

In cases where it is necessary to do more than one type of action, more than one submission button can be used. For this reason, submit buttons have names and values too. Each particular action can have a different name/value combination. The combination is sent as a parameter when the form is submitted. In this case:

```
Submit=Submit+Information
```

Other than the submit button, there are three more ways to submit information to a web application:

- Using an input `type=image` causes the form to be submitted when the user presses the mouse button while the mouse cursor is on the image. Submitting using an image causes the browser to send *the position where the user clicked in the image* as the submission parameter:

  ```
  …MyImage.x=24&MyImage.y=200…
  ```

This can be used very effectively for mapping purposes (e.g., a location on a map). When several images are used for submission, only the image used to submit the *form* will show up in this manner — allowing the programmer to test for that particular image's information.

- Most browsers support the feature in which forms that contain a single edit box cause the form to be submitted when the user presses the **Enter** button while in the edit box. In such an event, there is no specification as to what caused the form to be submitted (e.g., Submit=Submit+information). Usually, this causes a CR/LF to be concatenated to the end of the parameter list. This could be harmful, unless specifically noted. The oCGI library will automatically remove this CR/LF combination, preventing it from causing any subsequent problems in the application.

- The final way in which parameters can be passed to the server is by directly specifying the parameter information in the browser. An alternate way of doing this is by making a hyper-jump to a script with information:

```
<A HREF="/chapter2/guestbook.exe?Name=John+Doe&Contact=_
         ON&Remarks=none>
touch me to start the guest book
</A>
```

Pressing the text section causes the browser to launch the guest book application with the appropriate parameters.

When the form is submitted by the browser using either an IMG input, a Submit button, or the enter method, the form may specify the submission method between web server and server application.

When creating a hyper-link, or specifying the complete CGI application URL, the browser automatically submits this information via the GET submission method.

The oCGI library takes care of retrieving the text, regardless of the method of communication between server and application, as well as the restructuring of the parameters back to standard ASCII.

In order to retrieve a field, the *ReadParam* function is utilized:

```
sName= cgi.ReadParam("Name")
```

In this statement, *sName* is a string, and *cgi* is the reference object/variable to oCGI. The oCGI library has already retrieved and parsed the parameters (this occurs upon creation of the oCGI reference object: `set cgi= New oCGI` or `dim cgi as New oCGI`). The *ReadParam* function simply looks for the parameter "Name" in the parameter list and retrieves the value.

Another way to retrieve this information is to access the parameter collection in oCGI directly: `cgi.cParameters.Item(0).Value`. This is useful in situations where the names of the parameters are not known (for instance, the results of a query in which the item names may not be consecutive).

The *cParameters* collection has a *Count* property, which evaluates the number of items in the collection. The *Item* function allows access to these items. Each item in the collection is of type *ParamType;* each has a *Name* and *Value* property.

The following code is a simple implementation of the guest book application, using a localized file to store the guest book information. This application can just as easily be implemented using a simple database. The application has two types of functionality: storing the information from the guest book form, and displaying the guest book file. When the application senses that the Submit parameter is equivalent to "Submit Information," it stores the form information. Otherwise, the application simply displays the guest book.

```
Sub main()
On Error GoTo RegisterErr
   Dim cgi As new oCGI
On Error GoTo NormalErr
   cgi.ProcessCGI Command
   'Load frmVBCrash

   If cgi.ReadParam("Submit") = "Submit Information" Then
     ' this is the guest book signing application.
     StoreGuestBook cgi, "Guestbook.gbk"
     cgi.WriteCGI "<HTML><HEADER>"
     cgi.WriteCGI "Guestbook information _
         saved</HEADER><BODY>"
     cgi.WriteCGI "Information was saved to the guest book"
     cgi.WriteCGI "</BODY></HTML>"
   Else ' retrieve the guest book.
```

```
      cgi.WriteCGI "<HTML><BODY>"
      PipeFile cgi, App.Path + "\Guestbook.gbk"
      cgi.WriteCGI "</BODY></HTML>"
   End If

   Set cgi = Nothing
   End
NormalErr:
   cgi.WriteCGI "<HTML><BODY>Error:" + Error$ + _
         "</BODY></HTML>"
   Set cgi = Nothing ' Just in case
   End
RegisterErr:
   oCGIRegister
   End
End Sub


Sub PipeFile(cgi As oCGI, sFileName As String)
   ' pipe a web page.
On Error GoTo FileEmpty
   Open sFileName For Input As #1
   Dim sInfo As String
   Do While Not (EOF(1))
      Line Input #1, sInfo
      cgi.WriteCGI sInfo
   Loop
   Close #1
   Exit Sub
FileEmpty:
   cgi.WriteCGI "<h2>Nothing is currently stored in the guest_
         book</h2>"
   Exit Sub
End Sub


Sub StoreGuestBook(cgi As oCGI, sFileName As String)
   Open sFileName For Append As #1
   Print #1, "Name - "
   Print #1, cgi.ReadParam("Name") + vbCrLf + "<BR>"

   Print #1, "How much do you like the home page? - "
   Print #1, cgi.ReadParam("LikeFactor") + vbCrLf + "<BR>"
```

```
Print #1, "Browser type? - "
Print #1, cgi.ReadParam("BrowserType") + vbCrLf + "<BR>"

If (cgi.ReadParam("Contact") <> "") Then
  Print #1, "Would like to be contacted!" + vbCrlf + _
      "<BR>"
End If

Print #1, cgi.ReadParam("Remarks") + vbCrLf + "<BR><HR>"
Close #1
End Sub
```

The *PipeFile* subroutine simply pipes the contents of the guest book file to the browser. A simple modification of this subroutine enables it to pipe binary information to the server too (the content of GIF files).

The *StoreGuestBook* subroutine stores the content of a file as if it was an HTML file. It does, however, omit the very beginning and very end of the file. This is done so those new guest book items can be appended to the file without modification.

The guest book program can be easily tested from the command line by running:

```
Guestbook.exe "Name=test&Submit=Submit+Information" > _
    t.htm
```

You can view t.htm using any web browser (simply double-click this file from the Windows explorer).

Most directories for the web do not have sufficient security rights to allow the guest book application to write the guestbook.gbk file. One solution is to create the file in a location that does not present a security breach.

Keep in mind that the CGI application is running under a different user context than you yourself. The web server is actually a Windows NT service, and it logs on to the system as if it were another user. This permits the administrator to specify security rights for the web server, as well as for CGI applications.

Figure 2.5 shows the guest-book web page; Figure 2.6 shows the `guestbook.gbk` file contents.

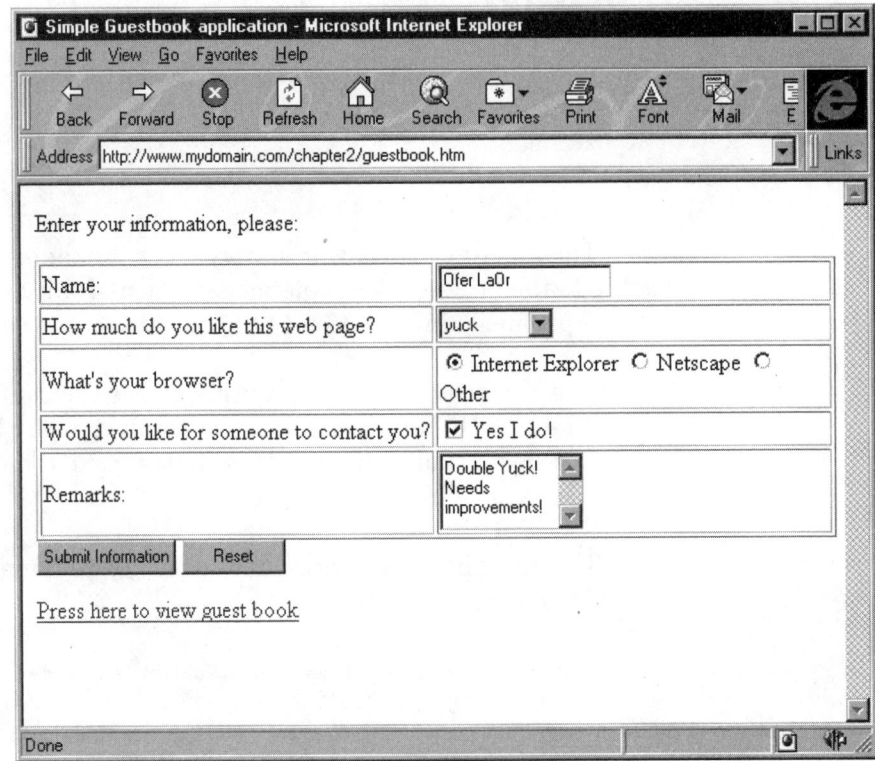

Figure 2.6
GUESTBOOK.GBK
sample

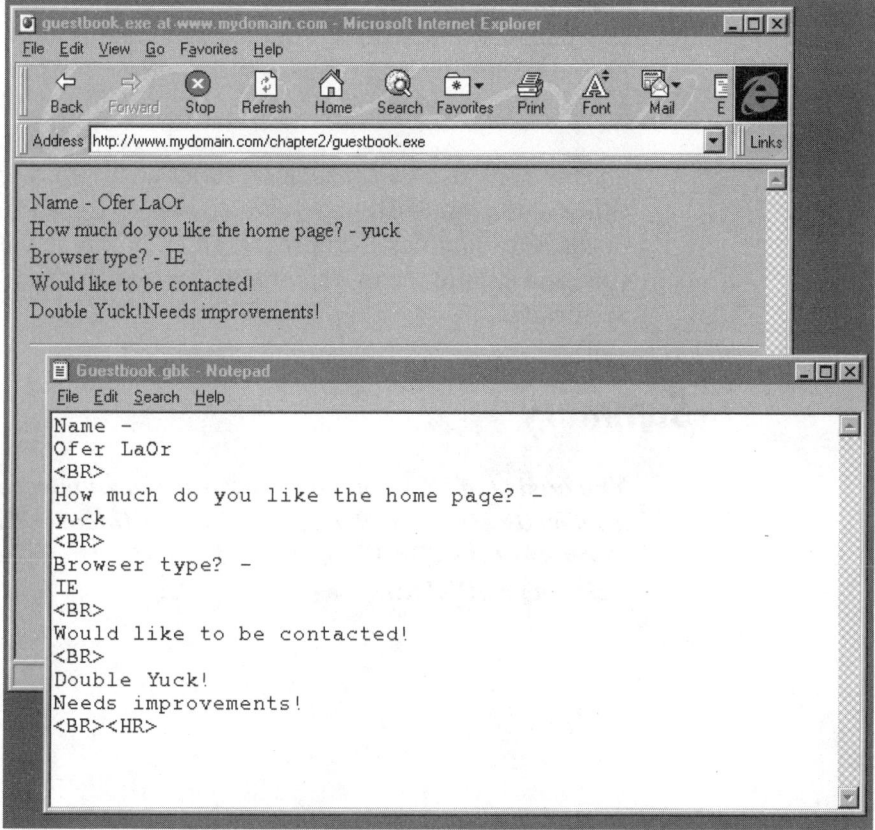

Security and the Guest Book Application

In order to grant the guest book application the rights to read/write a specific directory, give the service account the appropriate access rights for that directory. To prevent the application from creating new files through a bug or any other infiltration technique, you may create the **guestbook.gbk** file (using notepad) and grant the service account the rights to write and read *to just that file*. This allows you to use the default rights for the rest of the directory — leaving the system more secure.

Another option is to create a dedicated scripts directory for this application, and grant the service account full rights for that directory. This allows the application to screw itself up... but nothing else.

A programmer should distribute each level of secured functionality to a dedicated directory. This usually means that HTML files will be placed in one directory, images in another, scripts in a third directory, and data files in a fourth.

This book does not use such strict codes, and tends to place everything in the same directory. We do this to lessen the complexity factor in the code samples. The programmer, however, would do well to avoid this, and should try to implement a wise directory structure whenever applicable.

Summary

The basics of CGI code writing have been covered here. We can now write simple web applications with ease. What's missing is the actual details of what oCGI can do. The following chapter will cover oCGI and its functionality.

LEARNING *CGI* WITH THE O*CGI* LIBRARY

- Collections and classes in oCGI
- Accessing parameters and cookies
- Public methods in oCGI
- Methods of using oCGI in actual code

The oCGI library primarily takes care of encapsulating the communication between the server and the CGI application. As such, oCGI also hides some of the rougher details of CGI from the programmer, such as the method by which parameters are passed to the application, the decoding of parameters back to ASCII, as well as the details and limitations of cookies.

The encapsulation of oCGI can be viewed easily via Visual Basic's object browser (accessible by pressing **F2** from Visual Basic). This is shown in Figure 3.1.

Figure 3.1
Object browser view
of oCGI

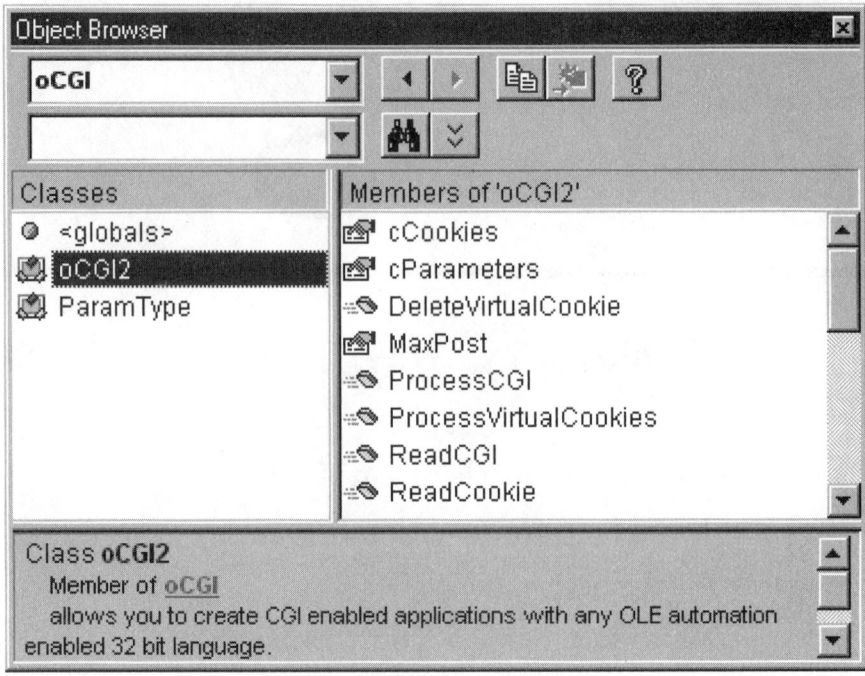

Collections and Classes within oCGI

The basis of oCGI is two collections: the *cCookies* and *cParameters* collections. Both contain objects of type *"ParamType."* Objects of type *ParamType* contain a *Name* string and a *Value* string. The *Name* string contains the name of a parameter, while the *Value* string contains the value for that particular parameter.

The *cParameters* collection contains the parameters passed to the browser by the browser, while the *cCookies* contains all of the cookies.

Cookies, briefly explained, are a list of items that an application can ask the remote user's browser to maintain locally. This information is sent to the application every time the application communicates with the server application.

Parameters, on the other hand, are those pieces of information particular to the form that was submitted, causing the server to execute the CGI application.

After the oCGI library initializes, the application usually calls the *ProcessCGI* subroutine. This subroutine makes oCGI retrieve the parameters and cookies, and proceed to process them.

Parameters are parsed and decoded into standard ASCII text and placed into the *cParameters* collection. Cookies are also parsed and decoded as needed, and placed by *ProcessCGI* into the *cCookies* collection. The application can manipulate these collections directly (although this is not recommended), or via the *ReadParam* and *ReadCookie* functions.

Public Methods in oCGI

Because the oCGI library does not have access to the command line parameters of the application, the command line parameters should be passed to the ProcessCGI call. In some situations, this command line information is required by oCGI to produce valid parameter results.

- *Sub ProcessCGI ([sCommand])*—This subroutine causes oCGI to process cookies and parameters. These are retrieved, parsed and processed. Once a parameter is ready, it is inserted into the cParameters collection. Similarly, cookies are inserted into the cCookies collection. This subroutine should be called immediately after creation of the oCGI variable. The command line parameter for the Visual Basic application should be placed as a parameter for this function in order to process the ISINDEX submission method, and for debug sessions:

```
cgi.ProcessCGI Command
```

The retrieval functions for cookies and parameters simply retrieve information from these collections. The collections are available to the user for more advanced manipulations. These include adding new cookies during the flow of the program (this has proved most useful when implementing shopping carts that utilize cookies), removing parameters based on outside factors, or implementing advanced constructs such as virtual cookies.

- *Function ReadParam (sName as string)* as string—This function retrieves the value of the parameter as specified by the *sName* parameter. If the parameter is not found in the *cParameters,* the function returns an empty string. Note that parameters are not required to have unique names. This means that there could potentially be two parameters with the same name and different values. Since this function can only return one value, a different approach is necessary to allow for non-unique names (i.e., two input controls that have the same name and could both be inserted into the parameter string during the same submission). An application using non-unique names will need to iterate through the *cParameters* collection in order to retrieve the parameters. This is also true in applications where the parameter name is not known.

- *Function ReadCookie (sName as string) as string*—This function retrieves the value of the cookie as specified by the *sName* parameter. If the cookie is not found in *cCookies,* the function returns an empty string.

Values of Cookies and Parameters

These functions allow the user to make queries about values of known cookies and parameters. Due to the fact that the *cCookies* and *cParameters* collections are thereby exposed to the user, direct access to cookies and parameters is easily provided. In addition, oCGI provides direct access to the raw, unprocessed cookie and parameter strings. This functionality can be accessed using the following functions:

- *Function ReadCookieString ( ) as string*—This function retrieves the raw cookie string. It is primarily useful in applications implementing their own scheme of cookies (or applications which require simple information from the cookie string).

- *Function ReadCGI ([sCommand]) as string*—This function retrieves the raw parameter string. It first determines the type of parameter passing method and then proceeds to retrieve the parameter string using that method. If no parameter passing technique is described, the function assumes that the user is debugging the system, and uses the command line parameters as the parameter string. In order to process the command line, the application's command line parameters should be passed to *sCommand:*

`cgi.ReadCGI Command`

This function is primarily used for debugging, because the prevailing method of form submission, POST, uses STOUT rather than the command line for parameter passing.

Since oCGI uses these two functions to retrieve cookie and parameter information, the user can replace these functions in order to enable the oCGI library to communicate with a server by a method other than CGI. One example of such functionality is a WINCGI interface.

CGI Output

The oCGI library provides simple functionality for outputting information from the CGI application:

- *Sub WriteCGI (sText as string,[fStartCGI])*—This subroutine allows the programmer to output information back to the server. The *fStartCGI* flag should not be used unless content types other than HTML are being transferred to the server (in which case, the application is in charge of writing the content type header to the server). The *sText* string is the text outputted to the server. This function should be used conservatively; the application should collect the text and minimize calls to this function in order to optimize performance. A long process should notify the user (using *WriteCGI* calls) as to its status; the server transmits this information to the browser right away. This allows a programmer to create "live" applications (e.g., chat programs). More information about how to do this can be found in later chapters.

- *Sub WriteCookie (sName As String, sValue As String, sDomain As String, [sPath], [expires])*—This subroutine allows the programmer to output cookie information to the server. There is a typical limit of 20 cookies per server/client combination (in addition to size limitations per each cookie). The *sName* parameter specifies the name of the cookie and *sValue* specifies the value. The *sDomain* parameter specifies the domain which receives this cookie (e.g., www.mydomain.com for a specific server, *.mydo-

main.com for all of the servers that end with mydomain.com).
Typically, the local server name is used—*ReadServerName*. The
sPath parameter specifies the path in the provided domain in
which applications receive this cookie (e.g., /scripts for all scripts
running under the scripts directory, / for all applications in the
specified domain). Typically, the script name is specified here—
ReadScriptName. If not specified, the subroutine assumes that
the current path is to be used. The *"expires"* parameter is a
date/time field specifying the persistence of a particular cookie.
If the *expires* parameter is not used, the cookie will be retained
in the browser's memory and will not persist beyond the current browser session!

Typical cookies expire within 1-30 days. This function must be
used prior to any *WriteCGI* call. This rule of thumb is useful for
all cookie operations (also including virtual cookies). Because
many complex applications determine the cookie usage after a
significant amount of processing — some of which will surely
result in output to the client — we recommend that such functions *not* interact directly with the oCGI library. Rather, they
should return their information in the form of HTML strings,
and proceed to do all of the cookie operations. The processed
HTML can be easily committed by a single *WriteCGI* call. Please
note that by writing these cookies to the browser, the cookies
will only take effect the next time the browser contacts the application. In order for the cookies to take effect immediately, the
user needs to create a new *ParamType* variable (`set
myParamType = new ParamType`) and insert it into the *cCookies*
collection (`cCookies.Add myParamType`) manually. This is usually
required for shopping cart-type applications. Cookies must have
unique names, as by writing a new cookie with the same name,
the browser automatically changes the value of the first cookie.
Cookies are deleted by specifying an expiration date that has
already passed (e.g., 2 days ago).

Virtual cookies overcome the limit of 20-cookie-per-client/server combination. Virtual cookies work by maintaining an internal virtual cookie string. This string is committed to the server right before the first
WriteCGI call, by way of one or more standard cookies. The oCGI library
commits as much of the string as possible into each cookie, after which
the library proceeds to create as many cookies as are needed. This allows

as many cookies to be created as the physical browser limit will permit. The oCGI library allows up to 19 physical cookies to be used as the canvas for virtual cookies. Netscape allows 4000 bytes to be kept in each cookie. For safety's sake, the oCGI library limits virtual cookies to 3800 bytes per physical cookie. This brings the theoretical limit of total browser contents to 80,000 bytes as the total maximum size for all cookies. The limit applies to the sum of bytes in both the name and value of each cookie.

It should be noted that cookies should retain **key** information rather than actual content. For example, a shopping cart application using virtual cookies should commit the key *value* for each item added to the shopping cart, not the description.

Since oCGI virtual cookies utilize 19 cookies, the application can utilize a single normal cookie in conjunction with virtual cookies, without fear that this will be erased due to lack of cookie memory.

When an application uses more cookies than the browser supports (the entire contents of the cookie file also has a limit), the browser proceeds to remove the oldest cookie from the list. Often, this is the first cookie committed to the server and, most likely, the most important (e.g., an identity cookie).

In some cases, actual information is still maintained on the server itself. The cookie is used to index this information. Information is cleared periodically on the server clearing indexes that had not been recently accessed. The primary reason for doing this is lack of room. The oCGI library's virtual cookie scheme overcomes this issue, however, minimizing the need for such server-based information. This reduces the overall requirements on the server to the information that the application process requires when the user is off-line (for instance, e-mail addresses or credit card numbers).

All of the operations on virtual cookies actually take place on the persistent virtual cookie string. When the first *WriteCGI* call occurs, this string is transformed into as many physical cookies as needed. Because all of the virtual cookies are maintained in the same physical cookie (or in several sequential cookies), virtual cookies cannot specify a domain or path. These are automatically assumed as the current server and the current script. In addition, all of the cookies have the same persistence (Time To Live = TTL). The default persistence for the virtual cookies is 14 days (this can be modified by the application).

Virtual cookies are constructed of one or several standard cookies containing the virtual cookie string. The *ProcessVirtualCookies* subroutine locates these standard cookies, orders them, and reconstructs the virtual cookie string. The subroutine then continues to insert individual cookies in the virtual cookie string into the *cCookies* collection. Finally, the physical cookies holding virtual cookies are removed from the cookie list. This turns the virtual cookies into standard cookies for the application.

Changes to virtual cookies are made by directly manipulating the virtual cookie string. The virtual cookie string is finally deconstructed and committed in one or more standard cookies, as needed.

Active Server Pages (ASP) provide a similar functionality by allowing the user to embed several pieces of information in a single cookie. Virtual cookies, on the other hand, provide a standard cookie compatible system and require significantly less effort to access, construct and deconstruct.

This feature is especially useful in situations where more than 20 cookies are required. An application that has been using a relatively large number of cookies can easily migrate to virtual cookies with little effort, allowing the application to utilize the vast amount of space in the browser's cookie "domain."

- *Sub ProcessVirtualCookies ([NewVirtualTTL])*—This subroutine turns virtual cookies into standard cookies, accessible via the normal cookie functions. This is necessary when virtual cookies are being used. The *NewVirtualTTL* allows the programmer to modify the persistence of all subsequent virtual cookies. If this parameter is not specified, the virtual cookies will cease to exist after the session between browser and web server terminates. This function must be executed before any potential access to virtual cookies is needed (*read* or *write*).

- *Sub WriteVirtualCookie (sName As String, sValue As String, [fNotUnique])*—This subroutine allows the programmer to output virtual cookie information to the server. The subroutine can only be called after *ProcessVirtualCookie* and before *WriteCGI*. The *sName* parameter specifies the name of the virtual cookie, and *sValue* specifies the value of that cookie. When *fNotUnique* is not specified (or is false), the system assumes that virtual cookies have unique names (as regular cookies do). When *fNotUnique* is *True,* the system will add the new virtual cookie *even if the same cookie name is already in use.* Since the *ReadCookie* function can only return one value when non-unique names are used, the user is required to iterate through the *cCookies* collection in order to retrieve the other, identically-named cookie information.

- *Sub DeleteVirtualCookie (sName As String, [sValue])*—Because virtual cookies cannot specify a localized expiration date, they need to be deleted differently than standard cookies. This subroutine provides the ability to delete a virtual cookie from the virtual cookie string. It must be done **after** a call to *ProcessVirtualCookies* (so that the virtual cookie string is filled) but **before** any call to *WriteCGI* (i.e., before virtual cookies are committed). Because virtual cookies don't necessarily have unique names, the programmer may also specify a value. If a value is specified, the subroutine will only remove the virtual cookie if both name *and* value are a match.

The oCGI library also provides several utility functions which provide the application with useful information from the server.

- *Function ReadRemoteAddress ( ) as string*—This function returns the client's remote IP address. It is primarily utilized for logging, security and validation purposes.

- *Function ReadRemoteFrom ( ) as string*—This function returns the client's email address. It is not a standard CGI construct. As such, it will return a relevant string only with Netscape servers in conjunction with clients running Netscape browsers.

- *Function ReadRemoteHost ( ) as string*—This function is very similar to *ReadRemoteAddress.* Instead of returning the client's IP address, it returns the client's host name if available. This is relevant primarily for non-dial-in clients (static IP addresses). This information is primarily utilized for logging, security and validation purposes.

- *Function ReadScriptName ( ) as string*—This function returns the running script name. You can determine the actual executable being run using the Visual Basic **App** object. However, many web servers have the ability to "redirect"—meaning that the script address and the application name do not necessarily have to match. In addition, the path to the script usually does not match the physical path to the script (i.e., virtual directories). To simplify things, this function always returns the path that the server sees to the CGI application. For example **/scripts/CGIapplication.exe.**

- *Function ReadServerName ( ) as string*—This function returns the host name for the currently running script. It is useful for determining the web server you are running on. Many applications have been created which allow them to move from one server to another easily. This enables many operations to be more generic, and less dependent on a specific machine. This information is also useful in situations where the web server is multi-homing. One such example is an application that behaves differently depending on the host that is communicating with it. If you have two Internet domains running off the same web server, each requiring a "dedicated" catalog system, you can create a generic catalog system. Now each web server will "see" a different catalog without knowing (or caring) that a single application and database are providing this functionality transparently. It can also save you from having to specify a vendor code for some applications (unless the same database and application need to service more than one vendor on the same IP address — for example, to minimize the cost of an SSL license for each IP address).

- *Function ReadGatewayInterface ( ) as string*—This function retrieves the interface type between server and application. With oCGI, it is most definitely a version of CGI. Typically, this function will return "CGI/1.0" or "CGI/1.1." (Please note that servers supporting the CGI 1.0 interface do not support cookies. This includes Microsoft IIS version 1.0.)

- *Function ReadServerPort ( ) as string*—This function retrieves the port which is being used to communicate between server and browser. (Unless modified, this is usually port 80 for non-secure communication.)

- *Function ReadServerSecured ( ) as Boolean*—This function allows the application to determine whether the communication between web server and browser is secured.

- *Function ReadUserAgent ( ) as String*—This function returns a string with the client's browser application name and version. The string may also include other information, such as the client's operating system. This allows the application to log browser types, or to control content based on the client's browser type.

Methods of Using the oCGI Library in Your Code

The oCGI library can be used in a few ways, the easiest of which is to include the oCGI source code in the project's code. This enables the programmer to step into oCGI code and debug things from there. An additional benefit is the ability to place a *debug.Print* statement in the WriteCGI function. This enables the programmer to follow up on what the CGI application is writing to the outside world in an easy to use manner. In addition, this way of activating the application does not require any registration on part of the application since it only utilizes components that are already included in the project. A DLL, however, is more efficient since when running multiple instances, the Windows NT memory manager can be more effective when an application is modularized. In addition, several instances of the same application (and other applications) require less load time and a smaller memory footprint.

An example of statically linking oCGI is presented in the chapter2 directory in the HelloWorldStatic Visual Basic project. Static linking is used in these examples to demonstrate this capability, in most situations a DLL is a more effective way of using an ActiveX component such as oCGI.

The alternative way of utilizing oCGI is by registering it in the way described in the previous chapter. This way, the oCGI library is referenced by the code and utilizes the `oCGI2.DLL` file. When using a referenced ActiveX library, such as oCGI, Visual Basic provides additional functionality, including online help that activates when the user presses **F1** while on a valid oCGI function (e.g., *ProcessCGI*). The `oCGI2.DLL` is an In-process DLL, meaning that it will operate in the same process context as applications that are using it. This provides the DLL the capability to write into the same STDOUT stream as the CGI application.

When using a referenced version of oCGI, the library must be registered (sample code for registering a control or other 32-bit ActiveX components such as oCGI is listed throughout the book). If the oCGI library is modified, Visual Basic will most likely change the CLSID for the ActiveX component. This is the identifier that correlates between oCGI2 and the actual code that activates it.

Visual Basic provides the option to maintain CLSID compatibility with older component versions. This capability only works when no design changes have been implemented (e.g., parameter changes to a public function, the addition or removal of a public method or variable). The component tab in the project options dialog box allows for version compatibility using the "binary compatibility" radio button. The edit box underneath should contain the full directory of the older component DLL.

When this identifier changes, the project lloses the connection with the oCGI library and must be re-referenced with the new DLL. This is important to note should changes be instigated into the oCGI DLL by the programmer.

Yet a third alternative is not to reference the oCGI during the design time. Binding the project to oCGI at runtime prevents any direct relationship with the CLSID and causes the project to search for the oCGI library at run time.

When using "late binding" (connecting to a library at run-time), the project will have a slightly slower load time. This is because Visual Basic is required to determine at run time what the application's CLSID is. With late binding, Visual Basic will not be able to validate oCGI function syntax, as well as prevents Visual Basic from being able to provide online context-sensitive help.

When using late binding, the CGI global parameter should be of type *object* (which is a generic type that will work for all types of ActiveX libraries). Creation of the CGI object library can be done as follows (this replaces the New oCGI2 specification):

```
dim cgi as Object
set cgi = CreateObject("oCGI.oCGI2")
```

Objects of type: *ParamType* can be created:

```
dim item as Object
set item = CreateObject("oCGI.ParamType")
```

This type of initialization would only be recommended to users who are likely to modify or extend the oCGI code—not allowing Visual Basic to retain its CLSID. Using this type of initialization prevents Visual Basic from depending on the CLSID.

When using the "binary compatibility" option, Visual Basic will attempt to retain the existing CLSID—so long as no structural changes had been integrated into the ActiveX library (e.g., the addition or removal of functions, modification of function's parameter or name).

In a situation where there may be more than one oCGI version on the server, the *CreateObject* method of connecting to oCGI will allow the currently registered version of oCGI to interact with the application while maintaining a different CLSID. As oCGI versions should be backward compatible, the application should still operate correctly even without depending on the specific CLSID version. In situations where there may be a revised oCGI library involved, it is recommended to either modify the class name or statically link with the oCGI library (i.e., by including the oCGI modules in the project).

References

When a Visual Basic application lists a library in the reference list, that library and all supporting files (DLLs, OCXs, etc.) should exist on the target system. The same rule applies to OCXs that are listed in Visual Basic controls list.

It is generally a good idea to remove unneeded controls from the control list and only list the necessary libraries in the reference list. Visual Basic will only attempt to load these controls/libraries when they are actually used. Minimizing the items listed in these locations will allow the programmer to verify during the development process which controls and libraries are required for distribution.

Summary

The reader should now be well versed with the oCGI library details. This enables the reader to write a well balanced application utilizing the entire breadth of functionality that oCGI offers. The next step is being able to retrieve information from previous screens (via parameters) and to be able to persist data in the end-user's browser (via cookies).

COOKIES AND PARAMETERS IN oCGI

- Interfacing with oCGI
- The user-security application (Access-based user security)
- Improved version of the user-security application: an introduction to cookies
- Removing the actual password from the communication

Ways of Interfacing with oCGI

The oCGI library can be used in many ways to produce a viable CGI application. It is presented here as a building tool that enables Visual Basic programmers to program applications for the Internet.

Because oCGI interfaces with Visual Basic, it can also be used to port existing applications onto the Internet. This, however, is only the case with well-written, modular applications.

As with every type of development tool, it is possible to develop applications that cannot be ported in any manner. Visual Basic provides application builders with many ways to create applications that use little or no code (using bound controls instead, for example). These types of applications require significant rewriting when ported to any other environment.

Most web applications rely heavily on the manner in which parameters are interfaced, parsed and used.

When the ProcessCGI subroutine is called, it first retrieves the parameter string (using the ReadCGI function). Once this string has been retrieved, it is parsed and inserted into the cParameters collection. This collection can be accessed directly, or by way of the interface function: ReadParam.

The UserSecurity Application

In order to demonstrate the usability of these options, this chapter will incrementally improve a simple, database-enabled CGI application. The *"UserSecurity"* application was created to allow a programmer control over users accessing a specific web page. The application is activated as soon as the user logs on — after which the user receives the web page requested.

UserSecurity provides an authentication method for the application, bypassing the NT security that standard authentication techniques require. When an application requires user authentication, it can either be blocked to the guest user (or the user that the web server utilizes to log browsers onto the system) via standard NTFS file security, or by sending the "401 access denied" HTTP status message.

This method of user authentication, however, requires tight integration with the Windows NT user database. Often, this is neither required nor needed. The NT user database is hard to manage programmatically, and sometimes lacks information that the system needs to track anyway. In most real-world situations, several server applications can work on the same server, but may require different user databases.

The *UserSecurity* system employs a database-oriented user database, allowing the system to work independently of the NT user database in the server where the application is running. This database can hold any information the application wants to record about the user (e.g., address, phone number, credit card number) and provides a simple way to manage the user database.

This application is "smart," since it creates its own log-on form (the reason for this will become clear when cookies enter the picture). Look over the *DoInitialLogonScreen* function for more information.

The UserSecurity Database Layout

The application uses a small users' database called USERS.MDB. Table 4.1 presents a column description of this:

Table 4.1

Users Table Layout

Table: USERS Field Name	Field Type	Remark
UserID	AutoNumber (long integer)	Primary key — identifies user.
UserName	Text(50), Indexed	User's log-on name.
FullName	Text(50)	User's full name.
Password	Text(50)	User's log-on password
Notes	Text(50)	Any additional information we would like to maintain about each user.

This database is placed in the same directory as the *"UserSecurity"* application. By providing only *execute* security on the scripts directory, client browsers will not be able to download the database itself.

In order for the Jet engine to open the database, the directory needs sufficient NTFS rights to allow new files to be created and removed.

If this is not possible, a copy of the USERS.LDB file should be placed in the directory where the database resides, while the application (or Access) is using the database. The user context under which the web server is running should be allowed *read* and *write* access to both the MDB and LDB files. This allows the application to open the database, without requiring it to create a new LDB file *or* access an existing one.

The server must also have DAO 3.0/3.5 (or higher) installed, as well as the run time for Visual Basic. Visual Basic 4.0 requires VB40032.DLL to be present (along with any other libraries the application may require).

Visual Basic 5.0 applications compiled with the native compiler do *not* require this run-time DLL. Instead, MSVBVM50.DLL is needed in order for the Visual Basic application to work correctly. In addition, DAO/RDO/ADO may be installed for use on the target machine.

Notes

MSVBVM50.DLL is necessary regardless of whether the application is being compiled to native code or utilizes PCode. This library contains not only the PCode parser, but also all of the run time libraries (other than some of the functionality that it utilizes MSVCRT20.DLL and MSVCRT40.DLL for—these are the Visual C++ run time library support files).

When a Visual Basic 5.0 application is compiled, the speed is increased, but file size becomes significantly larger. Since CGI applications primarily focus on the speed issue, compiled code is always recommended over PCode.

There are additional benefits to compiling an application, such as the ability to debug the application natively using a "CodeView" compatible debugger.

The following is the initial version of *UserSecurity*:

```
Option Explicit

Declare Function oCGI2Register Lib "oCGI2.dll" Alias _
    "DllRegisterServer" () As Long

Dim cgi As oCGI2
Dim db As Database

Sub DoInitialLogonScreen(Optional sError As Variant)
    ' this function displays the initial log on screen.
    ' this gets called to show the existing user screen.
    With cgi
        .WriteCGI "<HTML>" + vbCrLf
        If (IsMissing(sError)) Then
            .WriteCGI "<HEAD><TITLE>Creating a user database _
                with"
            .WriteCGI "the oCGI VB module</TITLE></HEAD><BODY _
                BGCOLOR=""#ffffff"">"
            .WriteCGI vbCrLf
        Else
```

```
            .WriteCGI "<HEAD><TITLE>" + sError + _
              "</TITLE></HEAD>"
          .WriteCGI "<BODY BGCOLOR=""#ffffff"">" + vbCrLf
          .WriteCGI "<H2>ERROR: " + sError + "</H2><HR>" + _
            vbCrLf
      End If


      .WriteCGI "<BR><H2>please enter your username and _
            password:<H2>" + vbCrLf
      .WriteCGI "<FORM ACTION=""" + .ReadScriptName
      .WriteCGI """ METHOD=""POST"">" + vbCrLf
      .WriteCGI "<INPUT TYPE=""HIDDEN"" NAME=""Action"" _
            VALUE=""LOGIN"">"
      .WriteCGI vbCrLf
      .WriteCGI "<TABLE><TR><TD>" + vbCrLf
      .WriteCGI "<B>User Name:</B></TD><TD><INPUT TYPE=TEXT _
            SIZE=20 "
      .WriteCGI "MAXLENGTH=50 NAME=""UserName"" "
      If (.ReadParam("UserName") <> "") Then ' is this a _
            "wrong login" error?!
        .WriteCGI " VALUE=""" + .ReadParam("UserName") + _
            """>" + vbCrLf
      Else
        .WriteCGI ">" + vbCrLf
      End If

      .WriteCGI "</TD></TR><TR><TD>" + vbCrLf
      .WriteCGI "<B>Password:</B></TD><TD><INPUT _
            TYPE=PASSWORD SIZE=20"
      .WriteCGI " MAXLENGTH=50 NAME=""Password"">" + vbCrLf
      .WriteCGI "</TD></TR><TR><TD> <P><INPUT TYPE=Submit _
            NAME=""Submit"""
      .WriteCGI " VALUE=""Log in as existing User"">" + _
            vbCrLf
      .WriteCGI "</TD><TD><INPUT TYPE=Reset NAME=""Reset"" _
            VALUE=""Reset"">"
      .WriteCGI vbCrLf
      .WriteCGI "</TD><TD>" + vbCrLf
      .WriteCGI "</TD></TR></TABLE>" + vbCrLf
      .WriteCGI "</FORM> </BODY></HTML>" + vbCrLf
  End With
```

```
        End Sub
        Sub DoUserSecurity()
          If (Not TryToLogin()) Then
            DoInitialLogonScreen
          Else
            Select Case cgi.ReadParam("Action")
              Case "LOGIN":
                HomePage
              Case Else: ' dunno what this is!
                DoInitialLogonScreen
            End Select
          End If
        End Sub

        Sub HomePage()
          With cgi
            .WriteCGI "<HTML>" + vbCrLf
            .WriteCGI "<TITLE> You have successfully logged on _
                  </TITLE>" + vbCrLf
            .WriteCGI "<BODY BGCOLOR=#fffff0>" + vbCrLf

            .WriteCGI "<H2>Success! You have logged on _
                  successfully!</H2>"

            .WriteCGI "</BODY></HTML>"
          End With
        End Sub

        Sub main()
        On Error GoTo RegisterErr ' register oCGI only if having _
                  problems!
          Set cgi = New oCGI2
        On Error GoTo NormalErr
          cgi.ProcessCGI Command
          'Load frmVBCrash
          Set db = Workspaces(0).OpenDatabase(App.Path + _
                  "\users.mdb")

          DoUserSecurity

          db.Close
```

```vb
    Set cgi = Nothing
    End
NormalErr:
  cgi.WriteCGI "<HTML><BODY>Error:" + Error$ + _
        "</BODY></HTML>"
  Set cgi = Nothing ' Just in case
  End
RegisterErr:
  oCGI2Register
  Set db = Nothing
  End
End Sub


' Try to login user. Return true if successful.
Function TryToLogin() As Boolean
  TryToLogin = UserPasswordMatch(cgi.ReadParam("UserName"), _
    cgi.ReadParam("Password"))
End Function


Function UserPasswordMatch(sUserName As String, sPassword _
        As String) As Boolean
  Dim rsUser As Recordset, sSQL As String
  UserPasswordMatch = False ' convince me otherwise!
  If (sUserName = "" And sPassword = "") Then Exit Function _
        ' no good for sure!

  sSQL = "select * from USERS where UserName='" + _
        DoubleQuote(sUserName) + "'"
  Set rsUser = db.OpenRecordset(sSQL, dbOpenDynaset)
  If Not rsUser.EOF Then
    If (rsUser("Password") = sPassword) Then
      UserPasswordMatch = True
    End If
  End If
  rsUser.Close
End Function


Function DoubleQuote(sData As String) As String
  Dim sOut As String, iPos As Integer

  For iPos = 1 To Len(sData)
```

```
        Select Case Mid$(sData, iPos, 1)
          Case "'":
             sOut = sOut + "'"
          Case """":
             sOut = sOut + """"""
          Case Else:
             sOut = sOut + Mid$(sData, iPos, 1)
        End Select
      Next
      DoubleQuote = sOut
  End Function
```

This application can be launched from a form that has the information built right into it, or launched directly (**http://www.myddomain.com/scripts/UserSecurity1.exe**).

The main function takes care of registering and initializing the CGI variable. In addition, the main subroutine also logs onto the database and launches the *DoUserSecurity* subroutine.

DoUserSecurity first determines whether the user is valid or not. If the user is valid, it checks the Action parameter. (This parameter is utilized so that many, completely different functions can be performed by the same application.) By checking this parameter — the application can determine what the form is requesting it to do. In this case, the form is requesting the application to log the user on. If the Action parameter is not recognized (or not specified), the log-on screen is displayed. This can be modified to show a different initial page when the user is logged on without further Action specification. In order to transfer the Action parameter *without* displaying a visible control, the **input=hidden** statement is used. This construct transfers information to the next form without explicitly displaying it on the screen. This type of control can serve many functions other than those displayed here.

When attempting to log a user on, the *UserPasswordMatch* function is used. This function attempts to locate a user with the given *UserName*. If it finds that user, it compares passwords. (If it does not, the recordset will not have any rows in it and `rsUser.EOF` would be True.) If they are equal, the user is successfully logged on to the system.

It should be noted that it is good policy to check for a valid username and password for each subsequent form/screen.One cannot assume that the user has reached a particular point in the application by stepping through the application. There are many ways to circumvent this (bypassing the security scheme) if it only checks for a valid user id/password once.

The home page subroutine can easily be replaced by the *PipeFile* subroutine from Chapter 2, enabling the user to jump ahead to a valid HTML file without requiring that the application be modified every time the home page is.

As can easily be seen in the code, when quotes need to be outputted to the server, two sets are used, so that Visual Basic recognizes that this is not the end of a string. The statement `cgi.WriteCGI ""“"test-ing"""`—yields "testing."

Similarly, since strings must use quotes to surround them when building SQL code, the parameters (e.g., the user name in this case) cannot contain single quotes. In order to prevent errors from occurring should users insert single quotes as parameters (e.g., "Joe's name" as a user name), the *DoubleQuote* function is utilized. This function duplicates any quotes it finds. It prevents an odd number of sequential quotes from causing errors in the SQL code.

When generating the SQL statement that searches for the text "Ofer's program," the following is sent to SQL server:

```
Select * from MYTABLE where SEARCHFIELD='Ofer's program'
```

If the system has actually been sending out fields in this manner, SQL server (or any other SQL-enabled database—e.g., Microsoft Access) cannot determine where the string ends. It will assume that it is looking for the text: "Ofer" and that the string "s program' " is erroneous.

In order to resolve this issue, the double quotes are used to form:

```
Select * from MYTABLE where SEARCHFIELD='Ofer''s program'
```

By doubling the number of quotes sent out to SQL server, the server becomes aware that the client is actually referring to the single quote character within the search string.

The Double quote function simply doubles any single quotes it finds. It should be utilized when doing direct SQL statements that use external text variables (or user parameters) which may or may not contain single quotes. This includes all types of select statements (select, delete, update, insert).

When using DAO constructs, it is not necessary to use *DoubleQuotes* since DAO contains its own double quote engine. For example, when doing:

```
myRecordset("MYFIELD")= "Ofer's program" 'may contain _
          single quotes, no difference.
sMyField= myRecordset("MYFIELD") ' may contain single _
          quotes, no difference.
```

When placing the select statement into the recordset object, though, double quotes must be used:

```
Set myRS= db.OpenRecordset("Select * from MYTABLE where _
          SEARCHFIELD='Ofer''s'")
```

Or when utilizing a string:

```
Set myRS= db.OpenRecordset("Select * from MYTABLE where _
          SEARCHFIELD='" + _ DoubleQuote(sSearchText) _
          + "'", dbOpenDynaset)
```

The *DoInitialLogonScreen* is designed to display error information (e.g., the user name was not found, vs. an error in password). If the user has not logged on correctly, this function also picks up the user name used previously (assuming that the password was mistyped).

Figures 4.1 and 4.2 demonstrate the initial form and log-on form.

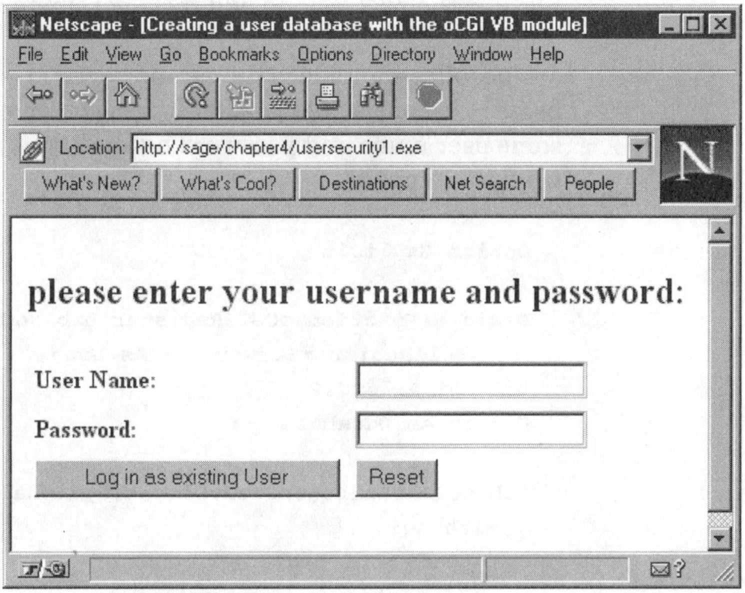

Figure 4.1
User security 1—initial
log-on screen

After logging in:

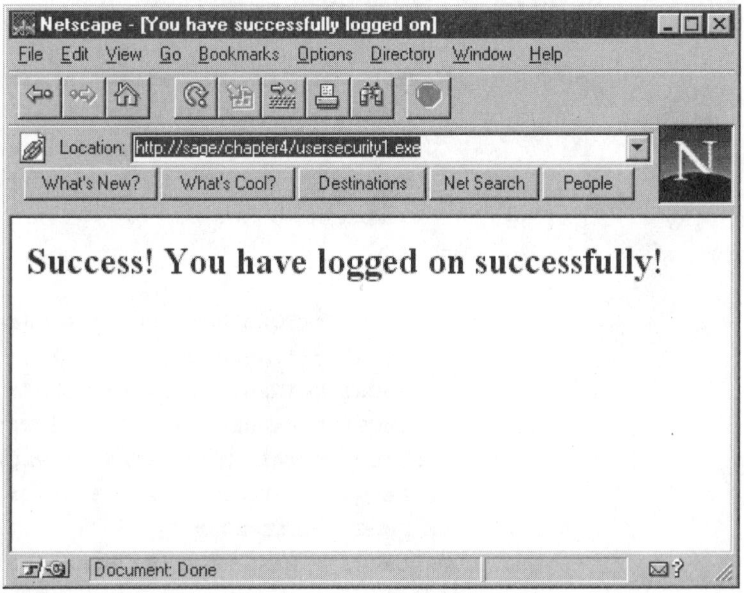

Figure 4.2
User security 1—after
logging on

This program lacks several features. For one, it does not allow for new users. The next phase of this system would be to enable guests to register themselves and add their parameters to the database.

The following code is the second revision of this program. It enables users to log on as guests. After logging on once, the user can employ the same user name and password he/she employed initially, and log on to the system again.

```
Option Explicit

Declare Function oCGI2Register Lib "oCGI2.dll" Alias _
    "DllRegisterServer" () As Long
Dim cgi As oCGI2
Dim db As Database


Sub DoInitialLogonGuestScreen(Optional sError As Variant)
  With cgi
    .WriteCGI "<HTML>" + vbCrLf
    If (IsMissing(sError)) Then
      .WriteCGI "<HEAD><TITLE>Creating a user database _
          with the oCGI VB module"
      .WriteCGI "</TITLE></HEAD><BODY BGCOLOR=""#ffffff"">"_
          + vbCrLf
    Else
      .WriteCGI "<HEAD><TITLE>" + sError + _
          "</TITLE></HEAD><BODY "
      .WriteCGI "BGCOLOR=""#ffffff"">" + vbCrLf
      .WriteCGI "<H2>ERROR: " + sError + "</H2><HR>" + _
          vbCrLf
    End If

    .WriteCGI "<FORM ACTION=""" + .ReadScriptName
    .WriteCGI """ METHOD=""POST"">" + vbCrLf
    .WriteCGI "<INPUT TYPE=""HIDDEN"" NAME=""Action"" "
    .WriteCGI " VALUE=""PROCESSGUEST"">" + vbCrLf
    .WriteCGI "<TABLE><TR><TD>" + vbCrLf
    .WriteCGI "<B>User Name:</B></TD><TD><INPUT TYPE=_
        TEXT SIZE=20 "
    .WriteCGI " MAXLENGTH=50 NAME=""UserName"" "
    If (.ReadParam("UserName") <> "") Then
```

```
        .WriteCGI " VALUE=""" + cgi.ReadParam("UserName") + _
            """">" + vbCrLf
    Else
        .WriteCGI ">" + vbCrLf
    End If


    .WriteCGI "</TD></TR><TR><TD>" + vbCrLf
    .WriteCGI "<B>Full Name:</B></TD><TD><INPUT TYPE=TEXT _
        SIZE=20 "
    .WriteCGI " MAXLENGTH=50 NAME=""FullName"" "
    If (.ReadParam("FullName") <> "") Then
        .WriteCGI " VALUE=""" + .ReadParam("FullName") + _
            """">" + vbCrLf
    Else
        .WriteCGI ">" + vbCrLf
    End If


    .WriteCGI "</TD></TR><TR><TD>" + vbCrLf
    .WriteCGI "<B>Password:</B></TD><TD><INPUT _
        TYPE=PASSWORD SIZE=20 "
    .WriteCGI " MAXLENGTH=50 NAME=""Password"">" + vbCrLf
    .WriteCGI "</TD></TR><TR><TD>" + vbCrLf
    .WriteCGI "<B>VerifyPassword:</B></TD><TD><INPUT _
        TYPE=PASSWORD "
    .WriteCGI " SIZE=20 MAXLENGTH=50 _
        NAME=""VerifyPassword"">" + vbCrLf
    .WriteCGI "</TD></TR><TR><TD>" + vbCrLf


    .WriteCGI "</TD></TR><TR><TD> <P><INPUT TYPE=Submit _
        NAME=""Submit"" "
    .WriteCGI " VALUE=""Create your new user"">" + vbCrLf
    .WriteCGI "</TD><TD><INPUT TYPE=Reset NAME=""Reset"" _
        VALUE=""Reset"">"
    .WriteCGI vbCrLf + "</TD><TD>" + vbCrLf
    .WriteCGI "</TD></TR></TABLE>" + vbCrLf
    .WriteCGI "</FORM> </BODY></HTML>" + vbCrLf
  End With
End Sub


Sub DoInitialLogonScreen(Optional sError As Variant)
  ' this function displays the initial log on screen.
```

```
' this gets called to show the existing user screen.
With cgi
    .WriteCGI "<HTML>" + vbCrLf
    If (IsMissing(sError)) Then
        .WriteCGI "<HEAD><TITLE>Creating a user database _
            with the oCGI "
        .WriteCGI " VB module</TITLE></HEAD><BODY _
            BGCOLOR=""#ffffff"">" + vbCrLf
    Else
        .WriteCGI "<HEAD><TITLE>" + sError + _
            "</TITLE></HEAD><BODY "
        .WriteCGI " BGCOLOR=""#ffffff"">" + vbCrLf
        .WriteCGI "<H2>ERROR: " + sError + "</H2><HR>" + _
            vbCrLf
    End If
    .WriteCGI "<BR><H2> If you've never logged in before, _
        press this:<H2>"
    .WriteCGI vbCrLf
    .WriteCGI "<FORM ACTION=""" + .ReadScriptName + """ _
        METHOD=""POST"">"
    .WriteCGI vbCrLf
    .WriteCGI "<INPUT TYPE=""HIDDEN"" NAME=""Action"" _
        VALUE=""LOGGUEST"">"
    .WriteCGI vbCrLf
    .WriteCGI "<INPUT TYPE=Submit NAME=""Submit"" _
        VALUE=""New User"">"
    .WriteCGI vbCrLf
    .WriteCGI "</FORM><BR><HR>" + vbCrLf

    .WriteCGI "<BR><H2> If you have logged in, please use _
        your username and "
    .WriteCGI "password:<H2>" + vbCrLf
    .WriteCGI "<FORM ACTION=""" + .ReadScriptName + """ _
        METHOD=""POST"">"
    .WriteCGI vbCrLf
    .WriteCGI "<INPUT TYPE=""HIDDEN"" NAME=""Action"" _
        VALUE=""LOGIN"">" + vbCrLf
    .WriteCGI "<TABLE><TR><TD>" + vbCrLf
    .WriteCGI "<B>User Name:</B></TD><TD><INPUT TYPE=TEXT _
        SIZE=20 "
    .WriteCGI " MAXLENGTH=50 NAME=""UserName"" "
```

```
        If (.ReadParam("UserName") <> "") Then ' is this a _
            "wrong login" error?!
          .WriteCGI " VALUE=""" + .ReadParam("UserName") + _
            """>" + vbCrLf
        Else
          .WriteCGI ">" + vbCrLf
        End If


        .WriteCGI "</TD></TR><TR><TD>" + vbCrLf
        .WriteCGI "<B>Password:</B></TD><TD><INPUT _
            TYPE=PASSWORD SIZE=20 MAXLENGTH=50 "
        .WriteCGI " NAME=""Password"">" + vbCrLf
        .WriteCGI "</TD></TR><TR><TD> <P><INPUT TYPE=Submit _
            NAME=""Submit"" "
        .WriteCGI " VALUE=""Log in as existing User"">" + _
            vbCrLf
        .WriteCGI "</TD><TD><INPUT TYPE=Reset NAME=""Reset"" _
            VALUE=""Reset"">" + vbCrLf
        .WriteCGI "</TD><TD>" + vbCrLf
        .WriteCGI "</TD></TR></TABLE>" + vbCrLf
        .WriteCGI "</FORM> </BODY></HTML>" + vbCrLf
    End With
End Sub


Sub DoProcessGuest()
    ' check validity of everything to start with...
    With cgi
        If (Trim$(.ReadParam("UserName")) = "") Then
          DoInitialLogonGuestScreen "Invalid User name _
            entered."
          Exit Sub
        ElseIf (Trim$(.ReadParam("FullName")) = "") Then
          DoInitialLogonGuestScreen "Invalid Full Name _
            entered."
          Exit Sub
        End If
        If (Trim(.ReadParam("Password") = "")) Then
          DoInitialLogonGuestScreen "An empty password cannot _
            be used"
          Exit Sub
        End If
```

```
If (.ReadParam("Password") <> _
      .ReadParam("VerifyPassword")) Then
  DoInitialLogonGuestScreen "Password and Verify _
      Password must be the same!"
  Exit Sub
End If
If (.ReadParam("Password") = .ReadParam("UserName")) _
      Then
  DoInitialLogonGuestScreen "UserName and Password _
      must be different!"
  Exit Sub
End If



' this function gets called to finalize the logging _
      in of the user!
Dim rs As Recordset, sSQL As String
sSQL = "select * from USERS where UserName='"
sSQL = sSQL + DoubleQuote(.ReadParam("UserName")) + "'"
Set rs = db.OpenRecordset(sSQL, dbOpenDynaset)



' make sure that there's no one by that same name...
If rs.EOF Then
  rs.AddNew ' no need for double quotes, DAO takes _
      care of it here!
  rs("UserName") = .ReadParam("UserName")
  rs("Password") = .ReadParam("Password")
  rs("FullName") = .ReadParam("FullName")
  rs("Notes") = "Host=[" + .ReadRemoteHost + "]"
  rs.Update
  Set rs = db.OpenRecordset(sSQL, dbOpenDynaset)
  If Not rs.EOF Then
    ' logged in, show home page!
    HomePage
  Else
    rs.Close
    DoInitialLogonGuestScreen "Could not add User to _
      system"
  End If
Else
```

```
         rs.Close
         DoInitialLogonGuestScreen "User Name already exists"
      End If
   End With
End Sub


Sub DoUserSecurity()
   If (Not TryToLogin()) Then
      Select Case (cgi.ReadParam("Action"))
         Case "LOGGUEST"
            DoInitialLogonGuestScreen
         Case "PROCESSGUEST"
            DoProcessGuest
         Case Else
            If (cgi.ReadParam("UserName") <> "") Then ' tried _
                  to log on, but couldn't
               DoInitialLogonScreen "UserName/Password could _
                  not be matched"
            Else
               DoInitialLogonScreen
            End If
      End Select
   Else
      Select Case cgi.ReadParam("Action")
         Case "LOGIN":
            HomePage
         Case Else: ' dunno what this is!
            DoInitialLogonScreen
      End Select
   End If
End Sub
```

This application can be launched from a form with the information built right into it, or launched directly (http://www.myddomain.com/scripts/UserSecurity2.exe).

The following functions remain unaffected by the change, and so were not included in this source code listing: *HomePage*, *main*, *TryToLogin*, *UserPasswordMatch* and *DoubleQuote*.

The *DoInitialLogonGuestScreen* subroutine was added to display the log-on screen for guests. Just as with *DoInitialLogon* screen, this function attempts to post control values. This lessens the retyping users are required to do in case of an error (such as not entering necessary information, or not verifying the password correctly). The guest form produces a "PROCESSGUEST" Action, which is handled by the *DoProcessGuest* subroutine.

The *DoInitialLogonScreen* function was modified to include a jump to *DoInitialLogonGuestScreen*, permitting new users (or "guests") to log on to the system using the "LOGGUEST" action.

The *DoUserSecurity* function was extended to include the "LOGGUEST" action, which displays the guest logon screen, and the "PROCESSGUEST" action, which creates and logs on a guest user. This function also detects whether the user has failed to log on, in which case an error appears.

The *DoProcessGuest* subroutine is the heart of this modification. It is separated into two logical parts: *validation* and *creation*. The subroutine first determines whether the log-on information is valid. Validity includes making sure that fields are filled in, that the user is not using an existing user name, that the password is identical to the password validation field and finally, that the user is not using his user name as the password, too. If any of these conditions are identified, the guest log-on screen reappears with an appropriate message explaining why the information could not be properly processed. If the new user's information is valid, the subroutine uses the *AddNew* recordset method to add the new user. When employing these functions, you do not need to use the *DoubleQuote* function, too, since this is only relevant for pure SQL calls. A more efficient alternative to *AddNew* is an SQL insertion statement (INSERT INTO). This can be executed using the following statement: `db.execute sSQL` and checked by `db.RowsEffected`.

Once the user is added, the *DoProcessGuest* function calls *HomePage* in order to display the home page to the newly created user.

Figure 4.3 shows the changes to the log-on screen:

Figure 4.3
User security 2—initial
log-on screen

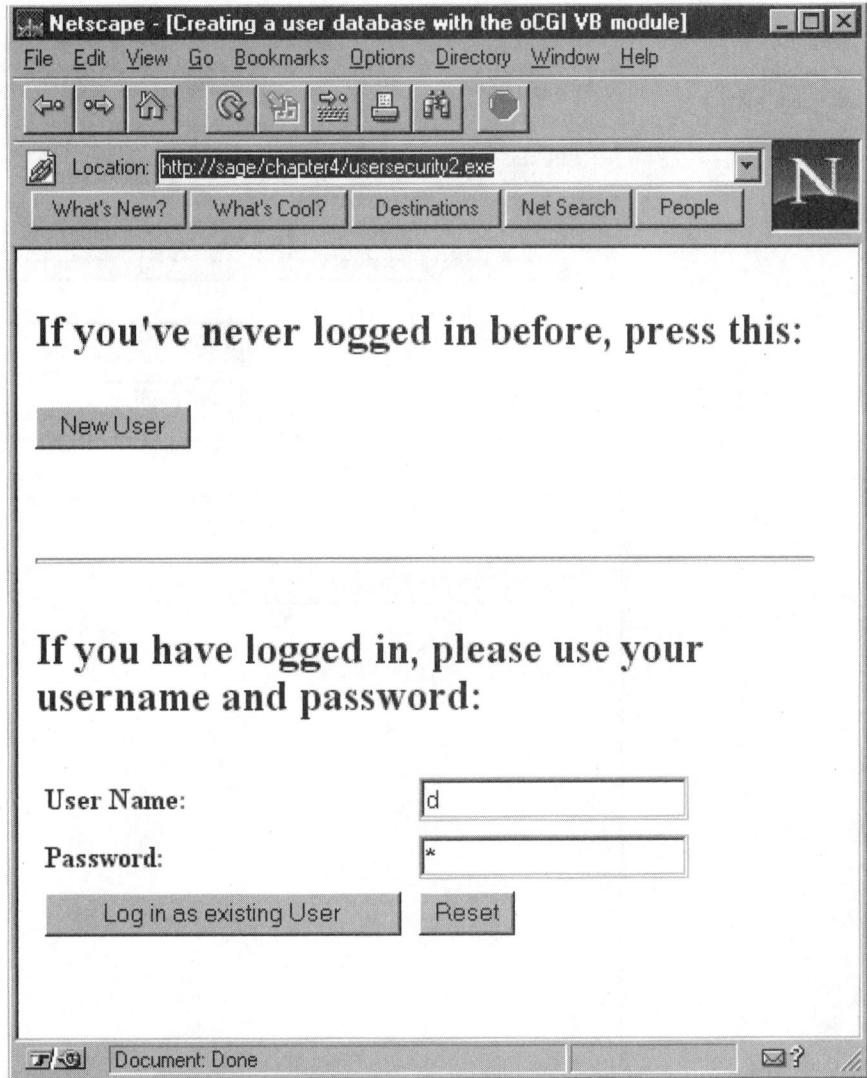

Figure 4.4 demonstrates the subsequent guest log-on page produced by clicking the guest button.

Figure 4.4
User security 2—
subsequent guest log-
on screen

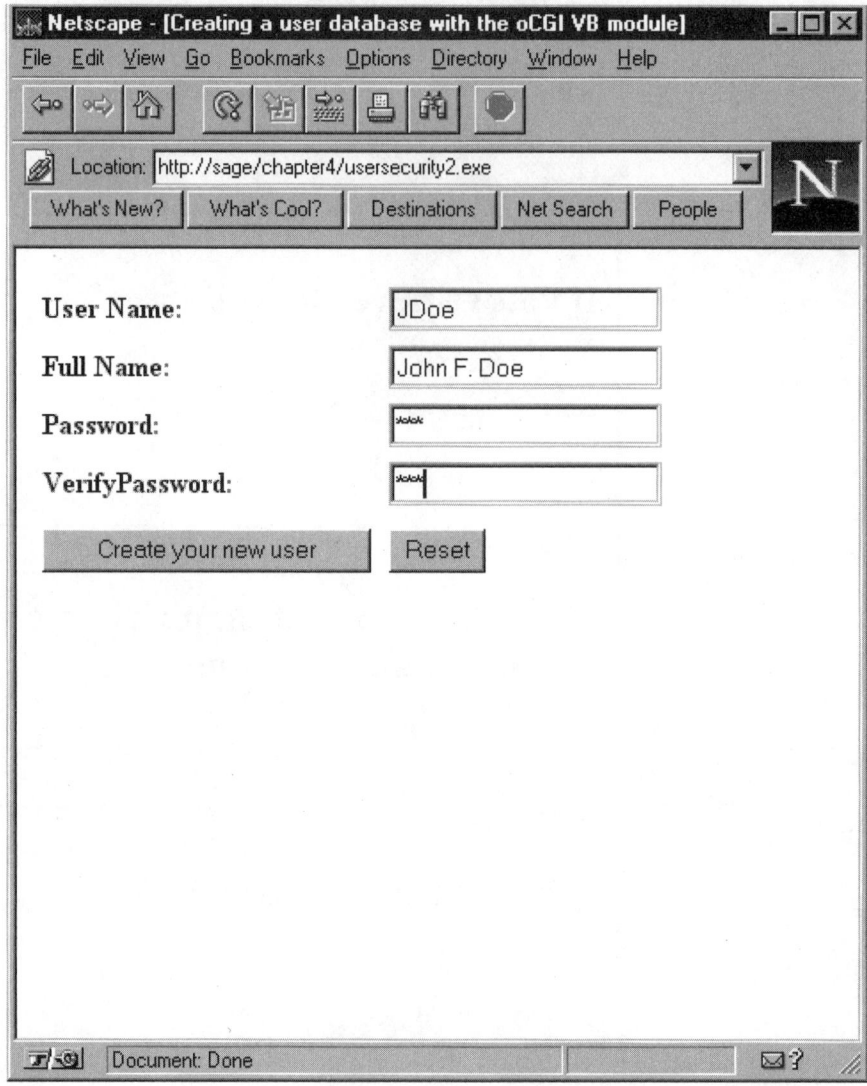

Improvements?

The *UserSecurity* program can still be improved somewhat. We can utilize cookies to improve some aspects of it. The user has to manually log in every time. While this may be required on some systems, persistent cookies will allow the user to log in just once, making subsequent logons automatic on the same machine/browser. This is because the browser will actually remember the user's security information (e.g., username/password).

As was mentioned previously, logging the user on once and subsequently assuming that the user was logged on is not very secure. The system may want to disable certain users, who would then still be able to use old bookmarks to get to certain locations in a "secured" system. This is especially true in situations involving many dynamic web pages.

Using persistent/non-persistent cookies, the system can always automatically validate the user's authenticity every time he logs on, and revalidate this every time the browser interacts with the server application (e.g., when a transaction is carried out). Due to the small number of available cookies, the cookie-enabled UserSecurity application will utilize a single cookie to retain all of the user's security information.

Since this is a simple security system, it must be noted that retaining the user's actual name and password on their local system as cookies would allow *anyone* with access to the browser's cookie file to see their user name and password.

Users are required to have many user names and passwords — one on each service they subscribe to — so they often choose identical user names and passwords for some or all of these systems.

Even if a particular service is relatively unimportant or unsecured, maintaining this information in a secure manner is of paramount importance. Securing information on the client side, as well as on the server side, should not be disregarded or taken lightly. The information can often be used elsewhere to imperil a user in other ways.

Since the application is most likely unsecured, it would be safe to say that the entire Internet can see the user's name and password.

When employing the user name and password in cookies for validation purposes, the information will be transmitted repeatedly between browser and server—increasing the possibility that it will be picked up by a "nasty" router or another Internet entity.

The application can minimize the chance of this occurring by preventing the information from traveling into the wrong hands. This can be accomplished by 1) not transmitting the information repeatedly to the Internet, and 2) not placing the information, as-is, on the client's workstation, where it can easily be picked up by any passer-by.

In order to avoid these problems, the system retains identifying information in the browser in such a way that *neither* user name nor password can be saved on the client side. This information is much safer on the client's workstation as well as when transmitted repeatedly between client and server. For purposes of identity, a unique number is assigned to the user and saved in the database, namely the *UserID*. This integer identifies the user just as well as a user name. A malicious entity listening in would not have much use for the information outside this particular system, since there is no direct correlation between ID and user name.

In order to replace the password, a random number is generated every time a user identifies himself (either when logging on as an already-existing user, or logging on for the first time as a guest). This technique allows the browser to retain this number — which, in itself, is inconsequential—and to accurately identify the user when utilized in conjunction with the *UserID*.

The Notes field can be used to retain the value of this cookie from session to session on the server side.

How Do We Fix It?

An alternative to this method is to generate the random number every time a user logs on (i.e., every time the user utilizes the *UserSecurity* CGI application). This technique adds to security, in the respect that only a single owner/browser will be able to retain the latest identifying cookie. This prevents someone from simply copying cookie information without knowing the right password — since the system cannot validate two browsers using different identification cookies. Should the cookie file be copied to another machine, the second user will be able to log on without knowing the password — until the other user logs in just once (in which case, the identifying cookie will no longer be valid).

Both techniques demonstrate alternatives to saving plain user name and password information on a local machine. In addition, these techniques do not compromise the user by continually transmitting user name and password over the Internet every time the application is accessed.

The second alternative is given here as more of a conceptual idea than a practical implementation. With browser frames (as well as other techniques), users can simultaneously access more than one instance of the script. This can cause a timing problem, which in turn causes the script to believe that two distinct browsers are accessing the application—causing one of the scripts to retain a previous value. This, of course, can be worked around by validating more pieces of information (client's IP address, validation against previous values, etc.). These techniques are beyond the scope of this book, but are described here for the sake of being complete

In addition to using the *UserID* and a random number to cause persistence, additional modifications have been entered into this code. These include a rewrite of the home page (which now displays user-specific information) and simplification of the validation process for empty fields.

The user has full control over the persistence of the user validation cookie (aka, *UserCookie*). The user can decide to forgo persistence altogether, in which case the program does not specify an expiration date. If the *RememberPassword* checkbox is on, the *RememberDuration* field is validated. If the duration is valid, the system specifies the expiration date as: `(Now + CInt(RememberDuration))`. If *RememberDuration* is equal to "14", this will specify the date occurring two weeks from today.

```
Option Explicit

Declare Function oCGI2Register Lib "oCGI2.dll" Alias _
        "DllRegisterServer" () As Long
Dim cgi As oCGI2
```

```
Dim db As Database
Dim sFullName As String

Sub DoInitialLogonGuestScreen(Optional sError As Variant)
   With cgi
      .WriteCGI "<HTML>" + vbCrLf
      If (IsMissing(sError)) Then
         .WriteCGI "<HEAD><TITLE>Creating a user database _
            with the oCGI VB module"
         .WriteCGI "</TITLE></HEAD><BODY BGCOLOR=""#ffffff"">"_
            + vbCrLf
      Else
         .WriteCGI "<HEAD><TITLE>" + sError + _
            "</TITLE></HEAD><BODY "
         .WriteCGI "BGCOLOR=""#ffffff"">" + vbCrLf
         .WriteCGI "<H2>ERROR: " + sError + "</H2><HR>" + _
            vbCrLf
      End If

      .WriteCGI "<FORM ACTION=""" + .ReadScriptName
      .WriteCGI """ METHOD=""POST"">" + vbCrLf
      .WriteCGI "<INPUT TYPE=""HIDDEN"" NAME=""Action"" "
      .WriteCGI " VALUE=""PROCESSGUEST"">" + vbCrLf
      .WriteCGI "<TABLE><TR><TD>" + vbCrLf
      .WriteCGI "<B>User Name:</B></TD><TD><INPUT TYPE=TEXT _
            SIZE=20 "
      .WriteCGI " MAXLENGTH=50 NAME=""UserName"" "
      If (.ReadParam("UserName") <> "") Then
         .WriteCGI " VALUE=""" + cgi.ReadParam("UserName") + _
            """>" + vbCrLf
      Else
         .WriteCGI ">" + vbCrLf
      End If

      .WriteCGI "</TD></TR><TR><TD>" + vbCrLf
      .WriteCGI "<B>Full Name:</B></TD><TD><INPUT TYPE=TEXT _
            SIZE=20 "
      .WriteCGI " MAXLENGTH=50 NAME=""FullName"" "
      If (.ReadParam("FullName") <> "") Then
         .WriteCGI " VALUE=""" + .ReadParam("FullName") + _
            """>" + vbCrLf
```

```
            Else
               .WriteCGI ">" + vbCrLf
            End If


            .WriteCGI "</TD></TR><TR><TD>" + vbCrLf
            .WriteCGI "<B>Password:</B></TD><TD><INPUT _
                TYPE=PASSWORD SIZE=20 "
            .WriteCGI " MAXLENGTH=50 NAME=""Password"">" + vbCrLf
            .WriteCGI "</TD></TR><TR><TD>" + vbCrLf
            .WriteCGI "</TD></TR><TR><TD> <input type=checkbox _
                name=""RememberPassword"" "
            .WriteCGI " value=""ON""> Remember my password for "
            .WriteCGI " <input type=TEXT SIZE=2 MAXLENGTH=2 _
                NAME=""RememberDuration"" "
            .WriteCGI " VALUE=14> days"
            .WriteCGI "</TD></TR><TR><TD>" + vbCrLf
            .WriteCGI "<B>VerifyPassword:</B></TD><TD><INPUT _
                TYPE=PASSWORD "
            .WriteCGI " SIZE=20 MAXLENGTH=50 _
                NAME=""VerifyPassword"">" + vbCrLf
            .WriteCGI "</TD></TR><TR><TD>" + vbCrLf


            .WriteCGI "</TD></TR><TR><TD> <P><INPUT TYPE=Submit _
                NAME=""Submit"" "
            .WriteCGI " VALUE=""Create your new user"">" + vbCrLf
            .WriteCGI "</TD><TD><INPUT TYPE=Reset NAME=""Reset"" _
                VALUE=""Reset"">"
            .WriteCGI vbCrLf + "</TD><TD>" + vbCrLf
            .WriteCGI "</TD></TR></TABLE>" + vbCrLf
            .WriteCGI "</FORM> </BODY></HTML>" + vbCrLf
        End With
    End Sub


    Sub DoInitialLogonScreen(Optional sError As Variant)
        ' this function displays the initial log on screen.
        ' this gets called to show the existing user screen.
        With cgi
            .WriteCGI "<HTML>" + vbCrLf
            If (IsMissing(sError)) Then
                .WriteCGI "<HEAD><TITLE>Creating a user database _
                    with the oCGI "
```

```
            .WriteCGI " VB module</TITLE></HEAD><BODY _
                BGCOLOR=""#ffffff"">" + vbCrLf
        Else
            .WriteCGI "<HEAD><TITLE>" + sError + _
                "</TITLE></HEAD><BODY "
            .WriteCGI " BGCOLOR=""#ffffff"">" + vbCrLf
            .WriteCGI "<H2>ERROR: " + sError + "</H2><HR>" + _
                vbCrLf
        End If
        .WriteCGI "<BR><H2> If you've never logged in before, _
                press this:<H2>"
        .WriteCGI vbCrLf
        .WriteCGI "<FORM ACTION=""" + .ReadScriptName + """ _
                METHOD=""POST"">"
        .WriteCGI vbCrLf
        .WriteCGI "<INPUT TYPE=""HIDDEN"" NAME=""Action"" _
                VALUE=""LOGGUEST"">"
        .WriteCGI vbCrLf
        .WriteCGI "<INPUT TYPE=Submit NAME=""Submit"" _
                VALUE=""New User"">"
        .WriteCGI vbCrLf
        .WriteCGI "</FORM><BR><HR>" + vbCrLf


        .WriteCGI "<BR><H2> If you have logged in, please use _
                your username and "
        .WriteCGI "password:<H2>" + vbCrLf
        .WriteCGI "<FORM ACTION=""" + .ReadScriptName + """ _
                METHOD=""POST"">"
        .WriteCGI vbCrLf
        .WriteCGI "<INPUT TYPE=""HIDDEN"" NAME=""Action"" _
                VALUE=""LOGIN"">" + vbCrLf
        .WriteCGI "<TABLE><TR><TD>" + vbCrLf
        .WriteCGI "<B>User Name:</B></TD><TD><INPUT TYPE=TEXT _
                SIZE=20 "
        .WriteCGI " MAXLENGTH=50 NAME=""UserName"" "
        If (.ReadParam("UserName") <> "") Then ' is this a _
                "wrong login" error?!
            .WriteCGI " VALUE=""" + .ReadParam("UserName") + _
                """>" + vbCrLf
        Else
            .WriteCGI ">" + vbCrLf
```

```
        End If

        .WriteCGI "</TD></TR><TR><TD>" + vbCrLf
        .WriteCGI "<B>Password:</B></TD><TD><INPUT _
            TYPE=PASSWORD SIZE=20 MAXLENGTH=50 "
        .WriteCGI " NAME=""Password"">" + vbCrLf
        .WriteCGI "</TD></TR><TR><TD> <input type=checkbox _
            name=""RememberPassword"" "
        .WriteCGI " value=""ON""> Remember my password for "
        .WriteCGI " <input type=TEXT SIZE=2 MAXLENGTH=2 _
            NAME=""RememberDuration"" "
        .WriteCGI " VALUE=14> days"
        .WriteCGI "</TD></TR><TR><TD> <P><INPUT TYPE=Submit _
            NAME=""Submit"" "
        .WriteCGI " VALUE=""Log in as existing User"">" + _
            vbCrLf
        .WriteCGI "</TD><TD><INPUT TYPE=Reset NAME=""Reset"" _
            VALUE=""Reset"">" + vbCrLf
        .WriteCGI "</TD><TD>" + vbCrLf
        .WriteCGI "</TD></TR></TABLE>" + vbCrLf
        .WriteCGI "</FORM> </BODY></HTML>" + vbCrLf
    End With
End Sub


Sub DoProcessGuest()
    ' check validity of everything to start with...
    With cgi
        ' this could be done better with JavaScript validation!
        Select Case "" ' find out if some of the fields are _
            empty!
          Case Trim$(.ReadParam("UserName"))
            DoInitialLogonGuestScreen "Invalid User name _
            entered."
            Exit Sub
          Case Trim$(.ReadParam("FullName"))
            DoInitialLogonGuestScreen "Invalid Full Name _
            entered."
            Exit Sub
          Case Trim$(.ReadParam("Password"))
            DoInitialLogonGuestScreen "An empty password _
            cannot be used"
```

```
        Exit Sub
    End Select
    If (.ReadParam("Password") <> _
        .ReadParam("VerifyPassword")) Then
      DoInitialLogonGuestScreen "Password and Verify _
        Password must be the same!"
      Exit Sub
    End If
    If (.ReadParam("Password") = .ReadParam("UserName")) _
        Then
      DoInitialLogonGuestScreen "UserName and Password _
        must be different!"
      Exit Sub
    End If

    ' this function gets called to finalize the logging _
        in of the user!
    Dim rs As Recordset, sSQL As String
    sSQL = "select * from USERS where UserName='"
    sSQL = sSQL + DoubleQuote(.ReadParam("UserName")) + "'"
    Set rs = db.OpenRecordset(sSQL, dbOpenDynaset)

    ' make sure that there's no one by that same name...
    If rs.EOF Then
      rs.AddNew ' no need for double quotes, DAO takes _
        care of it here!
      rs("UserName") = .ReadParam("UserName")
      rs("Password") = .ReadParam("Password")
      rs("FullName") = .ReadParam("FullName")
      rs.Update

      sFullName = .ReadParam("FullName")

      Set rs = db.OpenRecordset(sSQL, dbOpenDynaset)
      If Not rs.EOF Then
        rs.Close
        SetUserCookies .ReadParam("UserName") ' install _
          cookies!
        ' logged in, show home page!
        HomePage
      Else
```

```
               rs.Close
               DoInitialLogonGuestScreen "Could not add User _
                  to system"
             End If
           Else
             rs.Close
             DoInitialLogonGuestScreen "User Name already exists"
           End If
       End With
   End Sub


   Sub DoUserSecurity()
     If (Not TryToLogin()) Then
       Select Case (cgi.ReadParam("Action"))
         Case "LOGGUEST"
           DoInitialLogonGuestScreen
         Case "PROCESSGUEST"
           DoProcessGuest
         Case Else
           If (cgi.ReadParam("UserName") <> "") Then ' _
             tried to log on, but couldn't
            DoInitialLogonScreen "UserName/Password _
               could not be matched"
           Else
            DoInitialLogonScreen
           End If
       End Select
     Else
       Select Case cgi.ReadParam("Action")
         Case "LOGIN", "": ' the empty string is added for _
             cookie support!
           HomePage
         Case Else: ' dunno what this is!
           DoInitialLogonScreen
       End Select
     End If
   End Sub


   Sub HomePage()
     With cgi
       .WriteCGI "<HTML>" + vbCrLf
```

```
        .WriteCGI "<HEADER><TITLE> Welcome to the sample _
            users home page "
        .WriteCGI sFullName + "</TITLE></HEADER>" + vbCrLf
        .WriteCGI "<BODY BGCOLOR=#ffffff>" + vbCrLf
        .WriteCGI "<H2> Welcome to the sample users home page_
            " + sFullName
        .WriteCGI "</H2><P>" + vbCrLf
        .WriteCGI "<I>Note: if you close your browser and _
            come back later, you will"
        .WriteCGI " not have to go through the _
            username/password screen again!<P>"
        .WriteCGI vbCrLf
        .WriteCGI "The system automatically identifies you _
            utilizing cookies.</I><HR>"
        .WriteCGI vbCrLf
        If (Trim$(cgi.ReadRemoteFrom()) <> "") Then
          .WriteCGI "Your email address is: " + _
              .ReadRemoteFrom() + "<BR>" + vbCrLf
        End If

        cgi.WriteCGI "Your browser is: " + cgi.ReadUserAgent_
            () + "<BR>" + vbCrLf

        .WriteCGI "Your IP address is: " + .ReadRemoteAddress_
            () + "<BR>" + vbCrLf
        If ((.ReadRemoteHost() <> "")And(.ReadRemoteHost() _
            <> .ReadRemoteAddress())) Then
          .WriteCGI "Your machine's host name: " + _
              .ReadRemoteHost() + "<BR>" + vbCrLf
        End If

        .WriteCGI "</BODY>" + vbCrLf
        .WriteCGI "</HTML>"
    End With
End Sub

Sub SetUserCookies(sUser As String)
    ' randomize a UserCookie, then place it!
    Dim rsUser As Recordset, sSQL As String

    sSQL = "select * from USERS where UserName='" + _
```

```
                    DoubleQuote(sUser) + "'"
          Set rsUser = db.OpenRecordset(sSQL, dbOpenDynaset)
          If Not rsUser.EOF Then ' this shouldn't happen if we _
                  are here!
            Dim sUserCookie As String, sRandom As String
            Randomize CLng(Format(Now, "hhmmss"))
            sRandom = CStr(CLng((Rnd * 1000000000)) + 1)
            sUserCookie = CStr(rsUser("UserID")) + "=" + sRandom

            'Note, using Java script, this validation could be _
                  done client-side!
            Dim sCookie As String, sServer As String, sScript As _
                  String
            sCookie = "UserCookie"
            sServer = cgi.ReadServerName
            sScript = cgi.ReadScriptName
            If (cgi.ReadParam("RememberPassword") = "ON") And _
              (IsNumeric(cgi.ReadParam("RememberDuration"))) Then
                Dim expire As Date
                expire = CDate(Now + _
                CInt(cgi.ReadParam("RememberDuration")))
              cgi.WriteCookie sCookie, sUserCookie, sServer, _
                  sScript, expire
            Else ' no persistence!
              cgi.WriteCookie sCookie, sUserCookie, sServer, _
                  sScript
            End If
            rsUser.Edit
            rsUser("Notes") = sRandom
            rsUser.Update
          End If
          rsUser.Close
      End Sub

      ' Try to login user. Return true if successful.
      Function TryToLogin() As Boolean
        TryToLogin = False
        If (UserPasswordMatch(cgi.ReadParam("UserName"), _
              cgi.ReadParam("Password"))) Then
          SetUserCookies cgi.ReadParam("UserName")
          TryToLogin = True
```

```
      Else
         Dim sUserID As String, sCookieValue As String
         Dim sUserCookie As String, iPos As Integer
         sUserCookie = cgi.ReadCookie("UserCookie")
         If (sUserCookie <> "") Then
            iPos = InStr(sUserCookie, "=")
            sUserID = Left$(sUserCookie, iPos - 1)
            sCookieValue = Mid$(sUserCookie, iPos + 1)
            TryToLogin = UserCookieMatch(sUserID, sCookieValue)
         End If
      End If
   End Function


   Function UserCookieMatch(sUserID As String, sCookieValue _
            As String) As Boolean
      Dim rsUser As Recordset, sSQL As String
      UserCookieMatch = False ' convince me otherwise!
      sSQL = "select * from USERS where UserID=" + sUserID
      Set rsUser = db.OpenRecordset(sSQL, dbOpenDynaset)
      If Not rsUser.EOF Then
         If (rsUser("Notes") = sCookieValue) Then
            sFullName = rsUser("FullName")
            UserCookieMatch = True
         End If
      End If
      rsUser.Close
   End Function
```

This application can be launched from a form with the information built right into it, or launched directly (`http://www.myddomain.com/scripts/UserSecurity3.exe`).

The following functions were unaffected by the change, and so were not included in this source code listing: *main*, *UserPasswordMatch* and *DoubleQuote*.

There are a few other items worth noting. The "UserCookie" is composed of two numbers separated by an equal sign. The left side of this "equation" is the *UserID* (the identifying key for the user). The right side is a random number generated in *SetUserCookies*. The random number can range from 1 to 1,000,000,000 and is saved in the Notes field of the User table. The *SetUserCookies* subroutine calls Visual Basic's *randomize* subroutine with a seed derived by the current time. This causes the randomizing function to start differently each time the subroutine is executed, making the "randomness factor" higher.

It should be noted that a network sniffer can easily read the UserCookie and use it for access to the site (if he has not logged on normally, no new random cookie will be generated). By using the standard Socket Security Layer (SSL), this information can be secured as well.

Figure 4.5
Cookie being validated in Microsoft Internet Explorer

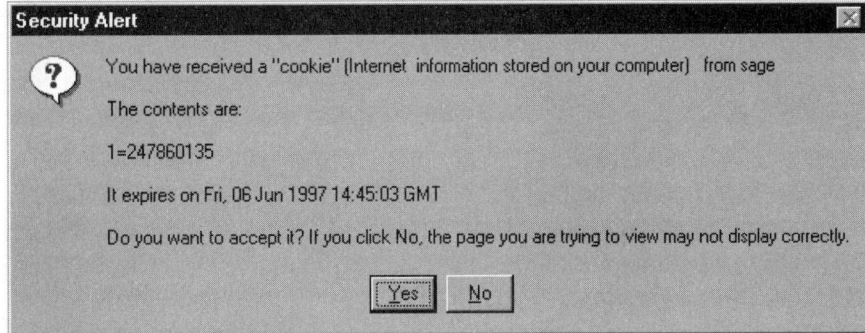

Netscape, Cookies and Localhost

Throughout the book, an imaginary IP address will be used, rather than localhost or a real domain address. This is important for those who want to completely develop an application locally, prior to rolling it out to the production server.

When referencing the local machine, developers often use the localhost (127.0.0.1), which is always forwarded to the local machine. Simply put, this is just another way to connect with the local machine *without* having to remember the actual IP address or the machine's URL.

Interestingly, Netscape browsers sometimes ignore certain HTTP headers (most importantly, cookies), when scripts are executed in this manner. If the actual IP address is used instead, the browser receives these headers. But Microsoft Internet explorer receives them regardless of how the machine is contacted.

When using the machine's logical name (a machine named SAGE can be contacted by `http://SAGE/`) the Netscape browser will, again, ignore these HTTP headers.

Summary

The reader should now be able to utilize both cookies and parameters for writing significantly more complex programming constructs. Our next hurdle to overcome involves errors the Visual Basic application may encounter. The following chapter discusses why some of these errors occur, and how the application can overcome them.

ERROR HANDLING

- Visual Basic error handling
- Common Visual Basic errors
- Using OCXs with CGI applications
- What happens when an error occurs in CGI applications
- Double faults

Until now, the error handling for the applications presented consisted of a single "on error" statement in the main subroutine. Due to the nature of Visual Basic language, the error handling consists of initiating a search for an error handler, stepping back through the call stack until the *main* routine is reached. If a valid error handler cannot be located in main, a global error handler catches the error and displays it in a message box. Once the user presses the **OK** button, the application is terminated. Figure 5.1 displays the typical Visual Basic error message box.

Figure 5.1
Typical VB error
message box

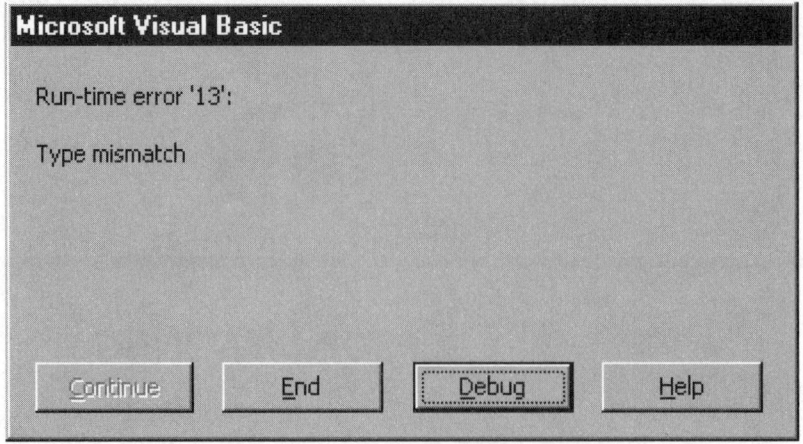

Figure 5.1
Typical VB error
message box

If an error occurs while the application is executing within the web server's context, this may cause several problems with both server and application. The web server will probably launch as a service (unless this is a Windows 95 machine, in which case it will execute as a standard application). As such, unless otherwise specified, forms or message boxes launched by the server remain invisible.

An application that requires a message box display can do so by specifying the **MB_SERVICE_NOTIFICATION** flag as one of the *MessageBox* (or *MsgBox* as it is called in Visual Basic) flags. Some types of messages can also be displayed when the service is made "interactive" by going to the Control Panel, the services icon, and the "World Wide Web Publishing Service" (this is the name for Microsoft's IIS web server, which would be named differently for every type of web server). Once there, press the **Startup** button and check on the **Allow service to interact with desktop** check box. (This does not affect web applications running on Microsoft's IIS web server in any way.)

Some flavors of web servers do not implement this feature fully (e.g., Microsoft IIS). In order to determine whether it has been fully implemented, one should experiment with this feature.

The simple placement of the main error handler is shown here primarily as a last resort. Anyone with significant Visual Basic development experience has encountered these errors. Some are the cause of the new type-safety that has been added to Visual Basic, starting with version 4.0. This prevents the conversion of standard data-types from one to another implicitly. It has been done to improve performance, as well as to improve the reliability of Visual Basic.

Type safety is a good thing; it prevents implicit type conversions and prevents many unexpected bugs from occurring. When a type error occurs, the user is prompted with the "Type Mismatch" message.

The error handler in main allows the user to know the type of error that has occurred, but this is a far cry from tracing the information back to the cause. When this occurs in a large project, the source of the error can be quite baffling.

The first objective of the error handler is to try and recover the error. When this fails or proves impossible, the application should shut down gracefully. Inability to recover from an error, regardless of its source, can be quite damaging to both the application and the web server hosting it.

Regular forms, when displayed by Visual Basic, will simply not show up on the screen. However, they are "out there." This feature is quite useful for applications which may require some interaction with ActiveX or OCX controls, or other tools or objects. These often require interaction with an actual form (such as communication with OCXs, communication via the prehistoric DDE interface, etc.).

Each time the user interacts with the web server, a dedicated web server thread is created to handle communication between server and browser. When this thread discovers that the user is requesting an action which should invoke a script, it launches that script.

Initially, the thread creates a memory block, which would serve as an environment for the soon-to-be-created CGI application. Next, the server thread launches the application and routes STDIN and STDOUT streams to itself. This allows the server to place information in the STDIN stream of the newly created process, and retrieve the information from the STDOUT stream.

As the application executes, the web server retrieves its output via the rerouted STDOUT stream. This information is immediately sent to the client browser via the HTTP protocol. The server determines that the application is finished when the CGI process terminates. At this point, the server also terminates the connection with the client, causing the browser to stop displaying the "Stop" button (which allows the browser to terminate the connection *before* the server terminates the connection.)

Non-Terminating Applications

Situations where the thread does not terminate are handled differently by each server. Originally, most servers had a time-out period of about five minutes. Should the server detect CGI applications which do not terminate after this time-out, the server terminates these processes forcefully, as well as terminating the connection with the client browser.

This feature has been removed from most modern web servers for many reasons. One is that each application takes its own time. The server cannot really tell whether the application is doing what it's supposed to or not. An application which uses SQL server stored procedures can easily cause a five-hour query to occur (and who's to say that this is a bad thing or an error?). In addition, several applications were specifically designed to never terminate! These included real-time applications (which feed more and more information to the client as they receive it). For example, a stock ticker or a chat application often terminates after a significant length of time. This type of application depends on the server to not cut it off after *any* period of time.

ASP scripts, for example, operate under a strict timeout regime. The ASP server terminates such runaway scripts (sometimes unwisely). This feature is limited, however, to ASP scripts, and does not apply to CGI applications executing under IIS version 3.0 or higher.

Any modal window will halt the CGI process indefinitely. Waiting for the user input can never release it, since even modal windows are hidden from the user. For this reason, CGI applications must try to prevent any modal interaction with the desktop. Should the application employ a modal form that requires some user interaction, it will cause the application to wait indefinitely and, in doing so, prevent the application thread from ever terminating.

Errors, message boxes and modal forms can all halt the web server thread in this way. When a thread stops, or waits indefinitely for user input that never arrives, the CGI application remains in memory, theoretically, for infinity — or at least until the next system reboot. Until such time, the application utilizes both CPU resources and the system's memory; both are quite expensive on a web server.

When a programmer attempts to replace the existing, running application with a newer version (attempting to fix the problem), she is unable to do so. As long as the application continues running, the operating system keeps the file locked. This allows the operating system to load sections of the application as needed without worrying about what other processes may be doing to the file. By not loading the entire application to memory, the operating system keeps the memory "footprint" of the application to a minimum.

The server needs to be able to access the application file at all times. For this purpose, the server effectively locks the application executable file until the application terminates. Even shutting down the web server service may not cause the application to cease running. Rebooting the machine is one way to ensure that the CGI application terminates. However, it is also the worst option for this server. Other techniques exist to terminate the process.

It should be noted that, in the opinion of this author, terminating a Visual Basic application without direct access to the web server machine is an impossible task.

Some servers allow interaction between the outside world and the CGI application. This allows the user to forcefully terminate the CGI process manually, thus allowing the server thread to terminate and, with it, the connection to the client. With IIS 1.0 running on Windows NT 3.51, the user can terminate the CGI application simply by using a process manager such as the one that comes with the NT resource kit. With this tool, given the security rights and access to the desktop, the user can terminate any process.

IIS 2.0 and higher spawn the CGI application under the context of the web server service. This causes the operating system to believe that the CGI process is, in fact, a service application — which prohibits the user from terminating the process via the standard operating system constructs (e.g., the task manager).

Unfortunately, the ability to terminate such tasks will not be available on every type of system, operating system or web server. Should an error occur in a CGI application, unloading the application can be a formidable task. One option is to simply create more and more CGI applications, each with a different executable file name, until the bug is resolved. Once the bug has been located and removed, the programmer can restart the machine, forcing all of the processes to terminate. Rebooting the machine, after all, is not possible in all situations and should only be used as a last resort.

For systems with a real debugger on them, the programmer can attach the debugger to the offending process and force it to terminate. There are quite a few stand-alone debuggers around today. The most popular one is embedded right in the Microsoft Developer's Studio (MSDEV) which comes with Visual C++ 4.X or the new Developer's Studio (containing, among other tools, Visual C++ 5).

To terminate an application, the Windows NT task manager must be loaded by pressing the **Control-Shift-Escape** combination, or right-clicking on the task bar and selecting **Task Manager**. Once there, the process tab shows all of the system's active tasks. The debugger can attach to the process by right-clicking on the appropriate entry in the list. Pressing the debug menu option will launch the active debugger if one exists (e.g., the Microsoft Developer's Studio). Closing the developer's studio causes the debugging process to terminate.

General protection faults can also trigger a debugging entity ("just in time" debugging), allowing the debugger to attach to an application mid-execution.

Both of these features can be used to natively debug a Visual Basic application mid-execution using the Microsoft Developer's Studio application.

In order to prevent errors, and to be able to pinpoint the location where an error has occurred, localized error handers should be installed at every location. Each function in the application should have a local error handler, allowing the programmer to determine which function is causing the offending error. This allows the application to recover gracefully while helping the programmer determine where the bug is located.

More Information

Visual Basic 5.0 introduces, among other things, two items that can help immensely when encountering run-time errors.

The first is *unattended execution*. Suffice it to say that this feature prevents run-time errors and message boxes from stopping an application (or server) and allows the application to vent error information into the NT event log or a separate log file.

The second is the ability for a CodeView-compatible debugger (e.g., Visual C++ 4 or higher) to debug compiled Visual Basic applications natively.

Both of these features will be discussed again, in greater detail, in Chapter 11.

Common Errors

As previously mentioned, type conversion errors (Type mismatch) are high on the list of frequently occurring errors. This is due to the fact that implicit conversions no longer work as of Visual Basic version 4. By doing this, Microsoft assisted Visual Basic in becoming a more efficient language, tolerating less implicit tasks that lower performance that the programmer would, in most cases, not be aware of. By forcing this out into the open, the programmer is forced to consider this and the language is better for it.

Since CGI applications are primarily text processing applications, the programmer may require many explicit text conversions. These often incur oversights, which can easily cause run-time errors to occur. Pinpointing the subroutine where the error has occurred is often instrumental in allowing the programmer to locate and fix the problem quickly.

The programmer should take special care in attempting to utilize error recovery techniques. They can often lead to bulletproof applications that can withstand *any* input the user throws at it.

Error handlers can resume at the next position (utilizing `on error resume next`). This often helps recover an application gracefully, but it can lead to other problems as well. It does not, however, resolve the bug that's causing the error. In fact, the error handler can bypass critical code that could be crucial to the application's operation. In addition, this type of error handler may erroneously convince the programmer that the application is working perfectly, when in fact errors are constantly occurring.

Often, errors can be located by simple debugging techniques. The oCGI library supports parameter passing through command line arguments. This allows the programmer to place the parameter string that seems to be causing the problem in the browser into the Command line arguments edit box in VB. The edit box is located in the advanced section of the options dialog box.

Disabling the error handlers (which can be done through the options dialog box) causes the development environment to halt in the position where the error is occurring. Alternatively, the programmer can place break points in the error handling routine and, when the development environment halts, executing the command: `resume 0`, allowing the programmer to determine what may be causing the error to occur.

Double-faults

Error handlers should contain minimal code, or recover quickly. If a second error occurs within the error handler, the global error handler takes over and the application will halt. This has always been the traditional manner in which systems handle secondary faults as a terminating offense.

One way to avoid this effect is by having the error handler resume into a "real error handler." This, however, prevents the error from being located or resumed. It is often useful in situations where the error handling routine needs to be able to do some potentially error-prone actions. These actions include sending the error message as an e-mail to the programmer, or logging the error in a database log. Both can subsequently cause additional errors, due to various reasons.

Localized sections of a subroutine may use different error handlers, or even a local variable, which tells the programmer precisely where the program has stopped.

Following is some sample code, which does this:

```
Dim sError As String, iError As Integer
On Error GoTo MainErrorHandler
   Dim sErrorCausing As String

   ' type conversion error
   sErrorCausing = "Testing" + 1.2

MainErrorHandler:
   sError = Error$
   iError = Err.Number
   Resume RealErrorHandler
RealErrorHandler:
   On Error GoTo SecondaryFault
   ' ERROR PRONE CODE HERE
   sErrorCausing = "ERROR HANDLING :" + sError + iError

   Exit Sub
SecondaryFault:
   Exit Sub
```

This type of error handling concept is useful in attempting to recover potentially erroneous operations with actions which are also potentially erroneous.

In addition to type mismatches, there are other popular error-prone operations that occur frequently and are worth noting. These include:

1. When creating ODBC sources for databases, the full database path should always be stated. When using databases, the *App.Path* variable can be used to specify the directory the executable file resides in (This is also, most often, the directory where the database file is located as well). When recovering this type of error, the error handler often neglects to assume that the database object was never opened and subsequently attempts to close the database object, causing a double fault.

   A similar error occurs when the database fails to open due to a host of possible problems. These can include attempting to read the database file from the wrong directory, or lacking properly installed ODBC database drivers for the particular database type. The application may fail to recover an error of this type. If it succeeds in recovery of this error, the application may still attempt to access some of the underlying objects in that database object, or may attempt to close the object erroneously. All of these errors will cause the server application to halt.

One way to detect whether an object is valid or not (e.g., whether it has been previously initialized) is to use the Visual Basic *TypeName* function, which returns the string "Nothing" if the object has not been initialized. This works because the type of the object is Nothing. If the object was of another type, the type of that object would be returned in a string ("oCGI", for example, if the object was initialized as an oCGI object).

VB5 also adds the *Is Nothing* statement, which checks if the object is of type Nothing (`if myObj Is Nothing then.`). This author does not know of a way of testing for "Nothing" under VB4, except for catching the error that results from trying to access an uninitialized object.

In any case, the optimal way of shutting down an object without knowing if the object is valid or not is by using the `set databaseObject = Nothing` statement. This works with every type of OLE automation object. Since a database object is simply another type of OLE automation object (residing in the DAO object library), it can be closed in this fashion.

Visual Basic uses reference counting and terminates all of the OLE automation objects that may still be active when the application terminates (e.g., when the `end` keyword is encountered, or when the final form is closed and no subroutine or function is still executing).

2. When creating ODBC sources, the ODBC driver may "decide" to prompt the user for more information. This can occur, for example, when the user is not validated correctly with SQL server or when the ODBC data source cannot be found.

Because the CGI application is launched by a service, it can only utilize ODBC data sources located in the DSN section of the ODBC administrator. ODBC data sources located in the DSN ODBC section are not dependent on any user currently logged on in Windows NT, and so is critical when accessing ODBC sources from services (for instance, CGI applications running under the web server context).

I could not locate an acceptable workaround for this issue, (at least, not when using just DAO alone). When faced with the possibility that an ODBC data source may or may not be active, the application should perform an additional test to determine whether the ODBC data source is active or not.

One way to do this is to contact the ODBC data sources directly, or else utilize a form of "helper component" to determine whether the data source is active or not (the DBLIB library). Using the Remote Data Objects (RDO) library is another alternative. Version 1.0 of this library exists in the Enterprise Edition of Visual Basic 4.0. Visual Basic 5.0 (Enterprise Edition) contains version 2.0 of this library, which further improves and optimizes it.

DAO 3.5 eliminates this problem by exposing the **dbDriverNoPrompt** option for ODBCDirect type databases. This allows the application to bypass the Jet Engine, and prevents the ODBC window from halting system execution. The following is an example:

```
Set dbsPubs = wrkJet.OpenDatabase("Publishers", _
    dbDriverNoPrompt, True, _
    "ODBC;DATABASE=pubs;UID=sa;PWD=;DSN=Publishers")
```

The following code demonstrates a simple test to determine if an ODBC data source (named SQLCONNECTION) is active. This is a useful code segment in determining that a SQL server is currently running:

```
On Error GoTo test
  Dim sConnect As String
  sConnect = "DSN=SQLCONNECTION;UID=Myself;PWD=MyPassword"
  Dim rdo As rdoConnection
  Set rdo = rdoEnvironments(0).OpenConnection("", _
      rdDriverNoPrompt,
```

```
                    False, sConnect)
    Set rdo = Nothing


    ' DAO, doing the same thing, the error here is _
            untrappable.
    Dim db As Database
    Set db = Workspaces(0).opendatabase("", False, False, _
            "ODBC;" + sConnect)
    Set db = Nothing
test:
    'error, trapping the RDO error, but not the DAO error!
    Resume Next
```

Remote Data Objects is not only more efficient than DAO, but also provides some functionality not available with DAO. The biggest reason to use DAO is for compatibility with Access databases. Often, a project starts with a simple Access database and later is upgraded to utilize the advanced features of a high-end server, such as SQL server. This is advisable in the case of high-usage web applications, or when several applications, systems or web servers access the database concurrently. The same application, running on several servers concurrently, can easily access the same SQL server database, but performance would be terrible if the system maintained Access as the database format.

One of the improvements in RDO vs. DAO 3.0 is the ability to prevent the data source from prompting the user; this causes a trappable error instead. (As mentioned previously, DAO 3.5 resolves this problem, but is significantly slower than RDO and ADO for SQL server type queries.)

In such situations, The RDO code listed earlier can be used to detect if the server is available. If it is not, the application prompts the user with an alternative DSN and user name/password combination. This also occurs if the SQL Server user name/password combination needs to be validated.

ADO is another new technology from Microsoft. This technology revolutionizes the way database access is executed, since most of the code actually executes *on the server*, rather than the client — bringing Client/Server technology much closer to its original premise. This is useful for ActiveX components running on a server or a client.

3. Security in Access and SQL server often cause trappable, (but often unexpected) errors. These come in the form of "ODBC call failed" errors in SQL server. Error handling code should surround every section of code that accesses the database. The security policy for tables must be carefully reviewed as needed. These errors can occur through improper use of indexes, duplicate keys, foreign key constraints or SQL server triggers.

4. When utilizing OLE automation objects, dedicated error handling should surround creation and initialization of the object. Bad or wrong Type Libraries (installed in the references dialog box) can cause errors when new versions of a library or tool are created.

5. Applications that access databases, either local or Client/Server, often encounter the "double quote" error. This often-overlooked error occurs when SQL statements contain text with double or single quotes. Since the communication between application and database also uses quotes as a string boundary, the server (or database) will not be able to tell where strings begin and where they end. This often occurs when the user enters quotes as one of the parameters to the CGI application. This type of problem is only relevant when actual SQL statements are used (using select, insert, update or delete statements) with a SQL server or an Access database. When accessing Recordset items directly (e.g., using the *AddNew* Visual Basic function), DAO maintains quotes automatically.

6. The recordset will sometimes reach an End Of File (EOF) state when selecting a group of rows from the database. This occurs when no rows have met the selection criteria. If the application tries to access the recordset without checking for an EOF condition beforehand, an error will be triggered. Checking for an EOF condition before accessing a recordset will ensure that the Recordset does indeed have data in it.

7. Most fields default to Null. If a Null is referenced as a string or converted into one, a trappable error occurs. More often than

not, Nulls could be referenced as empty strings. Creating a simple function for handling Null values resolves this easily:

```
Public Function CheckNull(vInformation As Variant) As String
    CheckNull = IIf(IsNull(vInformation), "", _
            CStr(vInformation))
End Function
```

8. Conversion from one type of variable to another (type conversion). It is easily handled using code similar to this:

```
Public Function ToInt(vInt As Variant) As Integer
    On Error GoTo ToIntErr
    ToInt = CInt(vInt)
    Exit Function
ToIntErr:
    ToInt = 0
    Exit Function
End Function
```

9. References for items beyond array boundaries, or access to items in collections that do not exist (via the key portion). These reference errors can be bypassed in much the same way as the previous ones.

```
Dim aInt(1 To 2) As Integer
aInt(3) = 3 ' Subscript out of range

Dim cTest As New Collection
cTest.Add Item:=100, Key:="One Hundred"
Dim iOneHundred As Integer
iOneHundred = cTest("One Hundred")
Dim iTwoHundred As Integer
iTwoHundred = cTest("Two Hundred") ' Invalid procedure _
        call or argument
```

Summary

The reader should now be able to produce error-free code that can overcome most of the internal bugs and typical errors the application will encounter throughout its life. Now that we have a full understanding of most of the technologies involved in writing CGI applications with Visual Basic, we will discuss the next level of web application — the search engine — in the next chapter.

PART II

USING CGI FOR REAL WORLD APPLICATIONS

6

SEARCH ENGINE

- The search engine: What is it?
- Types of searches the search engine makes
- SQL searches
- Enhanced search engine
- Reverse search
- Enhanced search engine: Catagorizing by number of matched keywords

What Am I Searching for?

Most web programmers require a search engine of one type or another. Some databases offer acceptable tools for search engines. These usually have several flaws and limitations, though, primarily in the level of customization that they will accept.

Providing a flexible, generic search tool is the focus of this chapter. It is a tool that can be easily ported and moved to accommodate any format or database. By understanding the mechanics behind this search engine, a programmer should be able to revise this code and modify it for his or her own needs.

The initial version of the search engine presented here will be fairly advanced. It includes three distinct types of searches: **And, Or** and **Exact match.**

- The **Exact match** search simply takes text written by the user and attempts to locate it in the column being searched.

- The **And** search attempts to locate every distinct word in the string. Only strings that are fully matched by *all* of the strings will be shown.

- The **Or** search attempts to match *any* of the words in the string with the column being searched.

When using the **And** and **Or** options, allow multiple words to be matched by using quotes or double quotes. Once these are located, the system attempts to match an equivalent quote. Several words, surrounded by quotes, will be matched as a whole (as in "Exact Match").

This engine also supports multiple pages. In order to do this, the search SQL statement actually specifies one item more than the number of items per screen. This final item, if it exists, is used to find out whether there are more items to display as well as to determine the first item on the next screen.

It should be noted that the Visual Basic jet engine is not exact in the number of returned items when a search specifies a "TOP #" of rows to be returned. For some queries, a few more items will be returned than are specified. For example, specifying TOP 3 could result in 5 or 6 items being returned. This has to do with the number of items found that actually match the same condition. If DAO (or the "Jet engine") retrieves more than the specified number of items, all of these items will be returned. Relying on the number of items returned to be less than or equal to the number specified by TOP# is a definite mistake. Imagine a user asking for 4 rows, and the system retrieving 6. The user will not develop much trust in it. For this reason, the system counts the number of items retrieved, to be sure that it is precise.

Alternatively, the user can use the *AbsolutePosition* Visual Basic property to set and get the position after a particular number of items. This property, however, is not available on Forward-only cursor recordsets (e.g., most ODBC based SQL servers).

The implementation for the *DoAndOr* function is interesting to detail. This function first creates the beginning of the SQL statement. The select statement always has "**WHERE 1=1**" as the first select statement condition. This is done to avoid having to determine, for each condition, whether a "WHERE" statement, an "OR" statement or an "AND" statement is needed.

By placing the "WHERE 1=1" at the beginning of the statement, an empty search results, returning all items in the database. But checking for this particular case in the following statement can prevent this:

```
'prevent empty search
  If (Trim$(sKeywords) = "") Then
    DoShowSearch
       Exit Sub
  End If
```

The function iterates through the keyword list. When the function determines that quotes are in use, it automatically looks for the end of these quotes and considers everything *within* the quotes a single "keyword" to be searched for as a whole. Other than this exception, words are separated by spaces.

Should the search be an **And** search, the *DoAndOr* function receives a true *fAnd* parameter. When the search starts, each keyword is located and placed in a search statement appended to the end of the SQL code. The statement consists of

```
AND INSTR( SEARCHCOL, 'data')
```

SEARCHCOL stands for the column being searched, and **data** is the data being searched for. Each keyword triggers another statement like this. The DAO engine attempts to locate all searched keywords within the given column.

When the search is an **Or** type search, the first filtering statement must be an **And**. Otherwise, doing an **Or** on "WHERE 1=1" would always provide a true result — causing the system to retrieve all of the data in the database. Because the system retains a flag, telling us whether or not this is the first statement the function is allowed to recover. The system uses the *fNextTimeOr* flag to retain this information. Initially, the flag is false and the system appends an **AND** to the end of the SQL code. Now, each keyword triggers an **OR** statement at the end. Finally, the parenthesis for the **AND** statement is closed.

Performance-wise, the **Or** search could have been better implemented. Several database engines (particularly, the Jet engine, Access and SQL server) generate less than ideal performance when **OR** conditions are found in the SQL statement. Often, SQL performance tuners convert such statements to UNION statements. These often allow the server's optimizer to use indexes in the most efficient manner.

In this situation, however, the type of implementation presents particular difficulties. The only way to specify the number of rows is by specifying *the number of rows that each union will return*. This makes it nearly impossible to build an effective Next # of rows system, because of the lack of any specific key to index.

The *DoEntire* function takes care of the **Exact match** search. Because double quotes function as keyword specifiers in the other search, they must be discarded here. In order to do this, the *RemoveDoubleQuotes* function is called. This strips the keyword string from any double quotes. Once these are removed, the rest of the string is inserted into an "INSTR" statement in the query.

The *RemoveDoubleQuotes* function removes double quotes from the keyword string by consistently searching for and removing them until no more quotes can be located.

After displaying the required number of items, the engine determines whether more are available. If so, the next item is the one that should be displayed first when the user presses the "Next 10 Rows" button. The key for this row is placed as a hidden object in a small form, which encapsulates this button. The button effectively runs the same script, which notes a "first row" item and uses it in its search.

In addition to the first row, the original form's keywords must be replaced here. These keywords are "de-scrambled" by oCGI in order for the application to view them as the user types them. They cannot simply be passed on to the newly created form without change. In fact, the keywords have to be partially *re*-scrambled in order for the search engine to retain the same information. The *ReadScrambledParam* function does just that — it takes an existing parameter and returns it in a partially scrambled form. *This function only scrambles single and double quotes that do not pass well into the browser.* (Rather, the browser assumes that these specify the end of the keyword field specification.)

The problem could be overcome by using a single line Textarea field. But this type of field does not utilize an `<input type=text name=name value="value">` format. Rather, it specifies the contents of the field in between `<textarea>` and `</textarea>` HTML statements. This, however, would allow the user to change the search context mid-search without the application ever knowing.

This concept can be easily ported in order to fill input HTML controls with information that may contain quotes.

The *DoEntire* function produces the SQL statement for the **Exact match** option. The *DoAndOr* function produces an equivalent SQL statement for the **And** and **Or** options. Once a SQL statement is created, the system uses it to traverse the rows resulting from this query. When the selected number of items is retrieved, the search engine determines whether more items are available. If so, the search engine proceeds to place a form, and the embedded button, in order to allow the "Next 10 rows" button to work.

Because the SQL code produced by these functions is fully ODBC compatible, it could be easily ported to high end systems with no change other than pointing the database to a SQL server.

The Search Applications Database Layout

The table structure for the Search database is as shown in Table 6.1:

Table 6.1
Data Table Layout

Table: DATA Field Name	Field Type	Remark
Key	Autonumber (long integer)	Primary key (identifies record).
Title	Text(50)	Title of the item.
Data	Memo	Description of item (this is what we're searching through).

The Source Code for SearchEngine1.bas

```
Option Explicit


Declare Function oCGI2Register Lib "oCGI2.dll" Alias _
        "DllRegisterServer" () As Long
```

```
Public cgi As oCGI2

Sub main()
On Error GoTo RegisterErr ' register oCGI only if having _
        problems!
   Set cgi = New oCGI2
On Error GoTo NormalErr
   cgi.ProcessCGI Command
   'Load frmVBCrash

   Select Case cgi.ReadParam("Action")
     Case "DOSEARCH":
       DoSearch
     Case Else:
       DoShowSearch
   End Select

   Set cgi = Nothing
   End
NormalErr:
   cgi.WriteCGI "<HTML><BODY>Error:" + Error$ + "</BODY></HTML>"
   Set cgi = Nothing ' Just in case
   End
RegisterErr:
   oCGI2Register
   End
End Sub


Function DoAndOr(fAnd As Boolean, sColumns As String, _
        sFrom As String, sData As String, sSearchRow _
        As String, Optional nRows As Variant, _
   Optional vFirstRow As Variant) As String
   Dim sQuery As String

   sQuery = "select " + IIf(IsMissing(nRows), "", "TOP " + _
        CStr(ToInt(nRows + 1)))
   sQuery = sQuery + " " + sColumns + " from " + sFrom + " _
        where 1=1 "

   If (Not IsMissing(vFirstRow)) Then
     If (vFirstRow <> "") Then
```

```
                  sQuery = sQuery + " AND (Key>=" + _
                     CStr(ToInt(vFirstRow)) + ") "
            End If
      End If


      Dim fNextTimeOr As Boolean
      Dim iPos As Integer
      Do While (1)
         If (Trim$(sData) = "") Then Exit Do
         If (Left$(sData, 1) = """") Then
            sData = Mid$(sData, 2)
            iPos = InStr(sData, """")
         Else
            iPos = InStr(sData, " ")
         End If


         Dim sWord As String

         If iPos <= 0 Then
            sWord = sData
            iPos = Len(sWord)
         Else
            sWord = Left(sData, iPos - 1)
         End If
      If (fAnd) Then
         sQuery = sQuery+ "AND INSTR("+ sSearchRow + ",'" + _
             DoubleQuote(sWord) + "') "
         Else
            ' it's an or, gotta check if this is the first time!
            If (fNextTimeOr) Then
               sQuery = sQuery + " OR INSTR(" + sSearchRow + ",'"
               sQuery = sQuery + DoubleQuote(sWord) + "') "
            Else ' first time.
               fNextTimeOr = True
               sQuery = sQuery + "AND (INSTR(" + sSearchRow + ",'"
               sQuery = sQuery + DoubleQuote(sWord) + "') "
            End If
         End If

         sData = Mid(sData, iPos + 1)
      Loop
```

```
    If (fNextTimeOr) Then
       sQuery = sQuery + ")"
    End If
    DoAndOr = sQuery
End Function


Function DoEntire(sColumns As String, sFrom As String, _
           sKeywords As String, sSearchRow As String, _
             Optional nRows As Variant, Optional_
                vFirstRow As Variant) _
    As String
    Dim sQuery As String

    'check for quotes
    sKeywords = RemoveDoubleQuotes(sKeywords)

    sQuery = "select " + IIf(IsMissing(ToInt(nRows)), "", _
          "TOP " + CStr(nRows + 1)) + " "
    sQuery = sQuery + sColumns + " from " + sFrom
    sQuery = sQuery+ " WHERE INSTR(" + sSearchRow + ",'" + _
          DoubleQuote(sKeywords) + "') "
    If (Not IsMissing(vFirstRow)) Then
      If (vFirstRow <> "") Then
        sQuery = sQuery + " and Key>=" + _
           CStr(ToInt(vFirstRow))
      End If
    End If
    DoEntire = sQuery
End Function


Function ReadScrambledParam(sParam As String) As String
   ' rescramble parameter.

   Dim sValue As String, iPos As Integer, sOut As String

   sValue = cgi.ReadParam(sParam)

   For iPos = 1 To Len(sValue)
     Select Case Mid$(sValue, iPos, 1)
       Case """":
         sOut = sOut + "%22"
```

```
            Case "'":
               sOut = sOut + "%27"
            Case Else
               sOut = sOut + Mid$(sValue, iPos, 1)
         End Select
      Next
      ReadScrambledParam = sOut
End Function

Sub DoSearch()
   ' max number of rows that a query returns.
   Const TOP_ROWS = 10

   Dim sQuery As String, sOut As String
   With cgi
      ' first break down the parameters.
      Dim sKeywords As String, sFirstRow As String
      sKeywords = .ReadParam("KeyWords")

      'prevent empty search
      If (Trim$(sKeywords) = "") Then
         DoShowSearch
         Exit Sub
      End If

      sFirstRow = .ReadParam("FirstRow")
      Select Case .ReadParam("Match")
         Case "A" ' and
            sQuery = DoAndOr(True, "*", "DATA", sKeywords, _
               "Data", TOP_ROWS, _ sFirstRow)
         Case "E" ' Entire
            sQuery = DoEntire("*", "DATA", sKeywords, _
               "Data", TOP_ROWS, sFirstRow)
         Case "O" ' or
            sQuery = DoAndOr(False, "*", "DATA", sKeywords, _
               "Data", TOP_ROWS, sFirstRow)

         Case Else ' error
            sOut = "<HTML>" + vbCrLf
            sOut = sOut + "<HEADER><TITLE> Sample Search "
            sOut = sOut + " results</TITLE></HEADER>" + vbCrLf
```

```
            sOut = sOut + "<BODY BGCOLOR=#ffffff>" + vbCrLf
            sOut = sOut + "<H2> Error: matching option was "
            sOut = sOut + " not selected correctly </H2>"
            sOut = sOut + "</BODY></HTML>"
            .WriteCGI sOut
            Exit Sub
    End Select

    Dim db As Database, rs As Recordset
    Set db = Workspaces(0).OpenDatabase(App.Path + _
            "\search.mdb")
    Set rs = db.OpenRecordset(sQuery, dbOpenDynaset)

    sOut = "<HTML>" + vbCrLf
    sOut = sOut + "<HEADER><TITLE> Sample Search _
            results</TITLE>"
    sOut = sOut + " </HEADER>" + vbCrLf
    sOut = sOut + "<BODY BGCOLOR=#ffffff>" + vbCrLf
    sOut = sOut + "<H2>Sample Search results</H2><HR>" + vbCrLf
    Dim iRows As Integer, fNextBunch As Boolean
    iRows = 0
    fNextBunch = False
    If rs.EOF Then
        sOut = sOut + "<H3>Search did not retrieve any _
            rows</H3>" + vbCrLf
    Else
        sOut = sOut + "<H3>Search resulted in the _
            following results</H3>" + vbCrLf
        sOut = sOut + "<TABLE BORDER=1 WIDTH=100%>" + vbCrLf
        Do While Not rs.EOF
            iRows = iRows + 1
            If iRows <= TOP_ROWS Then
            sOut = sOut + "<TR>"
            sOut = sOut + "<TD WIDTH=20%>" + rs("Title")_
            + "</TD>" + vbCrLf
            sOut = sOut + "<TD WIDTH=80%>" + rs("Data")_
            + "</TD>" + vbCrLf
            sOut = sOut + "</TR>"
            Else ' last row - instead, put up a next + _
            TOP_ROWS + button
            fNextBunch = True
```

```
            Exit Do
          End If
          rs.MoveNext
       Loop
       sOut = sOut + "</TABLE>"
       If (fNextBunch) Then
          sOut = sOut + "<FORM ACTION=""" + .ReadScriptName
          sOut = sOut + """ METHOD=""POST"">"
          sOut = sOut + "<INPUT TYPE=HIDDEN NAME=""Action"" _
            VALUE=""DOSEARCH"">"
          sOut = sOut + "<INPUT TYPE=HIDDEN _
            NAME=""KeyWords"" "
          sOut = sOut + "VALUE=""" + ReadScrambledParam_
            ("KeyWords") + """>"
          sOut = sOut + "<INPUT TYPE=HIDDEN NAME=""Match"" "
          sOut = sOut + " VALUE=""" + cgi.ReadParam("Match")_
            + """>"
          sOut = sOut + "<INPUT TYPE=HIDDEN _
            NAME=""FirstRow"" VALUE= "
          sOut = sOut + CStr(rs("Key")) + ">"
          sOut = sOut + "<INPUT TYPE=Submit NAME=Submit _
            VALUE=""View the next "
          sOut = sOut + CStr(TOP_ROWS) + " rows "">"
          sOut = sOut + "</FORM>"
        End If
      End If

      sOut = sOut + "</BODY></HTML>"
      cgi.WriteCGI sOut
      rs.Close
      db.Close
    End With
  End Sub

Function DoubleQuote(sData As String) As String
  Dim sOut As String, iPos As Integer

  For iPos = 1 To Len(sData)
    Select Case Mid$(sData, iPos, 1)
      Case "'":
        sOut = sOut + "''"
```

```vb
        Case """":
            sOut = sOut + """"""
        Case Else:
            sOut = sOut + Mid$(sData, iPos, 1)
      End Select
   Next
   DoubleQuote = sOut
End Function


Sub DoShowSearch()
   With cgi
      Dim sOut As String

      sOut = "<HTML>" + vbCrLf
      sOut = sOut + "<HEADER><TITLE> Sample Search page _
           </TITLE></HEADER>" + vbCrLf
      sOut = sOut + "<BODY BGCOLOR=#ffffff>" + vbCrLf
      sOut = sOut + "<H2> The search engine </H2>" + vbCrLf
      sOut = sOut + "Enter your search keywords here:<P>_
           <HR>" + vbCrLf

      sOut = sOut + "<FORM ACTION=""" + .ReadScriptName + _
           """ METHOD=""POST"">"
      sOut = sOut + "<INPUT TYPE=""HIDDEN"" NAME=""Action"" _
           VALUE=""DOSEARCH"">"
      sOut = sOut + vbCrLf + "<TABLE><TR><TD>"
      sOut = sOut + "<B>Search for:</B></TD><TD></TD><TD>"
      sOut = sOut + <INPUT TYPE=TEXT SIZE=20 MAXLENGTH=100 "
      sOut = sOut + "NAME=""KeyWords"" VALUE="""">"
      sOut = sOut + "</TD></TR><TR><TD><INPUT TYPE=""RADIO"" "
      sOut = sOut + "CHECKED NAME=""Match"" VALUE=""E"">_
           Exact Match"
      sOut = sOut + "</TD><TD><INPUT TYPE=""RADIO"" _
           NAME=""Match"" VALUE=""A"">And"
      sOut = sOut + "</TD><TD><INPUT TYPE=""RADIO"" _
           NAME=""Match"" VALUE=""O"">Or"
      sOut = sOut + "</TD></TR><TR><TD><P><INPUT _
           TYPE=Submit "
      sOut = sOut + "NAME=""Submit"" VALUE=""Search"">"
      sOut = sOut + "</TD><TD></TD></TR></TABLE> </FORM>"
      sOut = sOut + "<HR>"
```

```
     If (Trim$(.ReadRemoteFrom) <> "") Then
       sOut = sOut + "Your email address is: " + _
           .ReadRemoteFrom + "<BR>" + vbCrLf
     End If

     sOut = sOut + "Your browser is: " + .ReadUserAgent + _
          "<BR>" + vbCrLf

     sOut = sOut + "Your IP address is: " + _
           .ReadRemoteAddress + "<BR>" + vbCrLf
     If (.ReadRemoteHost <> "") And (.ReadRemoteHost <> _
           .ReadRemoteAddress) Then
       sOut = sOut + "Your machine's host name: " + _
          .ReadRemoteHost + "<BR>"
       sOut = sOut + vbCrLf
     End If

     sOut = sOut + "</BODY>" + vbCrLf
     sOut = sOut + "</HTML>"

     .WriteCGI sOut
   End With
End Sub

Function RemoveDoubleQuotes(sStrings As String) As String
   Dim iPos As Integer
   Do While (True)
     iPos = InStr(sStrings, """")
     If (iPos > 0) Then
       sStrings = Left$(sStrings, iPos - 1) + Mid$_
           (sStrings, iPos + 1)
     Else
       RemoveDoubleQuotes = sStrings
       Exit Function
     End If
   Loop
End Function

Function ToInt(vInteger As Variant) As Integer
On Error GoTo ToIntErr
   ToInt = CInt(vInteger)
```

```
      Exit Function
ToIntErr:
   ToInt = 0
   Exit Function
End Function
```

Snapshots from Search Engine 1

Figure 6.1 displays the search engine's initial page. Figure 6.2 shows the subsequent result page.

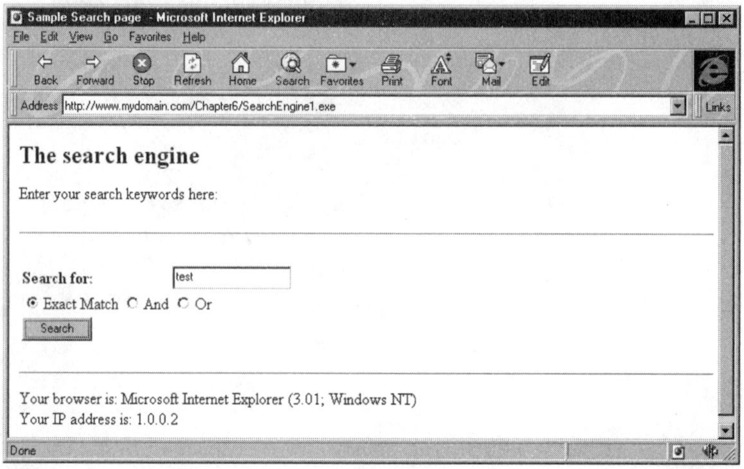

Figure 6.1
Search Engine 1 —
initial web page

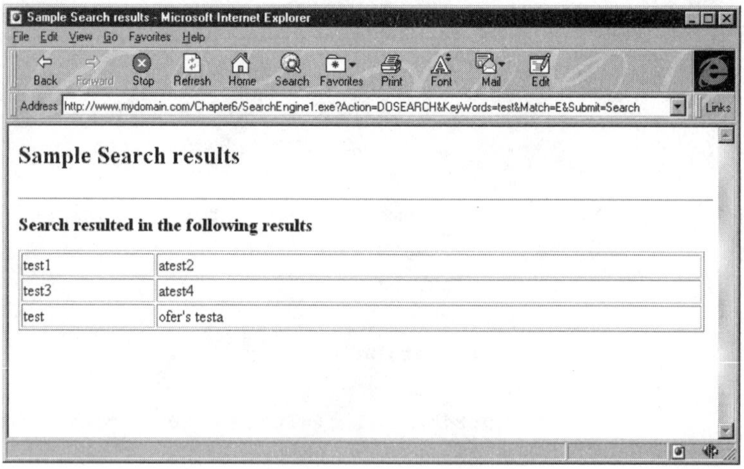

Figure 6.2
Subsequent
results page

Searching for More?

This version of the search engine could still be improved. First, the number of rows returned should be up to the user. In addition, the user should be able to search *back* a number of rows.

The tabular display of search results could also be improved somewhat. The current results shown make it difficult to detect where the matched keywords are located. The next revision of the search engine improves this, however, by highlighting the keywords in the search results.

DoShowSearch Routine

To allow the user to select the number of results returned, the *DoShowSearch* routine adds a combo box to the search display. This combo box lets the user select the number of rows returned from the options displayed. Ideally, this should be done in an edit box, in much the same way that the number of days were selected to identify the password in the User Security application.

Several browsers presently support a "button-less" submit. This type of submit occurs when the user is presented with a single edit box and, optionally, other types of input controls (e.g., combo boxes, radio buttons, etc.). When a user is presented with such a form, she may submit it by simply pressing the **Enter** (i.e., the Carriage Return key). This submits the form with a Carriage Return/Line Feed appended to the end of the parameter list. The CR/LF combination is automatically removed from the parameter list by oCGI.

Presenting a user with more than one edit box forces him or her to press the **Submit** button (or any other submission device — an image-input type, for example). Most power-users prefer the CR method of submitting the form because it is quicker and easier. This is doubly true when the objective of the form is a search of any kind. Therefore, edit boxes should be avoided in situations where this rule applies.

The information in this combo box is submitted in the *TopRows* parameter, which is tested and converted into the TOP_ROWS variable.

DoAndOr and DoEntire Functions

The implementation of backtracking is a bit more complex. First, the query *DoAndOr* and *DoEntire* functions are modified to account for descending order. Placing the results from the recordset in the opposite order they would normally be shown undid this. Additionally, the functions would assume that the last row, rather then the first row, was to be referenced. Therefore, when *fBackwards* is true, these functions change the query to show everything **before and including** *sFirstRow*.

Once the query functions return the proper SQL code, the result sets must be parsed correctly. The difference between backward motion and forward motion is delicate enough to warrant a new function to handle backtracking. The *DoSearch* function will handle forward motion, as before, while *DoSearchBack* takes care of backward motion.

Both functions utilize the *PrevBunch* and *NextBunch* functions. These functions create buttons, as well as the dedicated forms for them, to move forward and backward at each point.

NextBunch Function

The *NextBunch* function takes much of its functionality from the previous *DoSearch* implementation. *Nextbunch* maintains the form, which allows the user to proceed forward in the recordset. It perpetuates the Keywords, TopRows and Match parameters into the next phase. In addition, *Nextbunch* proceeds to pass the *FirstRow* for the next round. When the **Next** button is pressed, the *DoSearch* subroutine uses the *FirstRow* as a reference for the first row to compare with the key.

PrevBunch Function

The *PrevBunch* function has much the same functionality as *NextBunch*. One notable difference is that the form action for backtracking in *PrevBunch* is DOSEARCHBACK. This is translated in main into a call for the *DoSearchBack* function. This type of form contains a *LastRow* parameter, which specifies that the next *DoSearchBack* call must search for information occurring before *LastRow*.

The *DoSearch* subroutine ascertains whether or not there are more rows in the same manner as before: by selecting at least one more item and determining if it exists. The last item, not shown in this round, will be entered into *sTopRow*, to be shown as the top row for the next round should it occur. If the function senses that it has passed a first row (i.e., that this is not the first call to this function — meaning there are more items **behind** us), it will display the *PrevBunch* results. This function requires the value of the first key in the list *and* the number of rows. If the subroutine detects that there are more rows following the last one (the *fNextBunch* variable helps determine this using the last dummy row as a reference), the *NextBunch* function is called. The parameter in this call presents the last row detected (the one following the last row displayed) and proceeds to pass it along as the first row displayed in the next round.

The *DoSearchBack* subroutine requires that two new records be returned, in addition to the number of rows specified by the user. The subroutine retrieves rows in the order opposite from the order in which they are to be displayed. For this reason, the subroutine traverses the recordset from end to beginning. The last row retrieved in this way is only utilized in order to allow the user to proceed forward. (This row is going to be used as the first row in the next forward round.) The number of rows will be more than TOP_ROWS+1 if there are more items in the back. This is the reason for retrieving the second extra row — in order to determine whether a new move back is possible. In that case, the *fPrevBunch* becomes true and the next, previous row (since we are moving backwards) is retrieved. This prevents the row from being used erroneously.

The first row retrieved (the last or next to last row in the recordset) is used in order to reference the next *PrevBunch*, if there are more items behind these. The *fPrevBunch* flag determines this. Additionally, the first row is used for the next forward round, utilizing the *NextBunch* function.

The backward movement maintains the previous round's first displayed item, while the forward movement returns the next item that is **not** displayed. This permits these subroutines to complement each other, and makes the referencing process easier to maintain.

Going backwards through the list prevents this functionality from being ported to larger-scale servers (like the SQL server) that use *forward* only cursors. Several techniques can overcome this: the information can be restructured so that backtracking does not actually require it to be in descending order (rather than ascending). The BOTTOM SQL keyword can replace the TOP to enable correct backtracking. Another alternative is to reorder the information using a local collection, subsequently displaying the results from *that* collection instead of from the original recordset.

The key is now displayed with the information. The table column for the key does not have a width specification, so it varies according to the data width. In addition, the background color for this column was modified to "Aqua." This allows the user to determine quickly that the forward and backward movement is working.

The forward and backward buttons are placed in table cells to force them side by side.

MakeBold Function

Another addition to this revision of the Search Engine is the introduction of the *MakeBold* function. This function's objective is to locate the keywords in the data section of the result and make these keywords bold. The user can then locate where these keywords are in the search results.

The *MakeBold* function takes as input the raw data and the SQL query from the *DoAndOr* and *DoEntire* functions. The SQL statement is broken down into keywords, and the first instance of each keyword is located in the raw text. This information is stored in two collections: the *cStart* collection — holding the starting position of each keyword encountered; and the *cLength* collection — holding that specific keyword's length. The objective is to localize each keyword and to surround it with HTML statements that make it bold.

Direct modifications on the input string only work for a single replacement. Subsequent searches may replace information in the HTML code as well. For example, a search for the keyword "FONT" could enter an endless loop, because the HTML statement (which may be causing the "FONT" word to stand out) also contains this text. In order to prevent this, the subroutine first detects all of the appearances of first-instance keywords in the text, and later rebuilds the text, based on this information, to account for the HTML additions. This prevents interaction between the HTML and the searched-for keywords.

Once the list of starting points and keyword lengths is finalized, the subroutine traverses it from the smallest (closer to the beginning of the string) to the largest (closest to the end of the string). At each point, the subroutine reconstructs the text with the appropriate HTML code entered in. In order to make the "bold" text stand out better than standard bold, the subroutine uses the <FONT COLOR=RED> HTML statement instead. At each reconstruction, the old starting and length entries are removed from the list, enabling the subroutine to locate the next smallest ones.

The *MakeBold* subroutine is called once for every item displayed. Each item is then shown with the keywords that triggered its inclusion in the search results.

Source Code for SearchEngine2.bas

```
Option Explicit

Declare Function oCGI2Register Lib "oCGI2.dll" Alias _
        "DllRegisterServer" () As Long
Public cgi As oCGI2

Fun5ction DoError() As String
  Dim sOut As String

  sOut = "<HTML>" + vbCrLf
  sOut = sOut + "<HEADER><TITLE> Sample Search "
  sOut = sOut + " results</TITLE></HEADER>" + vbCrLf
  sOut = sOut + "<BODY BGCOLOR=#ffffff>" + vbCrLf
  sOut = sOut + "<H2> Error: matching option was "
  sOut = sOut + " not selected correctly </H2>"
  sOut = sOut + "</BODY></HTML>"

  DoError = sOut
End Function

Sub main()
```

```
    On Error GoTo RegisterErr ` register oCGI only if having _
            problems!
        Set cgi = New oCGI2
    On Error GoTo NormalErr
        cgi.ProcessCGI Command
        `Load frmVBCrash

        Select Case cgi.ReadParam("Action")
          Case "DOSEARCH":
            DoSearch
          Case "DOSEARCHBACK":
            DoSearchBack
          Case Else:
            DoShowSearch
        End Select

        Set cgi = Nothing
        End
    NormalErr:
        cgi.WriteCGI "<HTML><BODY>Error:" + Error$ + _
                "</BODY></HTML>"
        Set cgi = Nothing ` Just in case
        End
    RegisterErr:
        oCGI2Register
        End
    End Sub


    Function DoAndOr(fAnd As Boolean, sColumns As String, _
            sFrom As String,
        sData As String, sSearchCol As String, sKeyCol As String, _
        nRows As Variant, sFirstRow As String, fBackwards As _
            Boolean) As String

        Dim sQuery As String

        sQuery = "select TOP " + CStr(nRows + 1)
        sQuery = sQuery + " " + sColumns + " from " + sFrom + " _
            where 1=1 "

        If (sFirstRow <> "") Then
```

```
      sQuery = sQuery + " AND (" + sKeyCol + IIf(fBackwards, _
          "<=", ">=")
      sQuery = sQuery + CStr(ToInt(sFirstRow)) + ") "
  End If


  Dim fNextTimeOr As Boolean
  Dim iPos As Integer
  Do While (1)
    If (Trim$(sData) = "") Then Exit Do
    If (Left$(sData, 1) = """") Then
      sData = Mid$(sData, 2)
      iPos = InStr(sData, """")
    Else
      iPos = InStr(sData, " ")
    End If


    Dim sWord As String

    If iPos <= 0 Then
      sWord = sData
      iPos = Len(sWord)
    Else
      sWord = Left$(sData, iPos - 1)
    End If
    If (fAnd) Then
      sQuery = sQuery + "AND INSTR(" + sSearchCol + ",'"
      sQuery = sQuery + DoubleQuote(sWord) + "') "
    Else
        ' it's an or, gotta check if this is the first time!
      If (fNextTimeOr) Then
        sQuery = sQuery + " OR INSTR(" + sSearchCol + ",'"
        sQuery = sQuery + DoubleQuote(sWord) + "') "
      Else ' first time.
        fNextTimeOr = True
        sQuery = sQuery + "AND (INSTR(" + sSearchCol + _
          ",'"
        sQuery = sQuery + DoubleQuote(sWord) + "') "
      End If
    End If

    sData = Mid$(sData, iPos + 1)
```

```
      Loop

    If (fNextTimeOr) Then
       sQuery = sQuery + ")"
    End If
    sQuery = sQuery + " ORDER BY " + sKeyCol
    sQuery = sQuery + IIf(fBackwards, " DESC", " ASC")
    DoAndOr = sQuery
End Function


Function DoEntire(sColumns As String, sFrom As String, _
         sKeywords As String,
    sSearchCol As String, sKeyCol As String, nRows As Integer, _
    sFirstRow As String, fBackwards As Boolean) As String

    Dim sQuery As String

    'check for quotes
    sKeywords = RemoveDoubleQuotes(sKeywords)

    sQuery = "select TOP " + CStr(nRows + 1) + " "
    sQuery = sQuery + sColumns + " from " + sFrom
    sQuery = sQuery + " WHERE INSTR(" + sSearchCol + ",'"
    sQuery = sQuery + DoubleQuote(sKeywords) + "') "
    If (sFirstRow <> "") Then
       sQuery = sQuery + " and " + sKeyCol + IIf(fBackwards, _
            "<=", ">=")
       sQuery = sQuery + CStr(ToInt(sFirstRow))
    End If

    sQuery = sQuery + " ORDER BY " + sKeyCol
    sQuery = sQuery + IIf(fBackwards, " DESC", " ASC")
    DoEntire = sQuery
End Function


Function MakeBold(ByVal sMakeBold As String, ByVal sData _
         As String) As String
    ' make each found keyword in this thing bold.
    Dim cStart As New Collection, cLength As New Collection
    Dim sWord As String, iPos As Integer
    Do While (1)
```

```vb
iPos = InStr(sData, "INSTR(")
If (iPos < 1) Then Exit Do
sData = Mid$(sData, iPos)
iPos = InStr(sData, ",'")
sData = Mid$(sData, iPos + 2)

' not very safe!
' won't really work if the keywords have "')"
iPos = InStr(sData, "')")

sWord = Left$(sData, iPos - 1)

' now locate the first instance of sWord in sMakeBold
Dim iPosMakeBold As Integer

iPosMakeBold = InStr(sMakeBold, sWord)
If (iPosMakeBold > 0) Then
   cStart.Add iPosMakeBold
   cLength.Add Len(sWord)
End If
sData = Mid$(sData, iPos + 1)
Loop
' all of this is to prevent the search from locating
' — stuff in the modified string!

' now loop and implement modifications.
Dim i As Integer, iSmallestPosition As Integer
Dim sOut As String, iLastEnd As Integer
iLastEnd = 1
Do While (cStart.Count > 0)
   ' look for the smallest position.
   iSmallestPosition = 1
   For i = 2 To cStart.Count
     If (cStart.Item(i) < cStart.Item(iSmallestPosition)) _
        Then
        iSmallestPosition = i
     End If
   Next

   Dim iStart As Integer, iLen As Integer
   iStart = cStart.Item(iSmallestPosition)
```

```
        iLen = cLength.Item(iSmallestPosition)
        If (iStart < iLastEnd) Then
            iStart = iLastEnd
        End If
        sOut = sOut + Mid$(sMakeBold, iLastEnd, iStart - iLastEnd)
        sOut = sOut + "<FONT COLOR=RED>"
        If (iLastEnd < iStart + iLen) Then
            iLastEnd = iStart + iLen
        End If
        sOut = sOut + Mid$(sMakeBold, iStart, iLastEnd - sOut =_
            sOut + "</FONT>"

        ' kill this collection item!
        cStart.Remove iSmallestPosition
        cLength.Remove iSmallestPosition
    Loop

    ' add everything else!
    sOut = sOut + Mid$(sMakeBold, iLastEnd)


    MakeBold = sOut
End Function


Function NextBunch(sFirstRow As String, sTopRows As String)
    Dim sOut As String
    With cgi
        sOut = sOut + "<FORM ACTION=""" + .ReadScriptName
        sOut = sOut + """ METHOD=""POST"">" + vbCrLf
        sOut = sOut + "<INPUT TYPE=HIDDEN NAME=""Action"" "
        sOut = sOut + " VALUE=""DOSEARCH"">" + vbCrLf
        sOut = sOut + "<INPUT TYPE=HIDDEN NAME=""KeyWords"" "
        sOut = sOut + "VALUE=""" + _
            ReadScrambledParam("KeyWords")
        sOut = sOut + """>" + vbCrLf
        sOut = sOut + "<INPUT TYPE=HIDDEN NAME=""Match"" "
        sOut = sOut + " VALUE=""" + cgi.ReadParam("Match")
        sOut = sOut + """>" + vbCrLf
        sOut = sOut + "<INPUT TYPE=HIDDEN NAME=""TopRows"" "
        sOut = sOut + " VALUE=""" + sTopRows + """>" + vbCrLf
        sOut = sOut + "<INPUT TYPE=HIDDEN NAME=""FirstRow"" _
            VALUE= "
```

```
                sOut = sOut + sFirstRow + ">" + vbCrLf
                sOut = sOut + "<INPUT TYPE=Submit NAME=Submit "
                sOut = sOut + " VALUE=""View the next "
                sOut = sOut + sTopRows + " rows "">" + vbCrLf
                sOut = sOut + "</FORM>" + vbCrLf
        End With


        NextBunch = sOut
    End Function


    Function PrevBunch(sLastRow As String, sTopRows As String)
        Dim sOut As String
        With cgi
                sOut = sOut + "<FORM ACTION=""" + .ReadScriptName
                sOut = sOut + """ METHOD=""POST"">" + vbCrLf
                sOut = sOut + "<INPUT TYPE=HIDDEN NAME=""Action"" "
                sOut = sOut + " VALUE=""DOSEARCHBACK"">" + vbCrLf
                sOut = sOut + "<INPUT TYPE=HIDDEN NAME=""KeyWords"" "
                sOut = sOut + "VALUE=""" + ReadScrambledParam("KeyWords")
                sOut = sOut + """>" + vbCrLf
                sOut = sOut + "<INPUT TYPE=HIDDEN NAME=""Match"" "
                sOut = sOut + " VALUE=""" + cgi.ReadParam("Match")
                sOut = sOut + """>" + vbCrLf
                sOut = sOut + "<INPUT TYPE=HIDDEN NAME=""TopRows"" "
                sOut = sOut + " VALUE=""" + sTopRows + """>" + vbCrLf
                sOut = sOut + "<INPUT TYPE=HIDDEN NAME=""LastRow"" _
                        VALUE= "
                sOut = sOut + sLastRow + ">" + vbCrLf
                sOut = sOut + "<INPUT TYPE=Submit NAME=Submit"
                sOut = sOut + " VALUE=""View the previous "
                sOut = sOut + sTopRows + " rows "">" + vbCrLf
                sOut = sOut + "</FORM>" + vbCrLf
        End With


        PrevBunch = sOut
    End Function


    Function ReadScrambledParam(sParam As String) As String
        ' rescramble parameter.

        Dim sValue As String, iPos As Integer, sOut As String
```

```
        sValue = cgi.ReadParam(sParam)

    For iPos = 1 To Len(sValue)
      Select Case Mid$(sValue, iPos, 1)
        Case """":
           sOut = sOut + "%22"
        Case "'":
           sOut = sOut + "%27"
        Case Else
           sOut = sOut + Mid$(sValue, iPos, 1)
      End Select
    Next
    ReadScrambledParam = sOut
End Function


Sub DoSearch()
    ' max number of rows that a query returns.
    Dim TOP_ROWS As Integer

    Dim sQuery As String, sOut As String
    With cgi
        ' first break down the parameters.
        Dim sKeywords As String, sFirstRow As String
        sKeywords = .ReadParam("KeyWords")

      TOP_ROWS = ToInt(cgi.ReadParam("TopRows"))
      If (TOP_ROWS < 1) Then
        TOP_ROWS = 10
      End If


      'prevent empty search
      If (Trim$(sKeywords) = "") Then
        DoShowSearch
        Exit Sub
      End If


      sFirstRow = .ReadParam("FirstRow")
      Select Case .ReadParam("Match")
        Case "A" ' and
           sQuery = DoAndOr(True, "*", "DATA", sKeywords, _
            "Data", "Key", TOP_ROWS, sFirstRow, False)
```

```
        Case "E" ' Entire
        sQuery = DoEntire("*", "DATA", sKeywords, "Data", _
          "Key", TOP_ROWS, sFirstRow, False)
        Case "O" ' or
        sQuery = DoAndOr(False, "*", "DATA", sKeywords, _
          "Data", "Key", TOP_ROWS, sFirstRow, False)
        Case Else ' error
          sOut = DoError
          .WriteCGI sOut
          Exit Sub
    End Select

    Dim db As Database, rs As Recordset
    Set db = Workspaces(0).OpenDatabase(App.Path + _
          "\search.mdb")
    Set rs = db.OpenRecordset(sQuery, dbOpenDynaset)

    sOut = "<HTML>" + vbCrLf
    sOut = sOut + "<HEADER><TITLE> Sample Search _
          results</TITLE>"
    sOut = sOut + " </HEADER>" + vbCrLf
    sOut = sOut + "<BODY BGCOLOR=#ffffff>" + vbCrLf
    sOut = sOut + "<H2>Sample Search results</H2><HR>" + _
          vbCrLf
    Dim iRows As Integer, fNextBunch As Boolean
    iRows = 0
    fNextBunch = False
    If rs.EOF Then
      sOut = sOut + "<H3>Search did not retrieve any _
          rows</H3>" + vbCrLf
    Else
      Dim sTopRow As String
      rs.MoveFirst
      sOut = sOut + "<H3>Search resulted in the following _
          results</H3>"
      sOut = sOut + vbCrLf + "<TABLE BORDER=1 WIDTH=100%>" _
          + vbCrLf
      Do While Not rs.EOF
        iRows = iRows + 1
        If iRows <= TOP_ROWS Then
          sOut = sOut + "<TR>"
```

```
                    sOut = sOut + "<TD BGCOLOR=AQUA>" + _
                      CStr(rs("Key")) + "</TD>"
                    sOut = sOut + vbCrLf + "<TD WIDTH=20%>" + _
                      rs("Title") + "</TD>"
                    sOut = sOut + vbCrLf + "<TD WIDTH=80%>"
                    sOut = sOut + MakeBold(rs("Data"), sQuery)
                    sOut = sOut + "</TD>" + vbCrLf + "</TR>"
                  Else ' last row - instead, put up a next + _
                    TOP_ROWS + button
                    sTopRow = CStr(rs("Key"))
                    fNextBunch = True
                    Exit Do
                  End If
                  rs.MoveNext
                Loop
                sOut = sOut + "</TABLE>"
                sOut = sOut + "<TABLE BORDER=0><TR>"
                If (sFirstRow <> "") Then
                  rs.MoveFirst
                  sOut = sOut + "<TD>"
                  sOut = sOut + PrevBunch(CStr(rs("Key")), _
                    CStr(TOP_ROWS)) + "</TD>"
                End If
                If (fNextBunch) Then
                  sOut = sOut + "<TD>" + NextBunch(sTopRow, _
                    CStr(TOP_ROWS)) + "</TD>"
                End If
                sOut = sOut + "</TR></TABLE>"
              End If

              sOut = sOut + "</BODY></HTML>"
              cgi.WriteCGI sOut
              rs.Close
              db.Close
            End With
          End Sub


        'THIS WILL NOT WORK WITH FORWARD ONLY RECORDSETS!
        Sub DoSearchBack()
          ' max number of rows that a query returns.
          Dim TOP_ROWS As Integer
```

```vb
Dim sQuery As String, sOut As String
With cgi
  ' first break down the parameters.
  Dim sKeywords As String, sLastRow As String
  sKeywords = .ReadParam("KeyWords")

  TOP_ROWS = ToInt(cgi.ReadParam("TopRows"))
  If (TOP_ROWS < 1) Then
    TOP_ROWS = 10
  End If

  'prevent empty search
  If (Trim$(sKeywords) = "") Then
    DoShowSearch
    Exit Sub
  End If

  sLastRow = .ReadParam("LastRow")
  Select Case .ReadParam("Match")
    Case "A" ' and
      sQuery = DoAndOr(True, "*", "DATA", sKeywords, _
        "Data", "Key", TOP_ROWS + 1, sLastRow, True)
    Case "E" ' Entire
      sQuery = DoEntire("*", "DATA", sKeywords, "Data", _
        "Key", TOP_ROWS + 1, sLastRow, True)
    Case "O" ' or
      sQuery = DoAndOr(False, "*", "DATA", sKeywords, _
        "Data", "Key", TOP_ROWS + 1, sLastRow, True)
    Case Else ' error
      sOut = DoError
      .WriteCGI sOut
      Exit Sub
  End Select

  Dim db As Database, rs As Recordset
  Set db = Workspaces(0).OpenDatabase(App.Path + _
      "\search.mdb")
  Set rs = db.OpenRecordset(sQuery, dbOpenDynaset)

  sOut = "<HTML>" + vbCrLf
  sOut = sOut + "<HEADER><TITLE> Sample Search results</TITLE>"
```

```
sOut = sOut + " </HEADER>" + vbCrLf
sOut = sOut + "<BODY BGCOLOR=#ffffff>" + vbCrLf
sOut = sOut + "<H2>Sample Search results</H2><HR>" + _
    vbCrLf
Dim iRows As Integer, fPrevBunch As Boolean
iRows = 0
fPrevBunch = False
If rs.EOF Then
  sOut = sOut + "<H3>Search did not retrieve any _
    rows</H3>" + vbCrLf
Else
  Dim sBottomRow As String
  rs.MoveLast
  If (rs.RecordCount > (TOP_ROWS + 1)) Then
    fPrevBunch = True
    rs.MovePrevious
  End If

  sBottomRow = CStr(rs("Key"))
  sOut = sOut + "<H3>Search resulted in the following _
    results</H3>" + vbCrLf
  sOut = sOut + "<TABLE BORDER=1 WIDTH=100%>" + vbCrLf
  Do While Not rs.BOF
    iRows = iRows + 1
    If iRows <= (TOP_ROWS + 1) Then
     If (iRows <= TOP_ROWS) Then
      sOut = sOut + "<TR>"
      sOut = sOut + "<TD BGCOLOR=AQUA>" + _
        CStr(rs("Key"))
      sOut = sOut + "</TD>" + vbCrLf
      sOut = sOut + "<TD WIDTH=20%>" + _
        rs("Title") + "</TD>"
      sOut = sOut + vbCrLf
      sOut = sOut + "<TD WIDTH=80%>" + _
        MakeBold(rs("Data"), sQuery)
      sOut = sOut + "</TD>" + vbCrLf + "</TR>"
     End If
    Else
     Exit Do
    End If
    rs.MovePrevious
```

```
        Loop
        sOut = sOut + "</TABLE>"
        sOut = sOut + "<TABLE BORDER=0><TR>"
        If (fPrevBunch) Then
          sOut = sOut + "<TD>" + PrevBunch(sBottomRow, _
           CStr(TOP_ROWS))
          sOut = sOut + "</TD>"
        End If
        If (sLastRow <> "") Then
          rs.MoveFirst
          sOut = sOut + "<TD>" + NextBunch(CStr(rs("Key")), _
           CStr(TOP_ROWS))
          sOut = sOut + "</TD>"
        End If
        sOut = sOut + "</TR></TABLE>"
      End If

      sOut = sOut + "</BODY></HTML>"
      cgi.WriteCGI sOut
      rs.Close
      db.Close
    End With
End Sub


Function DoubleQuote(sData As String) As String
   Dim sOut As String, iPos As Integer

   For iPos = 1 To Len(sData)
     Select Case Mid$(sData, iPos, 1)
       Case "'":
         sOut = sOut + "''"
       Case """":
         sOut = sOut + """"""
       Case Else:
         sOut = sOut + Mid$(sData, iPos, 1)
     End Select
   Next
   DoubleQuote = sOut
End Function


Sub DoShowSearch()
```

```
With cgi
  Dim sOut As String

  sOut = "<HTML>" + vbCrLf
  sOut = sOut + "<HEADER><TITLE> Sample Search page _
      </TITLE></HEADER>" + vbCrLf
  sOut = sOut + "<BODY BGCOLOR=#ffffff>" + vbCrLf
  sOut = sOut + "<H2> The search engine </H2>" + vbCrLf
  sOut = sOut + "Enter your search keywords here:<P><HR>" _
      + vbCrLf

  sOut = sOut + "<FORM ACTION=""" + .ReadScriptName + _
      """ METHOD=""POST"">"
  sOut = sOut + "<INPUT TYPE=""HIDDEN"" NAME=""Action"" _
      VALUE=""DOSEARCH"">"
  sOut = sOut + vbCrLf + "<TABLE><TR><TD>"
  sOut = sOut + "<B>Search for:</B></TD><TD></TD><TD>_
      <INPUT TYPE=TEXT SIZE=20 "
  sOut = sOut + " MAXLENGTH=100 NAME=""KeyWords"" _
      VALUE="""" > "
  sOut = sOut + "</TD></TR><TR><TD><INPUT TYPE=""RADIO"" _
      CHECKED "
  sOut = sOut + "NAME=""Match"" VALUE=""E"">Exact Match"
  sOut = sOut + "</TD><TD><INPUT TYPE=""RADIO"" _
      NAME=""Match"" VALUE=""A"">And"
  sOut = sOut + "</TD><TD><INPUT TYPE=""RADIO"" _
      NAME=""Match"" VALUE=""O"">Or"
  sOut = sOut + "</TD></TR><TR><TD><P><INPUT TYPE=Submit "
  sOut = sOut + " NAME=""Submit"" VALUE=""Search"">"
  sOut = sOut + "</TD><TD># rows shown:"
  sOut = sOut + "</TD><TD><select name=""TopRows"" > "
  sOut = sOut + "<option SELECTED>5</option>"
  sOut = sOut + "<option>10</option>"
  sOut = sOut + "<option>20</option>"
  sOut = sOut + "<option>50</option></select>"
  sOut = sOut + "</TD></TR></TABLE> </FORM>"
  sOut = sOut + "<HR>"
  If (Trim$(.ReadRemoteFrom) <> "") Then
    sOut = sOut + "Your email address is: " + _
        .ReadRemoteFrom + "<BR>"
    sOut = sOut + vbCrLf
```

```
        End If

        sOut = sOut + "Your browser is: " + .ReadUserAgent + _
            "<BR>" + vbCrLf

        sOut = sOut + "Your IP address is: " + _
            .ReadRemoteAddress + "<BR>" + vbCrLf
        If (.ReadRemoteHost <> "") And (.ReadRemoteHost <> _
            .ReadRemoteAddress) Then
          sOut = sOut + "Your machine's host name: " + _
            .ReadRemoteHost
          sOut = sOut + "<BR>" + vbCrLf
        End If

        sOut = sOut + "</BODY>" + vbCrLf
        sOut = sOut + "</HTML>"

      .WriteCGI sOut
    End With
End Sub

Function RemoveDoubleQuotes(sStrings As String) As String
  Dim iPos As Integer
  Do While (True)
    iPos = InStr(sStrings, """")
    If (iPos > 0) Then
      sStrings = Left$(sStrings, iPos - 1) + Mid$(sStrings,_
        iPos + 1)
    Else
      RemoveDoubleQuotes = sStrings
      Exit Function
    End If
  Loop
End Function

Function ToInt(vInteger As Variant) As Integer
On Error GoTo ToIntErr
  ToInt = CInt(vInteger)
  Exit Function
ToIntErr:
  ToInt = 0
```

```
Exit Function
End Function
```

Since the *SearchBack* routine requires an ability to search back through the database, this type of system cannot work if forward-only cursors are used. When using SQL server (or similar Client/Server systems), and creating the recordset, special care is required in order to prevent this. Such a recordset cannot be created with the *dbSQLPassThrough* or *dbForwardOnly* options.

When the *SearchBack* routine executes the *MoveLast* operation on the *Resultset*, the server/DAO engine must commit the entire recordset to memory. This means backward movement is substantially more expensive, memory and CPU wise, than forward movement. This type of information, especially when containing Memo type fields (or SQL server TEXT type fields) should always be maintained in *Dynaset* or *KeySet* type Recordsets in order to minimize the application's memory requirements. This type of recordset maintains just the key portion of each field, and requires substantially less memory to work with.

When porting to SQL server, the *Key* field should be made into a long integer, the *Title* field into Varchar (50) and the *Data* field into a text field. To add new items onto the table, new *Key* fields can be determined using this simple technique:

```
Function NewKey(sKey As String, sFrom As String, db As _
        Database) As Long
  Dim sSQL As String, rsKey As Recordset
  sSQL = "SELECT MAX(" + sKey + ")+1 as MaxKey from " + _
      sFrom
  Set rsKey = db.OpenRecordset(sSQL, dbReadOnly)
  NewKey = IIf(rsKey.EOF, 1, rsKey("MaxKey"))
  rsKey.Close
End Function
```

The new key can be inserted after searching for it using:

```
lNewKey = NewKey("Key","Data", db)
```

Another option is to utilize stored procedures to determine and even insert the new key values into the database.

Snapshots of Search Engine 2

Figure 6.3 shows the initial Search Engine 2 page using **OR** for a search parameter. Figure 6.4 shows the subsequent results for that search.

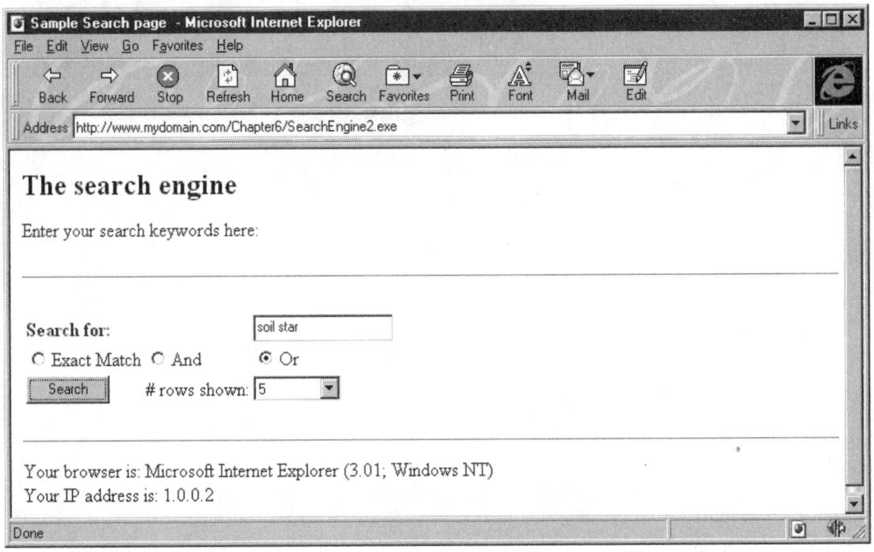

Figure 6.3
Search Engine 2 —
initial **OR** web page

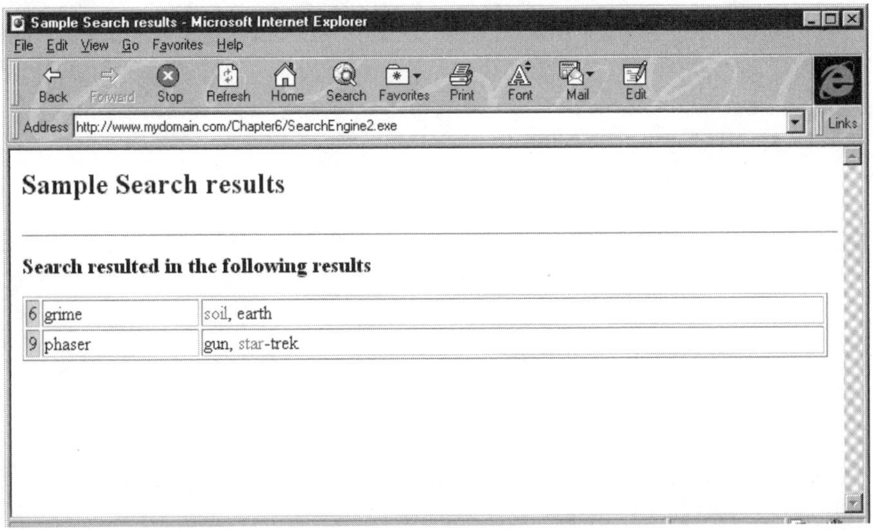

Figure 6.4
Search Engine 2 —
results page

Figure 6.5 shows the initial Search Engine 2 page using **AND** for a search parameter. Figure 6.6 shows the subsequent results for that search.

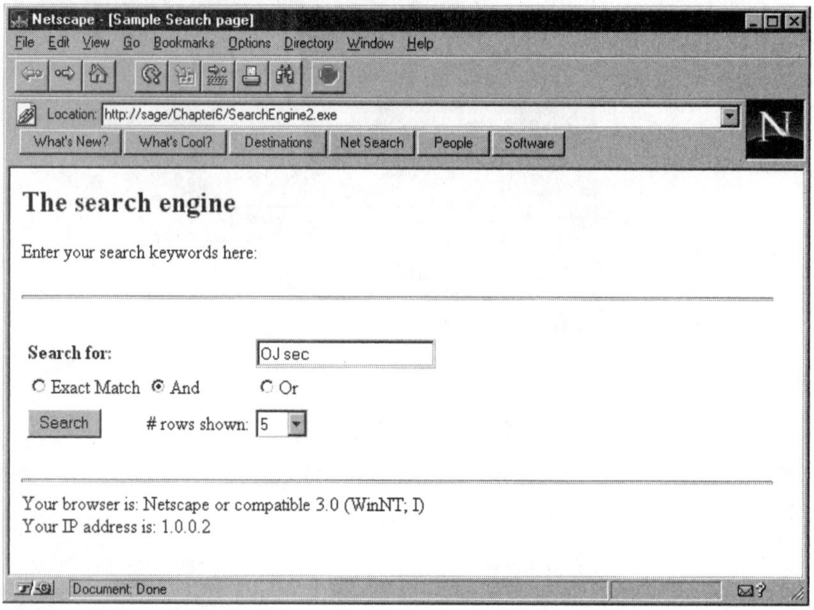

Figure 6.5
Search Engine 2 —
initial **AND** web page

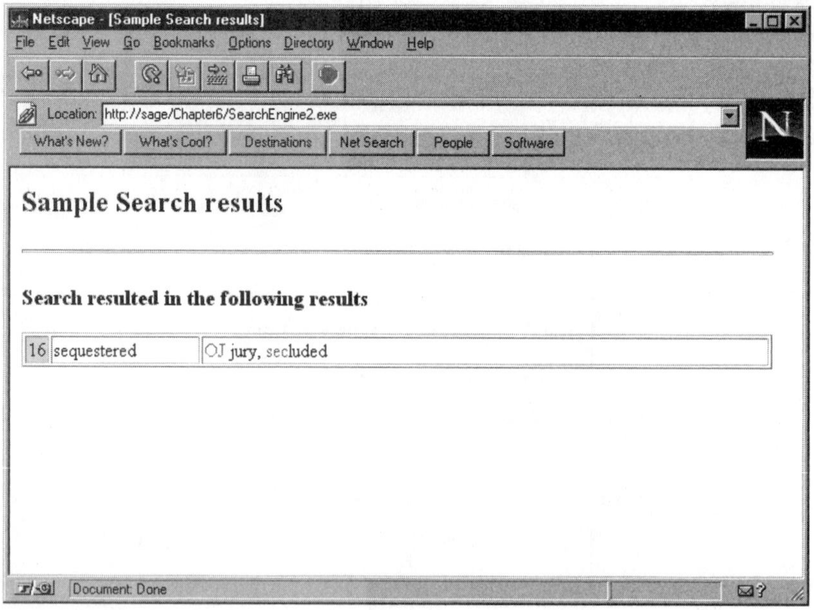

Figure 6.6
Search Engine 2 —
subsequent page

Figure 6.7 shows the initial Search Engine 2 page using **EXACT MATCH** for a search parameter. Figure 6.8 shows the subsequent results for that search.

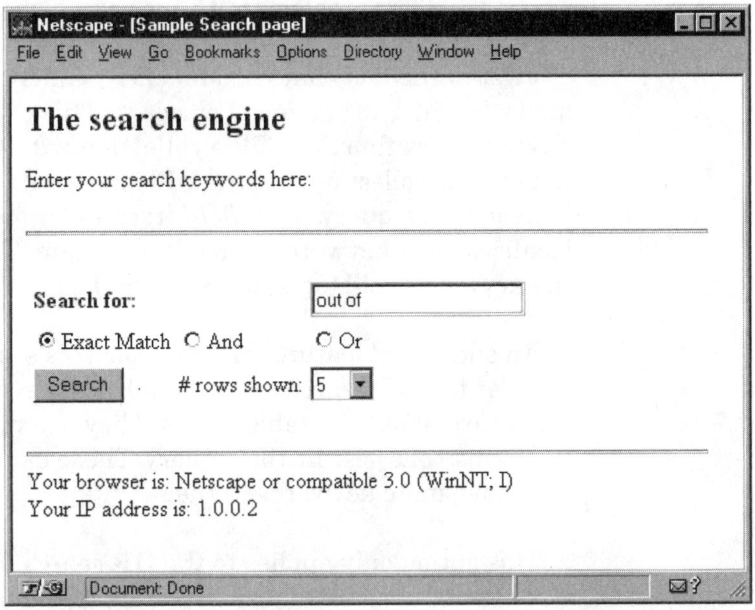

Figure 6.7
Search Engine 2 —
initial **EXACT MATCH** web page

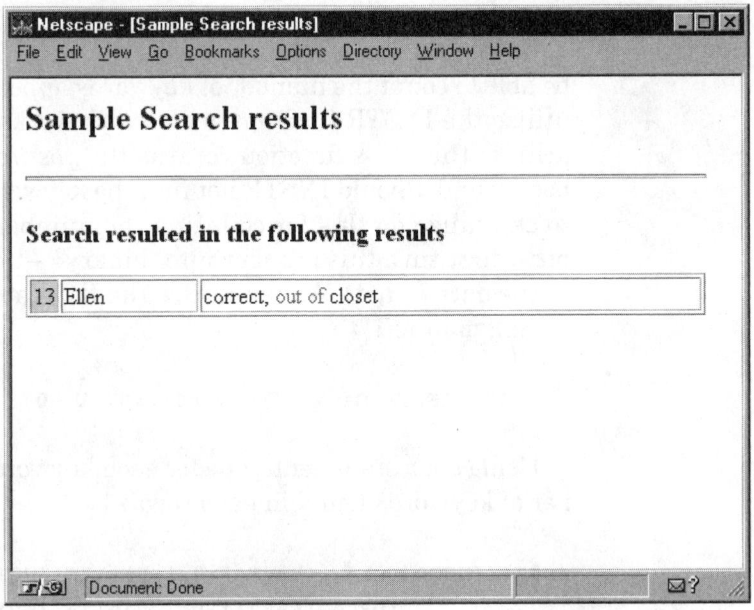

Figure 6.8
Search Engine 2 —
subsequent page

Completing the Search Engine with Still More Technology

There are a few problems with the search engine's current design.

First is the fact that the *MakeBold* function must parse an actual query in order to retrieve keywords. This can be easily overcome by having query functions fill a collection with the keywords they have found. This collection, in turn, will be passed to the *MakeBold* function instead of the query. *MakeBold* iterates through the keyword list and localizes each keyword in the data stream. The function then makes the keywords bold (or, to be exact, red).

An additional feature missing from this search engine is the ability to order the **OR** search by the number of keywords found. Users don't often care about the table's keys. They are more interested in seeing the items that best fit their query. These can be categorized as items that have more keywords in them.

This option only applies to the **OR** search. Both the **exact** and **and** type searches require that all keywords appear in the searched fields. This means there is no particular order in which these can be sorted through.

To sort the items by the number of keywords in them, we must first be able to count the number of keywords appearing in each row. We can utilize the INSTR function (which also works in ODBC databases) to achieve this. This function returns the *position* where a keyword had been found. Should INSTR not find the keyword, it returns (0). In order to capitalize on this for counting the number of keywords found, we must first turn this number into "binary" — (did this keyword appear in the data or not). We can utilize the IIF statement for this in the following manner:

```
IIF(INSTR(Data, 'keyword')>0, 1, 0)
```

Using such statements, one for each keyword, we can count the number of keywords found in each row:

```
IIF(INSTR(Data, 'key1')>0,1,0)+IIF(INSTR_
        (Data,'key2')>0,1,0)+IIF(INSTR(Data,'key3')>0,1,0)
```

This gives us a number from 0 (no keywords were found) to 3 (all keywords were found), we can utilize in order to sort the items in order.

Because this method is so different from the one used by the *DoAndOr* function to approach this problem, the **And** and **Or** searches must now be separated into two distinct functions.

The *DoAnd* function contains minor changes that account for the removal of the **Or** search.

The *DoOr* function acts quite differently than before. First, it organizes the string representing the number of keywords found in the data in the *sInStr* variable. Once this variable is filled, the function uses it to create the SQL statement.

This function first selects the summary as ISINSTR. This is in order to allow the search engine to determine the position for the next "bunch". Next, the select columns are specified and the WHERE clause is generated. The query now consists of three portions:

1. The number of keywords found (must be more than zero). This prevents the SQL statement from listing items that do not contain any of the requested keywords.

2. The first row is specified when this is the next round of a previous query.

3. The number of keywords found in the first row is specified.

The third section of the query is completely new. The sum of keywords found in the data field acts much like a second primary key for the query: it is completely distinct and separate from the "Key" field and must be used to identify the present location in the query. Since we would like to see each item show up once, we need an identifier, in addition to the "Key" field, to specify our present location. Since we can no longer rely on "Key" for the order of items, *not* maintaining a secondary position key causes items with a high number of keywords and a high "Key" value to show up on more than one query page!

In order to localize the search engine's present position, we must maintain the key value as well as the number of keywords found.

NextBunch places this number, called ISINSTR, in the query, so that the next round can use it.

The ORDER BY clause must also be changed to account for the keyword count. First, the number of keywords found is arranged in descending order. The Key column is sorted in ascending order.

This new feature does not come without a cost. The backtracking algorithm presented in the last section of this chapter cannot work in conjunction with it. It is, in fact, exclusive to single-key RecordSets.

One algorithm that *can* be used to resolve this is a bit complex, and beyond the scope of this book. In short, though, the entire RecordSet for the query can be generated. Next, the algorithm can locate an absolute position in the RecordSet and backtrack from there in order to generate the requested number of items in the correct order. This algorithm is costly in both CPU and memory requirements. In addition, absolute referencing does not work with forward-only cursors. With such cursors the only solution is to find out the total number of rows and *count* back the number of rows that have already been traversed; this enables the application to move forward the right number of records (using the Move recordset method).

The *DoSearchBack* function has been modified not to use the **or** type search. In addition, **or** searches do not utilize the *PreviousBunch* function, which places the backtracking button on the form.

NextBunch allows for an optional *sIsInstr* parameter, which it uses to determine the number of items, found — thus preventing items from being displayed more than once.

The *DoSearch* and *DoSearchBack* functions now create a collection of keywords, which is later passed to the *MakeBold* function. This prevents *MakeBold* from mistaking keywords for SQL statement, which was a potential bug in the previous implementation (since searching for the following keyword may present a problem: **INSTR ('** or **').** In addition, since the *DoOr* function utilizes INSTR statements throughout the SQL statement, keywords cannot be marked more than once!

It should be noted that the actual statement is used at every location in the select statement where there's a need for the summary — at three distinct locations. The way SELECT statements are structured prevents us from selecting the ISINSTR field once, and referencing it in the ORDER BY or WHERE clauses.

Source Code for SearchEngine3.bas

```
Option Explicit

Declare Function oCGI2Register Lib "oCGI2.dll" Alias _
        "DllRegisterServer" () As Long
Public cgi As oCGI2

Function DoAnd(sColumns As String, sFrom As String, _
   sData As String, sSearchCol As String, sKeyCol As String, _
   nRows As Variant, sFirstRow As String, _
   fBackwards As Boolean, cKeywords As Collection) As String

   Dim sQuery As String

   sQuery = "select TOP " + CStr(nRows + 1)
   sQuery = sQuery + " " + sColumns + " from " + sFrom + " _
         WHERE 1=1 "

   If (sFirstRow <> "") Then
      sQuery = sQuery + " AND (" + sKeyCol + IIf(fBackwards,_
            "<=", ">=")
      sQuery = sQuery + CStr(ToInt(sFirstRow)) + ") "
   End If

   Dim iPos As Integer
   Do While (1)
      If (Trim$(sData) = "") Then Exit Do
      If (Left$(sData, 1) = """") Then
         sData = Mid$(sData, 2)
         iPos = InStr(sData, """")
      Else
         iPos = InStr(sData, " ")
      End If

      Dim sWord As String
```

```
      If iPos <= 0 Then
        sWord = sData
        iPos = Len(sWord)
      Else
        sWord = Left$(sData, iPos - 1)
      End If


      cKeywords.Add sWord

      sQuery = sQuery + "AND INSTR(" + sSearchCol + ",'"
      sQuery = sQuery + DoubleQuote(sWord) + "') "

      sData = Mid$(sData, iPos + 1)
    Loop

    sQuery = sQuery + " ORDER BY " + sKeyCol
    sQuery = sQuery + IIf(fBackwards, " DESC", " ASC")
    DoAnd = sQuery
End Function


Function DoEntire(sColumns As String, sFrom As String, _
          sKeywords As String, _
    sSearchCol As String, sKeyCol As String, nRows As Integer, _
    sFirstRow As String, fBackwards As Boolean, cKeywords As _
          Collection) As String

    Dim sQuery As String

    'check for quotes
    sKeywords = RemoveDoubleQuotes(sKeywords)

    cKeywords.Add sKeywords

    sQuery = "select TOP " + CStr(nRows + 1) + " "
    sQuery = sQuery + sColumns + " from " + sFrom
    sQuery = sQuery + " WHERE INSTR(" + sSearchCol + ",'"
    sQuery = sQuery + DoubleQuote(sKeywords) + "') "
    If (sFirstRow <> "") Then
      sQuery = sQuery + " and " + sKeyCol + IIf(fBackwards, "<=", ">=")
      sQuery = sQuery + CStr(ToInt(sFirstRow))
    End If
```

```
      sQuery = sQuery + " ORDER BY " + sKeyCol
      sQuery = sQuery + IIf(fBackwards, " DESC", " ASC")
      DoEntire = sQuery
End Function

Function DoError() As String
    Dim sOut As String

    sOut = "<HTML>" + vbCrLf
    sOut = sOut + "<HEADER><TITLE> Sample Search "
    sOut = sOut + " results</TITLE></HEADER>" + vbCrLf
    sOut = sOut + "<BODY BGCOLOR=#ffffff>" + vbCrLf
    sOut = sOut + "<H2> Error: matching option was "
    sOut = sOut + " not selected correctly </H2>"
    sOut = sOut + "</BODY></HTML>"

    DoError = sOut
End Function

Function DoOr(sColumns As String, sFrom As String, _
    sData As String, sSearchCol As String, sKeyCol As String, _
    nRows As Variant, sFirstRow As String, _
    sFirstInStr As String, cKeywords As Collection) As String

    ' now create instr counter.
    Dim sInStr As String
    Dim iPos As Integer
    sInStr = "(0"
    Do While (1)
      If (Trim$(sData) = "") Then Exit Do
      If (Left$(sData, 1) = """") Then
        sData = Mid$(sData, 2)
        iPos = InStr(sData, """")
      Else
        iPos = InStr(sData, " ")
      End If

      Dim sWord As String

      If iPos <= 0 Then
        sWord = sData
```

```
            iPos = Len(sWord)
        Else
          sWord = Left$(sData, iPos - 1)
        End If


        cKeywords.Add sWord


        sInStr = sInStr + "+IIF(INSTR(" + sSearchCol + ",'"
        sInStr = sInStr + DoubleQuote(sWord) + "')>0,1,0)"


        sData = Mid$(sData, iPos + 1)
    Loop
    sInStr = sInStr + ")"


    Dim sQuery As String
    sQuery = "select TOP " + CStr(nRows + 1) + " "
    sQuery = sQuery + sInStr + " as ISINSTR,"
    sQuery = sQuery + " " + sColumns + " from " + sFrom + " WHERE "
    sQuery = sQuery + " (" + sInStr + ">0)"



    If (sFirstRow <> "") Then
        sQuery = sQuery + " AND (" + sKeyCol + ">="
        sQuery = sQuery + CStr(ToInt(sFirstRow)) + ") "
    End If
    If (sFirstInStr <> "") Then
        sQuery = sQuery + " AND (" + sInStr + "<="
        sQuery = sQuery + CStr(ToInt(sFirstInStr)) + ") "
    End If


    sQuery = sQuery + " ORDER BY (" + sInStr + ") DESC"
    sQuery = sQuery + "," + sKeyCol + " ASC"
    DoOr = sQuery
End Function

Sub DoSearch()
    ' max number of rows that a query returns.
    Dim TOP_ROWS As Integer

    Dim sQuery As String, sOut As String
    With cgi
```

```vb
' first break down the parameters.
Dim sKeywords As String, sFirstRow As String
Dim sFirstInStr As String
sKeywords = .ReadParam("KeyWords")

TOP_ROWS = ToInt(cgi.ReadParam("TopRows"))
If (TOP_ROWS < 1) Then
  TOP_ROWS = 10
End If

'prevent empty search
If (Trim$(sKeywords) = "") Then
  DoShowSearch
  Exit Sub
End If

sFirstRow = .ReadParam("FirstRow")
sFirstInStr = .ReadParam("IsInstr")

Dim cKeywords As Collection
Set cKeywords = New Collection
Select Case .ReadParam("Match")
  Case "A" ' and
    sQuery = DoAnd("*", "DATA", sKeywords, "Data", _
      "Key", TOP_ROWS, sFirstRow, False, cKeywords)
  Case "E" ' Entire
    sQuery = DoEntire("*", "DATA", sKeywords, "Data", _
      "Key", TOP_ROWS, sFirstRow, False, cKeywords)
  Case "O" ' or
    sQuery = DoOr("*", "DATA", sKeywords, "Data", "Key", _
      TOP_ROWS, sFirstRow, sFirstInStr, cKeywords)
  Case Else ' error
    sOut = DoError
    .WriteCGI sOut
    Exit Sub
End Select

Dim db As Database, rs As Recordset
Set db = Workspaces(0).OpenDatabase(App.Path + _
    "\search.mdb")
Set rs = db.OpenRecordset(sQuery, dbOpenDynaset)
```

```
sOut = "<HTML>" + vbCrLf
sOut = sOut + "<HEADER><TITLE> Sample Search _
    results</TITLE>"
sOut = sOut + " </HEADER>" + vbCrLf
sOut = sOut + "<BODY BGCOLOR=#ffffff>" + vbCrLf
sOut = sOut + "<H2>Sample Search results</H2><HR>" + _
    vbCrLf
Dim iRows As Integer, fNextBunch As Boolean
iRows = 0
fNextBunch = False
If rs.EOF Then
  sOut = sOut + "<H3>Search did not retrieve any _
    rows</H3>" + vbCrLf
Else
  Dim sTopRow As String, sTopIsInstr As String
  rs.MoveFirst
  sOut = sOut + "<H3>Search resulted in the following _
    results</H3>"
  sOut = sOut + vbCrLf + "<TABLE BORDER=1 WIDTH=100%>" _
    + vbCrLf
  Do While Not rs.EOF
    iRows = iRows + 1
    If iRows <= TOP_ROWS Then
      sOut = sOut + "<TR>"
      sOut = sOut + "<TD BGCOLOR=AQUA>" + _
        CStr(rs("Key")) + "</TD>"
      sOut = sOut + vbCrLf + "<TD WIDTH=20%>" + _
        rs("Title") + "</TD>"
      sOut = sOut + vbCrLf + "<TD WIDTH=80%>"
      sOut = sOut + MakeBold(rs("Data"), cKeywords)
      sOut = sOut + "</TD>" + vbCrLf + "</TR>"
    Else ' last row - instead, put up a next + _
        TOP_ROWS + button
      sTopRow = CStr(rs("Key"))
      If (.ReadParam("Match") = "O") Then
        sTopIsInstr = CStr(rs("ISINSTR"))
      Else
        sTopIsInstr = ""
      End If
      fNextBunch = True
      Exit Do
```

```
            End If
            rs.MoveNext
        Loop
        sOut = sOut + "</TABLE>"
        sOut = sOut + "<TABLE BORDER=0><TR>"
        If (sFirstRow <> "" And .ReadParam("Match") <> "O") _
            Then
            rs.MoveFirst
            sOut = sOut + "<TD>"
            sOut = sOut + PrevBunch(CStr(rs("Key")), _
            CStr(TOP_ROWS)) + "</TD>"
        End If
        If (fNextBunch) Then
            sOut = sOut + "<TD>" + NextBunch(sTopRow, _
            CStr(TOP_ROWS), _
            sTopIsInstr) + "</TD>"
        End If
        sOut = sOut + "</TR></TABLE>"
    End If

    sOut = sOut + "</BODY></HTML>"
    cgi.WriteCGI sOut
    rs.Close
    db.Close
  End With
End Sub


'THIS WILL NOT WORK WITH FORWARD ONLY RECORDSETS!
Sub DoSearchBack()
  ' max number of rows that a query returns.
  Dim TOP_ROWS As Integer

  Dim sQuery As String, sOut As String
  With cgi
    ' first break down the parameters.
    Dim sKeywords As String, sLastRow As String
    Dim sFirstInStr As String

    sKeywords = .ReadParam("KeyWords")

    TOP_ROWS = ToInt(cgi.ReadParam("TopRows"))
```

```
If (TOP_ROWS < 1) Then
  TOP_ROWS = 10
End If

'prevent empty search
If (Trim$(sKeywords) = "") Then
  DoShowSearch
  Exit Sub
End If

sLastRow = .ReadParam("LastRow")

Dim cKeywords As Collection
Set cKeywords = New Collection
Select Case .ReadParam("Match")
  Case "A" ' and
    sQuery = DoAnd("*", "DATA", sKeywords, "Data", _
    "Key", TOP_ROWS + 1, sLastRow, True, _
    cKeywords)
  Case "E" ' Entire
    sQuery = DoEntire("*", "DATA", sKeywords, "Data", _
    "Key", TOP_ROWS + 1, sLastRow, True, cKeywords)
  Case Else ' error
    sOut = DoError
    .WriteCGI sOut
    Exit Sub
End Select

Dim db As Database, rs As Recordset
Set db = Workspaces(0).OpenDatabase(App.Path + _
    "\search.mdb")
Set rs = db.OpenRecordset(sQuery, dbOpenDynaset)

sOut = "<HTML>" + vbCrLf
sOut = sOut + "<HEADER><TITLE> Sample Search _
    results</TITLE>"
sOut = sOut + " </HEADER>" + vbCrLf
sOut = sOut + "<BODY BGCOLOR=#ffffff>" + vbCrLf
sOut = sOut + "<H2>Sample Search results</H2><HR>" + _
    vbCrLf
Dim iRows As Integer, fPrevBunch As Boolean
```

```
iRows = 0
fPrevBunch = False
If rs.EOF Then
   sOut = sOut + "<H3>Search did not retrieve any _
      rows</H3>" + vbCrLf
Else
  Dim sBottomRow As String
  rs.MoveLast
  If (rs.RecordCount > (TOP_ROWS + 1)) Then
    fPrevBunch = True
    rs.MovePrevious
  End If


  sBottomRow = CStr(rs("Key"))
  sOut = sOut + "<H3>Search resulted in the following _
     results</H3>" + vbCrLf
  sOut = sOut + "<TABLE BORDER=1 WIDTH=100%>" + vbCrLf
  Do While Not rs.BOF
    iRows = iRows + 1
    If iRows <= (TOP_ROWS + 1) Then
     If (iRows <= TOP_ROWS) Then
       sOut = sOut + "<TR>"
       sOut = sOut + "<TD BGCOLOR=AQUA>" + _
         CStr(rs("Key"))
       sOut = sOut + "</TD>" + vbCrLf
       sOut = sOut + "<TD WIDTH=20%>" + _
         rs("Title") + "</TD>"
       sOut = sOut + vbCrLf
       sOut = sOut + "<TD WIDTH=80%>" + _
         MakeBold(rs("Data"), cKeywords)
       sOut = sOut + "</TD>" + vbCrLf + "</TR>"
     End If
    Else
     Exit Do
    End If
    rs.MovePrevious
  Loop
  sOut = sOut + "</TABLE>"
  sOut = sOut + "<TABLE BORDER=0><TR>"
  If (fPrevBunch) Then
```

```
                sOut = sOut + "<TD>" + PrevBunch(sBottomRow, _
                  CStr(TOP_ROWS))
                sOut = sOut + "</TD>"
            End If
            If (sLastRow <> "") Then
                rs.MoveFirst
                sOut = sOut + "<TD>" + NextBunch(CStr(rs("Key")), _
                  CStr(TOP_ROWS), "")
                sOut = sOut + "</TD>"
            End If
            sOut = sOut + "</TR></TABLE>"
        End If

        sOut = sOut + "</BODY></HTML>"
        cgi.WriteCGI sOut
        rs.Close
        db.Close
    End With
End Sub

Sub DoShowSearch()
    With cgi
        Dim sOut As String

        sOut = "<HTML>" + vbCrLf
        sOut = sOut + "<HEADER><TITLE> Sample Search page _
            </TITLE></HEADER>" + vbCrLf
        sOut = sOut + "<BODY BGCOLOR=#ffffff>" + vbCrLf
        sOut = sOut + "<H2> The search engine </H2>" + vbCrLf
        sOut = sOut + "Enter your search keywords here:<P><HR>" _
            + vbCrLf

        sOut = sOut + "<FORM ACTION=""" + .ReadScriptName + _
            """ METHOD=""POST"">"
        sOut = sOut + "<INPUT TYPE=""HIDDEN"" NAME=""Action"" _
            VALUE=""DOSEARCH"">"
        sOut = sOut + vbCrLf + "<TABLE><TR><TD>"
        sOut = sOut + "<B>Search for:</B></TD><TD></TD><TD>_
            <INPUT TYPE=TEXT SIZE=20 "
        sOut = sOut + " MAXLENGTH=100 NAME=""KeyWords"" _
            VALUE="""" > "
```

```
            sOut = sOut + "</TD></TR><TR><TD><INPUT TYPE=_
                """RADIO"" CHECKED "
            sOut = sOut + "NAME=""Match"" VALUE=""E"">Exact Match"
            sOut = sOut + "</TD><TD><INPUT TYPE=""RADIO"" _
                NAME=""Match"" VALUE=""A"">And"
            sOut = sOut + "</TD><TD><INPUT TYPE=""RADIO"" _
                NAME=""Match"" VALUE=""O"">Or"
            sOut = sOut + "</TD></TR><TR><TD><P><INPUT TYPE=Submit "
            sOut = sOut + " NAME=""Submit"" VALUE=""Search"">"
            sOut = sOut + "</TD><TD># rows shown:"
            sOut = sOut + "</TD><TD><select name=""TopRows"" > "
            sOut = sOut + "<option SELECTED>5</option>"
            sOut = sOut + "<option>10</option>"
            sOut = sOut + "<option>20</option>"
            sOut = sOut + "<option>50</option></select>"
            sOut = sOut + "</TD></TR></TABLE> </FORM>"
            sOut = sOut + "<HR>"
            If (Trim$(.ReadRemoteFrom) <> "") Then
              sOut = sOut + "Your email address is: " + _
                  .ReadRemoteFrom + "<BR>"
              sOut = sOut + vbCrLf
            End If


            sOut = sOut + "Your browser is: " + .ReadUserAgent + _
                "<BR>" + vbCrLf


            sOut = sOut + "Your IP address is: " + _
                .ReadRemoteAddress + "<BR>" + vbCrLf
            If (.ReadRemoteHost <> "") And (.ReadRemoteHost <> _
                .ReadRemoteAddress) Then
              sOut = sOut + "Your machine's host name: " + _
                  .ReadRemoteHost
              sOut = sOut + "<BR>" + vbCrLf
            End If


            sOut = sOut + "</BODY>" + vbCrLf
            sOut = sOut + "</HTML>"


            .WriteCGI sOut
        End With
    End Sub
```

```
Function DoubleQuote(sData As String) As String
   Dim sOut As String, iPos As Integer

   For iPos = 1 To Len(sData)
     Select Case Mid$(sData, iPos, 1)
        Case "'":
           sOut = sOut + "''"
        Case """":
           sOut = sOut + """"""
        Case Else:
           sOut = sOut + Mid$(sData, iPos, 1)
     End Select
   Next
   DoubleQuote = sOut
End Function


Sub main()
On Error GoTo RegisterErr ' register oCGI only if having _
           problems!
   Set cgi = New oCGI2
On Error GoTo NormalErr
   cgi.ProcessCGI Command
   'Load frmVBCrash

   Select Case cgi.ReadParam("Action")
     Case "DOSEARCH":
        DoSearch
     Case "DOSEARCHBACK":
        DoSearchBack
     Case Else:
        DoShowSearch
   End Select

   Set cgi = Nothing
   End
NormalErr:
   cgi.WriteCGI "<HTML><BODY>Error:" + Error$ + _
        "</BODY></HTML>"
   Set cgi = Nothing ' Just in case
   End
RegisterErr:
```

```
            oCGI2Register
        End
    End Sub


    Function MakeBold(ByVal sMakeBold As String, cKeywords As _
            Collection) As String
        ' make each found keyword in this thing bold.
        Dim cStart As New Collection, cLength As New Collection
        Dim sWord As Variant, iPos As Integer

        For Each sWord In cKeywords
            ' now locate the first instance of sWord in sMakeBold
            Dim iPosMakeBold As Integer

            iPosMakeBold = InStr(sMakeBold, sWord)
            If (iPosMakeBold > 0) Then
                cStart.Add iPosMakeBold
                cLength.Add Len(sWord)
            End If
        Next
        ' all of this is to prevent the search from locating
        ' — stuff in the modified string!


        ' now loop and implement modifications.
        Dim i As Integer, iSmallestPosition As Integer
        Dim sOut As String, iLastEnd As Integer
        iLastEnd = 1
        Do While (cStart.Count > 0)
            ' look for the smallest position.
            iSmallestPosition = 1
            For i = 2 To cStart.Count
                If (cStart.Item(i) < cStart.Item(iSmallestPosition))_
                    Then
                    iSmallestPosition = i
                End If
            Next


            Dim iStart As Integer, iLen As Integer
            iStart = cStart.Item(iSmallestPosition)
            iLen = cLength.Item(iSmallestPosition)
            If (iStart < iLastEnd) Then
```

```
            iStart = iLastEnd
        End If
        sOut = sOut + Mid$(sMakeBold, iLastEnd, iStart - _
            iLastEnd)
        sOut = sOut + "<FONT COLOR=RED>"
        If (iLastEnd < iStart + iLen) Then
            iLastEnd = iStart + iLen
        End If
        sOut = sOut + Mid$(sMakeBold, iStart, iLastEnd - _
            iStart)
        sOut = sOut + "</FONT>"

        ' kill this collection item!
        cStart.Remove iSmallestPosition
        cLength.Remove iSmallestPosition
    Loop

    ' add everything else!
    sOut = sOut + Mid$(sMakeBold, iLastEnd)

    MakeBold = sOut
End Function


Function NextBunch(sFirstRow As String, sTopRows As String, _
    sIsInstr As String)

    Dim sOut As String
    With cgi
        sOut = sOut + "<FORM ACTION=""" + .ReadScriptName
        sOut = sOut + """ METHOD=""POST"">" + vbCrLf
        sOut = sOut + "<INPUT TYPE=HIDDEN NAME=""Action"" "
        sOut = sOut + " VALUE=""DOSEARCH"">" + vbCrLf
        sOut = sOut + "<INPUT TYPE=HIDDEN NAME=""KeyWords"" "
        sOut = sOut + "VALUE=""" + ReadScrambledParam_
            ("KeyWords")
        sOut = sOut + """>" + vbCrLf
        sOut = sOut + "<INPUT TYPE=HIDDEN NAME=""Match"" "
        sOut = sOut + " VALUE=""" + cgi.ReadParam("Match")
        sOut = sOut + """>" + vbCrLf
        sOut = sOut + "<INPUT TYPE=HIDDEN NAME=""TopRows"" "
        sOut = sOut + " VALUE=""" + sTopRows + """>" + vbCrLf
```

```
            sOut = sOut + "<INPUT TYPE=HIDDEN NAME="""FirstRow"" _
                VALUE= "
            sOut = sOut + sFirstRow + ">" + vbCrLf

            If (sIsInstr <> "") Then
              sOut = sOut + "<INPUT TYPE=HIDDEN NAME="""IsInstr"" _
                VALUE= "
              sOut = sOut + sIsInstr + ">" + vbCrLf
            End If

            sOut = sOut + "<INPUT TYPE=Submit NAME=Submit "
            sOut = sOut + " VALUE=""View the next "
            sOut = sOut + sTopRows + " rows "">" + vbCrLf
            sOut = sOut + "</FORM>" + vbCrLf
        End With


        NextBunch = sOut
    End Function


    Function PrevBunch(sLastRow As String, sTopRows As String)

        Dim sOut As String
        With cgi
            sOut = sOut + "<FORM ACTION=""" + .ReadScriptName
            sOut = sOut + """ METHOD=""POST"">" + vbCrLf
            sOut = sOut + "<INPUT TYPE=HIDDEN NAME="""Action"" "
            sOut = sOut + " VALUE=""DOSEARCHBACK"">" + vbCrLf
            sOut = sOut + "<INPUT TYPE=HIDDEN NAME="""KeyWords"" "
            sOut = sOut + "VALUE=""" + _
                ReadScrambledParam("KeyWords")
            sOut = sOut + """>" + vbCrLf
            sOut = sOut + "<INPUT TYPE=HIDDEN NAME="""Match"" "
            sOut = sOut + " VALUE=""" + cgi.ReadParam("Match")
            sOut = sOut + """>" + vbCrLf
            sOut = sOut + "<INPUT TYPE=HIDDEN NAME="""TopRows"" "
            sOut = sOut + " VALUE=""" + sTopRows + """>" + vbCrLf
            sOut = sOut + "<INPUT TYPE=HIDDEN NAME="""LastRow"" _
                VALUE= "
            sOut = sOut + sLastRow + ">" + vbCrLf


            sOut = sOut + "<INPUT TYPE=Submit NAME=Submit"
```

```vb
        sOut = sOut + " VALUE=""View the previous "
        sOut = sOut + sTopRows + " rows "">" + vbCrLf
        sOut = sOut + "</FORM>" + vbCrLf
    End With

    PrevBunch = sOut
End Function

Function ReadScrambledParam(sParam As String) As String
    ' rescramble parameter.

    Dim sValue As String, iPos As Integer, sOut As String

    sValue = cgi.ReadParam(sParam)

    For iPos = 1 To Len(sValue)
      Select Case Mid$(sValue, iPos, 1)
        Case """":
           sOut = sOut + "%22"
        Case "'":
           sOut = sOut + "%27"
        Case Else
           sOut = sOut + Mid$(sValue, iPos, 1)
      End Select
    Next
    ReadScrambledParam = sOut
End Function

Function RemoveDoubleQuotes(sStrings As String) As String
    Dim iPos As Integer
    Do While (True)
      iPos = InStr(sStrings, """")
      If (iPos > 0) Then
         sStrings = Left$(sStrings, iPos - 1) + Mid$_
            (sStrings, iPos + 1)
      Else
         RemoveDoubleQuotes = sStrings
         Exit Function
      End If
    Loop
End Function
```

```
Function ToInt(vInteger As Variant) As Integer
On Error GoTo ToIntErr
   ToInt = CInt(vInteger)
   Exit Function
ToIntErr:
   ToInt = 0
   Exit Function
End Function
```

Snapshots of Search Engine 3

Figure 6.9 shows the initial Search Engine 3 search page using OR as a search parameter. Figures 6.10, 6.11 show the subsequent two search result pages.

Figure 6.9
Search Engine 3 —
initial **OR** search page

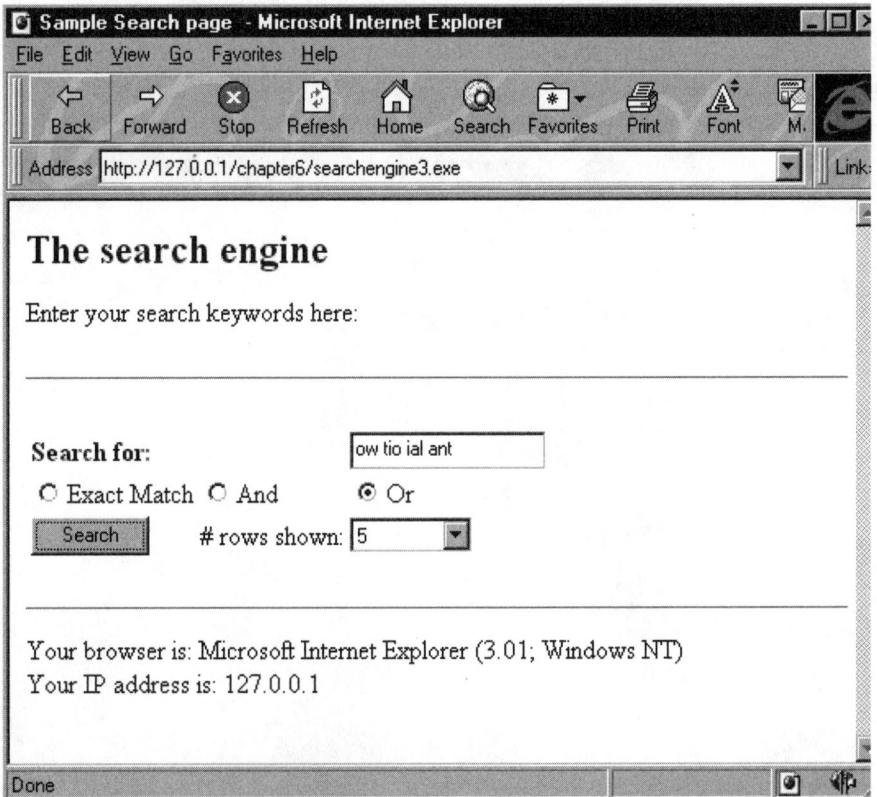

Figure 6.10
Search Engine 3 —
subsequent result page,
page 1

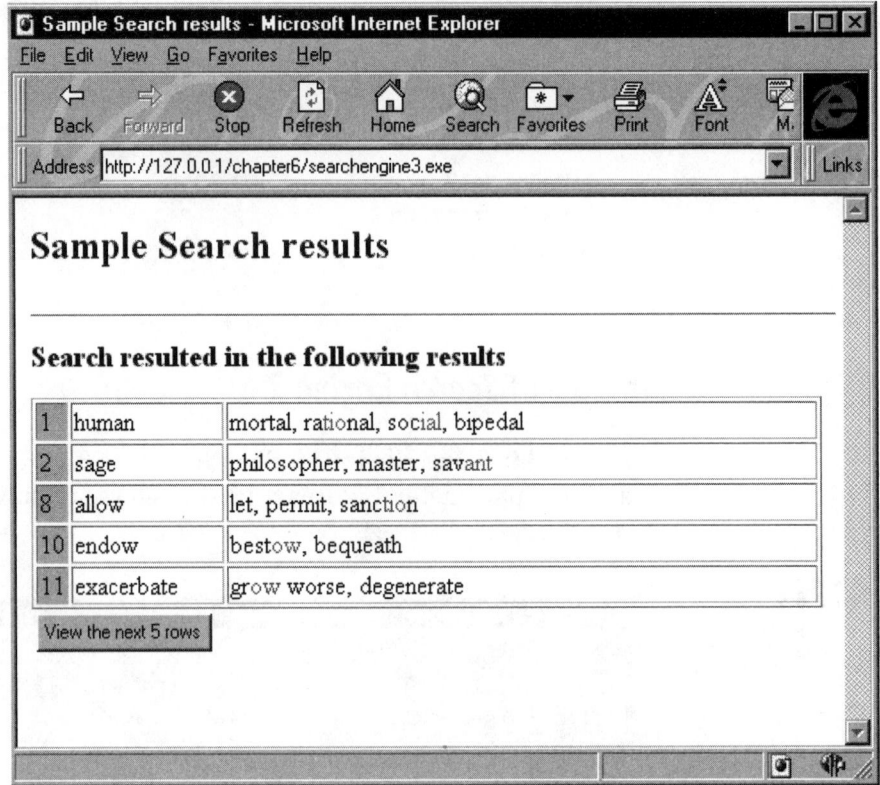

Figure 6.11
Search Engine 3 —
subsequent results
page, page 2

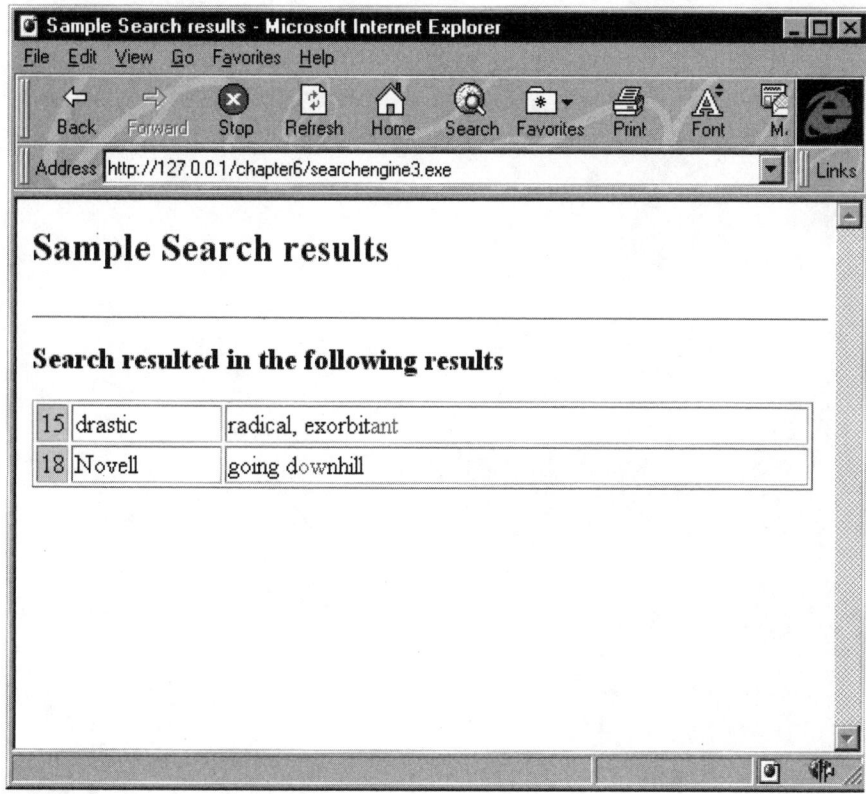

Summary

The reader should now be able to understand how to create a simple search engine using VB, and use CGI technology to interface with the Web. Additional technologies can assist the reader in producing more complex and interactive applications. The next chapter will deal with just such constructs and ways of utilizing them in a CGI application.

ADVANCED HTML AND
ADDITIONAL SERVER SIDE CONSTRUCTS

- Advanced HTML tags overview
- The cache meta tag
- Additional meta tags (metadata)
- The HTTP-EQUIV meta tag
- The refresh meta tag
- The meta pragma tag
- Frames and CGI applications
- Frames-enabled user-security application (with meta tags)
- Using ActiveX controls from the CGI application
- Sending e-mail from the server application
- Processing credit cards from the server application
- Mainframes, servers, and other external entities
- Alphanumeric pagers

As demonstrated previously, CGI applications can use standard HTML constructs to do anything that a normal HTML web page can. This allows the user to employ authoring tools to design the initial web page. Tools such as FrontPage utilize many of the advanced aspects of web design. FrontPage '97 also has the ability to integrate client side JavaScript and VB-Script into the mix.

Figure 7.1
Frontpage 97 Script
Wizard

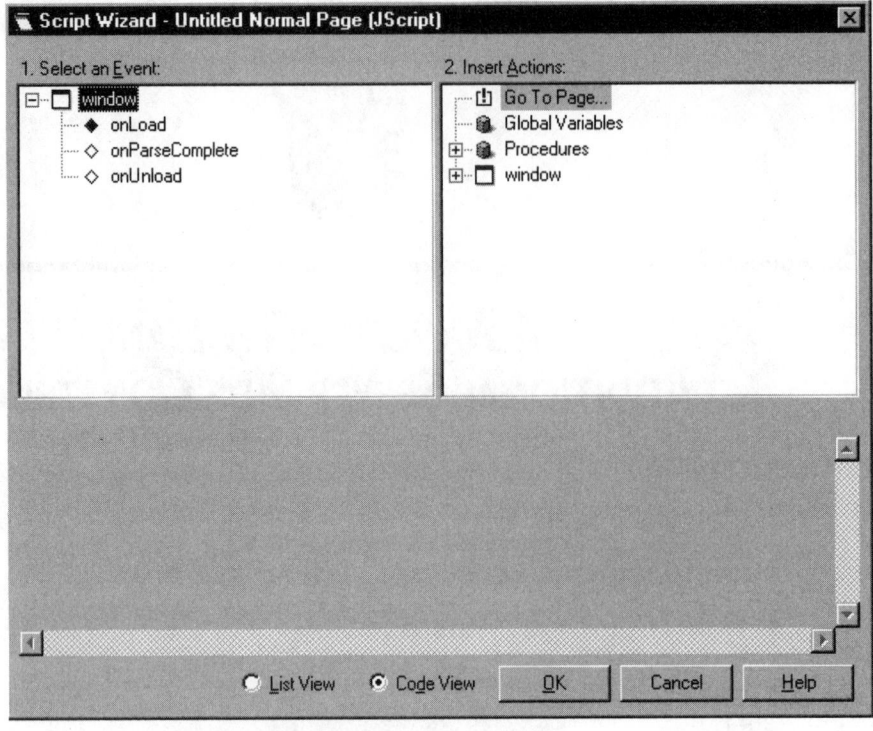

Figure 7.1
Frontpage 97 Script
Wizard

Figure 7.2
Frontpage 97 Event
Tree

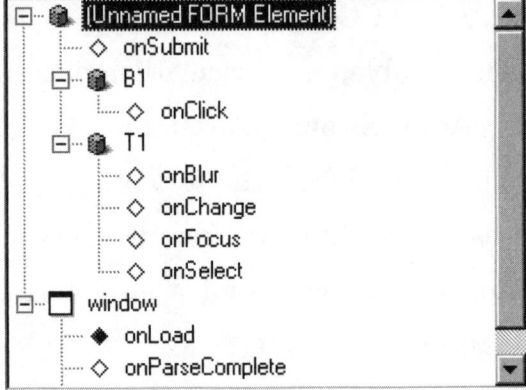

Often, the design process dictates features that are difficult to implement using a standard HTML authoring tool. For example, tables within tables are quite difficult to use outside of a simple HTML editor.
Luckily, some authoring tools (such as FrontPage '97) allow the user to
author HTML directly when necessary, without exiting into another
editor (such as Old Faithful — notepad).

Figure 7.3
Notepad Editing HTML

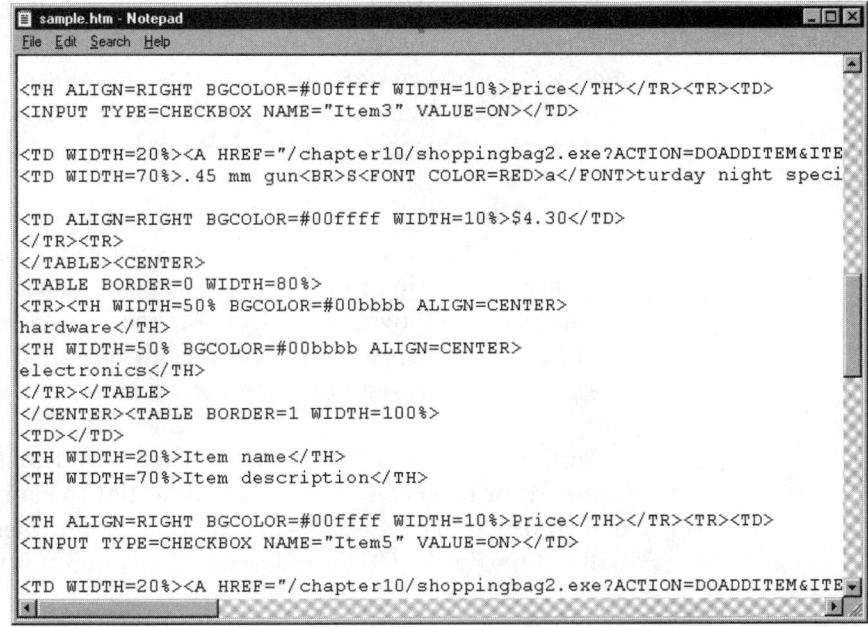

```
sample.htm - Notepad
File  Edit  Search  Help

<TH ALIGN=RIGHT BGCOLOR=#00ffff WIDTH=10%>Price</TH></TR><TR><TD>
<INPUT TYPE=CHECKBOX NAME="Item3" VALUE=ON></TD>

<TD WIDTH=20%><A HREF="/chapter10/shoppingbag2.exe?ACTION=DOADDITEM&ITE
<TD WIDTH=70%>.45 mm gun<BR>S<FONT COLOR=RED>a</FONT>turday night speci

<TD ALIGN=RIGHT BGCOLOR=#00ffff WIDTH=10%>$4.30</TD>
</TR><TR>
</TABLE><CENTER>
<TABLE BORDER=0 WIDTH=80%>
<TR><TH WIDTH=50% BGCOLOR=#00bbbb ALIGN=CENTER>
hardware</TH>
<TH WIDTH=50% BGCOLOR=#00bbbb ALIGN=CENTER>
electronics</TH>
</TR></TABLE>
</CENTER><TABLE BORDER=1 WIDTH=100%>
<TD></TD>
<TH WIDTH=20%>Item name</TH>
<TH WIDTH=70%>Item description</TH>

<TH ALIGN=RIGHT BGCOLOR=#00ffff WIDTH=10%>Price</TH></TR><TR><TD>
<INPUT TYPE=CHECKBOX NAME="Item5" VALUE=ON></TD>

<TD WIDTH=20%><A HREF="/chapter10/shoppingbag2.exe?ACTION=DOADDITEM&ITE
```

Once the design phase for the HTML is over (is it really over?), the design can simply be integrated into the application. This allows the application to support a new theme or support a new tag.

CGI programming can be used together with other techniques to produce a flawless, integrated application that looks perfect to the naked eye. Programmers are no longer limited to the old HTML tags. They can utilize the latest, greatest tags supported by both Netscape and Microsoft.

Advanced HTML Tags (the Meta Tag)

One all-important HTML tag enables the user to request that the browser *not* cache the CGI application's responses. Some browsers employ the same caching algorithm used for standard HTML pages in CGI applications as well. To a programmer, this can mean that in certain situations the browser never requests information from the CGI application, using a previously cached response in its stead.

A CGI application should use this tag in situations where the HTML response to a CGI "query" can change *even if it receives the same parameters*. This often occurs in databases where the information changes a lot — the browser must not assume that, given the same input parameters, the response from the CGI application will be identical.

Examples of this problem can be found when, for instance, a credit card transaction must take place a second time; since the information is identical, certain browsers may assume that the same transaction is taking place, and bypass the CGI application. More often than not, the user has simply pressed the refresh button, justifying this decision on the part of the browser development teams.

In this scenario, if the user expected the transaction to take place again, he or she is fooled into thinking that the submission for the second transaction *was* successful. The client's browser, on the other hand, will not notify the CGI application of any second transaction.

An application, or Web page, can use the Meta tag in situations where the browser may choose to handle the web page somewhat differently than the default.

The Meta tag is used primarily for three functions:

1. Specifying cache and other browser parameters (most of which are browser-specific).

2. Asking the browser to refresh the contents of a page after a given number of seconds. This can be used to create a "pull" (or constantly-refreshing web page or frame) or to create a presentation style web site ("PowerPoint" style). It is often used for redirection in web-servers, which neither support redirectors nor contain intrinsic support for several types of default pages.

3. In situations where an indexing search engine (used either internally or externally) references a specific web page, the Meta tag can be employed to set up keywords that the search engine then uses to index the page.

The Cache Meta Tag

Used primarily for preventing unwanted caching of pages by the browser, this tag was created primarily for standard HTML web pages that change all too often. Some browsers do not notice that a page has changed. The result is that the user believes the web page has *not* actually changed since the last time it was reviewed.

Most browsers cache the pages they encounter by simply placing every web page or file they reference into a cache directory. The browser uses this temporary cache directory to store all encountered web related files. These files contain the actual HTML scripts as the web server originally relayed them to the browser.

When a URL is referenced explicitly (by typing it in or using a bookmark) or implicitly (by way of hyperlink, Meta tag or form submission), the browser first attempts to locate that URL in its cache directory. If it is found, the browser uses proprietary methods to decide whether to use the cached file, or retrieve the information from the server again. In some scenarios the browser may actually start to download the web page, stopping after determining that it already has the latest version (e.g. using the head submission method). In most cases, a simple "timeout" is used for each cache file.

The browser can also use additional techniques to determine if the cached file is still effective (for instance, a session-wide cache refresh, time-based refreshes and other, less widely used techniques for discovering the web page's cache "expiration date").

Some browsers, such as Netscape, forego caching of CGI application responses altogether. This tends to be more useful than Internet Explorer, which often erroneously caches some of the responses it gets from CGI applications! The latest release seems to fix this problem.

The Meta-Pragma tag with no-cache contents specifies to the browser that a web page is likely to change every time the user references it. This is used in the home pages of many popular web sites (e.g., *www.microsoft.com* or *www.netscape.com*) since these pages are usually modified on a daily basis (even more than once a day).

Subsequent files and subdirectories in these web sites do not change as often, and so would not normally utilize this tag.

Database applications that seek to preserve the option of modifying the database on the fly will want to implement this tag for every modifiable page. However, since it prevents browsers from caching files, and slows down the page's performance, it should not be overused.

Meta tags are typically placed between the <HEAD> and </HEAD> tags. This allows the browser to absorb the Meta tag information before processing the actual document it pertains to.

The following tag, placed between <HEAD> and </HEAD>, will cause the browser to forego any caching on the following document. This may or may not also refer to the underlying components in that document (e.g., images), based on client browser implementation!

```
<META NAME="Pragma" CONTENT="no-cache">
```

Other tags are also relevant to CGI programmers. These are the "Author" and "Description" Meta tags. In CGI applications, such tags provide room for the CGI programmer to officially place his/her name (or company name), as well as a good description of the CGI application.

This is similar to the executable version information often found in normal Windows executables. Indexing servers can use the Author Meta tag information that enables managers and external users to quickly determine who is in charge of a specific web site development (or of a CGI application development, for that matter).

The description tag allows for a standard description of a web page or a web application.

```
<HEAD>
<meta name="Author" content="Ofer LaOr">
<meta name="Description" content="oCGI book samples and _
          source code">
<!- standard HEAD structures here ->
    .

    .
</HEAD>
```

An obvious alternative to these tags is the HTML remark clause (initiated by <!— and terminated by —>). This works well in most situations, since the information that must be maintained in the HTML source code varies for each project.

One important piece of information can be the version information (build number) of the CGI application itself. Visual Basic can be asked to increment the revision number each time the application is built (or compiled). This revision number is quite easily accessed from the VB application itself, utilizing the Visual Basic App object. The system variables: App.Major, App.Minor, App.Revision hold the complete version number for the current application. An application with version 2.1.125 will have App.Major=2, App.Minor=1, App.Revision=125.

It is a good idea to embed this number into the HTML stream. This can help resolve version issues and incompatibilities. It also helps to be able to know the version number in order to determine whether or not a new version is in place. All too often, the programmer believes a new version has been installed, when, in fact, the old version is still up and running. On the flip side, bugs can persist regardless of revision, in which case the programmer believes that the new version has not yet been installed.

The generator Meta tag allows a web page to specify the application that created this HTML stream. Usually, an HTML editor integrates this tag into the HTML document without bothering the author with details. FrontPage 97 places the following tag in every document it edits:

```
<meta name="GENERATOR" content="Microsoft FrontPage 2.0">
```

In the CGI application, this is equivalent to the description or name of the application itself.

The HTTP-EQUIV Meta Tag

Meta tags with the HTTP-EQUIV qualifier function by converting the tag into a virtual HTTP request header. This normally requires cooperation from both client and server in order to function properly. It gives the programmer the freedom to use Meta tags for most HTTP "instructions" while not restricting him to doing so in the HTTP header.

The original intent was to provide the HTML author with a way of notifying the browser on HTTP requests without resorting to programming. To the programmer, these tags are used primarily to avoid HTTP headers, which are hard to support, maintain and debug. In addition, the tags can be read on the client side, whereas an HTTP header instruction is "swallowed up" and processed by the browser.

Meta tags meant for HTTP response headers must be located in the HTML stream prior to the first <HTML> tag. This lets the browser know the instruction is to be handled in the same way as normal HTTP header instructions.

Notes

Some HTML editors prohibit the explicit placement of HTML tags outside of the <HTML> </HTML> range. This includes Microsoft's FrontPage 97.

These HTTP-EQUIV Meta tags can be used to set a document's expiration date (there is no way to tell for sure whether the browser will support this option). They can be used as a replacement to the no-cache tag in situations where it is impossible to detrmine the expiration date/time of the information.

Placing the following tag will cause the browser to expire the document in said date and time:

```
<META HTTP-EQUIV="Expires" CONTENT="Tue, 04 Dec 1996 _
         21:29:02 GMT">
```

This correlates to the following HTTP header field:

```
Expires: Tue, 04 Dec 1996 21:29:02 GMT
```

Additional, popular HTTP-EQUIV tags include content type:

```
<META HTTP-EQUIV="Content-Type" CONTENT="text/html; _
         charset=Windows-1251">
```

This can theoretically be used to modify the Content **type** (to something other than **text/html**). Unfortunately, this is not practical because the server and browser will disregard such information unless they already knows that it is an HTML-type document. The only use for this tag is to specify the char-set a specific page is using. It can easily be used to internationalize a web page.

The Refresh Meta Tag

This tag is the most popular of the Meta tags, and is often used to generate self-refreshing or "progressive" web pages. This is usually implemented within a specific frame, as to allow the user the comfort of static surroundings with a single changing frame.

In certain situations, a CGI application may require a periodic refresh. This can be used to update the display (e.g., update stock prices in an HTML stock ticker) or cause the web page to redraw (a chat application may use it to periodically clear the chat window).

A variant of this tag allows you to redirect a web page onto another location. (For more information about this, and other HTTP headers, refer to an HTTP 1.0 reference manual. Many such manuals are available for download, or are accessible via the web.)

Once again, the Meta tag is used. This time the HTTP-EQUIV option is utilized in order to cause the web page to refresh. The tag must be used in **between enclosing HEAD tags**. Unfortunately, this precludes utilizing the tag to refresh or redirect the page at will. In order to achieve this, a scripting language must be employed (such as JavaScript).

The syntax for this tag is as follows:

```
<META HTTP-EQUIV="Refresh" CONTENT="x; URL=http://y">
```

Where **x** is the number of seconds before the browser refreshes the view. Depending on the browser, refresh timing can start when the document finishes loading (since this only occurs after the CGI application terminates, it provides a neat way for refreshing the web page a few seconds afterwards). An alternative method for refresh starts the countdown when the browser begins receiving the document. In order to target a timing-critical CGI application for a specific browser set, the programmer must experiment with this option to make the application portable across a given set of browsers.

Luckily, both Netscape and Microsoft browsers start counting from the time the CGI application terminates. Since these two browsers dominate the market, most systems only target them.

The **y** variable signifies the URL to which the browser should load instead of the current one:

```
<META HTTP-EQUIV="Refresh" CONTENT="12; _
        URL=http://foo.bar/blatz.html">
```

The Meta tag described above can be translated into the following HTTP header:

```
Refresh: 12; URL=http://foo.bar/blatz.html
```

Notes

If the program needs to send HTTP headers to the browser, it may do so utilizing the **WriteCGI** *function with the* **fStartCGI = false.** *This should be done prior to any normal* **WriteCGI** *function calls. The HTTP header should be followed with at least one CR/LF combination (implemented in Visual Basic's* **vbCrLf** *constant).*

In order to load a CGI application this way, use the following syntax:

```
<META HTTP-EQUIV="Refresh" CONTENT="12; _
        URL=http://www.myweb.com/scripts/cgiapp.exe?_
        param1=true&Submit=Sumbit+Information">
```

This syntax is standard for directly referencing web applications.

If the URL qualifier is omitted, the browser will refresh the currently loaded CGI application. In order to allow for parameter passing in such a scenario, the CGI parameters should be explicitly called from within the URL. If this is the result of a form submission, the form should be submitted using the ISINDEX posting method.

The HTTP Return Code

The HTTP return code is an often-neglected header tag, since neither server nor browser requires it. This tag tells the browser the status of the HTTP transaction. When not specified, the browser assumes that a transaction has been successful. If the application needs to specifically place a successful HTTP transaction, it should place the following text before the first active *WriteCGI* call:

```
HTTP/1.0 200 OK
```

This string should be placed (with a CR/LF at the end) using the *WriteCGI* function with *fStartCGI* as false prior to the first standard *WriteCGI* call. A complete list of HTTP codes is as follows:

```
200 OK
201 created
202 accepted
204 no content
301 moved permanently
302 moved temporarily
304 not modified
400 bad request
401 unauthorized
403 forbidden
404 not found
500 internal server error
501 not implemented
502 bad gateway
503 service unavailable
```

Note that the code is all that's required, the text being a more detailed explanation for the human side of the equation. When a code is received by the browser with no subsequent text, the browser typically places its interpretation of the code (codes are standard).

This tag is representative of how most current Internet protocols (e.g., FTP, SMTP) return error codes. Browsers rarely check for these codes, and most applications do not bother to return them any more. In protocols such as SMTP, POP and FTP, however, these codes are crucial for proper communication between the two conversing sides.

Applications written in oCGI generally do not bother with this type of return code. The code can be returned using the Meta tag similar to the way in which other meta tags are used in this book. Since none of the samples shown here return this code, and because of the rare need for it, sample code for this option was omitted.

Frames and CGI Applications

Frames are often used from within applications to allow the user access to a static portion of the screen, along with a variable part. Most often, frames are used for a graphic menu (roughly equivalent to the toolbar in Windows applications), submenus or search buttons.

In order to create a frame-based application, a good overall design of the look and feel should be created prior to any actual code writing.

The first thing that must be determined is which frames are to be handled by the application, and which are to remain static HTML documents. A good approach usually utilizes a static web page design for as much of the system as possible. This allows the programmer to use conventional HTML editing programs. It also helps minimize the application size.

A frame-based document contains any number of references to the documents within each frame. Each frame can reference any URL, including standard HTML documents, as well as CGI applications. Each frame can theoretically be an independent CGI script (or, in our case, an actual application); this normally minimizes program size, but prevents reuse of system components, and defeats caching on the *web server*.

Our user-name/password application is extended to include two frames in the final document. For demonstration's sake, some of the frames are static and others dynamic.

Source Code of UserSecurity4.bas

```
Option Explicit

Declare Function oCGI2Register Lib "oCGI2.dll" Alias _
        "DllRegisterServer" () As Long
Dim cgi As oCGI2
Dim db As Database
Dim sFullName As String
```

```
Sub DoInitialLogonGuestScreen(Optional sError As Variant)
  With cgi
    .WriteCGI "<HTML>" + vbCrLf
    If (IsMissing(sError)) Then
      .WriteCGI "<HEAD><TITLE>Creating a user database _
          with the oCGI VB module"
      .WriteCGI "</TITLE></HEAD><BODY BGCOLOR=""_
          #ffffff"">" + vbCrLf
    Else
      .WriteCGI "<HEAD><TITLE>" + sError + _
          "</TITLE></HEAD><BODY "
      .WriteCGI "BGCOLOR=""#ffffff"">" + vbCrLf
      .WriteCGI "<H2>ERROR: " + sError + "</H2><HR>" + _
          vbCrLf
    End If


    .WriteCGI "<FORM ACTION=""" + .ReadScriptName
    .WriteCGI """ METHOD=""POST"">" + vbCrLf
    .WriteCGI "<INPUT TYPE=""HIDDEN"" NAME=""Action"" "
    .WriteCGI " VALUE=""PROCESSGUEST"">" + vbCrLf
    .WriteCGI "<TABLE><TR><TD>" + vbCrLf
    .WriteCGI "<B>User Name:</B></TD><TD><INPUT TYPE=TEXT _
          SIZE=20 "
    .WriteCGI " MAXLENGTH=50 NAME=""UserName"" "
    If (.ReadParam("UserName") <> "") Then
      .WriteCGI " VALUE=""" + cgi.ReadParam("UserName") + _
          """>" + vbCrLf
    Else
      .WriteCGI ">" + vbCrLf
    End If

    .WriteCGI "</TD></TR><TR><TD>" + vbCrLf
    .WriteCGI "<B>Full Name:</B></TD><TD><INPUT TYPE=TEXT _
          SIZE=20 "
    .WriteCGI " MAXLENGTH=50 NAME=""FullName"" "
    If (.ReadParam("FullName") <> "") Then
      .WriteCGI " VALUE=""" + .ReadParam("FullName") + _
          """>" + vbCrLf
    Else
      .WriteCGI ">" + vbCrLf
```

```
                 End If


           .WriteCGI "</TD></TR><TR><TD>" + vbCrLf
           .WriteCGI "<B>Password:</B></TD><TD><INPUT _
               TYPE=PASSWORD SIZE=20 "
           .WriteCGI " MAXLENGTH=50 NAME=""Password"">" + vbCrLf
           .WriteCGI "</TD></TR><TR><TD>" + vbCrLf
           .WriteCGI "</TD></TR><TR><TD>" + vbCrLf
           .WriteCGI "<B>VerifyPassword:</B></TD><TD><INPUT _
               TYPE=PASSWORD "
           .WriteCGI " SIZE=20 MAXLENGTH=50
               NAME=""VerifyPassword"">" + vbCrLf
           .WriteCGI "</TD></TR><TR><TD> <input type=checkbox _
               name=""RememberPassword"" "
           .WriteCGI " value=""ON""> Remember my password for "
           .WriteCGI " <input type=TEXT SIZE=2 MAXLENGTH=2 _
               NAME=""RememberDuration"" "
           .WriteCGI " VALUE=14> days"
           .WriteCGI "</TD></TR><TR><TD>" + vbCrLf

           .WriteCGI "</TD></TR><TR><TD> <P><INPUT TYPE=Submit _
               NAME=""Submit"" "
           .WriteCGI " VALUE=""Create your new user"">" + vbCrLf
           .WriteCGI "</TD><TD><INPUT TYPE=Reset NAME=""Reset"" _
               VALUE=""Reset"">"
           .WriteCGI vbCrLf + "</TD><TD>" + vbCrLf
           .WriteCGI "</TD></TR></TABLE>" + vbCrLf
           .WriteCGI "</FORM> </BODY></HTML>" + vbCrLf
       End With
   End Sub



   Sub DoInitialLogonScreen(Optional sError As Variant)
       ' this function displays the initial log on screen.
       ' this gets called to show the existing user screen.
       With cgi
           .WriteCGI "<HTML>" + vbCrLf
           If (IsMissing(sError)) Then
               .WriteCGI "<HEAD><TITLE>Creating a user database _
                   with the oCGI "
```

```
      .WriteCGI " VB module</TITLE></HEAD><BODY _
          BGCOLOR="""#ffffff""">" + vbCrLf
Else
    .WriteCGI "<HEAD><TITLE>" + sError + _
        "</TITLE></HEAD><BODY "
    .WriteCGI " BGCOLOR="""#ffffff""">" + vbCrLf
    .WriteCGI "<H2>ERROR: " + sError + "</H2><HR>" + vbCrLf
End If
.WriteCGI "<BR><H2> If you've never logged in before, _
        press this:<H2>"
.WriteCGI vbCrLf
.WriteCGI "<FORM ACTION=""" + .ReadScriptName + """ _
        METHOD=""POST"">"
.WriteCGI vbCrLf
.WriteCGI "<INPUT TYPE=""HIDDEN"" NAME=""Action"" _
        VALUE=""LOGGUEST"">"
.WriteCGI vbCrLf
.WriteCGI "<INPUT TYPE=Submit NAME=""Submit"" _
        VALUE=""New User"">"
.WriteCGI vbCrLf
.WriteCGI "</FORM><BR><HR>" + vbCrLf


.WriteCGI "<BR><H2> If you have logged in, please use _
        your username and "
.WriteCGI "password:<H2>" + vbCrLf
.WriteCGI "<FORM ACTION=""" + .ReadScriptName + """ _
        METHOD=""POST"">"
.WriteCGI vbCrLf
.WriteCGI "<INPUT TYPE=""HIDDEN"" NAME=""Action"" _
        VALUE=""LOGIN"">" + vbCrLf
.WriteCGI "<TABLE><TR><TD>" + vbCrLf
.WriteCGI "<B>User Name:</B></TD><TD><INPUT TYPE=TEXT _
        SIZE=20 "
.WriteCGI " MAXLENGTH=50 NAME=""UserName"" "
If (.ReadParam("UserName") <> "") Then ' is this a _
        "wrong login" error?!
    .WriteCGI " VALUE=""" + .ReadParam("UserName") + _
        """>" + vbCrLf
Else
    .WriteCGI ">" + vbCrLf
```

```
          End If

          .WriteCGI "</TD></TR><TR><TD>" + vbCrLf
          .WriteCGI "<B>Password:</B></TD><TD><INPUT _
               TYPE=PASSWORD SIZE=20 MAXLENGTH=50 "
          .WriteCGI " NAME=""Password"">" + vbCrLf
          .WriteCGI "</TD></TR><TR><TD> <input type=checkbox _
               name=""RememberPassword"" "
          .WriteCGI " value=""ON""> Remember my password for "
          .WriteCGI " <input type=TEXT SIZE=2 MAXLENGTH=2 _
               NAME=""RememberDuration"" "
          .WriteCGI " VALUE=14> days"
          .WriteCGI "</TD></TR><TR><TD> <P><INPUT TYPE=Submit _
               NAME=""Submit"" "
          .WriteCGI " VALUE=""Log in as existing User"">" + _
               vbCrLf
          .WriteCGI "</TD><TD><INPUT TYPE=Reset NAME=""Reset"" _
               VALUE=""Reset"">" + vbCrLf
          .WriteCGI "</TD><TD>" + vbCrLf
          .WriteCGI "</TD></TR></TABLE>" + vbCrLf
          .WriteCGI "</FORM> </BODY></HTML>" + vbCrLf
     End With
End Sub


Sub DoProcessGuest()
  ' check validity of everything to start with...
  With cgi
     ' this could be done better with JavaScript validation!
     Select Case "" ' find out if some of the fields are empty!
        Case Trim$(.ReadParam("UserName"))
           DoInitialLogonGuestScreen "Invalid User name _
              entered."
           Exit Sub
        Case Trim$(.ReadParam("FullName"))
           DoInitialLogonGuestScreen "Invalid Full Name _
              entered."
           Exit Sub
        Case Trim$(.ReadParam("Password"))
           DoInitialLogonGuestScreen "An empty password _
           cannot be used"
```

```
          Exit Sub
End Select
If (.ReadParam("Password") <>
        .ReadParam("VerifyPassword")) Then
   DoInitialLogonGuestScreen "Password and Verify _
        Password must be the same!"
   Exit Sub
End If
If (.ReadParam("Password") = .ReadParam("UserName")) _
        Then
   DoInitialLogonGuestScreen "UserName and Password _
        must be different!"
   Exit Sub
End If



' this function gets called to finalize the logging _
        in of the user!
Dim rs As Recordset, sSQL As String
sSQL = "select * from USERS where UserName='"
sSQL = sSQL + DoubleQuote(.ReadParam("UserName")) + "'"
Set rs = db.OpenRecordset(sSQL, dbOpenDynaset)



' make sure that there's no one by that same name...
If rs.EOF Then
   rs.AddNew ' no need for double quotes, DAO takes _
        care of it here!
   rs("UserName") = .ReadParam("UserName")
   rs("Password") = .ReadParam("Password")
   rs("FullName") = .ReadParam("FullName")
   rs.Update

   sFullName = .ReadParam("FullName")



   Set rs = db.OpenRecordset(sSQL, dbOpenDynaset)
   If Not rs.EOF Then
      rs.Close
      SetUserCookies .ReadParam("UserName") ' install _
      cookies!
```

```
                            ' logged in, show home page!
                            HomePage
                        Else
                            rs.Close
                            DoInitialLogonGuestScreen "Could not add User _
                                to system"
                        End If
                    Else
                        rs.Close
                        DoInitialLogonGuestScreen "User Name already exists"
                    End If
                End With
            End Sub



            Sub DoUserSecurity()
                If (Not TryToLogin()) Then
                    Select Case (cgi.ReadParam("Action"))
                        Case "LOGGUEST"
                            DoInitialLogonGuestScreen
                        Case "PROCESSGUEST"
                            DoProcessGuest
                        Case Else
                            If (cgi.ReadParam("UserName") <> "") Then ' _
                                    tried to log on, but couldn't
                                DoInitialLogonScreen "UserName/Password could _
                                    not be matched"
                            Else
                                DoInitialLogonScreen
                            End If
                    End Select
                Else
                    Select Case cgi.ReadParam("Action")
                        Case "LOGIN", "": ' the empty string is added for _
                                cookie support!
                            HomePage
                        Case Else: ' dunno what this is!
                            If InStr(cgi.ReadParam("Action"), "FRAME") = 1 Then
                                DoFrame cgi.ReadParam("Action")
                            Else
                                DoInitialLogonScreen
```

```
                    End If
              End Select
          End If
    End Sub


Sub HomePage()
   With cgi
      .WriteCGI "<HTML>" + vbCrLf
      .WriteCGI "<HEADER><TITLE> Welcome to the frame home _
              page " + sFullName
      .WriteCGI "</TITLE></HEADER>" + vbCrLf
      .WriteCGI "<FRAMESET ROWS=20%,200,* BORDER=0>"
      .WriteCGI " <FRAME BORDER=0 FRAMEBORDER=0 _
              NORESIZE SCROLLING=NO SRC="""
      .WriteCGI .ReadScriptName + "?ACTION=FRAME1"" _
              NAME=""FRAME1"">"
      .WriteCGI " <FRAME BORDER=1 SCROLLING=YES _
              FRAMEBORDER=0 SRC="""
      .WriteCGI .ReadScriptName + "?ACTION=FRAME2"" _
              NAME=""FRAME2"">"
      .WriteCGI " <FRAMESET COLS=30%,50%,*>"
      .WriteCGI " <FRAME FRAMEBORDER=0 NORESIZE _
              SCROLLING=NO SRC="""
      .WriteCGI .ReadScriptName + "?ACTION=FRAME3"" _
              NAME=""FRAME3"">"
      .WriteCGI " <FRAME SRC=""" + .ReadScriptName + _
              "?ACTION=FRAME4"" _ NAME=""FRAME4"">"
      .WriteCGI " <FRAME SCROLLING=YES FRAMEBORDER=0 _
              SRC=""http://"
      .WriteCGI .ReadServerName + """ NAME=""FRAME4"">"
      .WriteCGI " </FRAMESET>"
      .WriteCGI "<NOFRAMES>"
      .WriteCGI "<BODY BGCOLOR=#ffffff>" + vbCrLf
      .WriteCGI "<H2> Welcome to the sample users home _
              page " + sFullName
      .WriteCGI "</H2><P>" + vbCrLf
      .WriteCGI "<I>Note: if you close your browser and _
              come back later, "
      .WriteCGI "you will not have to go through the _
              username/password "
```

```
          .WriteCGI "screen again!<P>"
          .WriteCGI vbCrLf
          .WriteCGI "The system automatically identifies you _
                utilizing cookies.</I><HR>"
          .WriteCGI vbCrLf
          .WriteCGI "<H1> Your browser does not support frames! _
                </H1>"




          If (Trim$(cgi.ReadRemoteFrom()) <> "") Then
            .WriteCGI "Your email address is: " + _
                .ReadRemoteFrom() + "<BR>" + vbCrLf
          End If




          cgi.WriteCGI "Your browser is: " + cgi.ReadUserAgent_
                () + "<BR>" + vbCrLf


          .WriteCGI "Your IP address is: " + .ReadRemoteAddress_
                () + "<BR>" + vbCrLf
          If ((.ReadRemoteHost()<>"") And (.ReadRemoteHost() <> _
                .ReadRemoteAddress())) Then
            .WriteCGI "Your machine's host name: " + _
                .ReadRemoteHost() + "<BR>" + vbCrLf
          End If


          .WriteCGI "</BODY>"
          .WriteCGI "</NOFRAMES>"
          .WriteCGI "</FRAMESET>"

          .WriteCGI "</HTML>"
      End With
  End Sub


  Sub DoFrame(sFrame As String)
      With cgi
          .WriteCGI "<HTML>" + vbCrLf
          .WriteCGI "<HEADER>" + vbCrLf
```

```
Dim iCounter As Integer
If sFrame = "FRAME1" Then


  If IsNumeric(.ReadParam("Counter")) Then
    iCounter = CInt(.ReadParam("Counter"))
  Else
    iCounter = 0
  End If
  .WriteCGI "<META HTTP-EQUIV=""Refresh"" "
  .WriteCGI "CONTENT=""1; URL=" + .ReadScriptName
  .WriteCGI "?ACTION=FRAME1&Counter="
  .WriteCGI CStr(iCounter + 1) + """>"
End If



.WriteCGI "</HEADER>" + vbCrLf
Select Case sFrame
  Case "FRAME1":
    .WriteCGI "<BODY BGCOLOR=#ffffff>" + vbCrLf
    .WriteCGI "<h4>Counter= " + CStr(iCounter) + "</h4>"
    .WriteCGI "this will keep going and going and _
      going and going..."
    .WriteCGI "</BODY>" + vbCrLf
    .WriteCGI "</HTML>"
    Beep
    Sleep 5000 ' sleep 5 seconds, + 1 sec refresh _
      meta tag = 6 seconds total.
  Case "FRAME2":
    .WriteCGI "<BODY BGCOLOR=#ffffff>" + vbCrLf
    .WriteCGI "Your browser is: " + .ReadUserAgent()_
      + "<BR>" + vbCrLf
    .WriteCGI "Your IP address is: " + _
      .ReadRemoteAddress()
    .WriteCGI "<BR>" + vbCrLf
    .WriteCGI "</BODY>" + vbCrLf
    .WriteCGI "</HTML>"
  Case "FRAME3":
    .WriteCGI "<BODY BGCOLOR=#ffff00>" + vbCrLf
    If ((.ReadRemoteHost() <> "") _
```

```vb
      And (.ReadRemoteHost() <> _
        .ReadRemoteAddress())) Then
      .WriteCGI "Your machine's host name: "
      .WriteCGI .ReadRemoteHost() + "<BR>" + vbCrLf
    Else
      .WriteCGI "<H1>FRAME3</H1>"
    End If
    .WriteCGI "</BODY>" + vbCrLf
    .WriteCGI "</HTML>"
  Case "FRAME4":
    .WriteCGI "<FRAMESET COLS=50%,50% BORDER=1>_
      " + vbCrLf
    .WriteCGI " <FRAME SRC=""" + .ReadScriptName
    .WriteCGI "?ACTION=FRAME5"" NAME=""FRAME5"">" + _
      vbCrLf
    .WriteCGI " <FRAME SRC=""" + .ReadScriptName
    .WriteCGI "?ACTION=FRAME6"" NAME=""FRAME6"">" + _
        vbCrLf
    .WriteCGI "</FRAMESET>" + vbCrLf
    .WriteCGI "</HTML>"
  Case "FRAME5":
    .WriteCGI "<BODY BGCOLOR=#00ffff>" + vbCrLf
    .WriteCGI "<A HREF=""" + .ReadScriptName
    .WriteCGI "?ACTION=FRAME5"" target=_parent> _
        change parent "
    .WriteCGI " </A><BR>" + vbCrLf
    .WriteCGI "<A HREF=""" + .ReadScriptName + _
        "?ACTION=FRAME5"" "
    .WriteCGI " target=FRAME1> change frame1 </A>" _
        + vbCrLf
    .WriteCGI "</BODY>" + vbCrLf
    .WriteCGI "</HTML>"
  Case "FRAME6":
    .WriteCGI "<BODY BGCOLOR=#00ffff>" + vbCrLf
    .WriteCGI "<A HREF=""" + .ReadScriptName + _
        "?ACTION=FRAME6"" "
    .WriteCGI " target=_top> change top frame _
        </A><BR>" + vbCrLf
    .WriteCGI "<A HREF=""" + .ReadScriptName + _
      "?ACTION=FRAME6"" "
    .WriteCGI " target=_blank> create new page </A>"_
```

```
                                + vbCrLf
                    .WriteCGI "</BODY>" + vbCrLf
                    .WriteCGI "</HTML>"
        End Select
    End With
End Sub


Sub main()
On Error GoTo RegisterErr ' register oCGI only if having _
            problems!
    Set cgi = New oCGI2
On Error GoTo NormalErr
    cgi.ProcessCGI Command
    'Load frmVBCrash
    Set db = Workspaces(0).OpenDatabase(App.Path + _
            "\users.mdb")

    DoUserSecurity

    db.Close
    Set cgi = Nothing
    End
NormalErr:
    cgi.WriteCGI "<HTML><BODY>Error:" + Error$ + _
            "</BODY></HTML>"
    Set cgi = Nothing ' Just in case
    End
RegisterErr:
    oCGI2Register
    Set db = Nothing ' this works for uninitialized objects _
            too!
    End
End Sub


Sub SetUserCookies(sUser As String)
    ' randomize a UserCookie, then place it!
    Dim rsUser As Recordset, sSQL As String

    sSQL = "select * from USERS where UserName='" + _
            DoubleQuote(sUser) + "'"
    Set rsUser = db.OpenRecordset(sSQL, dbOpenDynaset)
```

```
    If Not rsUser.EOF Then ' this shouldn't happen if we _
            are here!
      Dim sUserCookie As String, sRandom As String
      Randomize CLng(Format(Now, "hhmmss"))
      sRandom = CStr(CLng((Rnd * 1000000000)) + 1)
      sUserCookie = CStr(rsUser("UserID")) + "=" + sRandom

      'Note, using Java script, this validation could be _
            done client-side!
      Dim sCookie As String, sServer As String, sScript _
            As String
      sCookie = "UserCookie"
      sServer = cgi.ReadServerName
      sScript = cgi.ReadScriptName
      If (cgi.ReadParam("RememberPassword") = "ON") And _
        (IsNumeric(cgi.ReadParam("RememberDuration"))) Then
          Dim expire As Date
          expire = CDate(Now + CInt(cgi.ReadParam_
            ("RememberDuration")))
          cgi.WriteCookie sCookie, sUserCookie, sServer, _
            sScript, expire
      Else ' no persistence!
          cgi.WriteCookie sCookie, sUserCookie, sServer, _
            sScript
      End If
      rsUser.Edit
      rsUser("Notes") = sRandom
      rsUser.Update
    End If
    rsUser.Close
End Sub

' Try to login user. Return true if successful.
Function TryToLogin() As Boolean
    TryToLogin = False
    If (UserPasswordMatch(cgi.ReadParam("UserName"), _
            cgi.ReadParam("Password"))) Then
      SetUserCookies cgi.ReadParam("UserName")
      TryToLogin = True
    Else
      Dim sUserID As String, sCookieValue As String
```

```
      Dim sUserCookie As String, iPos As Integer
      sUserCookie = cgi.ReadCookie("UserCookie")
      If (sUserCookie <> "") Then
        iPos = InStr(sUserCookie, "=")
        sUserID = Left$(sUserCookie, iPos - 1)
        sCookieValue = Mid$(sUserCookie, iPos + 1)
        TryToLogin = UserCookieMatch(sUserID, sCookieValue)
      End If
    End If
End Function


Function UserCookieMatch(sUserID As String, sCookieValue _
          As String) As Boolean
    Dim rsUser As Recordset, sSQL As String
    UserCookieMatch = False ' convince me otherwise!
    sSQL = "select * from USERS where UserID=" + sUserID
    Set rsUser = db.OpenRecordset(sSQL, dbOpenDynaset)
    If Not rsUser.EOF Then
      If (rsUser("Notes") = sCookieValue) Then
        sFullName = rsUser("FullName")
        UserCookieMatch = True
      End If
    End If
    rsUser.Close
End Function


Function UserPasswordMatch(sUserName As String, sPassword _
          As String) As Boolean
    Dim rsUser As Recordset, sSQL As String
    UserPasswordMatch = False ' convince me otherwise!
    If (sUserName = "" And sPassword = "") Then Exit _
          Function ' no good for sure!

    sSQL = "select * from USERS where UserName='" + _
          DoubleQuote(sUserName) + "'"
    Set rsUser = db.OpenRecordset(sSQL, dbOpenDynaset)
    If Not rsUser.EOF Then
      If (rsUser("Password") = sPassword) Then
        sFullName = rsUser("FullName")
        UserPasswordMatch = True
      End If
```

```
        End If
        rsUser.Close
    End Function

    Function DoubleQuote(sData As String) As String
        Dim sOut As String, iPos As Integer

        For iPos = 1 To Len(sData)
            Select Case Mid$(sData, iPos, 1)
                Case "'":
                    sOut = sOut + "\'"
                Case """":
                    sOut = sOut + """"""
                Case Else:
                    sOut = sOut + Mid$(sData, iPos, 1)
            End Select
        Next
        DoubleQuote = sOut
    End Function
```

Note how a frame structure can be structured *within* a frame structure (e.g., the *HomePage* function) or created locally (as in frame number 4).

Note, too, the use of the *DoFrame* function in the system. This type of function, handling a specific subsection of a web page, is useful in frame applications and other applications where a few pages are very close in nature.

Frame 1 continually updates itself. The frame-1 process will beep, pause for 5 seconds and then terminate. The browser then takes over and refreshes the screen after one second. Since the timer increments itself once every 6-7 seconds with Microsoft and Netscape browsers, this shows that the browser waits for the application to terminate before starting the count-down.

Neither type of browser shows the last section of the HTML stream before the application terminates. This prevents a situation in which the browser decides on a layout for a page *before* it ascertains that something new will not modify that layout. A dummy text line (or graphic) that forces the browsers to commit prior information can be placed on the bottom of the screen in order to resolve this problem.

Figure 7.4

Frames in action

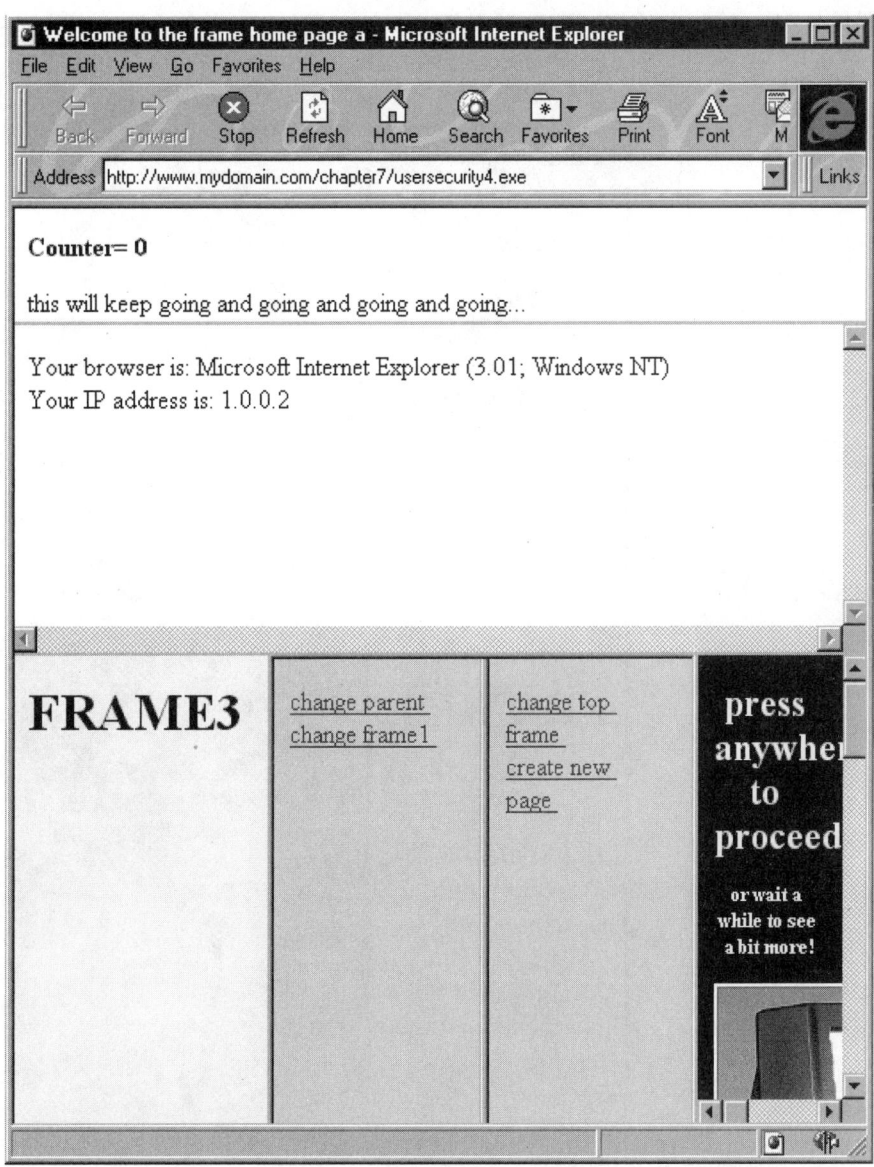

Figure 7.5
The frame incremented
using the timer

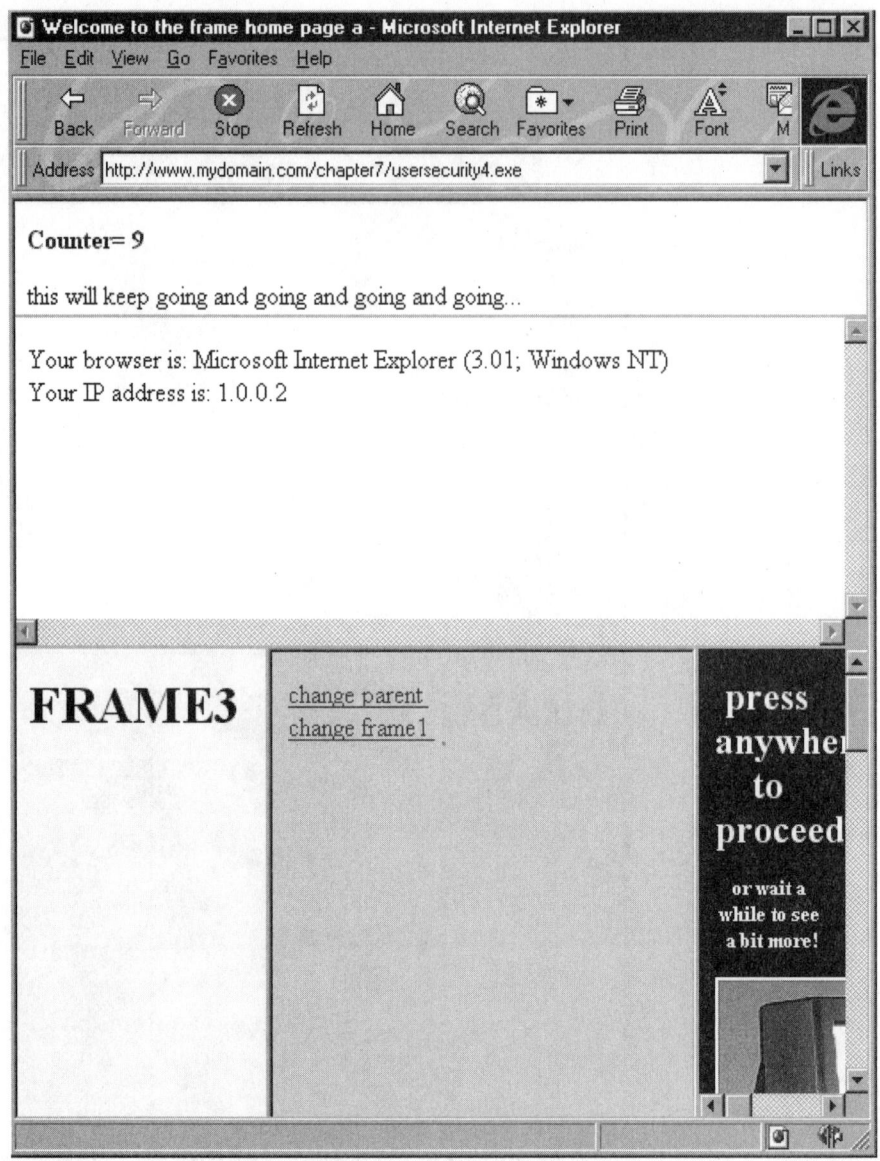

As seen here, frames may or may not contain borders, background
colors or scroll bars, as required by the application.

Additional Ideas

The Meta refresh tag can be seen, in the previous example, to cause a web page to increment a counter. While this is a nifty idea, what can this feature be used for in real life?

The browser only refreshes the form once the CGI application that created it has ceased running. This enables a CGI application to process tasks incrementally, allowing the user to receive notifications about each step.

A simple example of this is an application that takes a long time to validate a user or perform a task. For example, a bank application can retrieve client information from a remote site into a local "cache" database. The application validates the user against the slow mainframe computer, and imports the information into the local cache database. Each step of the way, the application can display a status web page to the user (updating him or her about what's going on, since the application could be taking a long period of time). The user can now view the status of the procedure as it is occurring.

This can be implemented by breaking down the tasks for the application, causing the web page to proceed to the next stage instantaneously. Once the CGI application dumps the HTML stream onto the browser, it goes on to process the current state. As soon as the current state completes, the application terminates and the browser refreshes the screen — causing the application to proceed onto the next state.

A simpler application can utilize this simply to log on users. The first page displays the log-on information while the user is being validated. Once the user is validated, the refresh tag causes the browser to display user-specific information.

Another application can refresh a frame containing a live image. Since the live image takes a while to download, a small refresh time-out provides a nearly live image for smaller images with quick download times.

The World is Your ActiveX-Oyster

Server side constructs also enable communication with the outside world via the server rather than the client. This is especially useful when the server needs to communicate primarily with external entities (which may be protected by a firewall, or another type of security construct).

Some entities the server application may want to contact include e-mail servers, credit card companies or banks, mainframes, and external sensors (e.g., stock ticker).

The server application may want to interface with these entities for a number of reasons. An error condition might require the system to page the administrator via his e-mail account; the system could very well handle all of the actual credit card transactions with no human interaction; the interface with the mainframe could determine whether or not the transaction succeeded, etc.

Visual Basic can handle all of these chores using standard communication techniques. Most entities that allow Visual Basic to communicate with them provide the programmer with a DLL, OCX or ActiveX library encapsulating that entity's functionality.

Sending E-mail from the Server

There are various ways to do this. Since we are dealing with the Internet, most e-mails coming out of the server will use the SMTP protocol. If we are dealing with a MAPI compatible system (utilizing the Exchange client to communicate with the outside) — an OLE automation MAPI interface will allow the programmer access to the local mailbox.

This type of solution covers most e-mail cases, since there are drivers for practically any e-mail system that will talk MAPI. If the e-mail needs to go to the Internet, an Exchange server, or a MAPI compatible system, this would be a fairly good solution. Microsoft provides a full type-library and documentation for the enhanced MAPI interface that comes with NT 4 (as well as Windows 95). This library can be found on the VB CD-ROM under the name "OLE Messaging."

This type of solution however, requires interaction with a local mailbox. It can lead to a "paper trail" auditing all sent items in the "sent items" folder. This can be both a blessing (in situations where an e-mail log, such as an error log, would be appropriate) and a curse (since you may not want such important information in a file on your system).

A simpler, albeit more expensive, alternative is to use a third party control that talks SMTP. There are many such controls around. At one point, Microsoft had a beta Internet Control Pack. This pack was originally to be included in Visual Basic 5. When VB5 came out, it had two Internet-oriented controls: the transfer control (for transferring files from web servers and FTP servers) and the WinSock control. The web browser control is also available if Internet Explorer 3.02 is installed on the machine.

The original pack contained many more features that were excluded from final release. The pack was transferred over to NetManage, which is currently selling it as a part of their Visual Basic Internet SDK.

Some of the controls in this package were the POP and SMTP controls and the NNTP control (for interacting with USENET servers). Since there is no SMTP control built into VB, one can either:

a. Build it yourself using the WinSock control.
   This can be fairly easy so long as you have the proper specs. These are found in `http://nic.ddn.mil/rfc/rfc821.txt`

b. Use an existing control. Any Internet pack for Visual Basic will work, including packages from NetManage, Mabry, Dart, Distinct and a wide assortment of other vendors. Some of these allow for file attachments, and most provide for a simple and elegant way of sending mail from Visual Basic.

c. Use a freeware control. There are several "floating out there."

d. Use a command line automated mailer tool (you can run it via shell). There are several of these (search `http://www.shareware.com` using keyword "SMTP" for more information).

For the purpose of showing how to use such a control, Microsoft's old Internet Control Package can be used. This should be compatible with NetManage's current offerings (although I have not verified this).

To use such a control, two things must happen — it must be registered (and available) prior to usage, and it must have a form to reside in. The registration part is easy — simply use the same technique as in registering oCGI.

First, declare the control you would like to register:

```
Declare Function RegisterSMTP Lib "SMTP.OCX" Alias _
        "DllRegisterServer" () As Long
```

The application should execute this function before displaying the form. The control must reside in the same directory as the application (or anywhere else in the path) for this registration process to work.

To utilize this control, a form must be added to the project. The system loads (show is usually not needed) the form and can start utilizing the control right away. The form will not be displayed on the monitor since the CGI application is running under the context of the Web server (which is a service, so it cannot create visible windows).

The following is sample code that's been tested with Microsoft's ICP (Internet Control Pack) SMTP control. It is shown here as a sample of what should be done. The Microsoft ICP is now obsolete, and other types of controls must be used instead:

```
Sub SendEmail(sEmail As String, sSubject As String, _
        sContent As String, Optional sCC As Variant)
    Load frmEmail
    With frmEmail
        .smtpOutgoing.Cancel ' cancel any outstanding operations!
        .smtpOutgoing.DocInput.Headers.Clear
        .smtpOutgoing.DocInput.Headers.Add "From", _
            "test<test@test.com>"
        .smtpOutgoing.DocInput.Headers.Add "X-Comments1", _
            "version 1.0"
        .smtpOutgoing.DocInput.Headers.Add "X-MyWebPage", _
            "http://test.com"
```

```
      .smtpOutgoing.DocInput.Headers.Add "To", sEmail

   If (Not IsMissing(sCC)) Then
     .smtpOutgoing.DocInput.Headers.Add "CC", CStr(sCC)
   End If

   .smtpOutgoing.DocInput.Headers.Add "Subject", sSubject
   Dim fStartChecking As Boolean
   fStartChecking = True
   Do While (.smtpOutgoing.ProtocolState <> 0) And _
         (.smtpOutgoing.State <> 6)
     Sleep DELAY
   Loop
   .smtpOutgoing.SendDoc , , (sContent)
   Do While (1)
     If (fStartChecking) Then

       If (.smtpOutgoing.ProtocolState = 0) And _
         (.smtpOutgoing.State = 6) Then Exit Do

     End If
     ' wait a while, try again!
     Sleep DELAY
     Dim i As Integer
     For i = 1 To 1000
       DoEvents
     Next
   Loop
 End With

   Unload frmEmail
End Sub
```

The above code sets the SMTP headers as needed, waits for the control to become ready (this is especially important when sending consecutive e-mails) and unloads the form when it detects that the e-mail had been sent.

In terms of programming, the Microsoft ICP controls are very close to the actual protocols they work with. Other SMTP controls probably would not require this level of complexity for sending e-mail out.

It should be noted, though, that this type of control allows one to send all types of e-mail with a great amount of flexibility. (The programmer should not abuse this feature. After all, there is enough junk mail going around these days without more being generated by yet another system.)

Hardcore programmers can use the WinSock control that comes with Visual Basic to implement the SMTP protocol themselves. This is tedious work, especially if files need to be attached (using the MIME/UUEN-CODE formats). The SMTP protocol is quite primitive, and incredibly easy to implement using Visual Basic. For more information, please refer to Appendix C.

Credit Card Transactions

Often, the actual transaction does not require human interaction in order to charge the credit card. Rather, an automated process can do most of the work. There are quite a few ways to implement this feature, including use of virtual money solutions, merchant systems and web vendors.

Most of these solutions require a kludgy interface between application and vendor. Some transfer the user over to another web server to do the actual monetary transaction. Others communicate with an external server (via TCP/IP) and resolve the problem that way. Still other solutions require the user to purchase a block of "virtual money" that he or she can use when purchasing items from a vendor. When the user is required to exert some effort in the procurement process, he may reconsider and go to a competing vendor where he will likely exert less of an effort.

Often, these solutions are either very complex to implement, or require too much effort on the part of the user (or programmer). If a system requires such a solution, it often involves quite a bit of interaction between vendor and programmer.

On the flip side, there are various, simple, ActiveX solutions to this problem. These often require that the server have a modem port and a dedicated line for communication with the credit card company. These types of solutions can be as interactive (or even more interactive) than a real-life credit card transaction.

Using real, plastic credit-card money requires the programmer to place various securities into the system. It does, however, give the user an easy purchasing experience, with minimal "harassment factor." The user can get a receipt code immediately, rather than waiting for it via e-mail or other forms.

The application can also batch-process these transactions, or move them to a distributed system for processing (via DCOM / remote OLE automation, or even a secondary web server solution).

There are many such controls, including **Go software's PC-Charge**. The following code demonstrates how to charge a credit card using this OCX.

The application uses a form with the OCX on it called *frmOrderProcessor*.

```
Function ChargeCreditCard(lTicketNum As Long, _
            sCreditCardNumber As String, sExpirationDate _
            As String, cCreditCharge As Currency, _
            sAuthorization As String) As Integer


    ChargeCreditCard = CREDIT_ERROR
    sAuthorization = ""


    If (sExpirationDate = "0000") Then Exit Function
    Load frmOrderProcessor


    frmOrderProcessor.chargeCredit.ShowError = false
    With frmOrderProcessor.chargeCredit
        .Path = PCCW_PATH
        .PROCESSOR = PROCESSOR
        .MerchantNumber = MERCHANT_ACCOUNT
        ' bad credit card number.
        If (Not .LuhnMod_10(sCreditCardNumber)) Then _
                Exit Function
        ' cancel any previous, pending transactions
        .Cancel
        .Action = 1
        .Card = sCreditCardNumber
        .Member = ""
```

```
        .ExpDate = sExpirationDate
        .Reference = CStr(lTicketNum)
        .Amount = Format$(cCreditCharge, "#######.00")

        .send
    End With


    ' find out if successful or not!
    If frmOrderProcessor.chargeCredit.GetCaptured Then
        ChargeCreditCard = CREDIT_SUCCESSFUL
        sAuthorization = Trim$(frmOrderProcessor._
                chargeCredit.GetAuth)
    Else
        ChargeCreditCard = CREDIT_DECLINED
        sAuthorization = Trim$(frmOrderProcessor._
                chargeCredit.GetAuth)
    End If
    Unload frmOrderProcessor
End Function
```

Mainframes, Servers and External Entities

The server application may require some interaction with mainframes, servers or other external entities. This might include placing the order directly in the company's mainframe-based order system, validation against a server backend, or interaction with other entities such as stock tickers, robotic arms, etc.

Visual Basic has been able to communicate with all types of mainframes since version 3.0, using a variety of controls and other tools. Several types of 3270 emulation packages (for interaction with IBM mainframes) now provide an OCX that is easily interfaced with. Other terminal types, such as VT220, can be used with standard communication controls (even the COM port control that comes with Visual Basic).

When communicating with servers over TCP/IP often, a simple ANSI interface is used, but a TCP/IP socket control is needed for physical communication between machines. Internet tool packs (excluding Microsoft's ICP) often include such a control, which makes communication with TCP/IP machines easy to accomplish. VBS also includes such a control: WinSock.

When dealing with this kind of communication, security should not be overlooked. A localized, secure network for this type of communication may be needed to prevent unwanted access. Additionally, a virtual private network can be set up using two firewalls (Windows NT and Windows 95 can both use tunneling PPTP to accomplish this). This allows servers to communicate securely with one another over a routed, unsecured network configuration.

Visual Basic 5.0 comes with a simple WinSock control that enables an application to communicate with practically any TCP/IP enabled entity. Some such entities (e.g., mainframes) require a translation layer or terminal emulator (3270), for which several brands of emulating OCXs exist.

Other types of devices may require a different approach, depending on how they communicate with the machine. Often, such devices (unless they communicate through the PC's serial interface = COM port) have some kind of DLL or ActiveX library that one can utilize. When building customized cards, or when requiring direct access to such devices, Blue Water System's WinRT OCX does the trick quite nicely by providing I/O port, memory access as well as access to Interrupts, using a customized Windows NT device driver. When dealing with this kind of device, access to the hardware and setup of the Windows NT machine is mandatory.

Pagers

Alphanumeric pagers are quite useful in interacting with a program. A supervisor can be notified when an important system event occurs (for instance, if a particular user is logging into the system, a fatal error has just occurred, another server is not responding, etc.). This allows the supervisor to respond with optimum speed.

Additional functionalities for pagers are limited. Some include applications like paging a particular user when his order arrives (or when his "wakeup call" has been triggered), or when an important event occurs (i.e., a particular stock has dropped below that user's buy point).

Pagers can be communicated with using several varied techniques. Most big alphanumeric pager services already have an e-mail gateway to their pagers. This enables the system to use the same VB code for both e-mail *and* pagers. Other options include a pager gateway (for Exchange server, or even Exchange/Outlook client) that is usually communicated with via MAPI or the OLE messaging interface (documentation about this can be found in the Tools\olemsg directory on the VB5 CD). There are also some command line pager parsers (e.g., CONPAGE) where the application prepares the message in a file and executes the WIN32 console application with particular command line parameters which activate that application. These are usually a bit more cumbersome to interface with, but are generally extremely cheap (in the range of $15 per licensed server).

Summary

The reader should now be able to utilize advanced tags in her application. In addition, your CGI application is now able to communicate with the outside world whenever necessary. The next logical application to create is the **shopping** *bag.* *The next chapter will present a simple, yet powerful, shopping bag CGI application.*

SHOPPING BAG

- Virtual cookies
- Big brother and cookies
- Designing the shopping bag
- The shopping bag database layout
- Displaying the shopping bag contents

VIRTUAL COOKIES

As CGI programs became more and more complex, the Internet community began searching for a method in which information collected about the client could be more easily manipulated and referenced.

Servers wanted to know the user's previously-established preferences. They also wanted to be able to track the user's actions across several, non-contiguous, connections.

In order to do this, cookies were introduced. Cookies allowed servers to store information locally on the client. This enabled servers to maintain persistence across sessions — resulting in several initiatives, such as a personalized home page (showing personalized information based on previous selections), saving states, etc.

For security purposes, this construct was created to be inflexible. Servers would only be allowed access to the server that created the cookie (or another server within the same domain). Because of this, the common belief that cookies are a tool for companies to perform "big brother" operations — such as tracking where users go or what they do — is erroneous; in actuality, this is *less* likely to occur with cookies.

This assumes, of course, that the browser makers did not make specific modifications in order to be able to monitor cookies. This, however, would have been easily detected by networking hackers long ago — putting such a vendor quickly out of business.

Previously, servers would track user information by having them log on, and then maintaining their state on the server. One such example is maintaining a user ID, and keeping shopping bag items on the server that are easily retrievable by the ID number (supplied by the user every time he enters the system).

Moving such information to the client allows the client to have **more** control over it; and this also alleviates storage capacity problems on the server. Since users now have more control over the information retained, this is in fact a case of "little brother" being mistaken for a "bigger brother."

Cookies were created to maintain very limited amounts of information. To prevent abuse of this construct by unruly servers, a server or a group of servers can create only 20 cookies at any one time. Each cookie, however, can retain information of up to 4000 bytes. This allows for a maximum of 80 Kilobytes to be retained on the client side in any particular application.

When using this information effectively, the server application should utilize as little of that storage space as possible (to minimize the chance that the browser will erase information due to client storage constraints).

When creating a shopping bag, the programmer is presented with two options: keeping the contents of this shopping bag on the server, or keeping it on the client.

Keeping it on the server requires the creation of a new table that will retain shopping bag contents. The key for such a table will be an *item number* and the items will be indexed by the *user name*. A user can have as many items as he wants in his shopping bag. Once he or she orders these files, the files are removed from the shopping bag and moved to a second table where ordering information, as well as additional parameter about each requested item in the bag (e.g., quantity), can be maintained.

Maintaining this information on the server is costly, since it necessarily stores shopping bag contents for people who never order anything and are simply "checking things out." This ultimately requires a cleanup process that periodically cleans out old shopping bags to make room for new ones (on Windows NT, this scheduling can be easily done with the schedule service and the "AT" command line interface).

Maintaining this information on the server provides the system with two features that would be harder to implement otherwise. The system can monitor each user's order, and locate items that are most frequently added to the shopping bag. (This feature is less effective than following up on actual, ordered, items.) The second feature, which cannot be implemented using client side constructs, is the ability of the user to log in, utilizing any browser at any location, and maintain a persistent shopping bag. Most likely, this will deter users who do not expect their selections to be maintained across several computers (they may even be alarmed by it!).

Maintaining this information on the client side alleviates the need to clean up after orders that were never followed through. It also gives the user more control over information (via the cookie file). The cookie file is cleaned up automatically by the browser as needed.

When maintaining the shopping bag information in a distributed form, rather than centralized on the server, the system can usually store more information than it ever could otherwise.

Since the client browser limits us in terms of cookie capacity, a programming construct is needed to make all 80K of "cookie space" available without the constraint of 20 cookies. It is more than likely that a user's shopping bag will contain far *more than* 20 items. Also, we may want to add more persistent information about the user (i.e., user ID, and the random key from the User Security module).

Virtual Cookies

The oCGI library presents us with a programming construct that handles virtual cookies instead of ordinary ones. The virtual cookies are fully maintained by oCGI and are transformed into "normal" cookies before the first *WriteCGI* call. This feature enhances the standard cookie construct, allowing it to provide the server with many more cookies than are actually allowed on the browser, with minimal changes to the CGI application.

Virtual cookies provide a greater amount of persistent data for the application, but not without some cost. When utilizing standard cookies, each cookie may have a different expiration date and time. All virtual cookies in oCGI, however, must have the same expiration date (an internal "time to live" variable in oCGI determines the number of days that virtual cookies will persist for a particular oCGI application session).

Both standard cookies and virtual cookies can set up cookies that will not be written on the end-user's hard drive. These cookies will persist for as long as the user maintains a particular session in the browser. The browser keeps these in the end user's system memory *only*, so if the session is cut off, the browser terminated, or the machine shut off, these cookies are lost forever.

Setting the "time to live" virtual cookie value to zero causes all virtual cookie operations to be session based; they will not persist beyond the user's current session. This is a great way to prevent a shopping bag from being maintained after the user leaves the site. Also, some paranoid users will not accept cookies that are written to the harddrive (because of the "big brother syndrome"). Since there is no way to link non-persistent cookies from one session to another, this problem is also eliminated. In standard cookies, not specifying an expiration date means that the cookies will be removed at the end of the user's session.

Virtual cookies, in fact, normally default to session based cookies. In order to rectify this, simply enter the number of days you want the cookies to persist on the end user's machine when processing virtual cookies (using the *ProcessVirtualCookies* method).

Shopping Bag — A How-to Manual

To track user interaction across multiple purchases and maintain that information, the *UserSecurity* module can be employed. Only minor changes are required of this module to make it interact well within the system.

First, the main function is moved to the ShoppingBag1 basic file, but no further changes are made to the *UserSecurity* module. After all, this module is the first to operate in this system each time the user interacts with it. In addition, the module now maintains a global variable containing user ID — the unique number identifying the user. This makes it easier to reference the user, and to modify the user's information as needed.

The *UserSecurity* database table (USERS) has been merged into ShoppingBag1.MDB. Also, new fields have been added to this table to account for the extra information that needs to be maintained about each user. Since a user would be reluctant to enter this information upfront, without selecting items for purchase, no additional information is acquired from the user prior to purchase time.

Note the lack of credit card information in the USERS table. This information can be different for each purchase, so it is maintained in the purchase session table.

A new function, *NoCache* is used to place the no-cache Meta tag into each web page produced by the application.

The Shopping Bag Database Layout

Table 8.1 shows the fields in the USERS table layout. The fields marked in gray are needed at the time of purchase only.

Table 8.1

The shopping bag USERS table layout

Table: USERS Field Name	Field Type	Remark
UserID	Autonumber (long integer)	Primary key- identifies user.
UserName	Text(50), Indexed	User's logon name.
FullName	Text(50)	User's full name.
Password	Text(50)	User's logon password
Notes	Text(50)	Will contain IP information about the user.
Address	Text(50)	User's address.
CityState	Text(35)	User's city and state.
Zip	Text(11)	User's zip code.
Email	Text(50)	User's email address.
Phone	Text(15)	User's phone number

HomePage Function

The *HomePage* function has been moved into the Shopping bag module and references all of the possible ACTION values back into their appointed functions.

The search engine module has also been imported into the system with minimal changes. The main routine has been eliminated, and the *HomePage* function now calls the *DoShowSearch* function and references other search action values.

DoShowSearch Function

A few changes were necessary in order to make the search engine more compatible with this type of application. The *DoShowSearch* function now uses a virtual cookie (assigned in the forward search routine *DoSearch*) to retain previous keyword searches. When a user wants to search for something, the system defaults to the last search keywords he or she was using.

Search Functions

The *SearchTop* and *SearchBottom* functions are called by both the forward and backward searching routines. These functions implement the top and bottom of the search page, and prevent a duplicate effort.

The *SearchRow* function manages display of the actual rows in the page. The optional *vTop* parameter causes this function to display the page header. The search functions (both forward and backward) handle the table tags — both start and finish.

The *SearchRow* function also hyperlinks each of the displayed items so that when clicked upon, a selected item is inserted into the shopping bag. Finally, the function also displays each item's cost.

The search engine's DATA table (Table 8.2) has been modified to allow for an associated cost for each of the available items:

Table 8.2
The shopping bag
DATA table layout

Table: DATA Field Name	Field Type	Remark
Key	AutoNumber (long integer)	Primary key- identifies record.
Title	Text(50)	Title of the item.
Data	Memo	Description of item (this is what we're searching through).
Price	Currency	Associated cost of item.

DoShow Functions

Once the user successfully logs on, the system initiates the *DoShowFrames* function. This function handles the display of the top and bottom frames. The top frame is linked to the *DoShowButtons* function and displays program options (search, empty shopping bag and check out).

The bottom frame defaults to *DoShowSearch* and enables the user to start searching right away. It is usually a good idea to display (by default) the first frame selection in the button bar as the default for the main frame.

The *DoShowButtons* function works by placing hyperlinked text in such a way as to cause different pages to display in the main frame (named "MAIN"). The buttons shown here are very simplistic. Most similar applications utilize images or image maps so that the user can select a main option.

Simple image hyperlinks are easy to implement — simply switch the text between the anchor tags (<A ...> text </A>) with an image tag (<IMG SRC=... BORDER=0>; the border command prevents an outline from being displayed around the hyperlink image). Similarly, client-side image maps can be implemented by using something like:

```
<IMG SRC="/image.gif" USEMAP="#Imagemap" BORDER="0">
<MAP NAME="Imagemap">
<AREA SHAPE=RECT COORDS="0,2,119,98" TARGET="MAIN" _
        HREF="CGIapp.exe?ACTION=DOKEYWORDS">
<AREA SHAPE=RECT COORDS="0,100,119,200" TARGET="MAIN" _
        HREF="CGIapp.exe?ACTION=DOCATEGORIES">
<AREA SHAPE=RECT COORDS="0,201,119,335" TARGET="MAIN" _
        HREF="CGIapp.exe?ACTION=DOEMPTYSHOPPINGBAG">
</MAP>
```

Should real buttons be required on the button frame, the programmer can use small forms for each of the buttons; these will jump directly to the target frame and target ACTION:

```
<FORM METHOD=POST TARGET=MAIN
        ACTION="CGIapp.exe?ACTION=DOEMPTYSHOPPINGBAG">
<INPUT TYPE=BUTTON NAME=Submit Value="Empty Shopping _
        Bag">
</FORM>
```

An alternative to explicitly calling the script "CGIapp.exe? ACTION=DOEMPTYSHOPPINGBAG", is:

```
<FORM METHOD=POST TARGET=MAIN ACTION="CGIapp.exe">
<INPUT TYPE=HIDDEN NAME=ACTION VALUE="DOEMPTYSHOPPINGBAG">
<INPUT TYPE=BUTTON NAME=Submit Value="Empty Shopping Bag">
</FORM>
```

This is a nicer option, albeit lengthy, since some browsers show you the target URL when your mouse is over a target (most prominent, in that respect, is Microsoft Internet Explorer). It simply looks cleaner to the user when explicit parameters are eliminated altogether.

Shopping bag items are kept as virtual cookies using the following naming convention: "Item#", where # is the unique key for the selected item. The value for this cookie is the quantity of the particular item.

GetShoppingBag Function

The first important function displays the items in the shopping bag. This is done by the *GetShoppingBag* function. This function returns the HTML for shopping bag contents. It is used when emptying the shopping bag, when viewing the contents of the shopping bag, when checking out, when adding new items, and when finalizing the purchase.

The *GetShoppingBag* function essentially loops through all of the items in *cCookies*. Once it finds anything that starts with the word "Item" it identifies it as a valid shopping bag item. The first item it encounters automatically becomes the head of the shopping bag table. Should no items be detected, this function returns an empty string.

Each time that *GetShoppingBag* function finds a valid item, it locates the information for it in the DATA table and displays the name of the item. After that, the function sets up an edit box specifying the current quantity in it and the cost per item. This allows the user to select or modify quantities of each item. When the user selects a quantity of zero, the application subsequently clears the item from the list.

DoEmpty and ClearShoppingBag Subroutines

Emptying out the shopping bag is much easier. The *DoEmptyShoppingBag* subroutine is called from the button frame, and clears the shopping bag using the *ClearShoppingBag* subroutine.

The *ClearShoppingBag* subroutine operates by going through each of the items in the cCookies collection and removing any that adhere to the shopping bag item naming convention (i.e., any that start with the word "Item"). This uniquely identifies the item as part of the shopping bag.

Once the shopping bag has been cleared using the *ClearShoppingBag* subroutine, the *DoEmptyShoppingBag* subroutine calls the *DoCheckOut* subroutine, which (since the shopping bag is now empty) displays the standard display for an empty shopping bag. Of course, if the user rejects the particular cookie change (they can do that, you know!), the system displays an erroneously updated shopping bag list.

Clicking on an item title automatically adds that item to the shopping bag. The hyperlink for each item is placed there by the *SearchRow* function. This is done by using the DOADDITEM action in conjunction with the ITEM parameter (ITEM=4 means - add the item with Key=4 to the shopping bag).

AddShoppingBagItem Subroutine

The *DoAddItem* function works by using *AddShoppingBagItem* to add the item to the shopping bag. It then utilizes *GetShoppingBag* to display the contents of the shopping bag *after* the addition.

The *AddShoppingBagItem* subroutine first determines if the item being added already starts with the shopping bag identifier ("Item"). If it does not, the "Item" identifier is added to the front of the item number. The *WriteVirtualCookie* function is used to add the item to the shopping bag. In order to be able to view this item in the subsequent *GetShoppingBag* function call, the system must also add it to the cookie list. This only simulates the effect of adding it into the list, since the browser has not yet accepted the updated virtual cookie. Once the virtual cookie is accepted by the browser, it will receive the updated cookie with the new item added the *next time* the script is executed.

In order for the system to recognize the cookie in the current session, the item must be entered "manually" into the cookie list as if it was originally parsed during the current session.

Adding the item onto the current cookie list requires the creation of a new instance of the *ParamType* object. Using the following statement creates the new *ParamType* instance:

```
Set pParam = New ParamType
```

Once this parameter has been created, its values can be filled in and it can be added to the cookie list:

```
pParam.Name = sName
pParam.Value = CStr(nQuantity)
.cCookies.Add item:=pParam, Key:=sName
```

The final statement also enables the system to search for the particular cookie by referencing the hash key for that cookie:

```
sTest= .cCookies("MyKey")
```

This statement allows the program to locate the particular, previously queued-in hash key by referencing it by name. This permits access to the cookie by using the *ReadCookie* function.

Once the item is inserted onto the cookie list, it can be viewed as if it was just another item in the shopping bag.

GetShoppingBag Function

When the user checks out, the *DoCheckOut* subroutine handles the shopping bag display (if it is not empty, otherwise, an appropriate message is displayed) using the *GetShoppingBag* function.

When utilized in this context, the *GetShoppingBag* function allows the user to proceed and purchase the selected items. It also allows the user to modify the quantity values for each of the items in the shopping bag. The user proceeds by executing the DOSUBMIT action.

The *DoSubmit* function handles the DOSUBMIT action. First, this function "refreshes" the shopping bag, utilizing the *RefreshShoppingBag* subroutine.

RefreshShoppingBag Subroutine

The *RefreshShoppingBag* subroutine goes into the shopping bag and updates the items to the actual quantities specified in the quantity edit box. The subroutine first completely clears out the shopping bag with a call to *ClearShoppingBag*. Then, the function proceeds to go over the parameters in the *cParameters* collection to find any valid item specification. It finds these in the form of the quantity edit boxes that are presented with the shopping bag. Once located, each item quantity is verified. If the item quantity is more than zero, the item and quantity are reinserted into the shopping bag via the *AddShoppingBagItem* subroutine.

Next, the *DoSubmit* subroutine uses the *GetShoppingBag* function to view the updated shopping bag. This time, however, the shopping bag proceeds to the next step — using the DOVERIFYSUMBIT action, rather than the default action.

ShowInformation Functions

If there are actual items in the shopping bag, the *ShowUserInformation* function can display and query updated user information, and the *ShowCreditCardInformation* function requests credit card information. These functions are separated due to their separation as pieces of data in the database.

The *ShowUserInformation* function simply builds an HTML table with the user fields that have not yet been filled. Those items already in the database will be displayed as values in the appropriate edit boxes. This enables the user to update the system with new information as needed. The user is *not* required to modify these boxes if his or her information has remained unchanged since the last time the form was filled.

The *ShowCreditCardInformation* function simply displays the edit box for credit card information — the card number and expiration date. For security reasons, this information is not transferred back to the user. This function also places the submit button on the form, allowing the user to proceed to the DOVERIFYSUBMIT action.

DoVerifySubmit Subroutine

Once the user verifies the information, he or she may submit the form to actually purchase items in the shopping bag. This is done in the *DoVerifySubmit* subroutine. This routine first uses the *RefreshShoppingBag* subroutine in order to update quantity information. It is now assumed that the user actually has items in his shopping bag. Next, the *UpdateUserInformation* subroutine is used to update the user's information as submitted.

The *UpdateUserInformation* subroutine locates the user in question, and updates the user's information with all of the parameters that he or she has filled in on the HTML form.

SubmitShoppingBag Subroutine

Next, the *SubmitShoppingBag* subroutine is called to submit the contents of the shopping bag to the system. In this case, the system simply adds the information to the database, to be picked up by the administrator. In other cases, the system may be required to send an e-mail to the vendor or, in certain circumstances, even charge the credit card and ship the items directly to the user, with no human interaction.

The *SubmitShoppingBag* subroutine first creates a new ORDER_SESSION row which contains user information, purchase date, and credit card information. Next, the unique identifier for the session row is determined, and new rows are added to the PURCHASE_ITEMS table — one for each item the user had ordered.

The unique key for each shopping bag item is determined by the *GetItemKey* function, which simply trims the "Item" header from the beginning of the item and converts the rest into a numeric form that correlates to the item's key identifier.

Each row in the PURCHASE_ITEMS table also contains the session identifier and quantity. This way, the administrator can easily browse the database for unfilled order sessions (this will soon be done automatically). Once such a session is identified, the administrator can locate all of the items attached to this session and proceed to prepare the order. When done, the administrator can set the "Filled" flag to true.

As soon as the shopping bag is submitted, there is nothing left but to clear it and notify the user that his order is being processed.

SearchEngine4.bas Source Code

```
Option Explicit
Function DoError() As String
   Dim sOut As String

   sOut = "<HTML>" + vbCrLf
   sOut = sOut + "<HEADER><TITLE> Sample Search "
   sOut = sOut + " results</TITLE></HEADER>" + vbCrLf
   sOut = sOut + "<BODY BGCOLOR=#ffffff>" + vbCrLf
   sOut = sOut + "<H2> Error: matching option was "
   sOut = sOut + " not selected correctly </H2>"
   sOut = sOut + "</BODY></HTML>"

   DoError = sOut
End Function


Function DoAnd(sColumns As String, sFrom As String, sData_
         As String, sSearchCol As String, sKeyCol As _
            String, nRows As Variant, sFirstRow As String, _
            fBackwards As Boolean, cKeywords As _
            Collection) As String
```

```
Dim sQuery As String

sQuery = "select TOP " + CStr(nRows + 1)
sQuery = sQuery + " " + sColumns + " from " + sFrom + " _
        WHERE 1=1 "

If (sFirstRow <> "") Then
  sQuery = sQuery + " AND (" + sKeyCol + _
        IIf(fBackwards, "<=", ">=")
  sQuery = sQuery + CStr(ToInt(sFirstRow)) + ") "
End If

Dim iPos As Integer
Do While (1)
  If (Trim$(sData) = "") Then Exit Do
  If (Left$(sData, 1) = """") Then
    sData = Mid$(sData, 2)
    iPos = InStr(sData, """")
  Else
    iPos = InStr(sData, " ")
  End If

  Dim sWord As String

  If iPos <= 0 Then
    sWord = sData
    iPos = Len(sWord)
  Else
    sWord = Left$(sData, iPos - 1)
  End If

  cKeywords.Add sWord

  sQuery = sQuery + "AND INSTR(" + sSearchCol + ",'"
  sQuery = sQuery + DoubleQuote(sWord) + "') "

  sData = Mid$(sData, iPos + 1)
Loop

sQuery = sQuery + " ORDER BY " + sKeyCol
sQuery = sQuery + IIf(fBackwards, " DESC", " ASC")
```

```
        DoAnd = sQuery
End Function


Function DoOr(sColumns As String, sFrom As String, sData _
            As String, sSearchCol As String, sKeyCol As _
            String, nRows As Variant, sFirstRow As _
              String, sFirstInstr As String, cKeywords _
              As Collection) As String


    ' now create instr counter.
    Dim sInStr As String
    Dim iPos As Integer
    sInStr = "(0"
    Do While (1)
        If (Trim$(sData) = "") Then Exit Do
        If (Left$(sData, 1) = """") Then
            sData = Mid$(sData, 2)
            iPos = InStr(sData, """")
        Else
            iPos = InStr(sData, " ")
        End If

        Dim sWord As String

        If iPos <= 0 Then
            sWord = sData
            iPos = Len(sWord)
        Else
            sWord = Left$(sData, iPos - 1)
        End If

        cKeywords.Add sWord

        sInStr = sInStr + "+IIF(INSTR(" + sSearchCol + ",'"
        sInStr = sInStr + DoubleQuote(sWord) + "')>0,1,0)"

        sData = Mid$(sData, iPos + 1)
    Loop
    sInStr = sInStr + ")"

    Dim sQuery As String
```

```
      sQuery = "select TOP " + CStr(nRows + 1) + " "
      sQuery = sQuery + sInStr + " as ISINSTR,"
      sQuery = sQuery + " " + sColumns + " from " + sFrom + " _
            WHERE "
      sQuery = sQuery + " (" + sInStr + ">0)"

      If (sFirstRow <> "") Then
         sQuery = sQuery + " AND (" + sKeyCol + ">="
         sQuery = sQuery + CStr(ToInt(sFirstRow)) + ") "
      End If
      If (sFirstInStr <> "") Then
         sQuery = sQuery + " AND (" + sInStr + "<="
         sQuery = sQuery + CStr(ToInt(sFirstInStr)) + ") "
      End If

      sQuery = sQuery + " ORDER BY (" + sInStr + ") DESC"
      sQuery = sQuery + "," + sKeyCol + " ASC"
      DoOr = sQuery
End Function


Function DoEntire(sColumns As String, sFrom As String, _
            sKeywords As String, sSearchCol As String, _
               sKeyCol As String, nRows As Integer, _
                  sFirstRow As String, fBackwards As Boolean,_
                     cKeywords As Collection) As String


   Dim sQuery As String

   'check for quotes
   sKeywords = RemoveDoubleQuotes(sKeywords)

   cKeywords.Add sKeywords

   sQuery = "select TOP " + CStr(nRows + 1) + " "
   sQuery = sQuery + sColumns + " from " + sFrom
   sQuery = sQuery + " WHERE INSTR(" + sSearchCol + ",'"
   sQuery = sQuery + DoubleQuote(sKeywords) + "') "
   If (sFirstRow <> "") Then
      sQuery = sQuery + " and " + sKeyCol + IIf(fBackwards, _
            "<=", ">=")
      sQuery = sQuery + CStr(ToInt(sFirstRow))
```

```
        End If

    sQuery = sQuery + " ORDER BY " + sKeyCol
    sQuery = sQuery + IIf(fBackwards, " DESC", " ASC")
    DoEntire = sQuery
End Function


Function MakeBold(ByVal sMakeBold As String, cKeywords _
            As Collection) As String
  ' make each found keyword in this thing bold.
  Dim cStart As New Collection, cLength As New Collection
  Dim sWord As Variant, iPos As Integer

  For Each sWord In cKeywords
    ' now locate the first instance of sWord in sMakeBold
    Dim iPosMakeBold As Integer

    iPosMakeBold = InStr(sMakeBold, sWord)
    If (iPosMakeBold > 0) Then
      cStart.Add iPosMakeBold
      cLength.Add Len(sWord)
    End If
  Next
  ' all of this is to prevent the search from locating
  ' — stuff in the modified string!

  ' now loop and implement modifications.
  Dim i As Integer, iSmallestPosition As Integer
  Dim sOut As String, iLastEnd As Integer
  iLastEnd = 1
  Do While (cStart.Count > 0)
    ' look for the smallest position.
    iSmallestPosition = 1
    For i = 2 To cStart.Count
      If (cStart.item(i) < cStart.item(iSmallestPosition)) _
          Then
        iSmallestPosition = i
      End If
    Next

    Dim iStart As Integer, iLen As Integer
```

```
      iStart = cStart.item(iSmallestPosition)
      iLen = cLength.item(iSmallestPosition)
      If (iStart < iLastEnd) Then
        iStart = iLastEnd
      End If
      sOut = sOut + Mid$(sMakeBold, iLastEnd, iStart - _
          iLastEnd)
      sOut = sOut + "<FONT COLOR=RED>"
      If (iLastEnd < iStart + iLen) Then
        iLastEnd = iStart + iLen
      End If
      sOut = sOut + Mid$(sMakeBold, iStart, iLastEnd - _
          iStart)
      sOut = sOut + "</FONT>"

      ' kill this collection item!
      cStart.Remove iSmallestPosition
      cLength.Remove iSmallestPosition
    Loop

    ' add everything else!
    sOut = sOut + Mid$(sMakeBold, iLastEnd)

    MakeBold = sOut
End Function

Function NextBunch(sFirstRow As String, sTopRows As String, _
    sIsInstr As String)

    Dim sOut As String
    With cgi
      sOut = sOut + "<FORM ACTION=""" + .ReadScriptName
      sOut = sOut + """ METHOD=""POST"">" + vbCrLf
      sOut = sOut + "<INPUT TYPE=HIDDEN NAME=""Action"" "
      sOut = sOut + " VALUE=""DOSEARCH"">" + vbCrLf
      sOut = sOut + "<INPUT TYPE=HIDDEN NAME=""KeyWords"" "
      sOut = sOut + "VALUE=""" + _
          ReadScrambledParam("KeyWords")
      sOut = sOut + """>" + vbCrLf
      sOut = sOut + "<INPUT TYPE=HIDDEN NAME=""Match"" "
      sOut = sOut + " VALUE=""" + cgi.ReadParam("Match")
```

```
        sOut = sOut + """">" + vbCrLf
        sOut = sOut + "<INPUT TYPE=HIDDEN NAME=""TopRows"" "
        sOut = sOut + " VALUE=""" + sTopRows + """">" + vbCrLf
        sOut = sOut + "<INPUT TYPE=HIDDEN NAME=""FirstRow"" _
            VALUE= "
        sOut = sOut + sFirstRow + ">" + vbCrLf

        If (sIsInstr <> "") Then
          sOut = sOut + "<INPUT TYPE=HIDDEN NAME=""IsInstr"" _
            VALUE= "
          sOut = sOut + sIsInstr + ">" + vbCrLf
        End If

        sOut = sOut + "<INPUT TYPE=Submit NAME=Submit "
        sOut = sOut + " VALUE=""View the next "
        sOut = sOut + sTopRows + " rows """>" + vbCrLf
        sOut = sOut + "</FORM>" + vbCrLf
      End With

    NextBunch = sOut
End Function


Function PrevBunch(sLastRow As String, sTopRows As String)

    Dim sOut As String
    With cgi
      sOut = sOut + "<FORM ACTION=""" + .ReadScriptName
      sOut = sOut + """ METHOD=""POST"">" + vbCrLf
      sOut = sOut + "<INPUT TYPE=HIDDEN NAME=""Action"" "
      sOut = sOut + " VALUE=""DOSEARCHBACK"">" + vbCrLf
      sOut = sOut + "<INPUT TYPE=HIDDEN NAME=""KeyWords"" "
      sOut = sOut + "VALUE=""" + ReadScrambledParam _
            ("KeyWords")
      sOut = sOut + """">" + vbCrLf
      sOut = sOut + "<INPUT TYPE=HIDDEN NAME=""Match"" "
      sOut = sOut + " VALUE=""" + cgi.ReadParam("Match")
      sOut = sOut + """">" + vbCrLf
      sOut = sOut + "<INPUT TYPE=HIDDEN NAME=""TopRows"" "
      sOut = sOut + " VALUE=""" + sTopRows + """">" + vbCrLf
      sOut = sOut + "<INPUT TYPE=HIDDEN NAME=""LastRow"" _
            VALUE= "
```

```
            sOut = sOut + sLastRow + ">" + vbCrLf


            sOut = sOut + "<INPUT TYPE=Submit NAME=Submit"
            sOut = sOut + " VALUE=""View the previous "
            sOut = sOut + sTopRows + " rows "">" + vbCrLf
            sOut = sOut + "</FORM>" + vbCrLf
        End With


    PrevBunch = sOut
End Function


Sub DoSearch()
    ' max number of rows that a query returns.
    Dim TOP_ROWS As Integer

    Dim sQuery As String, sOut As String
    With cgi
        ' first break down the parameters.
        Dim sKeywords As String, sFirstRow As String
        Dim sFirstInStr As String
        sKeywords = .ReadParam("KeyWords")

        If (Trim$(sKeywords) <> "") Then
            .WriteVirtualCookie "Keywords", sKeywords
        End If

        TOP_ROWS = ToInt(cgi.ReadParam("TopRows"))
        If (TOP_ROWS < 1) Then
            TOP_ROWS = 10
        End If

        'prevent empty search
        If (Trim$(sKeywords) = "") Then
            DoShowSearch
            Exit Sub
        End If

        sFirstRow = .ReadParam("FirstRow")
        sFirstInStr = .ReadParam("IsInstr")

        Dim cKeywords As Collection
```

```
Set cKeywords = New Collection
Select Case .ReadParam("Match")
  Case "A" ' and
    sQuery = DoAnd("*", "DATA", sKeywords, "Data", _
      "Key", TOP_ROWS, sFirstRow, False, cKeywords)
  Case "E" ' Entire
    sQuery = DoEntire("*", "DATA", sKeywords, "Data", _
      "Key", TOP_ROWS, sFirstRow, False, cKeywords)
  Case "O" ' or
    sQuery = DoOr("*", "DATA", sKeywords, "Data", _
      "Key", TOP_ROWS, sFirstRow, sFirstInStr, _
        cKeywords)
  Case Else ' error
    sOut = DoError
    .WriteCGI sOut
    Exit Sub
End Select


Dim rs As Recordset
Set rs = db.OpenRecordset(sQuery, dbOpenDynaset)


sOut = SearchTop


Dim iRows As Integer, fNextBunch As Boolean
iRows = 0
fNextBunch = False
If rs.EOF Then
  sOut = sOut + "<H3>Search did not retrieve any _
      rows</H3>" + vbCrLf
Else
  Dim sTopRow As String, sTopIsInstr As String
  rs.MoveFirst
  sOut = sOut + "<H3>Search resulted in the following _
      items</H3>"
  sOut = sOut + vbCrLf + "<TABLE BORDER=1 WIDTH=100%>" _
      + vbCrLf
  sOut = sOut + SearchRow(rs, cKeywords, True)
  Do While Not rs.EOF
    iRows = iRows + 1
    If iRows <= TOP_ROWS Then
      sOut = sOut + SearchRow(rs, cKeywords)
```

```
              Else ' last row - instead, put up a next + _
                  TOP_ROWS + button
                sTopRow = CStr(rs("Key"))
                If (.ReadParam("Match") = "O") Then
                    sTopIsInstr = CStr(rs("ISINSTR"))
                Else
                    sTopIsInstr = ""
                End If
                fNextBunch = True
                Exit Do
            End If
            rs.MoveNext
        Loop
        sOut = sOut + "</TABLE>"
        sOut = sOut + "<TABLE BORDER=0><TR>"
        If (sFirstRow <> "" And .ReadParam("Match") <> "O") _
            Then
            rs.MoveFirst
            sOut = sOut + "<TD>"
            sOut = sOut + PrevBunch(CStr(rs("Key")), _
                CStr(TOP_ROWS)) + "</TD>"
        End If
        If (fNextBunch) Then
            sOut = sOut + "<TD>" + NextBunch(sTopRow, CStr_
                (TOP_ROWS), sTopIsInstr) + "</TD>"
        End If
        sOut = sOut + "</TR></TABLE>"
    End If

    sOut = sOut + SearchBottom
    cgi.WriteCGI sOut
    rs.Close
  End With
End Sub


'THIS WILL NOT WORK WITH FORWARD ONLY RECORDSETS!
Sub DoSearchBack()
   ' max number of rows that a query returns.
   Dim TOP_ROWS As Integer

   Dim sQuery As String, sOut As String
```

```vb
With cgi
  ' first break down the parameters.
  Dim sKeywords As String, sLastRow As String
  Dim sFirstInStr As String

  sKeywords = .ReadParam("KeyWords")

  TOP_ROWS = ToInt(cgi.ReadParam("TopRows"))
  If (TOP_ROWS < 1) Then
    TOP_ROWS = 10
  End If

  'prevent empty search
  If (Trim$(sKeywords) = "") Then
    DoShowSearch
    Exit Sub
  End If

  sLastRow = .ReadParam("LastRow")

  Dim cKeywords As Collection
  Set cKeywords = New Collection
  Select Case .ReadParam("Match")
    Case "A" ' and
      sQuery = DoAnd("*", "DATA", sKeywords, "Data", _
        "Key", TOP_ROWS + 1, sLastRow, True, cKeywords)
    Case "E" ' Entire
      sQuery = DoEntire("*", "DATA", sKeywords, "Data", _
        "Key", TOP_ROWS + 1, sLastRow, True, cKeywords)
    Case Else ' error
      sOut = DoError
      .WriteCGI sOut
      Exit Sub
  End Select

  Dim rs As Recordset
  Set rs = db.OpenRecordset(sQuery, dbOpenDynaset)
  sOut = SearchTop
  Dim iRows As Integer, fPrevBunch As Boolean
  iRows = 0
  fPrevBunch = False
```

```
If rs.EOF Then
   sOut = sOut + "<H3>Search did not retrieve any _
      rows</H3>" + vbCrLf
Else
   Dim sBottomRow As String
   rs.MoveLast
   If (rs.RecordCount > (TOP_ROWS + 1)) Then
      fPrevBunch = True
      rs.MovePrevious
   End If

   sBottomRow = CStr(rs("Key"))
   sOut = sOut + "<H3>Search resulted in the following _
      items</H3>"
   sOut = sOut + "<TABLE BORDER=1 WIDTH=100%>" + vbCrLf
   sOut = sOut + SearchRow(rs, cKeywords, True)
   Do While Not rs.BOF
      iRows = iRows + 1
      If iRows <= (TOP_ROWS + 1) Then
         If (iRows <= TOP_ROWS) Then
            sOut = sOut + SearchRow(rs, cKeywords)
         End If
      Else
         Exit Do
      End If
      rs.MovePrevious
   Loop
   sOut = sOut + "</TABLE>"
   sOut = sOut + "<TABLE BORDER=0><TR>"
   If (fPrevBunch) Then
      sOut = sOut + "<TD>" + PrevBunch(sBottomRow, _
         CStr(TOP_ROWS))
      sOut = sOut + "</TD>"
   End If
   If (sLastRow <> "") Then
      rs.MoveFirst
      sOut = sOut + "<TD>" + NextBunch(CStr(rs("Key")), _
         CStr(TOP_ROWS), "")
      sOut = sOut + "</TD>"
   End If
   sOut = sOut + "</TR></TABLE>"
```

```
            End If

            sOut = sOut + SearchBottom
            cgi.WriteCGI sOut
            rs.Close
        End With
    End Sub


    Sub DoShowSearch()
        With cgi
            Dim sOut As String

            sOut = "<HTML>" + vbCrLf
            sOut = sOut + "<HEADER></HEADER>" + vbCrLf
            sOut = sOut + "<BODY BGCOLOR=#ffffff>" + vbCrLf
            sOut = sOut + "<H2> Search for items </H2>" + vbCrLf
            sOut = sOut + "Enter your search keywords here:<P><HR>" _
                    + vbCrLf

            sOut = sOut + "<FORM ACTION=""" + .ReadScriptName + _
                    """ METHOD=""POST"">"
            sOut = sOut + "<INPUT TYPE=""HIDDEN"" NAME=""Action"" _
                    VALUE=""DOSEARCH"">"
            sOut = sOut + vbCrLf + "<TABLE><TR><TD>"
            sOut = sOut + "<B>Search for:</B></TD><TD></TD><TD>_
                    <INPUT TYPE=TEXT SIZE=20 "
            sOut = sOut + " MAXLENGTH=100 NAME=""KeyWords"" _
                    VALUE=""" +
            sOut = sOut + .ReadCookie("Keywords") + """ > "
            sOut = sOut + "</TD></TR><TR><TD><INPUT TYPE=""RADIO"" _
                    CHECKED "
            sOut = sOut + "NAME=""Match"" VALUE=""E"">Exact Match"
            sOut = sOut + "</TD><TD><INPUT TYPE=""RADIO"" _
                    NAME=""Match"" VALUE=""A"">And"
            sOut = sOut + "</TD><TD><INPUT TYPE=""RADIO"" _
                    NAME=""Match"" VALUE=""O"">Or"
            sOut = sOut + "</TD></TR><TR><TD><P><INPUT TYPE=Submit "
            sOut = sOut + " NAME=""Submit"" VALUE=""Search"">"
            sOut = sOut + "</TD><TD># rows shown:"
            sOut = sOut + "</TD><TD><select name=""TopRows"" > "
            sOut = sOut + "<option SELECTED>5</option>"
```

```
        sOut = sOut + "<option>10</option>"
        sOut = sOut + "<option>20</option>"
        sOut = sOut + "<option>50</option></select>"
        sOut = sOut + "</TD></TR></TABLE> </FORM>"
        sOut = sOut + "<HR>"

        sOut = sOut + "</BODY>" + vbCrLf
        sOut = sOut + "</HTML>"


        .WriteCGI sOut
    End With
End Sub


Function SearchBottom() As String
    SearchBottom = "</BODY></HTML>"
End Function


Function SearchRow(rs As Recordset, cKeywords As _
            Collection, Optional vTop As Variant)
    Dim sOut As String, fTop As Boolean
    fTop = False
    If Not IsMissing(vTop) Then fTop = vTop

    sOut = "<TR>"
    If (fTop) Then
        sOut = sOut + vbCrLf + "<TH WIDTH=20%>"
        sOut = sOut + "Item name"
        sOut = sOut + "</TH>"
    Else
        sOut = sOut + vbCrLf + "<TD WIDTH=20%>"
        sOut = sOut + "<A HREF=""" + cgi.ReadScriptName
        sOut = sOut + "?ACTION=DOADDITEM&ITEM=" + _
            CStr(rs("Key")) + """>"

        sOut = sOut + rs("Title")

        sOut = sOut + "</A>"
        sOut = sOut + "</TD>"
    End If
    sOut = sOut + vbCrLf
    If (fTop) Then
```

```
              sOut = sOut + "<TH WIDTH=70%>Item description</TH>" _
                     + vbCrLf
        Else
           sOut = sOut + "<TD WIDTH=70%>"
           sOut = sOut + MakeBold(rs("Data"), cKeywords)
           sOut = sOut + "</TD>" + vbCrLf
        End If
        If (fTop) Then
           sOut = sOut + vbCrLf
           sOut = sOut + "<TH ALIGN=RIGHT BGCOLOR=#00ffff _
                   WIDTH=10%>Price</TH>"
        Else
           sOut = sOut + vbCrLf
           sOut = sOut + "<TD ALIGN=RIGHT BGCOLOR=#00ffff _
                   WIDTH=10%>"
           sOut = sOut + Format$(CheckNull(rs("Price"), ""), _
                   "Currency")
           sOut = sOut + "</TD>" + vbCrLf
        End If
        sOut = sOut + "</TR>"

     SearchRow = sOut
   End Function


   Function SearchTop() As String
     Dim sOut As String

     sOut = "<HTML>" + vbCrLf
     sOut = sOut + "<HEADER><TITLE> Search results</TITLE>"
     sOut = sOut + " </HEADER>" + vbCrLf
     sOut = sOut + "<BODY BGCOLOR=#ffffff>" + vbCrLf
     sOut = sOut + "<H2>Search results</H2><HR>" + vbCrLf

     SearchTop = sOut
   End Function
```

UserSecurity5.bas Source Code

```
     Option Explicit


     Dim sFullName As String
```

```
Public sUID As String
Sub DoInitialLogonGuestScreen(Optional sError As Variant)
   With cgi
      .WriteCGI "<HTML>" + vbCrLf
      If (IsMissing(sError)) Then
         .WriteCGI "<HEAD><TITLE>Creating a user database _
             with the oCGI VB module"
         .WriteCGI "</TITLE></HEAD><BODY BGCOLOR=""""#ffffff"""">"_
             + vbCrLf
      Else
         .WriteCGI "<HEAD><TITLE>" + sError + _
             "</TITLE></HEAD><BODY "
         .WriteCGI "BGCOLOR=""""#ffffff"""">" + vbCrLf
         .WriteCGI "<H2>ERROR: " + sError + "</H2><HR>" + _
             vbCrLf
      End If

      .WriteCGI "<FORM ACTION=""""" + .ReadScriptName
      .WriteCGI """" METHOD="""POST""">" + vbCrLf
      .WriteCGI "<INPUT TYPE="""HIDDEN"" NAME="""Action"" "
      .WriteCGI " VALUE="""PROCESSGUEST"">" + vbCrLf
      .WriteCGI "<TABLE><TR><TD>" + vbCrLf
      .WriteCGI "<B>User Name:</B></TD><TD><INPUT TYPE=TEXT _
             SIZE=20 "
      .WriteCGI " MAXLENGTH=50 NAME="""UserName"" "
      If (.ReadParam("UserName") <> "") Then
         .WriteCGI " VALUE="""" + cgi.ReadParam("UserName") + _
             """">" + vbCrLf
      Else
         .WriteCGI ">" + vbCrLf
      End If

      .WriteCGI "</TD></TR><TR><TD>" + vbCrLf
      .WriteCGI "<B>Full Name:</B></TD><TD><INPUT TYPE=TEXT _
             SIZE=20 "
      .WriteCGI " MAXLENGTH=50 NAME="""FullName"" "
      If (.ReadParam("FullName") <> "") Then
         .WriteCGI " VALUE="""" + .ReadParam("FullName") + _
             """">" + vbCrLf
      Else
         .WriteCGI ">" + vbCrLf
```

```vb
            End If

            .WriteCGI "</TD></TR><TR><TD>" + vbCrLf
            .WriteCGI "<B>Password:</B></TD><TD><INPUT _
                TYPE=PASSWORD SIZE=20 "
            .WriteCGI " MAXLENGTH=50 NAME=""Password"">" + vbCrLf
            .WriteCGI "</TD></TR><TR><TD>" + vbCrLf
            .WriteCGI "</TD></TR><TR><TD>" + vbCrLf
            .WriteCGI "<B>VerifyPassword:</B></TD><TD><INPUT _
                TYPE=PASSWORD "
            .WriteCGI " SIZE=20 MAXLENGTH=50
                NAME=""VerifyPassword"">" + vbCrLf
            .WriteCGI "</TD></TR><TR><TD>" + vbCrLf
            .WriteCGI "</TD></TR><TR><TD> <input type=checkbox _
                name=""RememberPassword"" "
            .WriteCGI " value=""ON""> Remember my password for "
            .WriteCGI " <input type=TEXT SIZE=2 MAXLENGTH=2 _
                NAME=""RememberDuration"" "
            .WriteCGI " VALUE=14> days"
            .WriteCGI "</TD></TR><TR><TD> <P><INPUT TYPE=Submit _
                NAME=""Submit"" "
            .WriteCGI " VALUE=""Create your new user"">" + vbCrLf
            .WriteCGI "</TD><TD><INPUT TYPE=Reset NAME=""Reset"" _
                VALUE=""Reset"">"
            .WriteCGI vbCrLf + "</TD><TD>" + vbCrLf
            .WriteCGI "</TD></TR></TABLE>" + vbCrLf
            .WriteCGI "</FORM> </BODY></HTML>" + vbCrLf
        End With
End Sub

Sub DoInitialLogonScreen(Optional sError As Variant)
    ' this function displays the initial log on screen.
    ' this gets called to show the existing user screen.
    With cgi
        .WriteCGI "<HTML>" + vbCrLf
        If (IsMissing(sError)) Then
            .WriteCGI "<HEAD><TITLE>Creating a user database _
                with the oCGI "
            .WriteCGI " VB module</TITLE></HEAD><BODY BGCOLOR= _
                ""#ffffff"">" + vbCrLf
        Else
```

```
        .WriteCGI "<HEAD><TITLE>" + sError + _
            "</TITLE></HEAD><BODY "
        .WriteCGI " BGCOLOR=""#ffffff"">" + vbCrLf
        .WriteCGI "<H2>ERROR: " + sError + "</H2><HR>" + _
            vbCrLf
    End If
    .WriteCGI "<BR><H2> If you've never logged in before, _
            press this:<H2>"
    .WriteCGI vbCrLf
    .WriteCGI "<FORM ACTION=""" + .ReadScriptName + """ _
            METHOD=""POST"">"
    .WriteCGI vbCrLf
    .WriteCGI "<INPUT TYPE=""HIDDEN"" NAME=""Action"" _
            VALUE=""LOGGUEST"">"
    .WriteCGI vbCrLf
    .WriteCGI "<INPUT TYPE=Submit NAME=""Submit"" _
            VALUE=""New User"">"
    .WriteCGI vbCrLf
    .WriteCGI "</FORM><BR><HR>" + vbCrLf

    .WriteCGI "<BR><H2> If you have logged in, please use _
            your username and "
    .WriteCGI "password:<H2>" + vbCrLf
    .WriteCGI "<FORM ACTION=""" + .ReadScriptName + """ _
            METHOD=""POST"">"
    .WriteCGI vbCrLf
    .WriteCGI "<INPUT TYPE=""HIDDEN"" NAME=""Action"" _
            VALUE=""LOGIN"">" + vbCrLf
    .WriteCGI "<TABLE><TR><TD>" + vbCrLf
    .WriteCGI "<B>User Name:</B></TD><TD><INPUT TYPE=TEXT _
            SIZE=20 "
    .WriteCGI " MAXLENGTH=50 NAME=""UserName"" "
    If (.ReadParam("UserName") <> "") Then ' is this a _
            "wrong login" error?!
        .WriteCGI " VALUE=""" + .ReadParam("UserName") + _
            """>" + vbCrLf
    Else
        .WriteCGI ">" + vbCrLf
    End If

    .WriteCGI "</TD></TR><TR><TD>" + vbCrLf
```

```
            .WriteCGI "<B>Password:</B></TD><TD><INPUT _
                TYPE=PASSWORD SIZE=20 MAXLENGTH=50 "
            .WriteCGI " NAME=""Password"">" + vbCrLf
            .WriteCGI "</TD></TR><TR><TD> <input type=checkbox _
                name=""RememberPassword"" "
            .WriteCGI " value=""ON""> Remember my password for "
            .WriteCGI " <input type=TEXT SIZE=2 MAXLENGTH=2 _
                NAME=""RememberDuration"" "
            .WriteCGI " VALUE=14> days"
            .WriteCGI "</TD></TR><TR><TD> <P><INPUT TYPE=Submit _
                NAME=""Submit"" "
            .WriteCGI " VALUE=""Log in as existing User"">" + _
                vbCrLf
            .WriteCGI "</TD><TD><INPUT TYPE=Reset NAME=""Reset"" _
                VALUE=""Reset"">" + vbCrLf
            .WriteCGI "</TD><TD>" + vbCrLf
            .WriteCGI "</TD></TR></TABLE>" + vbCrLf
            .WriteCGI "</FORM> </BODY></HTML>" + vbCrLf
        End With
    End Sub


    Sub DoProcessGuest()
        ' check validity of everything to start with...
        With cgi
            ' this could be done better with JavaScript validation!
            Select Case "" ' find out if some of the fields are empty!
                Case Trim$(.ReadParam("UserName"))
                    DoInitialLogonGuestScreen "Invalid User name _
                        entered."
                    Exit Sub
                Case Trim$(.ReadParam("FullName"))
                    DoInitialLogonGuestScreen "Invalid Full Name _
                        entered."
                    Exit Sub
                Case Trim$(.ReadParam("Password"))
                    DoInitialLogonGuestScreen "An empty password _
                        cannot be used"
                    Exit Sub
            End Select
            If (.ReadParam("Password") <> _
                    .ReadParam("VerifyPassword")) Then
```

```
          DoInitialLogonGuestScreen "Password and Verify _
              Password must be the same!"
          Exit Sub
      End If
      If (.ReadParam("Password") = .ReadParam("UserName")) _
          Then
          DoInitialLogonGuestScreen "UserName and Password
              must be different!"
          Exit Sub
      End If

      ' this function gets called to finalize the logging _
              in of the user!
      Dim rs As Recordset, sSQL As String
      sSQL = "select * from USERS where UserName='"
      sSQL = sSQL + DoubleQuote(.ReadParam("UserName")) + "'"
      Set rs = db.OpenRecordset(sSQL, dbOpenDynaset)

      ' make sure that there's no one by that same name...
      If rs.EOF Then
        rs.AddNew ' no need for double quotes, DAO takes _
              care of it here!
        rs("UserName") = .ReadParam("UserName")
        rs("Password") = .ReadParam("Password")
        rs("FullName") = .ReadParam("FullName")
        rs.Update
        ' change back to what I've just added so that I can _
              get the UID
        rs.Bookmark = rs.LastModified

        sFullName = .ReadParam("FullName")
        sUID = rs("UserID")

        Set rs = db.OpenRecordset(sSQL, dbOpenDynaset)
        If Not rs.EOF Then
          rs.Close
          SetUserCookies .ReadParam("UserName") ' install _
              cookies!
          ' logged in, show home page!
          HomePage
        Else
```

```
              rs.Close
              DoInitialLogonGuestScreen "Could not add User to _
                 system"
            End If
          Else
            rs.Close
            DoInitialLogonGuestScreen "User Name already exists"
          End If
      End With
  End Sub


  Sub DoUserSecurity()
     If (Not TryToLogin()) Then
        Select Case (cgi.ReadParam("Action"))
          Case "LOGGUEST"
            DoInitialLogonGuestScreen
          Case "PROCESSGUEST"
            DoProcessGuest
          Case Else
            If (cgi.ReadParam("UserName") <> "") Then ' tried _
               to log on, but couldn't
               DoInitialLogonScreen "UserName/Password could _
                  not be matched"
            Else
               DoInitialLogonScreen
            End If
        End Select
     Else
        HomePage ' let this handle things from now on!
     End If
  End Sub


  Sub SetUserCookies(sUser As String)
     ' randomize a UserCookie, then place it!
     Dim rsUser As Recordset, sSQL As String

     sSQL = "select * from USERS where UserName='" + _
             DoubleQuote(sUser) + "'"
     Set rsUser = db.OpenRecordset(sSQL, dbOpenDynaset)
     If Not rsUser.EOF Then ' this shouldn't happen if we _
             are here!
```

```
          Dim sUserCookie As String, sRandom As String
          Randomize CLng(Format(Now, "hhmmss"))
          sRandom = CStr(CLng((Rnd * 1000000000)) + 1)
          sUserCookie = CStr(rsUser("UserID")) + "=" + sRandom


          'Note, using Java script, this validation could be _
                done client-side!
          Dim sCookie As String, sServer As String, sScript _
                As String
          sCookie = "UserCookie"
          sServer = cgi.ReadServerName
          sScript = cgi.ReadScriptName
          If (cgi.ReadParam("RememberPassword") = "ON") And _
             (IsNumeric(cgi.ReadParam("RememberDuration"))) Then
               Dim expire As Date
               expire = CDate(Now + CInt(cgi.ReadParam_
                  ("RememberDuration")))
               cgi.WriteCookie sCookie, sUserCookie, sServer, _
                  sScript, expire
          Else ' no persistence!
               cgi.WriteCookie sCookie, sUserCookie, sServer, _
                  sScript
          End If
          rsUser.Edit
          rsUser("Notes") = sRandom
          rsUser.Update
        End If
        rsUser.Close
End Sub


' Try to login user. Return true if successful.
Function TryToLogin() As Boolean
   TryToLogin = False
   If (UserPasswordMatch(cgi.ReadParam("UserName"), _
           cgi.ReadParam("Password"))) Then
      SetUserCookies cgi.ReadParam("UserName")
      TryToLogin = True
   Else
      Dim sUserID As String, sCookieValue As String
      Dim sUserCookie As String, iPos As Integer
      sUserCookie = cgi.ReadCookie("UserCookie")
```

```
      If (sUserCookie <> "") Then
        iPos = InStr(sUserCookie, "=")
        sUserID = Left$(sUserCookie, iPos - 1)
        sCookieValue = Mid$(sUserCookie, iPos + 1)
        TryToLogin = UserCookieMatch(sUserID, sCookieValue)
      End If
    End If
End Function


Function UserCookieMatch(sUserID As String, sCookieValue _
          As String) As Boolean
  Dim rsUser As Recordset, sSQL As String
  UserCookieMatch = False ' convince me otherwise!
  sSQL = "select * from USERS where UserID=" + sUserID
  Set rsUser = db.OpenRecordset(sSQL, dbOpenDynaset)
  If Not rsUser.EOF Then
    If (rsUser("Notes") = sCookieValue) Then
      sFullName = rsUser("FullName")
      sUID = sUserID
      UserCookieMatch = True
    End If
  End If
  rsUser.Close
End Function


Function UserPasswordMatch(sUserName As String, sPassword _
          As String) As Boolean
  Dim rsUser As Recordset, sSQL As String
  UserPasswordMatch = False ' convince me otherwise!
  If (sUserName = "" And sPassword = "") Then Exit _
          Function ' no good for sure!

  sSQL = "select * from USERS where UserName='" + _
          DoubleQuote(sUserName) + "'"
  Set rsUser = db.OpenRecordset(sSQL, dbOpenDynaset)
  If Not rsUser.EOF Then
    If (rsUser("Password") = sPassword) Then
      sFullName = rsUser("FullName")
      sUID = rsUser("UserID")
      UserPasswordMatch = True
    End If
```

```
        End If
        rsUser.Close
    End Function
```

ShoppingBag1.bas Source Code

```
Option Explicit

Declare Function oCGI2Register Lib _
   "oCGI2.dll" Alias "DllRegisterServer" () As Long

Public cgi As oCGI2
Public db As Database

Const COOKIE_TTL = 14 ' cookies will persist for 14 days.
Sub AddShoppingBagItem(sKey As String, nQuantity As Integer)
   With cgi
      Dim sName As String
      If (InStr(sKey, "Item") = 1) Then
         sName = sKey
      Else
         sName = "Item" + sKey
      End If
      .WriteVirtualCookie sName, CStr(nQuantity)

      ' add to current cookie list...
      ' — so that it shows up in this session too!
      If .ReadCookie(sName) = "" Then
         Dim pParam As ParamType
         Set pParam = New ParamType

         pParam.Name = sName
         pParam.Value = CStr(nQuantity)
         .cCookies.Add item:=pParam, Key:=sName
      End If
   End With
End Sub

Sub ClearShoppingBag()
   ' loop through the virtual cookie list
   ' kill anything that starts with Item*
```

```
              With cgi
                Dim item As Object, i As Integer
                i = 1
                Do While (True)
                  If (i > .cCookies.Count) Then Exit Do
                  Set item = .cCookies.item(i)
                  If (InStr(item.Name, "Item") = 1) Then ' has to _
                      be the beginning.

                    ' shopping bag item. Delete by setting expiration _
                      to two weeks back!
                    .DeleteVirtualCookie item.Name, item.Value
                    .cCookies.Remove i
                    i = 1
                  End If
                  i = i + 1
                Loop
              End With
            End Sub


            Sub DoAddItem()
              With cgi
                Dim sOut As String
                sOut = "<HTML>" + vbCrLf
                sOut = sOut + "<HEAD>" + NoCache + "</HEAD>" + vbCrLf
                sOut = sOut + "<BODY BGCOLOR=#ffdd99>" + vbCrLf
                sOut = sOut + "<H2> Shopping bag contents after item _
                      addition<HR></H2>" + vbCrLf

                ' add the single item to teh shopping bag
                AddShoppingBagItem .ReadParam("ITEM"), 1
                ' now display the contents for the shopping bag
                sOut = sOut + GetShoppingBag

                .WriteCGI sOut + "</BODY>" + vbCrLf
                .WriteCGI "</HTML>"
              End With
            End Sub


            Sub DoCheckOut()
              Dim sOut As String, sShoppingBag As String
```

```
                ' get the contents of the shopping bag
                sShoppingBag = GetShoppingBag


                sOut = "<HTML>" + vbCrLf
                sOut = sOut + "<HEAD>" + NoCache + "</HEAD>" + vbCrLf


                ' if empty, show err.
                If sShoppingBag <> "" Then
                   sOut = sOut + "<BODY BGCOLOR=#ffdd99>" + vbCrLf
                   sOut = sOut + "<H2> Shopping bag contents<HR></H2>" + vbCrLf
                   sOut = sOut + sShoppingBag
                   sOut = sOut + "</BODY>" + vbCrLf
                   sOut = sOut + "</HTML>" + vbCrLf
                Else
                   sOut = sOut + "<BODY BGCOLOR=#ffdddd>" + vbCrLf
                   sOut = sOut + "<H2> Shopping bag is empty!</H2><HR>" _
                          + vbCrLf
                   sOut = sOut + "</BODY>" + vbCrLf
                   sOut = sOut + "</HTML>" + vbCrLf
                End If
                cgi.WriteCGI sOut
            End Sub


            Sub DoEmptyShoppingBag()
                ClearShoppingBag


                ' it should be empty so this should show a clear...
                ' - shopping bag.
                DoCheckOut
            End Sub


            Sub DoSubmit()
                ' an actual order!
                With cgi
                   RefreshShoppingBag


                   ' now show a quote for entries in shopping bag
                   Dim sOut As String
                   sOut = GetShoppingBag("DOVERIFYSUMBIT", False)


                   .WriteCGI "<HTML>" + vbCrLf
```

```
        .WriteCGI "<HEAD>" + NoCache + "</HEAD>" + vbCrLf

     If (sOut = "") Then
       ' empty shopping bag!
       sOut = sOut + "<BODY BGCOLOR=#ffdddd>" + vbCrLf
       sOut = sOut + "<H2> Shopping bag is empty!</H2><HR>"_
             + vbCrLf
     Else
       ' sOut contains the entire shopping bag

        .WriteCGI "<BODY BGCOLOR=#ffffff>" + vbCrLf
        .WriteCGI "<H2>Shopping bag contents</H2><HR>"
        .WriteCGI sOut
        .WriteCGI "<H2>User Information</H2><HR>"
        .WriteCGI ShowUserInformation
        .WriteCGI ShowCreditCardInformation

        .WriteCGI "</FORM>"
     End If

        .WriteCGI "</BODY>" + vbCrLf
        .WriteCGI "</HTML>"
   End With
End Sub


Sub DoVerifySubmit()
   Dim sOut As String

   ' update the information in shopping bag.
   RefreshShoppingBag
   ' update the user information (to what was submitted)
   UpdateUserInformation
   ' submit the shopping bag information to database
   SubmitShoppingbag

   sOut = "<HTML>" + vbCrLf
   sOut = sOut + "<HEAD>" + NoCache + "</HEAD>" + vbCrLf
   sOut = sOut + "<BODY BGCOLOR=#ffffff>" + vbCrLf

   sOut = sOut + "<H2>Information has been successfuly _
             submitted </H2>"
```

```vb
      sOut = sOut + "</BODY>" + vbCrLf
      sOut = sOut + "</HTML>"
      cgi.WriteCGI sOut
End Sub

Function GetItemKey(ByVal sName As String) As Integer
   ' look for the number after "Item"
   GetItemKey = CInt(Mid$(sName, Len("Item") + 1))
End Function

Function GetShoppingBag(Optional vSubmitText As Variant, _
   Optional vTerminateForm As Variant) As String

   Dim sOut As String, sSubmitText As String
   If IsMissing(vSubmitText) Then
      ' default submission instruction
      sSubmitText = "DOSUBMIT"
   Else
      sSubmitText = vSubmitText
   End If

   With cgi
      Dim item As Object, fItems As Boolean
      Dim fItemsExist As Boolean
      fItemsExist = False
      Dim rs As Recordset
      Set rs = db.OpenRecordset("select * from DATA", _
            dbOpenDynaset, dbReadOnly)
      For Each item In .cCookies
        ' has to be the beginning.
        If (InStr(item.Name, "Item") = 1) Then
          If Not fItemsExist Then
             ' start it all out

             sOut = sOut + "<FORM METHOD=POST ACTION="""
             sOut = sOut + .ReadScriptName + "?ACTION=" + _
                sSubmitText
             sOut = sOut + """">" + vbCrLf
             sOut = sOut + "<CENTER><TABLE BORDER=1 WIDTH=_
                80%>" + vbCrLf
             sOut = sOut + "<TR>" + vbCrLf
```

```
      sOut = sOut + "<TH WIDTH=80% BGCOLOR=#ffffff>"
      sOut = sOut + "Item name"
      sOut = sOut + "</TH>" + vbCrLf
      sOut = sOut + "<TH WIDTH=10% BGCOLOR=#ffffff>"
      sOut = sOut + "Quantity"
      sOut = sOut + "</TH>" + vbCrLf
      sOut = sOut + "<TH WIDTH=10% BGCOLOR=#ffffff>"
      sOut = sOut + "Cost/item"
      sOut = sOut + "</TH>" + vbCrLf
      sOut = sOut + "</TR>" + vbCrLf
   End If

   Dim iItemKey As Integer
   iItemKey = GetItemKey(item.Name)
   rs.FindFirst "Key=" + CStr(iItemKey)

   sOut = sOut + "<TR>" + vbCrLf
   'fatal error!
   If Not rs.NoMatch Then
      ' item information.
      sOut = sOut + "<TD WIDTH=80%>"
      sOut = sOut + rs("Title")
      sOut = sOut + "</TD>" + vbCrLf
      sOut = sOut + "<TD WIDTH=10% ALIGN=CENTER>"
      sOut = sOut + "<INPUT TYPE=TEXT NAME="""
      sOut = sOut + item.Name + """ VALUE="""
      sOut = sOut + item.Value
      sOut = sOut + """>"
      sOut = sOut + "</TD>" + vbCrLf
      sOut = sOut + "<TD WIDTH=10% ALIGN=CENTER _
         BGCOLOR=#00ffff>"
      sOut = sOut + Format$(item.Value, "Currency")
      sOut = sOut + "</TD>" + vbCrLf
   Else
      sOut = sOut + "<TD>Error locating Item!</TD>" _
         + vbCrLf
   End If
   sOut = sOut + "</TR>" + vbCrLf

   fItemsExist = True
End If
```

```
        Next
        rs.Close
    End With

    ' if nothing exists, I don't need to close anything out!
    If fItemsExist Then
        'close it out.
        sOut = sOut + "</CENTER></TABLE><BR>"
        Dim fTerminateForm As Boolean
        fTerminateForm = True
        If Not IsMissing(vTerminateForm) Then fTerminateForm _
            = vTerminateForm

        If fTerminateForm Then
            sOut = sOut + "<CENTER><INPUT TYPE=SUBMIT NAME=SUBMIT _
                VALUE="""
            sOut = sOut + "Purchase files"
            sOut = sOut + """">"
            sOut = sOut + "</CENTER></FORM>"
        End If
    Else

    End If
    GetShoppingBag = sOut
End Function



Sub main()
On Error GoTo RegisterErr ' register oCGI only if _
            having problems!
    Set cgi = New oCGI2
On Error GoTo NormalErr
    cgi.ProcessCGI Command
    cgi.ProcessVirtualCookies COOKIE_TTL
    'Load frmVBCrash
    Set db = Workspaces(0).OpenDatabase(App.Path + _
            "\ShoppingBag1.mdb")

    ' security is first and foremost, it will delegate _
            authority later on!
    DoUserSecurity
```

```
            db.Close
            Set cgi = Nothing
            End
    NormalErr:
            cgi.WriteCGI "<HTML><BODY>Error:" + Error$ + "_
                        </BODY></HTML>"
            Set cgi = Nothing ' Just in case
            End
    RegisterErr:
            oCGI2Register
            Set db = Nothing ' this works for uninitialized objects too!
            End
    End Sub


    Sub DoShowButtons()
        With cgi
            .WriteCGI "<HTML>" + vbCrLf
            .WriteCGI "<BODY BGCOLOR=#aaaaaa>" + vbCrLf
            .WriteCGI "<H3>"

            ' change hyperlinks into images by using <IMG SRC=> tag.
            .WriteCGI "<A HREF=""" + .ReadScriptName
            .WriteCGI "?ACTION=DOSHOWSEARCH"" _
                        TARGET=MAIN>[Search]</A> * "

            ' jump to empty shopping bag instruction.
            .WriteCGI "<A HREF=""" + .ReadScriptName
            .WriteCGI "?ACTION=DOEMPTYSHOPPINGBAG"" _
                        TARGET=MAIN>[Empty Shopping Bag]</A> * "

            ' view the shopping bag.
            .WriteCGI "<A HREF=""" + .ReadScriptName
            .WriteCGI "?ACTION=DOCHECKOUT"" TARGET=MAIN>_
                        [View shopping bag / Checkout]</A>"

            .WriteCGI "</H3>" + vbCrLf

            .WriteCGI "</BODY>" + vbCrLf
            .WriteCGI "</HTML>"
        End With
    End Sub
```

```
Sub HomePage()
   Select Case cgi.ReadParam("Action")
      Case "DOSEARCH":
         DoSearch ' perform a forward search
      Case "DOSEARCHBACK":
         DoSearchBack ' perform a backwards search.
      Case "DOSHOWSEARCH":
         DoShowSearch ' show search HTML screen (could be _
               done externally!).
      Case "DOSHOWBUTTONS":
         DoShowButtons ' show button frame (could be done _
               externally!).
      Case "DOCHECKOUT":
         DoCheckOut ' check out (aka, view shopping bag)
      Case "DOEMPTYSHOPPINGBAG":
         DoEmptyShoppingBag ' empty shopping bag
      Case "DOADDITEM"
         DoAddItem ' add items.
      Case "DOSUBMIT"
         DoSubmit ' submit items (after viewing shopping bag)
      Case "DOVERIFYSUMBIT"
         DoVerifySubmit ' final verification of information _
               (+credit card)
      Case Else: ' anything else!
         DoShowFrames ' default home page!
   End Select
End Sub

Sub DoShowFrames()
   With cgi
      ' expire everything tomorrow!
      .WriteCGI "<HTML>" + vbCrLf
      .WriteCGI "<HEAD>" + NoCache + vbCrLf
      .WriteCGI "<TITLE>Shopping Bag oCGI sample _
            application</TITLE>" + vbCrLf
      .WriteCGI "</HEAD>" + vbCrLf
      ' first frame = 20%, the other will take up the rest _
            of the location
      .WriteCGI "<FRAMESET BORDER=1 ROWS=20%,*>"
      .WriteCGI " <FRAME NAME=""BUTTONS"" SCROLLING=NO SRC="""
      .WriteCGI .ReadScriptName + "?ACTION=DOSHOWBUTTONS"">"
```

```
        .WriteCGI " <FRAME NAME=""MAIN"" SRC="""
        .WriteCGI .ReadScriptName + "?ACTION=DOSHOWSEARCH"">"
        .WriteCGI "</FRAMESET>"

        .WriteCGI "</HTML>"
    End With
End Sub


Function NoCache() As String
    NoCache = "<META NAME=""Pragma"" CONTENT=""no-cache"">" _
            + vbCrLf
End Function


Sub RefreshShoppingBag()
    ClearShoppingBag

    ' transfer parameters BACK into shopping bag
    Dim item As Object
    For Each item In cgi.cParameters
        If (InStr(item.Name, "Item") = 1) Then ' has to be _
                the beginning.
            If (IsNumeric(item.Value)) Then
                If (CInt(item.Value) > 0) Then
                    AddShoppingBagItem item.Name, CInt(item.Value)
                End If
            End If
        End If
    Next
End Sub


Function ShowCreditCardInformation() As String
    Dim sOut As String
    sOut = "<H3>Credit card information</H3><HR>"

    sOut = sOut + "<TABLE BORDER=1 WIDTH=80% BGCOLOR=#aaffff>"
    sOut = sOut + "<TR><TH WIDTH=30%>Credit Card _
            number</TH><TD>"
    sOut = sOut + "<INPUT TYPE=TEXT MAXLENGTH=20 _
            NAME=""CreditCard"""
    sOut = sOut + " VALUE="""">"</TD></TR>"
    sOut = sOut + "<TR><TH>Expiration date</TH><TD>"
```

```
sOut = sOut + "<INPUT TYPE=TEXT MAXLENGTH=5 _
        NAME=""ExpirationDate"""
sOut = sOut + " VALUE=""""></TD></TR>"
sOut = sOut + "</TABLE>"
sOut = sOut + "<BR><CENTER>"
sOut = sOut + "<INPUT TYPE=SUBMIT NAME=SUBMIT _
        VALUE=""Purchase files"">"
sOut = sOut + "</CENTER>"


    ShowCreditCardInformation = sOut
End Function


Function ShowUserInformation() As String
    Dim sOut As String, rsUser As Recordset
    Set rsUser = db.OpenRecordset("select * from USERS _
            where UserID=" + sUID)
    If rsUser.EOF Then
      ' fatal error!
      sOut = "<H2><FONT COLOR=RED>"
      sOut = sOut + "Error retrieving information about _
            user!<BR>"
      sOut = sOut + "Please log in and try again!"
      sOut = "</FONT></H2>"
    Else
      ' form should already be set up for us...
      sOut = "<TABLE BORDER=1 WIDTH=80% BGCOLOR=#ffff00>"
      sOut = sOut + "<TR><TH>Full Name</TH><TD WIDTH=30%>"
      sOut = sOut + "<INPUT TYPE=TEXT MAXLENGTH=50 _
            NAME=""FullName"""
      sOut = sOut + " VALUE=""" + CheckNull _
            (rsUser("FullName"), "")
      sOut = sOut + """></TD></TR>"
      sOut = sOut + "<TR><TH>Address</TH><TD>"
      sOut = sOut + "<INPUT TYPE=TEXT SIZE=50 MAXLENGTH= _
            50 NAME=""Address"""
      sOut = sOut + " VALUE=""" + CheckNull(rsUser _
            ("Address"), "")
      sOut = sOut + """></TD></TR>"
      sOut = sOut + "<TR><TH>City/State</TH><TD>"
      sOut = sOut + "<INPUT TYPE=TEXT MAXLENGTH=35 _
            NAME=""CityState"""
```

```
      sOut = sOut + " VALUE=""" + CheckNull(rsUser _
            ("CityState"), "")
      sOut = sOut + """></TD></TR>"
      sOut = sOut + "<TR><TH>Zip</TH><TD>"
      sOut = sOut + "<INPUT TYPE=TEXT MAXLENGTH=11 _
            NAME=""Zip"""
      sOut = sOut + " VALUE=""" + CheckNull(rsUser("Zip"), "")
      sOut = sOut + """></TD></TR>"
      sOut = sOut + "<TR><TH>Email</TH><TD>"
      sOut = sOut + "<INPUT TYPE=TEXT MAXLENGTH=50 _
            NAME=""Email"""
      sOut = sOut + " VALUE=""" + CheckNull(rsUser("Email"), "")
      sOut = sOut + """></TD></TR>"
      sOut = sOut + "<TR><TH>Phone</TH><TD>"
      sOut = sOut + "<INPUT TYPE=TEXT MAXLENGTH=15 _
            NAME=""Phone"""
      sOut = sOut + " VALUE=""" + CheckNull(rsUser("Phone"), "")
      sOut = sOut + """></TD></TR>"
      sOut = sOut + "</TABLE>"
   End If

   rsUser.Close
   ShowUserInformation = sOut
End Function

Sub SubmitShoppingbag()
   Dim rsOrder As Recordset, lOrderSession As Long
   Set rsOrder = db.OpenRecordset("ORDER_SESSION")

   rsOrder.AddNew
   rsOrder("UserID") = sUID
   rsOrder("Filled") = False
   rsOrder("PurchaseDate") = Now
   rsOrder("CreditCard") = cgi.ReadParam("CreditCard")
   rsOrder("ExpirationDate") = cgi.ReadParam _
            ("ExpirationDate")
   rsOrder.Update

   ' move to the last modified item (so I can pick up _
            OrderSession
   rsOrder.Bookmark = rsOrder.LastModified
```

```
      lOrderSession = rsOrder("OrderSession")


      Set rsOrder = db.OpenRecordset("PURCHASE_ITEMS")
      Dim item As Object
      For Each item In cgi.cCookies
        If (InStr(item.Name, "Item") = 1) Then ' has to be_
            the beginning.
          rsOrder.AddNew
          rsOrder("OrderSession") = lOrderSession
          rsOrder("ItemKey") = GetItemKey(item.Name)
          rsOrder("Quantity") = item.Value
          rsOrder.Update
        End If
      Next
      rsOrder.Close
      ' empty everything out!
      ClearShoppingBag
    End Sub


    Sub UpdateUserInformation()
      Dim rsUser As Recordset
      Set rsUser = db.OpenRecordset("select * from USERS _
            where UserID=" + sUID)
      If Not rsUser.EOF Then
        rsUser.Edit
        rsUser("FullName") = cgi.ReadParam("FullName")
        rsUser("Address") = cgi.ReadParam("Address")
        rsUser("CityState") = cgi.ReadParam("CityState")
        rsUser("Zip") = cgi.ReadParam("Zip")
        rsUser("Email") = cgi.ReadParam("Email")
        rsUser("Phone") = cgi.ReadParam("Phone")
        rsUser.Update
      End If


      rsUser.Close
    End Sub
```

Sample Screen Shots

Figures 8.1 - 8.3 display the search and ordering process in the shopping bag application.

Figure 8.1
The result page from a shopping bag search

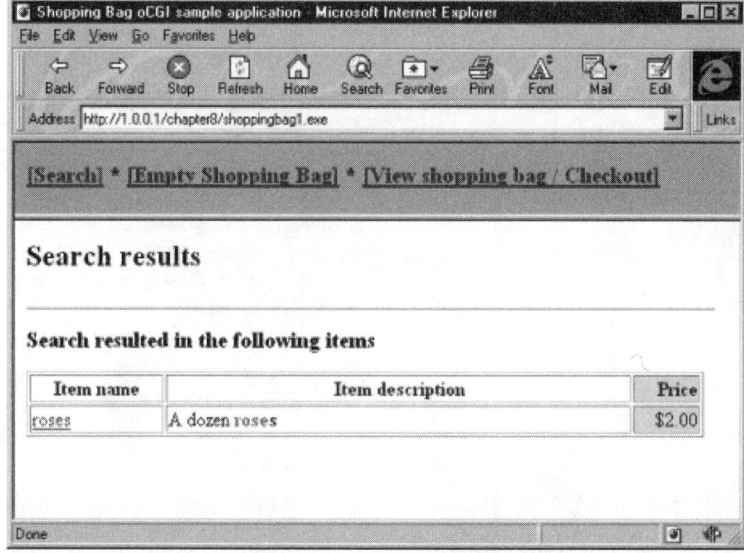

Figure 8.2
Ordering an item, selecting the quantity

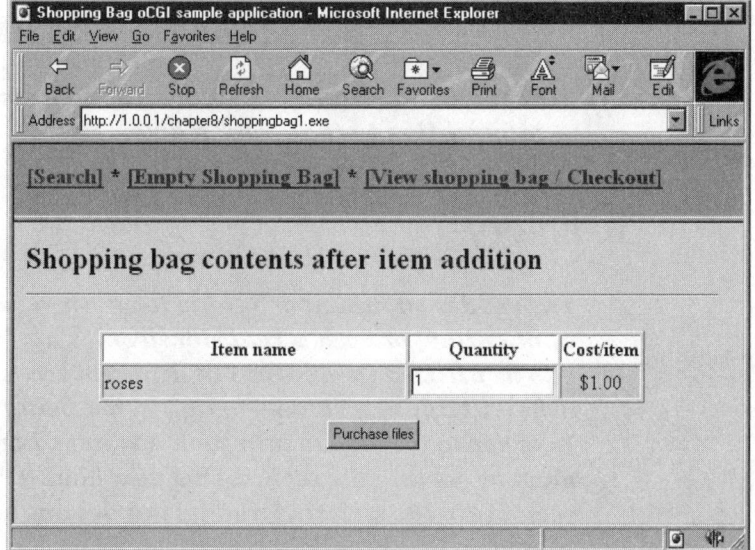

Figure 8.3
Filling out the order
information

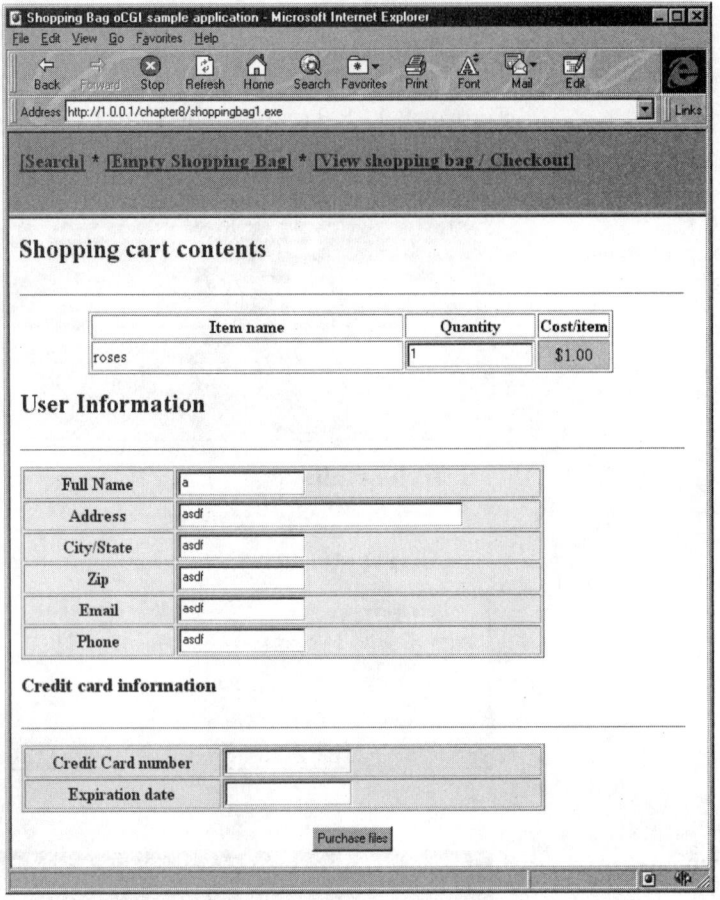

Notes

*Securing the final page requires the form to submit the
information to the "_top" frame.*

Summary

*The reader should now be able to create a full-blown shopping bag
application, or even a real storefront. This technology, of course,
can be utilized in a variety of different ways, and for completely
different applications — imagination being the limit to ingenuity.
In order to lure users into such a system, however, the application
must be completely secure. Our next chapter deals with adding
security to the web site, and its impact on the CGI applications in
that site.*

SECURITY AND CGI APPLICATIONS

- Securing CGI applications
- Routing TCP/IP packets
- Secure sockets layer
- Shopping bag administrator

A NOTE ABOUT SECURITY

The structure of the Internet is designed so that the transmission between client browser and web server passes through multiple junction points. These are handled by routers, and are physically located so that transmitting a TCP/IP packet from one peer on the Internet to another is done via a route path. This route is easily demonstrated using the tracert utility found in Windows NT. Just try using it to locate the path between you and **www.microsoft.com**:

```
Tracert www.microsoft.com
```

Figure 9.1 shows the results of a sample trace-route to **www.microsoft.com**.

Figure 9.1
Tracert to Microsoft's site

```
D:\WINNT\System32\cmd.exe
Microsoft(R) Windows NT(TM)
(C) Copyright 1985-1996 Microsoft Corp.

D:\>tracert www.microsoft.com

Tracing route to www.microsoft.com [207.68.156.51]
over a maximum of 30 hops:

  1   210 ms   201 ms   200 ms  ts024.pop4a.netvision.net.il [199.203.102.182]
  2   201 ms   200 ms   200 ms  haifa-cs4500-2-e2.pop4a.netvision.net.il [199.20
3.102.1]
  3   200 ms   200 ms   221 ms  hfa-e1-1.NetVision.net.il [199.203.4.71]
  4   451 ms   430 ms   431 ms  nyc-mci-ipl.NetVision.net.il [194.90.0.1]
  5     *      380 ms   401 ms  166.48.38.13
  6   521 ms   521 ms   691 ms  bordercore2-loopback.Seattle.mci.net [166.48.208
.1]
  7  1052 ms   510 ms   561 ms  microsoft.Seattle.mci.net [166.48.209.250]
  8   550 ms   491 ms   521 ms  207.68.145.54
  9   661 ms   551 ms   541 ms  207.68.156.51

Trace complete.

D:\>
```

Because of the distributed nature of the Internet transport protocol, information between browser and web server can be intercepted and logged in at any junction along the route. A typical route between two points can range from 10 to 20 distinct routing junctions (or hops). The maximum number of routing hops is typically 30 distinct hops. This prevents infinite loops from being implemented by a "nasty packet" or erroneous routing table (in one of the routers along the route).

Sensitive information, such as credit card numbers and passwords, can be fairly easily snagged utilizing a network monitor embedded directly within a router, or by using a network "sniffer" on one of the sub-networks along the route. In either case, a hacker with access to a router can potentially read *anything* that passes through that junction point.

Keep in mind that vendors directly receiving credit card information can far more easily abuse that information. Do you really know what a vendor's employee is doing after you hand him your credit card and he walks off with it? It seems silly to worry about such a high-tech way of stealing credit card numbers, when there are much easier ways to get this information!

It should be noted, however, that as the Internet commerce community grows larger, more and more transactions will start taking place over the Internet — making these unsecured transactions a prime target for high-tech thieves.

Security on the Internet

In order to secure transactions, a civilian encryption scheme called *SSL* (Secure Sockets Layer) has been introduced onto the net. This protocol simulates standard socket technology (the technology that makes the Internet "work") and adds encryption to that protocol. Because of this, no great changes need to be made by the participating browser or server in order to support the new protocol. Purchasing or gaining secure keys and installing them on the server allows a server to support this protocol.

SSL version 3 further enhances the protocol by allowing a client to have localized keys as well. This effectively doubles the security level between client and server.

In order to support SSL, a server must have a secure key installed. This key allows the server to support these protocols (a second key certificate may be needed on the client's browser in order to support SSL version 3). The key can be purchased from certificate companies such as Verisign `(http://www.verisign.com)`.

Alternatively, a certificate server can be purchased (such as Netscape certificate server) which allows a medium-to-large site to create its own certificates as needed. These certificates support all types of servers, but are typically less portable when it comes to the client browser (i.e., for personal certificates).

A certificate includes the name of the signing certificate authority, name and address of the site, and may also contain several variations of key size (depending on international export policies.)

Not all server versions support all types of SSL technology. For example, Netscape's lower level servers do *not* support SSL; in this case, a merchant server may be required. Microsoft's servers support SSL out of the box (although IIS version 1.0 requires the user to employ a cryptic command line utility in order to create the certificate request and install the certificate itself).

Microsoft web servers (IIS) version 2.0 and higher all have a GUI utility that handles the certificate requests, as well as installing and maintaining them. Figure 9.2 shows the server connection information for a particular certificate.

Figure 9.2

Selecting the secure server connection information

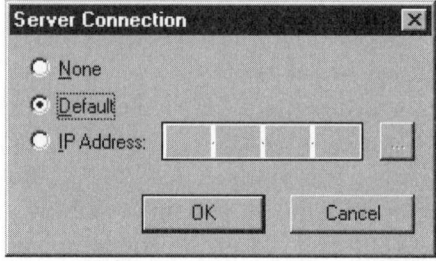

Once the certificate is installed, the administrator must delegate a certificate for each virtual IP for the server (or one can delegate a default key for a particular server). Figure 9.3 shows the key certificate manager, and demonstrates how a key is registered for a particular web server.

Figure 9.3

The key manager

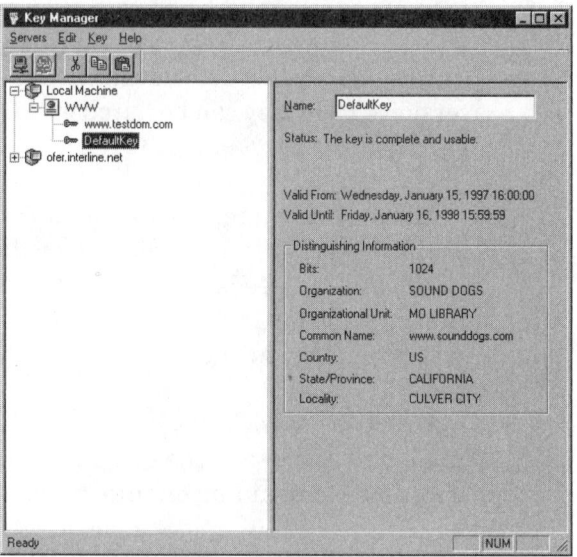

Once a key is enabled for a particular server/virtual IP, a secure connection can be established to a server by specifying https (rather than http) as the communication protocol:

```
https://www.mydomain.com
```

Figure 9.4 demonstrates how security is noted in a Netscape browser. Figure 9.5 shows how security is noted in a Microsoft browser.

Figure 9.4
Netscape browser showing a secure document

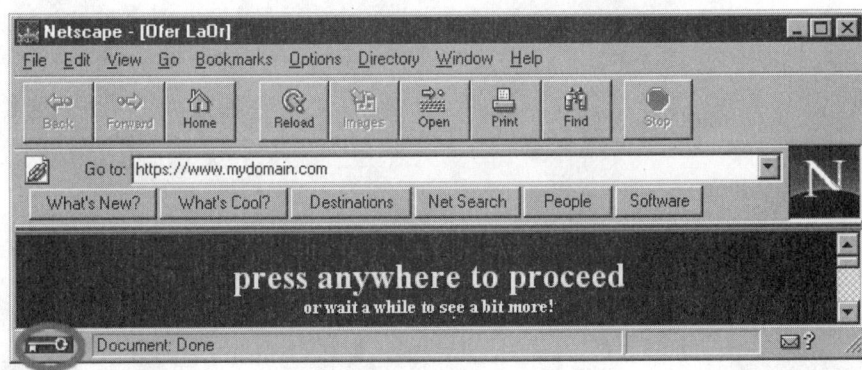

Figure 9.5
Microsoft browser showing a secure document

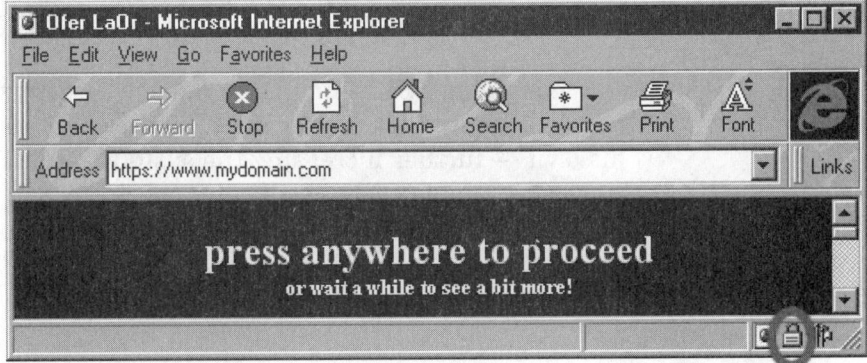

Under IIS, an administrator can specify that a certain directory requires a secure channel (i.e., a secure scripts directory). Figure 9.6 displays the security dialog box in IIS with the mandatory secure checkbox checked on.

Figure 9.6
The directory security
settings with the
mandatory SSL
checkbox

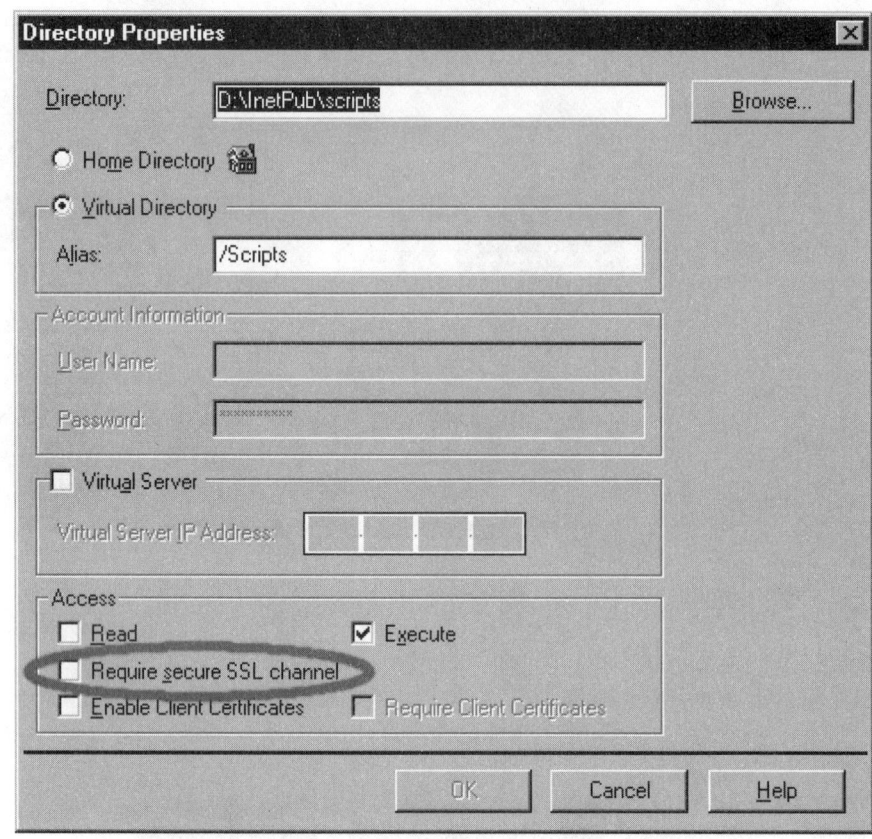

When using SSL version 2 or 3, each directory can specify that it requires (or, for that matter, enables) the client to have a certificate of his own — further increasing the system's security factor. Figure 9.7 shows the enable client certificates check box.

Figure 9.7
The enable client
certificates checkbox

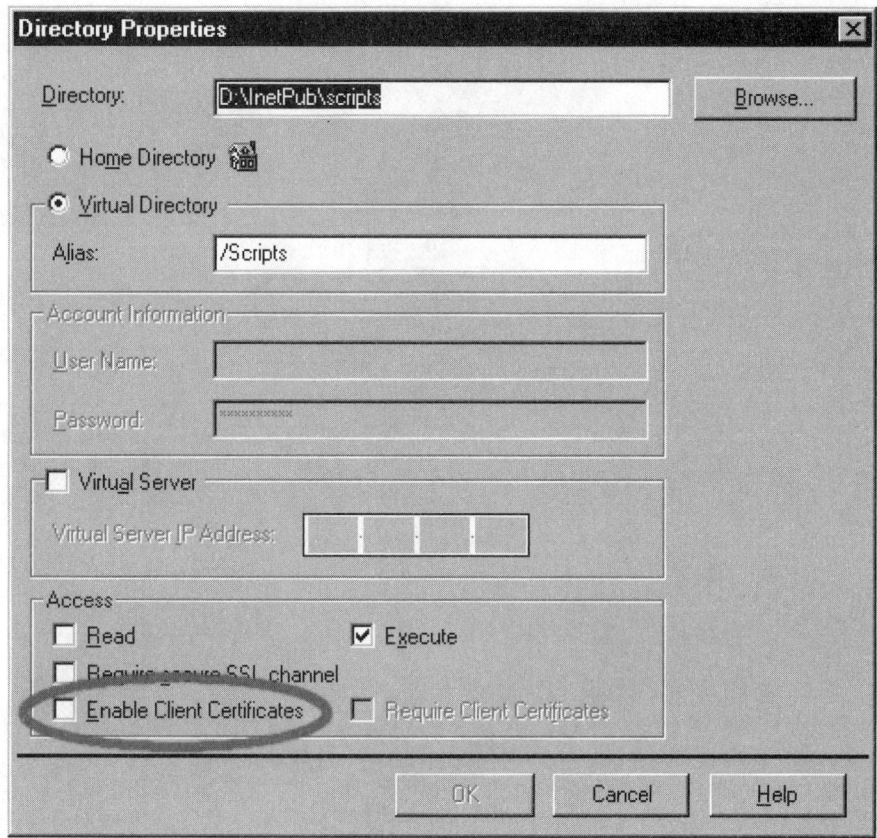

A web server can enforce security on particular directories. This causes the server to reject everything that is not using HTTPS security, before such requests can reach the CGI application or HTML document.

Alternatively, a CGI application can check for HTTPS by itself, without having the server enforcing the issue. Figures 9.8 and 9.9 demonstrate what happens when someone attempts to connect to a mandatory secured web site without security.

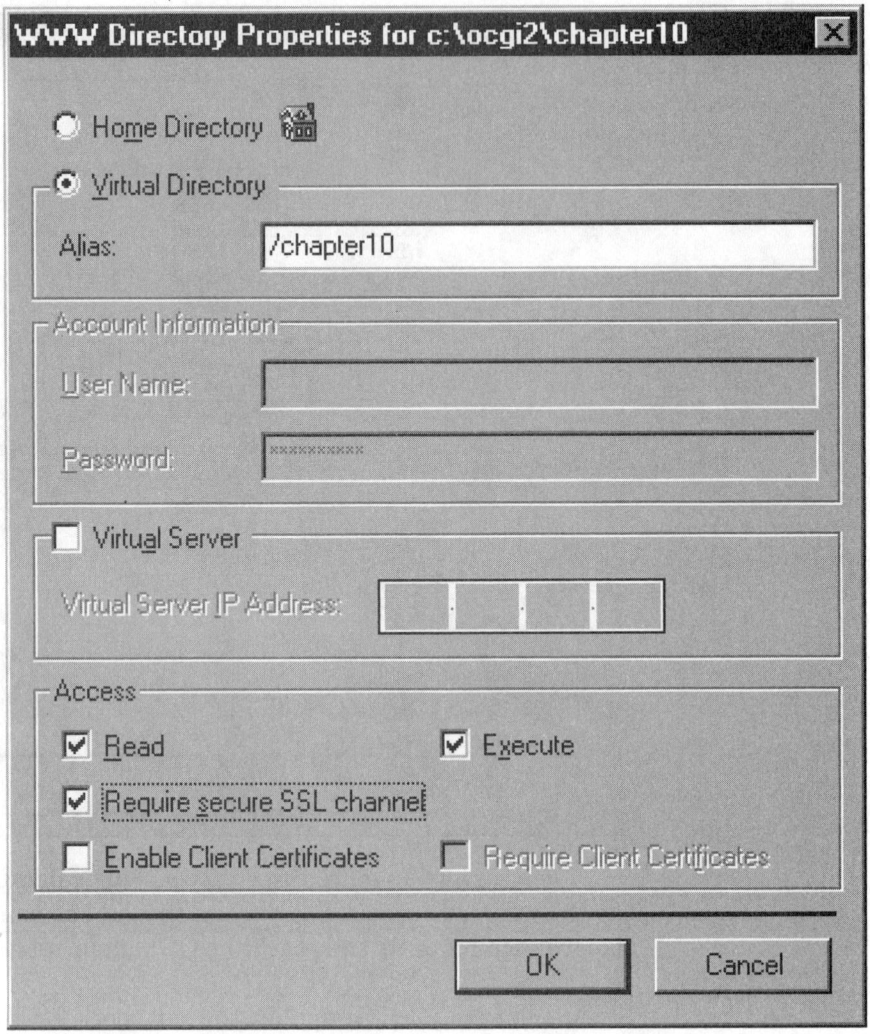

Figure 9.8
Setting mandatory
HTTPS

WWW Directory Properties for c:\ocgi2\chapter10

○ Home Directory

◉ Virtual Directory

Alias: /chapter10

Account Information

User Name:

Password: **********

☐ Virtual Server

Virtual Server IP Address:

Access

☑ Read   ☑ Execute

☑ Require secure SSL channel

☐ Enable Client Certificates   ☐ Require Client Certificates

OK   Cancel

Figure 9.9
Rejection by web
server due to security

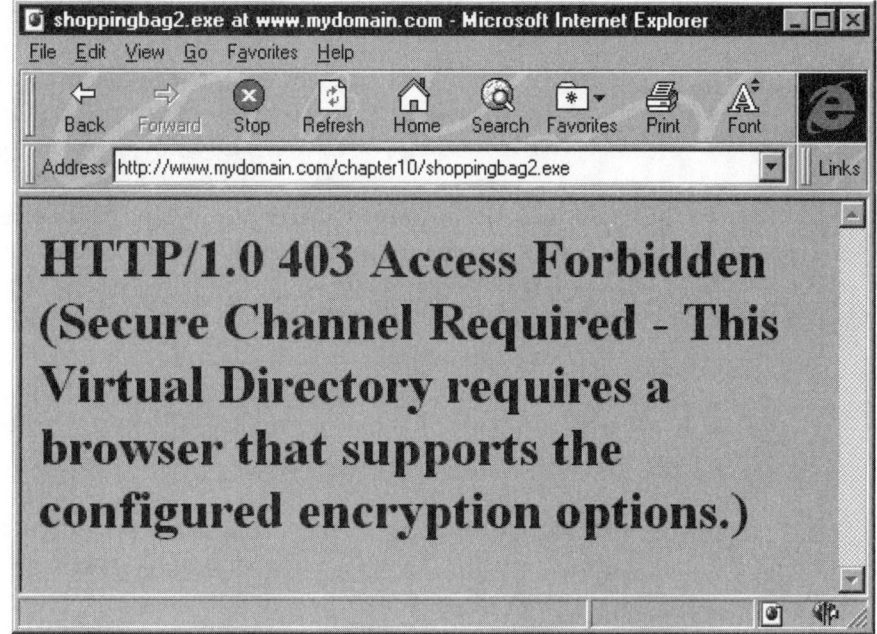

It should be noted that most browsers only use security for *all frames* on a given page. Should one frame on a given page need to be secured — it is more than likely that the browser will:

1. Ignore security and keep all frames "insecure."

2. Complain and error out.

3. Secure the selected frame.

In several tests, I was only able to get option number 3 out of *older* versions of browsers. All updated browser implementations choose option 1 most often, which is the worse of the lot.

It should also be noted that the browser usually rejects any mix of insecure elements in a secure page (or vice versa). In order to prevent such problems, the application should reference graphics and embedded objects without specifying a protocol:

```
<IMG SRC="/IMAGES/MYIMAGE.GIF">
```

There is no difference whether the security runs on a script or a standard HTML. Both cause the browser to display the same information. Actually, this is not exactly true; there are documented instances of "bugs" in Microsoft IIS 1.0 where IIS did not, in fact, behave the same way with or without SSL. Generally, however, the rule proves accurate.

To secure a form on a particular web page (regardless of its source — an HTML document or CGI application), the page that led the user to this information must specify that the URL be secured.

This relays to the user that the information he is currently filling in is, in fact, secure. The next document should also be secured, in order to verify that the information will actually be submitted securely over the Internet.

If the informational page is unsecured, the user will distrust the entire security scheme. Unsecuring the second page, for instance, would defeat the entire purpose of this feature.

In order to modify the application so that it works with SSL, the following change should be implemented:

The *DoSubmit* function currently implements the form in the following manner:

```
sOut = sOut + "<FORM METHOD=POST ACTION="""
sOut = sOut + .ReadScriptName + "?ACTION=" + sSubmitText
sOut = sOut + """>" + vbCrLf
```

Which translates to the following HTML tag:

```
<FORM METHOD=POST ACTION="/scripts/ShoppingBag1.exe?_
        ACTION=DOSUBMIT">
```

In order to make the process secure from this point onward, the previous statement should be modified to produce the following:

```
<FORM METHOD=POST ACTION="https://www.myweb.com/scripts
        /ShoppingBag1.exe?ACTION=DOSUBMIT">
```

No further changes are needed, since subsequent interactions with the server will default to the secured protocol.

It should be noted that if the server does not support the HTTPS protocol (i.e., it does not have a valid certificate), placing HTTPS will cause the form submission to fail. Neither the server nor the browser will accept an insecure connection under the HTTPS protocol.

The modified code will now be:

```
sOut = sOut + "<FORM METHOD=POST ACTION="""

sOut = sOut + "https://" + .ReadServerName

sOut = sOut + .ReadScriptName + "?ACTION=" + sSubmitText
sOut = sOut + """">" + vbCrLf
```

The Administration Piece

In order to retrieve information, an administrator with direct access to the server can easily use a product such as Microsoft Access (or create a dedicated client application using Visual Basic).

In most cases, however, the vendor that requires access to the orders does not have direct access to the database file. In order to give the vendor access to the file, a few options can be implemented:

1. Send the purchase information via e-mail. This is the most often-used implementation. Once the user submits final order information (i.e., *DoVerifySubmit* is executed), the system sends an e-mail with the contents of the order to a built-in address.

   Security-wise, this option is disastrous. Sensitive information is transferred from the web server to the mail server without security, and when the client retrieves his e-mail, the information is transferred from the mail server to the client's e-mail package without security. SSL technology is now being encorporated into mail systems. This can be a great way to resolve this issue in the future.

2. The second option is to provide a front end to the database. This option is more difficult to implement, but is gaining more and more supporters because of the increased security it provides.

   Because a web interface is involved here, the script output can be secured using SSL technology.

The first option is quite easy to implement. There are various ways to do this:

1. Use form e-mail submission. This is a special option that allows a form to be submitted via an e-mail message, rather than via a web interface. This is the least secure among all of the options, however, since it involves a remote mail server and subsequently causes the information to be transferred insecurely by a long-distance route!

   Additionally, the information in the message is submitted as a raw CGI string, which is fairly difficult to decode by hand.

2. Use a mail utility. There are various sendmail applications that save a text file before executing, causing the mail to be sent.

   A variation on this theme is a mail script that sends mail from the server and is referenced directly from the submitting form. An example of this is mailto.exe.

3. Use an e-mail control. This includes DLLs and OCXs that allow the script to send Internet e-mail directly from the server. Various types of such controls exist, including Microsoft's never-to-be released Internet Control Pack (which was later supposed to be merged with Netmanage's Internet development kit). Chameleon and Catalyst offer similar controls.

   These allow the system more direct control over the connection — permitting verification that the mail has reached its destination. Registration for such controls can be done in the manner demonstrated in registering oCGI. Appendix C will present a simple mail control that can be used for this purpose.

In some situations, sending this type of secure information over an e-mail interface make sense. For example, when the web server and mail server are within the same local network, and the manager receiving the information also logs onto that network. In this scenario, the information is only accessible to people who are physically *on* the local network. If the network is "trusted" (e.g., the local network is your own), this information can never be insecure in a "non-trusted" environment.

In most situations, however, the mail server and web server do not reside in a trusted environment; frequently, some routing is done between the e-mail package and the mail server — causing insecure information to be transferred via non-trusted environments.

The obvious solution is to provide a web front end which can be easily secured via SSL technology.

When dealing with a SQL server database, though, a third alternative exists: a TCP/IP connection can be utilized to connect directly to the server. This is easily done via the ODBC administration control panel applet, specifying the IP address of the target server. However, this still presents a security problem, because SQL server only provides a "secret" socket number with which to communicate with the server. While this is instrumental in deflecting "novice" hackers, information between server and client can still be tapped rather easily — giving the hacker easy access to your credit card numbers.

Notes

There are third party ODBC drivers that allow an encrypted conversation to take place between an ODBC client and server via TCP/IP.

The shopping bag administration application is a simple web front-end to the Shopping bag database. This application immediately displays the first order that it finds, enabling the administrator to fill the order and charge the credit card. Then, the application allows the administrator to move on to the next order, or else to mark the current order as filled *before* continuing. The administrator may then pass over specific orders that are hard to fill and simply proceed to others.

The main subroutine executes the *ViewCurrentPurchase* subroutine, which displays the subsequent purchase. This subroutine first starts up the web page, then calls the *CheckSecurity* subroutine.

CheckSecurity displays a blinking message that notifies the user of the current security status. It blinks SECURED if the application is being accessed via SSL. If not, the message NOT SECURED is displayed. An optional enhancement is to preclude use of this application on an unsecured channel.

The *ViewCurrentPurchase* subroutine attempts to read the *OrderSession* parameter. When this parameter is not specified, the first session is displayed by filling the *sSession* variable with -1 (a value that cannot be assigned to an AutoNumber type variable in an Access database). If the user had pressed the **Remove this purchase and proceed** button, the system will set the *Filled* flag in the database to true, so that the order will not show up anymore. By not actually removing the purchase from the database, though, the order is still in the system, and a history report can be generated as needed.

Next, the first order session *after* the previously shown one (as specified by the *OrderSession* CGI parameter) is requested. If no more orders exist, the **No more orders are pending** message is displayed. Otherwise, the user information and credit card information is retrieved and shown, and the *DisplayPurchaseInformation* subroutine is called to display purchase-specific information.

The *DisplayPurchaseInformation* subroutine selects purchase information from a given order session. This information is retrieved and displayed for each of the items in the order session. A running total is kept in the *totalCost* variable.

Finally the buttons are displayed, both of which reference the current order session. Once the user submits forms (there are two separate forms that can do this, although they can be consolidated into a single form, differing only on the Submit button's value), the application is executed again, finding the next order session and setting the *Filled* field to true, as needed.

Shopping Bag Administrator Source Code

```
Option Explicit

Declare Function oCGI2Register Lib _
```

```
              "oCGI2.dll" Alias "DllRegisterServer" () As Long

      Public cgi As oCGI2
      Public db As Database

      Sub CheckSecurity()
        With cgi
          .WriteCGI "<H2><BLINK>"
          If .ReadServerSecured Then
            .WriteCGI "SECURED"
          Else
            .WriteCGI "NOT SECURED"
          End If
          .WriteCGI "</BLINK></H2>" + vbCrLf
        End With
      End Sub

      Sub DisplayPurchaseInformation(lOrderSession As Long)
        With cgi
          Dim rs As Recordset, sSQL As String
          Dim totalCost As Currency

          ' start with a fresh total cost.
          totalCost = 0
          sSQL = "select * from PURCHASE_ITEMS, DATA"
          sSQL = sSQL + " where DATA.Key=PURCHASE_ITEMS.ItemKey "
          sSQL = sSQL + " and OrderSession=" + CStr(lOrderSession)

          ' start the purchase information table
          .WriteCGI "<BR><TABLE BORDER=1 WIDTH=70%>"
          Set rs = db.OpenRecordset(sSQL)
          Do While Not rs.EOF
            ' for every row, display the information.

            .WriteCGI "<TR>"
            .WriteCGI "<TD>" + CheckNull(rs("Title"), "") + "</TD>"
            .WriteCGI "<TD>" + CStr(rs("Quantity")) + "</TD>"
            .WriteCGI "<TD>"
            totalCost = totalCost + rs("Quantity") * rs("Price")
            .WriteCGI Format$(rs("Quantity") * rs("Price"), _
                "Currency")
```

```
        .WriteCGI "</TD>"
        .WriteCGI "</TR>"
      rs.MoveNext
Loop

' display the total charge:
.WriteCGI "<TR><TD BGCOLOR=#ffff00></TD><TD _
      BGCOLOR=#ffff00 ALIGN=RIGHT>"
.WriteCGI "Total charge:"
.WriteCGI "</TD><TD BGCOLOR=#ffff00>"
.WriteCGI Format$(totalCost, "Currency")
.WriteCGI "</TD></TR></TABLE>"

' place the buttons
.WriteCGI "<TABLE BORDER=0> <TR><TD>"

' the first button- which removes the purchase and _
      views the next one.
.WriteCGI "<FORM METHOD=POST ACTION=""" + _
      .ReadScriptName + """>"
.WriteCGI "<INPUT TYPE=HIDDEN NAME=OrderSession _
      VALUE="""
.WriteCGI CStr(lOrderSession) + """>"
.WriteCGI "<INPUT TYPE=SUBMIT NAME=SUBMIT "
.WriteCGI "VALUE=""Remove this purchase and proceed"">"
.WriteCGI "</FORM>"

' next button.
.WriteCGI "</TD><TD>"

' ... which proceeds without removing the purchase.
.WriteCGI "<FORM METHOD=POST ACTION=""" + _
      .ReadScriptName + """>"
.WriteCGI "<INPUT TYPE=HIDDEN NAME=OrderSession _
      VALUE="""
.WriteCGI CStr(lOrderSession) + """>"
.WriteCGI "<INPUT TYPE=SUBMIT NAME=SUBMIT "
.WriteCGI "VALUE=""Proceed without removing _
      purchase"">"
.WriteCGI "</FORM>"
.WriteCGI "</TD></TR></TABLE>"
```

```
        rs.Close
   End With
End Sub


Sub main()
On Error GoTo RegisterErr ' register oCGI only if having _
            problems!
   Set cgi = New oCGI2
On Error GoTo NormalErr
   cgi.ProcessCGI Command
   'Load frmVBCrash
   Set db = Workspaces(0).OpenDatabase(App.Path + _
            "\ShoppingBag1.mdb")


   ViewCurrentPurchase


   db.Close
   Set cgi = Nothing
   End
NormalErr:
   cgi.WriteCGI "<HTML><BODY>Error:" + Error$ + _
            "</BODY></HTML>"
   Set cgi = Nothing ' Just in case
   End
RegisterErr:
   oCGI2Register
   Set db = Nothing ' this works for uninitialized objects too!
   End
End Sub


Sub ViewCurrentPurchase()
   With cgi
      ' write top.
      .WriteCGI "<HTML>" + vbCrLf
      .WriteCGI "<HEAD> "
      .WriteCGI "<TITLE> Shopping Bag administration _
            application </TITLE>"
      .WriteCGI "</HEAD>" + vbCrLf
      .WriteCGI "<BODY BGCOLOR=#ffffff>" + vbCrLf

      ' check whether we are secured via SSL
```

```
CheckSecurity

' find the first purchase with order session.
Dim sSession As String, sSQL As String
sSession = .ReadParam("OrderSession")

' make up a dummy session number so we can view the _
        first session instead
If sSession = "" Then sSession = "-1"
If (.ReadParam("SUBMIT") = "Remove this purchase and _
        proceed") Then
  ' kill this one (set filled to true)
  sSQL = "Update ORDER_SESSION set Filled=-1 where _
        OrderSession="
  sSQL = sSQL + sSession
  db.Execute sSQL
End If


Dim rs As Recordset

' view the first order session that fits our goal
sSQL = "select TOP 1 * from ORDER_SESSION where _
        Filled=0 and OrderSession>"
sSQL = sSQL + sSession
Set rs = db.OpenRecordset(sSQL)
If rs.EOF Then
    .WriteCGI "<H2> No more orders are pending</H2>"
Else
  Dim rsUser As Recordset

  ' get user information
  sSQL = "select * from USERS where UserID=" + _
      CStr(rs("UserID"))
  Set rsUser = db.OpenRecordset(sSQL)
  .WriteCGI "<H1> User information </H1>" + vbCrLf
  ' print the user information
  .WriteCGI "<TABLE BORDER=1 WIDTH=90%>" + vbCrLf
  .WriteCGI "<TR><TH>Full Name:</TH><TD>" + vbCrLf
  .WriteCGI rsUser("FullName") + vbCrLf
  .WriteCGI "</TD></TR><TR><TH>Address:</TH><TD>" + _
      vbCrLf
```

```
        .WriteCGI rsUser("Address") + vbCrLf
        .WriteCGI "</TD></TR><TR><TH>City/State:</TH><TD>" + _
            vbCrLf
        .WriteCGI rsUser("CityState") + vbCrLf
        .WriteCGI "</TD></TR><TR><TH>Zip:</TH><TD>" + vbCrLf
        .WriteCGI rsUser("Zip") + vbCrLf
        .WriteCGI "</TD></TR><TR><TH>Email:</TH><TD>" + _
            vbCrLf
        .WriteCGI rsUser("Email") + vbCrLf
        .WriteCGI "</TD></TR><TR><TH>Phone:</TH><TD>" + _
            vbCrLf
        .WriteCGI rsUser("Phone") + vbCrLf


        ' print credit card information

        .WriteCGI "</TD></TR><TR><TH>Purchase date:</TH>_
            <TD>" + vbCrLf
        .WriteCGI rs("PurchaseDate")
        .WriteCGI "</TD></TR><TR><TH BGCOLOR=#00ffff>Credit _
            Card:</TH>"
        .WriteCGI "<TD BGCOLOR=#00ffff>" + vbCrLf
        .WriteCGI rs("CreditCard")
        .WriteCGI "</TD></TR><TR><TH _
            BGCOLOR=#00ffff>Expiration date:</TH>"
        .WriteCGI "<TD BGCOLOR=#00ffff>" + vbCrLf
        .WriteCGI rs("ExpirationDate")
        .WriteCGI "</TD></TABLE>"


    rsUser.Close
        .WriteCGI "<H1> Items ordered </H1>" + vbCrLf

    DisplayPurchaseInformation rs("OrderSession")
    End If

    rs.Close
        .WriteCGI "</BODY>" + vbCrLf
        .WriteCGI "</HTML>"
    End With
End Sub
```

Shopping Bag Administrator Screen Shots

Notes

The code for the shopping bag administration application has been placed in the same directory as Chapter 8's code in order to allow the applications to share the same database.

Figure 9.10 demonstrates the administrator page when connected to the server securely. Figure 9.11 demonstrates the same connection without security.

Figure 9.10
Secured shopping bag administrator page

Netscape - [Shopping Bag administration application]

File Edit View Go Bookmarks Options Directory Window Help

Location: https://1.0.0.1/chapter8/shoppingbagadmin.exe

What's New?   What's Cool?   Destinations   Net Search   People   Software

SECURED

User information

Full Name:	ofer laor
Address:	1234 Hidden ln #10991
City/State:	
Zip:	
Email:	
Phone:	
Purchase date:	02/28/97 10:54:20
Credit Card:	1234
Expiration date:	1234

Items ordered

roses	1		$2.00
		Total charge:	$2.00

Remove this purchase and proceed	Proceed without removing purchase

Document: Done

Figure 9.11
Non-secured shopping
bag administrator page

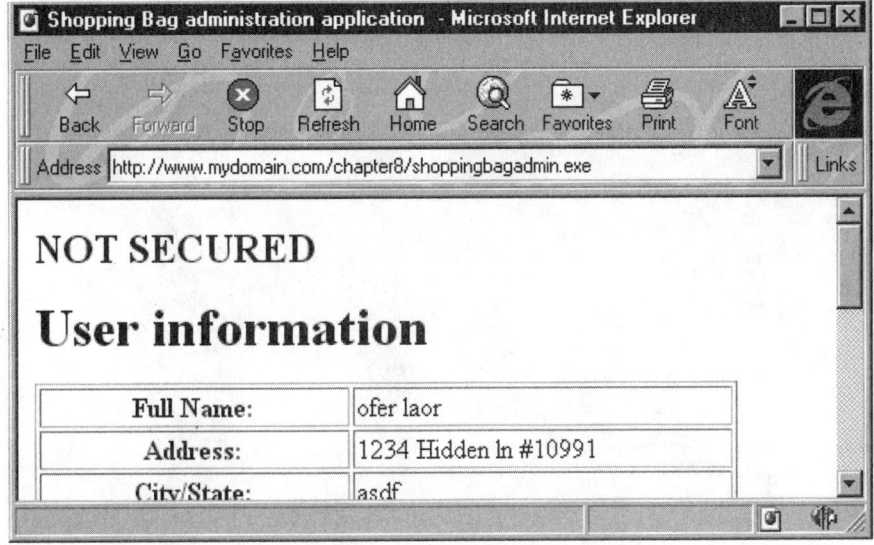

Summary

Having a secure site is a must. No experienced user orders anything from a non-secured site. Organizations dealing with sensitive information require security for most of their applications. With some of the tough export regulations are becoming more lax in recent years, better-secured sites are a requirement.

The reader should now be able to create remarkably complex applications for the web. Additional, non-traditional technologies can be added to the reader's application to make them more interactive. The next chapter deals with some of these technologies.

SHOPPING BAG, IMPROVED

- Adding categories and subcategories to the shopping bag
- Adding the capacity to order several items at a time
- Adding JavaScripts to the shopping bag
- Validation JavaScripts
- Iteration JavaScripts

WHAT'S WRONG WITH THE CURRENT SHOPPING BAG?

Nothing is really wrong with the current shopping bag implementation. Its design, however, can be much improved, and can include quite a few additions that allow users to order items easier and quicker.

First, the user should be able to select multiple items with one shot. In order to implement this, a new way of ordering files can be added. One way is by adding a checkbox to each of the displayed items. By default, this check box is turned off — if the user wants to purchase a number of items at once, she can do so by checking on the selected items and pressing a button. This adds the items to the shopping bag, after which the shopping bag contents are displayed, allowing the user to modify or review the quantity of each item.

The user should also be able to search for items using alternative methods. Keywords are hard to remember or come up with at times. This is especially true in situations where the database being searched has non-intuitive contents. In such cases, the user cannot find the item and purchase it, because he is limited to keyword searches.

But this can be resolved quite easily with the introduction of category and subcategory-based searches. Each item is assigned a category and subcategory. The user can now select items from a list in a given category/subcategory combination. This permits users to browse through the database without having to come up with keywords. Some types of shopping bags readily yield themselves to this type of implementation, while others still require keywords; therefore, the system easily implements *both* types of search concepts.

The user must be able to determine the price "on the fly" (he or she should be able to determine the price for a specific item, with a given quantity, without having to pick up a calculator). This requires implementation of some client side code. To do this, JavaScript can be utilized (it is, after all, much more universal than VB-Script), demonstrating how client-side scripts can be integrated into CGI applications.

Improvements, Improvements

First, the database has been modified in order to be able to search and index categories and subcategories. Two new tables have been added to the database to allow this to occur:

Table 10.1

The Shopping bag CATEGORIES table

Table: CATEGORIES

Field Name	Field Type	Remark
CategoryCode	AutoNumber (long integer)	Primary key: identifies record.
Category	Text(50)	Description of category.

Table 10.2

The Shopping bag SUBCATEGORIES table

Table: SUBCATEGORIES

Field Name	Field Type	Remark
SubCategoryCode	AutoNumber (long integer)	Primary key: identifies record.
CategoryCode	Long integer	Indexed (duplicates ok), Identifies the category to which this subcategory belongs.
SubCategory	Text(50)	Description of subcategory.

The SUBCATEGORIES table has its own unique identifier. This identifier is indexed in the DATA table. In order to link back to categories, each subcategory now contains an index to the category it belongs to.

In order to search through a specific category for all of the subcategories that belong to it:

```
Select * from SUBCATEGORIES where CategoryCode=1
```

The DATA table has been modified in the following manner:

Table 10.3

The Shopping bag modified DATA table

Table: DATA Field Name	Field Type	Remark
Key	AutoNumber (long integer)	Primary key: identifies record.
Title	Text(50)	Title of the item.
Data	Memo	Description of item (this is what we're searching through).
Price	Currency	Associated cost of item.
SubCategoryCode	Long integer	This is the code for the subcategory that this item belongs to.

DoSearch Subroutine

The search routines have been modified to account for the new changes. Both have been modified in the same way. For simplicity's sake, these changes are described only in the *DoSearch* subroutine context:

DoSearch now adds the subcategory code to order by. This groups together similar items, since the category and subcategory names are now displayed every time they change.

The *DoSearch* subroutine tracks the last subcategory code, and determines if it has changed between each item displayed. If it has, the *SearchRow* function is called with the *vTop* parameter set to TRUE. This causes *SearchRow* to add the category and subcategory descriptions for display.

SearchRow Function

The *SearchRow* function has been modified in two ways. First, when it is asked to display the top portion of the table (i.e., when the *vTop* parameter is set to TRUE), it now displays the Category and Subcategory descriptions for the current row. In addition, the function now adds a checkbox to each of the items shown, allowing the user to order several items using fewer mouse clicks.

A table has already been created to display the top portion of the search results. *SearchRow* first closes out the table definition from previous calls (be it *SearchRow* or the search routines that created it). Next, *SearchRow* determines the subcategory code for the current item, for which it will then determine the Category and Subcategory descriptions. This, the function displays in a new table. Once done with that, the function creates the actual top portion (or "caption") of the table.

The new table is created, and the text for the top portion added. The checkbox is added with the name of "Item#" (where # is the ItemCode for these items) with value ON.

The *SearchRow* function calls are encapsulated within a new form that submits data via the DOMASSORDER action. In order to submit this form and order a number of items at any given time, a SUBMIT button named **Order checked items** has been added after the last table was closed. Once this button is pressed, the entire form is submitted — allowing the *DoMassOrder* subroutine to add all of the selected items to the user's shopping bag.

DoMassOrder Subroutine

The *DoMassOrder* subroutine goes through the list of checkboxes and verifies that they are turned on; it then adds the items to the shopping bag and check out (displaying the shopping bag contents).

The browser will not return a checkbox name if it is not checked on. That means that an **OFF** checkbox will not even show up in the *cParameters* collection. Therefore, checking the **ON** value of the checkbox is not really necessary.

DoSearch Routines

The *DoSearch* and *DoSearchBack* routine also add a new concept: JavaScript code that will provide simple interaction with the user and simple validation. This is, in most cases, a perfect reason to use the JavaScript tool — its strength is in validation and simple interaction.

JavaScript

As yet, there is no official specification for JavaScript. The language was created primarily to tie up loose ends in Java applets and afford the end user simple interaction with a web page. Netscape's specification (on the Netscape web page) is version specific. Each version of Netscape's browser modifies the syntax and adds new functionality to this language. Unfortunately, this makes JavaScript applications hard to port between versions of browsers.

Microsoft's competing scripting language is identical to that of Netscape's in language structure. Similarly, Microsoft has produced subsequent releases to their JavaScript interpreter (Microsoft calls the language JScript, probably to prevent users from complaining of incompatibilities between Netscape's version of the language and their own). These releases attempted to clear the gap between Microsoft's JScript and Netscape's JavaScript.

Since Netscape has been the leader in implementing and using this language, Netscape's specification of JavaScript was used by Microsoft in the creation of JScript. Interestingly, due to this fact, Microsoft's implementation is often more in tune with Netscape's specification than Netscape themselves. On the other hand, Netscape's JavaScript version is more advanced and feature-rich than Microsoft's JScript.

In order to perform validation, the JavaScript specification provides an "OnClick" event for each button (including the submit buttons). This is useful when several submit buttons exist on the same form (all of which will submit the form to the same CGI application), each requiring its own particular validation routine. Alternatively, the entire form can be validated before submitting it via the "OnSubmit" event.

It should be noted that, in this author's tests, the JavaScript implementation in Netscape Navigator 2.x browsers did *not* allow the JavaScript code to stop the browser from submitting the form to the server. This prevented any real validation from taking place since, regardless of the validation results, the form was submitted anyway!

JavaScript code can exist in three locations when running on the client side (several JavaScript implementations executing on web servers can modify the HTML before it ever gets to the client — this includes Microsoft's Active Server Pages solution):

1. Within the event code

2. In a dedicated location in the HTML stream

3. In a separate .JS file that is loaded separately by the browser

All current JavaScript browsers support the first two options. The third option has been created so that advanced libraries of JavaScript code can be added to the system *without* requiring that all the routines be physically declared in the HTML stream.

For compatibility's sake, the shopping bag CGI application only uses the first two options. It should be noted, however, that the third option gives the programmer more freedom in modifying the JavaScript code, and significantly eases the developmental efforts on JavaScript intensive applications. Since a separate JavaScript file is easily implemented, the programmer should refer to a JavaScript reference book to see how the issue should be approached.

The JavaScript code for validating submission of the *DoSearch* and *DoSearchBack* subroutines is executed by the following statement:

```
OnClick="return AtLeastOneCheckBox();"
```

AtLeastOneCheckBox Function

This causes the browser to call the *AtLeastOneCheckBox* JavaScript function in order to validate the submission for that button. If the function determines that the browser cannot submit the form (for lack of validation), the function returns a **false** value. If the form *can* be submitted, the function returns a **true** value.

The *AtLeastOneCheckBox* validation function has been created in order to keep the browser from submitting the form when none of the checkboxes are checked on. The function simply returns true if it finds at least one check box that's turned on.

The *AtLeastOneCheckBox* JavaScript function is referenced by the OnClick event, and physically resides in a special "JavaScript" script section in the HTML stream. This section can exist anywhere, and is surrounded by the following tags:

```
<SCRIPT language="JavaScript">
<!—

                    Java Script Functions Here!


//—>
</SCRIPT>
```

Many such sections can be created; each of them can contain any number of JavaScript variables and functions. Because of this structure, non-JavaScript enabled browsers will ignore these tags.

For portability's sake, each of the JavaScript functions implemented in the Shopping Bag CGI application contains its own script tag section. Each such function starts with the Java word and returns a complete JavaScript section, containing the functions involved, with that functionality. These can be used together or apart.

The *AtLeastOneCheckBox* JavaScript function first determines the number of elements (or form controls) in the current form. It then determines whether the control's name starts with the text Item. Once it ascertains that an element is an Item checkbox, it will determine whether or not that checkbox is turned on. If it is, the FOR loop breaks and the function returns true (submitting the form is permitted). If the FOR loop does not find a valid checkbox, the function returns a **false** value (the browser cannot submit the form).

In determining the type of element, this code uses the name rather than element type. There are two reasons for this. First, this function can be useful when more than one set of check boxes need to be validated. Additionally, a complete lack of compatibility between browsers prevents a single code base from being used to determine the "TypeOf" a given element.

In this particular case, Microsoft's implementation, which came about much later than Netscape's, turns out to be closer to the specifications than Netscape's implementation.

The Microsoft Windows NT service Pack 2 (containing the IIS 3.0 and Active Server Pages) also contains a great JavaScript reference manual. This manual primarily covers the functionality of the language, whereas the script wizard in FrontPage 97 is a useful tool for determining objects, properties and events. Netscape's web site contains an additional, online JavaScript reference book that is fairly accurate, and contains a good reference on events in:

```
http://www.netscape.com/eng/mozilla/3.0/handbook/javascript/_
index.html
```

CheckAll Function

The *CheckAll* JavaScript function works in much the same way as *AtLeastOneCheckBox*. The *JavaCheckAll* Routine manages this script and adds it to the HTML stream. The function operates by iterating through the current form's controls, and locates Item checkboxes. Once found, the checked status of each such checkbox is modified to either *true* or *false* (depending on the *fCheckAll* parameter).

GetShoppingBag Function

The next modification in the shopping bag application is the *GetShoppingBag* function. This function has been modified to display an updated price edit box. The box changes as the user modifies the order quantity for each item. The price is calculated accordingly.

This is accomplished with the help of two JavaScript functions. Both are encapsulated in the *JavaNumberValidate* function.

Validate Function

The first JavaScript function is *Validate,* which determines whether or not the quantity text written by the user is a valid number. If it is not, the function converts that text into the number 1.

The *Dollar* JavaScript function rounds out the price to the nearest cent, and returns a dollar amount for the value of the text — similar to Visual Basic's Format$(myCurrency, "Currency").

The *GetShoppingBag* demonstrates how JavaScript code can be placed directly into a control's event. The Item edit boxes now contain an *OnChange* that will fire off when the contents of the edit box are changed by the user. This makes the contents of the quantity edit box equal to the "validated" value of what the user had written. Then, the equivalent price edit box (named BItem#, to prevent this edit box from being picked up in any way by the checkout routines) is modified to equal the item's price times the quantity.

The price edit box defaults to the currency value of the previous quantity (it defaults to one item if the user just ordered this item, but it may have been modified by the user beforehand). The maximum length is 1 character, the minimum number of characters that an edit box can be limited to (placing a 0 as the maximum length will not force any limit on the edit box contents). This makes it more difficult to change the contents manually. Upcoming specifications will allow read-only fields. But this is as close to it as current specifications allow.

The *OnChange* event for the price edit box has the exact same code, preventing the user from modifying the price edit box directly. In any case, even if this edit box is modified, the contents of the shopping bag are calculated again.

The *DoShowButtons* subroutine now adds a new "button" which jumps to the CGI application with ACTION = DOCATEGORIES.

DoCategories Subroutine

The *DoCategories* subroutine handles the call and displays a list of categories. It does this by creating a table containing 3 columns (changing the ITEMS_PER_LINE constant may modify the number of columns). Each item is surrounded with <A HREF> tags that will jump to the DOSUBCATEGORIES action, and also set the Category parameter to the current category value.

This approach allows the user to add graphics as needed.

There are a few other approaches — such as setting up localized (cellular) forms, each with a submit button that causes the requested category to be selected. Another alternative is to have a single form and multiple submit buttons. Yet another option is to have a single form and place check boxes next to each of the categories. This allows the user to view all of the subcategories from the selected categories.

The *DoSubCategories* subroutine works in much the same way. It does, however, submit the form to the DOITEMS action, and display subcategories for the given category code. It then passes the subcategory code for each of the displayed subcategories to the *DoItems* routine.

DoItems Subroutine

The *DoItems* subroutine is a simplified copy of the *DoSearch* routine. It bypasses some of the keyword specific information and simply displays items that qualify based on the Subcategory code. This subroutine uses *SearchRow* and the JavaScript codes in much the same way, to produce search results that are identical in functionality to the search engine. Similarly, the number of rows can be specified (as well as forward and backward traversal of the list) by modifying the code in a fashion similar to that of *DoSearch* and *DoSearchBack*.

Finally, the main routine has been slightly changed to utilize the Meta refresh tag when the oCGI library is being registered. This causes a message to be displayed for a second before the application is activated again. This time, the oCGI library is registered and everything will work. If the registration process fails for some reason, the error handler *RegisterOCGI2Err* is called and the application immediately terminates. This is instead of creating a "double fault," which would cause a message box to be displayed; which, in turn, might halt the web server process).

Following is the source code for the modified shopping bag application. Since the Utils and UserSecurity modules have not been changed, they will not be listed here again.

The SearchEngine5.bas Source Code

```
Option Explicit

Function DoError() As String
   Dim sOut As String

   sOut = "<HTML>" + vbCrLf
   sOut = sOut + "<HEADER><TITLE> Sample Search "
   sOut = sOut + " results</TITLE></HEADER>" + vbCrLf
   sOut = sOut + "<BODY BGCOLOR=#ffffff>" + vbCrLf
   sOut = sOut + "<H2> Error: matching option was "
   sOut = sOut + " not selected correctly </H2>"
   sOut = sOut + "</BODY></HTML>"

   DoError = sOut
End Function


Function DoAnd(sColumns As String, sFrom As String, _
         sData As String, sSearchCol As String, sKeyCol _
         As String, nRows As Variant, sFirstRow As _
             String, fBackwards As Boolean, cKeywords As _
             Collection) As String

   Dim sQuery As String

   sQuery = "select TOP " + CStr(nRows + 1)
   sQuery = sQuery + " " + sColumns + " from " + sFrom + " _
         WHERE 1=1 "
```

```
    If (sFirstRow <> "") Then
        sQuery = sQuery + " AND (" + sKeyCol + IIf(fBackwards, _
            "<=", ">=")
        sQuery = sQuery + CStr(ToInt(sFirstRow)) + ") "
    End If

    Dim iPos As Integer
    Do While (1)
      If (Trim$(sData) = "") Then Exit Do
      If (Left$(sData, 1) = """") Then
        sData = Mid$(sData, 2)
        iPos = InStr(sData, """")
      Else
        iPos = InStr(sData, " ")
      End If

      Dim sWord As String

      If iPos <= 0 Then
        sWord = sData
        iPos = Len(sWord)
      Else
        sWord = Left$(sData, iPos - 1)
      End If

      cKeywords.Add sWord

      sQuery = sQuery + "AND INSTR(" + sSearchCol + ",'"
      sQuery = sQuery + DoubleQuote(sWord) + "') "

      sData = Mid$(sData, iPos + 1)
    Loop

    sQuery = sQuery + " ORDER BY " + sKeyCol
    sQuery = sQuery + IIf(fBackwards, " DESC", " ASC")
    DoAnd = sQuery
End Function

Function DoOr(sColumns As String, sFrom As String, _
            sData As String, sSearchCol As String, sKeyCol _
            As String, nRows As Variant, sFirstRow As _
```

```
                        String, sFirstInStr As String, cKeywords _
                            As Collection) As String


    ' now create instr counter.
    Dim sInStr As String
    Dim iPos As Integer
    sInStr = "(0"
    Do While (1)
      If (Trim$(sData) = "") Then Exit Do
      If (Left$(sData, 1) = """") Then
        sData = Mid$(sData, 2)
        iPos = InStr(sData, """")
      Else
        iPos = InStr(sData, " ")
      End If

      Dim sWord As String

      If iPos <= 0 Then
        sWord = sData
        iPos = Len(sWord)
      Else
        sWord = Left$(sData, iPos - 1)
      End If

      cKeywords.Add sWord

      sInStr = sInStr + "+IIF(INSTR(" + sSearchCol + ",'"
      sInStr = sInStr + DoubleQuote(sWord) + "')>0,1,0)"

      sData = Mid$(sData, iPos + 1)
    Loop
    sInStr = sInStr + ")"

    Dim sQuery As String
    sQuery = "select TOP " + CStr(nRows + 1) + " "
    sQuery = sQuery + sInStr + " as ISINSTR,"
    sQuery = sQuery + " " + sColumns + " from " + sFrom + " _
            WHERE "
    sQuery = sQuery + " (" + sInStr + ">0)"
```

```vb
      If (sFirstRow <> "") Then
         sQuery = sQuery + " AND (" + sKeyCol + ">="
         sQuery = sQuery + CStr(ToInt(sFirstRow)) + ") "
      End If
      If (sFirstInStr <> "") Then
         sQuery = sQuery + " AND (" + sInStr + "<="
         sQuery = sQuery + CStr(ToInt(sFirstInStr)) + ") "
      End If

      sQuery = sQuery + " ORDER BY (" + sInStr + ") DESC"
      sQuery = sQuery + "," + sKeyCol + " ASC"
      DoOr = sQuery
End Function


Function DoEntire(sColumns As String, sFrom As String, _
          sKeywords As String, sSearchCol As String, _
            sKeyCol As String, nRows As Integer, sFirstRow _
              As String, fBackwards As Boolean, cKeywords _
                As Collection) As String

    Dim sQuery As String

    'check for quotes
    sKeywords = RemoveDoubleQuotes(sKeywords)

    cKeywords.Add sKeywords

    sQuery = "select TOP " + CStr(nRows + 1) + " "
    sQuery = sQuery + sColumns + " from " + sFrom
    sQuery = sQuery + " WHERE INSTR(" + sSearchCol + ",'"
    sQuery = sQuery + DoubleQuote(sKeywords) + "') "
    If (sFirstRow <> "") Then
      sQuery = sQuery + " and " + sKeyCol + IIf(fBackwards, _
           "<=", ">=")
      sQuery = sQuery + CStr(ToInt(sFirstRow))
    End If

    sQuery = sQuery + " ORDER BY " + sKeyCol
    sQuery = sQuery + IIf(fBackwards, " DESC", " ASC")
    DoEntire = sQuery
End Function
```

```
Function MakeBold(ByVal sMakeBold As String, cKeywords As _
        Collection) As String
  ' make each found keyword in this thing bold.
  Dim cStart As New Collection, cLength As New Collection
  Dim sWord As Variant, iPos As Integer

  For Each sWord In cKeywords
    ' now locate the first instance of sWord in sMakeBold
    Dim iPosMakeBold As Integer

    iPosMakeBold = InStr(sMakeBold, sWord)
    If (iPosMakeBold > 0) Then
      cStart.Add iPosMakeBold
      cLength.Add Len(sWord)
    End If
  Next
  ' all of this is to prevent the search from locating
  ' - stuff in the modified string!

  ' now loop and implement modifications.
  Dim i As Integer, iSmallestPosition As Integer
  Dim sOut As String, iLastEnd As Integer
  iLastEnd = 1
  Do While (cStart.Count > 0)
    ' look for the smallest position.
    iSmallestPosition = 1
    For i = 2 To cStart.Count
      If (cStart.item(i) < cStart.item(iSmallestPosition)) _
          Then
        iSmallestPosition = i
      End If
    Next

    Dim iStart As Integer, iLen As Integer
    iStart = cStart.item(iSmallestPosition)
    iLen = cLength.item(iSmallestPosition)
    If (iStart < iLastEnd) Then
      iStart = iLastEnd
    End If
    sOut = sOut + Mid$(sMakeBold, iLastEnd, iStart - _
        iLastEnd)
```

```
        sOut = sOut + "<FONT COLOR=RED>"
        If (iLastEnd < iStart + iLen) Then
          iLastEnd = iStart + iLen
        End If
        sOut = sOut + Mid$(sMakeBold, iStart, iLastEnd - _
              iStart)
        sOut = sOut + "</FONT>"

        ' kill this collection item!
        cStart.Remove iSmallestPosition
        cLength.Remove iSmallestPosition
    Loop

    ' add everything else!
    sOut = sOut + Mid$(sMakeBold, iLastEnd)

    MakeBold = sOut
End Function



Function NextBunch(sFirstRow As String, sTopRows As String, _
        sIsInstr As String)

    Dim sOut As String
    With cgi
        sOut = sOut + "<FORM ACTION=""" + .ReadScriptName
        sOut = sOut + """ METHOD=""POST"">" + vbCrLf
        sOut = sOut + "<INPUT TYPE=HIDDEN NAME=""ACTION"" "
        sOut = sOut + " VALUE=""DOSEARCH"">" + vbCrLf
        sOut = sOut + "<INPUT TYPE=HIDDEN NAME=""KeyWords"" "
        sOut = sOut + "VALUE=""" + ReadScrambledParam _
              ("KeyWords")
        sOut = sOut + """>" + vbCrLf
        sOut = sOut + "<INPUT TYPE=HIDDEN NAME=""Match"" "
        sOut = sOut + " VALUE=""" + cgi.ReadParam("Match")
        sOut = sOut + """>" + vbCrLf
        sOut = sOut + "<INPUT TYPE=HIDDEN NAME=""TopRows"" "
        sOut = sOut + " VALUE=""" + sTopRows + """>" + vbCrLf
        sOut = sOut + "<INPUT TYPE=HIDDEN NAME=""FirstRow"" _
              VALUE= "
        sOut = sOut + sFirstRow + ">" + vbCrLf
```

```
        If (sIsInstr <> "") Then
          sOut = sOut + "<INPUT TYPE=HIDDEN NAME=""IsInstr"" _
             VALUE= "
          sOut = sOut + sIsInstr + ">" + vbCrLf
        End If


        sOut = sOut + "<INPUT TYPE=Submit NAME=Submit "
        sOut = sOut + " VALUE=""View the next "
        sOut = sOut + sTopRows + " rows "">" + vbCrLf
        sOut = sOut + "</FORM>" + vbCrLf
      End With


      NextBunch = sOut
    End Function


    Function PrevBunch(sLastRow As String, sTopRows As String)

      Dim sOut As String
      With cgi
        sOut = sOut + "<FORM ACTION=""" + .ReadScriptName
        sOut = sOut + """ METHOD=""POST"">" + vbCrLf
        sOut = sOut + "<INPUT TYPE=HIDDEN NAME=""ACTION"" "
        sOut = sOut + " VALUE=""DOSEARCHBACK"">" + vbCrLf
        sOut = sOut + "<INPUT TYPE=HIDDEN NAME=""KeyWords"" "
        sOut = sOut + "VALUE=""" + ReadScrambledParam _
             ("KeyWords")
        sOut = sOut + """>" + vbCrLf
        sOut = sOut + "<INPUT TYPE=HIDDEN NAME=""Match"" "
        sOut = sOut + " VALUE=""" + cgi.ReadParam("Match")
        sOut = sOut + """>" + vbCrLf
        sOut = sOut + "<INPUT TYPE=HIDDEN NAME=""TopRows"" "
        sOut = sOut + " VALUE=""" + sTopRows + """>" + vbCrLf
        sOut = sOut + "<INPUT TYPE=HIDDEN NAME=""LastRow"" _
             VALUE= "
        sOut = sOut + sLastRow + ">" + vbCrLf


        sOut = sOut + "<INPUT TYPE=Submit NAME=Submit"
        sOut = sOut + " VALUE=""View the previous "
        sOut = sOut + sTopRows + " rows "">" + vbCrLf
        sOut = sOut + "</FORM>" + vbCrLf
      End With
```

```
        PrevBunch = sOut
    End Function

    Sub DoSearch()
        ' max number of rows that a query returns.
        Dim TOP_ROWS As Integer

        Dim sQuery As String, sOut As String
        With cgi
            ' first break down the parameters.
            Dim sKeywords As String, sFirstRow As String
            Dim sFirstInStr As String
            sKeywords = .ReadParam("KeyWords")

            If (Trim$(sKeywords) <> "") Then
                .WriteVirtualCookie "Keywords", sKeywords
            End If

            TOP_ROWS = ToInt(cgi.ReadParam("TopRows"))
            If (TOP_ROWS < 1) Then
                TOP_ROWS = 10
            End If

            'prevent empty search
            If (Trim$(sKeywords) = "") Then
                DoShowSearch
                Exit Sub
            End If

            sFirstRow = .ReadParam("FirstRow")
            sFirstInStr = .ReadParam("IsInstr")

            Dim cKeywords As Collection
            Set cKeywords = New Collection
            Select Case .ReadParam("Match")
                Case "A" ' and
                    sQuery = DoAnd("*", "DATA", sKeywords, "Data", _
                        "Key", TOP_ROWS, sFirstRow, False, cKeywords)
                Case "E" ' Entire
                    sQuery = DoEntire("*", "DATA", sKeywords, "Data",_
                        "Key", TOP_ROWS, sFirstRow, False, cKeywords)
```

```
      Case "O" ' or
        sQuery = DoOr("*", "DATA", sKeywords, "Data",_
          "Key", TOP_ROWS, sFirstRow, sFirstInStr, _
            cKeywords)
      Case Else ' error
        sOut = DoError
        .WriteCGI sOut
        Exit Sub
  End Select


  Dim rs As Recordset
  Set rs = db.OpenRecordset(sQuery + ",SubCategoryCode _
        ASC", dbOpenDynaset)


  sOut = SearchTop


  Dim iRows As Integer, fNextBunch As Boolean
  iRows = 0
  fNextBunch = False
  If rs.EOF Then
    sOut = sOut + "<H3>Search did not retrieve any _
        rows</H3>" + vbCrLf
  Else
    Dim sTopRow As String, sTopIsInstr As String
    rs.MoveFirst
    sOut = sOut + "<H3>Search resulted in the following _
        items</H3>"

    ' mass ordering
    sOut = sOut + "<FORM METHOD=POST ACTION="""
    sOut = sOut + .ReadScriptName + """>" + vbCrLf
    sOut = sOut + "<INPUT TYPE=HIDDEN NAME=ACTION "
    sOut = sOut + "VALUE=""DOMASSORDER"">" + vbCrLf

    ' this will be corrected by search row!
    sOut = sOut + vbCrLf + "<TABLE BORDER=0>" + vbCrLf
    sOut = sOut + SearchRow(rs, cKeywords, True)
    Dim SubCategory As Integer
    SubCategory = rs("SubCategoryCode")


    Do While Not rs.EOF
```

```
          iRows = iRows + 1
          If iRows <= TOP_ROWS Then
            ' show category/subcategory codes?
            If (SubCategory <> rs("SubCategoryCode")) Then
              sOut = sOut + SearchRow(rs, cKeywords, True)
              SubCategory = rs("SubCategoryCode")
            End If


            sOut = sOut + SearchRow(rs, cKeywords)
          Else ' last row - instead, put up a next + _
              TOP_ROWS + button
            sTopRow = CStr(rs("Key"))
            If (.ReadParam("Match") = "O") Then
              sTopIsInstr = CStr(rs("ISINSTR"))
            Else
              sTopIsInstr = ""
            End If
            fNextBunch = True
            Exit Do
          End If
          rs.MoveNext
        Loop
        sOut = sOut + "</TABLE>"


        ' mass order
        sOut = sOut + "<BR><CENTER>"
        sOut = sOut + "<INPUT TYPE=SUBMIT NAME=SUBMIT"
        sOut = sOut + " VALUE=""Order checked items"""
        sOut = sOut + " OnClick=""return AtLeastOneCheckBox _
          ();"">"
        sOut = sOut + "<INPUT TYPE=BUTTON NAME=ALLON _
            VALUE=""Select all"""
        sOut = sOut + " OnClick=""return CheckAll(true);"">"
        sOut = sOut + "<INPUT TYPE=BUTTON NAME=ALLOFF _
            VALUE=""Unselect all"""
        sOut = sOut + " OnClick=""return CheckAll(false);"">"


        sOut = sOut + "</CENTER></FORM>" + vbCrLf
        sOut = sOut + JavaAtLeastOneCheckBox
        sOut = sOut + JavaCheckAll
```

```
            sOut = sOut + "<TABLE BORDER=0><TR>"
            If (sFirstRow <> "" And .ReadParam("Match") <> "0") _
                Then
                rs.MoveFirst
                sOut = sOut + "<TD>"
                sOut = sOut + PrevBunch(CStr(rs("Key")), _
                    CStr(TOP_ROWS)) + "</TD>"
            End If
            If (fNextBunch) Then
                sOut = sOut + "<TD>" + NextBunch(sTopRow, _
                    CStr(TOP_ROWS), sTopIsInstr) + "</TD>"
            End If
            sOut = sOut + "</TR></TABLE>"
        End If

        sOut = sOut + SearchBottom
        cgi.WriteCGI sOut
        rs.Close
    End With
End Sub


'THIS WILL NOT WORK WITH FORWARD ONLY RECORDSETS!
Sub DoSearchBack()
    ' max number of rows that a query returns.
    Dim TOP_ROWS As Integer

    Dim sQuery As String, sOut As String
    With cgi
        ' first break down the parameters.
        Dim sKeywords As String, sLastRow As String
        Dim sFirstInStr As String

        sKeywords = .ReadParam("KeyWords")

        TOP_ROWS = ToInt(cgi.ReadParam("TopRows"))
        If (TOP_ROWS < 1) Then
            TOP_ROWS = 10
        End If

        'prevent empty search
        If (Trim$(sKeywords) = "") Then
```

```
        DoShowSearch
        Exit Sub
    End If

    sLastRow = .ReadParam("LastRow")

Dim cKeywords As Collection
Set cKeywords = New Collection
Select Case .ReadParam("Match")
   Case "A" ' and
       sQuery = DoAnd("*", "DATA", sKeywords, "Data", _
          "Key", TOP_ROWS + 1, sLastRow, True, cKeywords)
   Case "E" ' Entire
       sQuery = DoEntire("*", "DATA", sKeywords, "Data",_
          "Key", TOP_ROWS + 1, sLastRow, True, cKeywords)
   Case Else ' error
       sOut = DoError
       .WriteCGI sOut
       Exit Sub
End Select

Dim rs As Recordset
Set rs = db.OpenRecordset(sQuery + ",SubCategoryCode _
      ASC", dbOpenDynaset)
sOut = SearchTop
Dim iRows As Integer, fPrevBunch As Boolean
iRows = 0
fPrevBunch = False
If rs.EOF Then
   sOut = sOut + "<H3>Search did not retrieve any _
      rows</H3>" + vbCrLf
Else
   Dim sBottomRow As String
   rs.MoveLast
   If (rs.RecordCount > (TOP_ROWS + 1)) Then
      fPrevBunch = True
      rs.MovePrevious
   End If

   sBottomRow = CStr(rs("Key"))
   sOut = sOut + "<H3>Search resulted in _
```

```
        the following items</H3>"

' mass ordering
sOut = sOut + "<FORM METHOD=POST ACTION="""
sOut = sOut + .ReadScriptName + """>" + vbCrLf
sOut = sOut + "<INPUT TYPE=HIDDEN NAME=ACTION "
sOut = sOut + "VALUE=""DOMASSORDER"">" + vbCrLf


' this will be corrected by Search row.
sOut = sOut + vbCrLf + "<TABLE BORDER=0>" + vbCrLf
sOut = sOut + SearchRow(rs, cKeywords, True)
Dim SubCategory As Integer
SubCategory = rs("SubCategoryCode")
Do While Not rs.BOF
  iRows = iRows + 1
  If iRows <= (TOP_ROWS + 1) Then
    If (iRows <= TOP_ROWS) Then
      ' show category/subcategory codes?
      If (SubCategory <> rs("SubCategoryCode")) Then
        sOut = sOut + SearchRow(rs, cKeywords, True)
        SubCategory = rs("SubCategoryCode")
      End If

      sOut = sOut + SearchRow(rs, cKeywords, False)
    End If
  Else
    Exit Do
  End If
  rs.MovePrevious
Loop
sOut = sOut + "</TABLE>"

' mass order
' mass order
sOut = sOut + "<BR><CENTER>"
sOut = sOut + "<INPUT TYPE=SUBMIT NAME=SUBMIT "
sOut = sOut + "VALUE=""Order checked items"""
sOut = sOut + " OnClick=""return _
    AtLeastOneCheckBox();"">"
sOut = sOut + "<INPUT TYPE=BUTTON NAME=ALLON _
    VALUE=""Select all"""
```

```
                              sOut = sOut + " OnClick=""return CheckAll(true);"">"
                              sOut = sOut + "<INPUT TYPE=BUTTON NAME=ALLOFF _
                                  VALUE=""Unselect all"""
                              sOut = sOut + " OnClick=""return CheckAll(false);"">"
                              sOut = sOut + "</CENTER></FORM>" + vbCrLf
                              sOut = sOut + JavaAtLeastOneCheckBox
                              sOut = sOut + JavaCheckAll

                              sOut = sOut + "<TABLE BORDER=0><TR>"
                              If (fPrevBunch) Then
                                sOut = sOut + "<TD>" + PrevBunch(sBottomRow, _
                                  CStr(TOP_ROWS))
                                sOut = sOut + "</TD>"
                              End If
                              If (sLastRow <> "") Then
                                rs.MoveFirst
                                sOut = sOut + "<TD>" + NextBunch(CStr(rs("Key")), _
                                  CStr(TOP_ROWS), "")
                                sOut = sOut + "</TD>"
                              End If
                              sOut = sOut + "</TR></TABLE>"
                          End If

                          sOut = sOut + SearchBottom
                          cgi.WriteCGI sOut
                          rs.Close
                      End With
                  End Sub

                  Sub DoShowSearch()
                      With cgi
                          Dim sOut As String

                          sOut = "<HTML>" + vbCrLf
                          sOut = sOut + "<HEADER></HEADER>" + vbCrLf
                          sOut = sOut + "<BODY BGCOLOR=#ffffff>" + vbCrLf
                          sOut = sOut + "<H2> Search for items </H2>" + vbCrLf
                          sOut = sOut + "Enter your search keywords here:<P><HR>" _
                                  + vbCrLf

                          sOut = sOut + "<FORM ACTION=""" + .ReadScriptName + """ _
```

```
                                    METHOD="""POST""">"
                sOut = sOut + "<INPUT TYPE="""HIDDEN""" NAME="""ACTION""" _
                       VALUE="""DOSEARCH""">"
                sOut = sOut + vbCrLf + "<TABLE><TR><TD>"
                sOut = sOut + "<B>Search for:</B></TD><TD></TD><TD>_
                       <INPUT TYPE=TEXT SIZE=20 "
                sOut = sOut + " MAXLENGTH=100 NAME="""KeyWords""" "
                sOut = sOut + "VALUE=""" + .ReadCookie("Keywords") + _
                       """ > "
                sOut = sOut + "</TD></TR><TR><TD><INPUT TYPE="""RADIO""" _
                       CHECKED "
                sOut = sOut + "NAME="""Match""" VALUE="""E""">Exact Match"
                sOut = sOut + "</TD><TD><INPUT TYPE="""RADIO""" _
                       NAME="""Match""" VALUE="""A""">And"
                sOut = sOut + "</TD><TD><INPUT TYPE="""RADIO""" _
                       NAME="""Match""" VALUE="""O""">Or"
                sOut = sOut + "</TD></TR><TR><TD><P><INPUT TYPE=Submit "
                sOut = sOut + " NAME="""Submit""" VALUE="""Search""">"
                sOut = sOut + "</TD><TD># rows shown:"
                sOut = sOut + "</TD><TD><select name="""TopRows""" > "
                sOut = sOut + "<option SELECTED>5</option>"
                sOut = sOut + "<option>10</option>"
                sOut = sOut + "<option>20</option>"
                sOut = sOut + "<option>50</option></select>"
                sOut = sOut + "</TD></TR></TABLE> </FORM>"
                sOut = sOut + "<HR>"

                sOut = sOut + "</BODY>" + vbCrLf
                sOut = sOut + "</HTML>"


            .WriteCGI sOut
        End With
    End Sub

    Function SearchBottom() As String
        SearchBottom = "</BODY></HTML>"
    End Function

    Function SearchRow(rs As Recordset, cKeywords As _
                Collection, Optional vTop As Variant)
        Dim sOut As String, fTop As Boolean
```

```
fTop = False
If Not IsMissing(vTop) Then fTop = vTop

sOut = "<TR>"
If (fTop) Then
  ' category/SubCategory information!
  Dim rsCategory As Recordset, sSQL As String
  sSQL = "select * from CATEGORIES, SUBCATEGORIES where"
  sSQL = sSQL + " CATEGORIES.CategoryCode=_
         SUBCATEGORIES.CategoryCode "
  sSQL = sSQL + " and SUBCATEGORIES.SubCategoryCode="
  sSQL = sSQL + CStr(rs("SubCategoryCode"))
  Set rsCategory = db.OpenRecordset(sSQL)

  sOut = sOut + vbCrLf + "</TABLE><CENTER>"
  sOut = sOut + vbCrLf + "<TABLE BORDER=0 WIDTH=80%>"
  sOut = sOut + vbCrLf + "<TR><TH WIDTH=50% _
         BGCOLOR=#00bbbb ALIGN=CENTER>"
  sOut = sOut + vbCrLf + CheckNull(rsCategory_
         ("Category"),"") + "</TH>"
  sOut = sOut + vbCrLf + "<TH WIDTH=50% BGCOLOR=#00bbbb _
         ALIGN=CENTER>"
  sOut = sOut + vbCrLf + CheckNull(rsCategory_
         ("SubCategory"), "") + "</TH>"
  rsCategory.Close

  sOut = sOut + vbCrLf + "</TR></TABLE>"
  sOut = sOut + vbCrLf + "</CENTER><TABLE BORDER=_
         1 WIDTH=100%>"

  sOut = sOut + vbCrLf + "<TD></TD>"
  sOut = sOut + vbCrLf + "<TH WIDTH=20%>"
  sOut = sOut + "Item name"
  sOut = sOut + "</TH>"
Else
  ' mass ordering
  sOut = sOut + "<TD>" + vbCrLf
  sOut = sOut + "<INPUT TYPE=CHECKBOX NAME=""Item"
  sOut = sOut + CStr(rs("Key")) + """ VALUE=ON>"
  sOut = sOut + "</TD>" + vbCrLf
```

```
         sOut = sOut + vbCrLf + "<TD WIDTH=20%>"
         sOut = sOut + "<A HREF=""" + cgi.ReadScriptName
         sOut = sOut + "?ACTION=DOADDITEM&ITEM=" + CStr_
               (rs("Key")) + """>"

         sOut = sOut + rs("Title")


         sOut = sOut + "</A>"
         sOut = sOut + "</TD>"
      End If
      sOut = sOut + vbCrLf
      If (fTop) Then
         sOut = sOut + "<TH WIDTH=70%>Item description</TH>" + _
               vbCrLf
      Else
         sOut = sOut + "<TD WIDTH=70%>"
         If cKeywords.Count = 0 Then
            sOut = sOut + CheckNull(rs("Data"), "")
         Else
            sOut = sOut + MakeBold(rs("Data"), cKeywords)
         End If
         sOut = sOut + "</TD>" + vbCrLf
      End If
      If (fTop) Then
         sOut = sOut + vbCrLf
         sOut = sOut + "<TH ALIGN=RIGHT BGCOLOR=#00ffff _
               WIDTH=10%>Price</TH>"
      Else
         sOut = sOut + vbCrLf
         sOut = sOut + "<TD ALIGN=RIGHT BGCOLOR=#00ffff _
               WIDTH=10%>"
         sOut = sOut + Format$(CheckNull(rs("Price"), ""), _
               "Currency")
         sOut = sOut + "</TD>" + vbCrLf
      End If
      sOut = sOut + "</TR>"

      SearchRow = sOut
   End Function


   Function SearchTop() As String
```

```
            Dim sOut As String

            sOut = "<HTML>" + vbCrLf
            sOut = sOut + "<HEADER><TITLE> Search results</TITLE>"
            sOut = sOut + " </HEADER>" + vbCrLf
            sOut = sOut + "<BODY BGCOLOR=#ffffff>" + vbCrLf
            sOut = sOut + "<H2>Search results</H2><HR>" + vbCrLf

            SearchTop = sOut
        End Function
```

The ShoppingBag2.bas Source Code

```
        Option Explicit

        Declare Function oCGI2Register Lib "oCGI2.dll" Alias _
                "DllRegisterServer" () As Long

        Public cgi As oCGI2
        Public db As Database

        Const COOKIE_TTL = 14 ' cookies will persist for 14 days.

        Const ITEMS_PER_LINE = 3

        Sub AddShoppingBagItem(sKey As String, nQuantity As Integer)
          With cgi
            Dim sName As String
            If (InStr(sKey, "Item") = 1) Then
              sName = sKey
            Else
              sName = "Item" + sKey
            End If
            .WriteVirtualCookie sName, CStr(nQuantity)

            ' add to current cookie list...
            ' — so that it shows up in this session too!
            If .ReadCookie(sName) = "" Then
              Dim pParam As ParamType
```

```
            Set pParam = New ParamType

            pParam.Name = sName
            pParam.Value = CStr(nQuantity)
            .cCookies.Add item:=pParam, Key:=sName
        End If
    End With
End Sub


Sub ClearShoppingBag()
    ' loop through the virtual cookie list
    ' kill anything that starts with Item*
    With cgi
        Dim item As Object, i As Integer
        i = 1
        Do While (True)
            If (i > .cCookies.Count) Then Exit Do
            Set item = .cCookies.item(i)
            If (InStr(item.Name, "Item") = 1) Then ' has to be _
                the beginning.

                ' shopping bag item. Delete by setting expiration _
                  to two weeks back!
                .DeleteVirtualCookie item.Name, item.Value
                .cCookies.Remove i
                 i = 1
            End If
            i = i + 1
        Loop
    End With
End Sub


Sub DoAddItem()
    With cgi
        Dim sOut As String
        sOut = "<HTML>" + vbCrLf
        sOut = sOut + "<HEAD>" + NoCache + "</HEAD>" + vbCrLf
        sOut = sOut + "<BODY BGCOLOR=#ffdd99>" + vbCrLf
        sOut = sOut + "<H2> Shopping bag contents after item _
                addition<HR></H2>"
        sOut = sOut + vbCrLf
```

```
                    ' add the single item to teh shopping bag
                    AddShoppingBagItem .ReadParam("ITEM"), 1
                    ' now display the contents for the shopping bag
                    sOut = sOut + GetShoppingBag

                    .WriteCGI sOut + "</BODY>" + vbCrLf
                    .WriteCGI "</HTML>"
            End With
        End Sub


        Sub DoCategories()
            With cgi
                Dim sOut As String
                sOut = "<HTML>" + vbCrLf
                sOut = sOut + "<HEAD>" + NoCache + "</HEAD>" + vbCrLf
                sOut = sOut + "<BODY BGCOLOR=#ffdd99>" + vbCrLf
                sOut = sOut + "<H2> The following Categories are _
                        available<HR></H2>" + vbCrLf
                sOut = sOut + "<TABLE BORDER=1 WIDTH=90%>" + vbCrLf

                Dim rsCategories As Recordset
                Set rsCategories = db.OpenRecordset("CATEGORIES")
                Dim iPos As Integer
                iPos = 0
                Do While Not rsCategories.EOF
                    If (iPos Mod ITEMS_PER_LINE) = 0 Then
                        If iPos <> 0 Then sOut = sOut + "</TR>"

                        sOut = sOut + "<TR>"
                    End If
                    sOut = sOut + "<TD WIDTH=" + CStr(100 \ ITEMS_PER_LINE) _
                        + "%>"
                    sOut = sOut + "<A HREF=""" + cgi.ReadScriptName
                    sOut = sOut + "?ACTION=DOSUBCATEGORIES&Category="
                    sOut = sOut + CStr(rsCategories("CategoryCode")) + _
                        """>"
                    sOut = sOut + CheckNull(rsCategories("Category"), "")
                    sOut = sOut + "</A></TD>"
                    iPos = iPos + 1
                    rsCategories.MoveNext
                Loop
```

```
            sOut = sOut + "</TABLE>" + vbCrLf
            rsCategories.Close

            .WriteCGI sOut + "</BODY>" + vbCrLf
            .WriteCGI "</HTML>"
        End With
    End Sub

    Sub DoSubCategories()
        With cgi
            Dim sOut As String
            sOut = "<HTML>" + vbCrLf
            sOut = sOut + "<HEAD>" + NoCache + "</HEAD>" + vbCrLf
            sOut = sOut + "<BODY BGCOLOR=#ffdd99>" + vbCrLf
            sOut = sOut + "<H2> The following Sub Categories are _
                available<HR></H2>"
            sOut = sOut + vbCrLf
            sOut = sOut + "<TABLE BORDER=1 WIDTH=90%>" + vbCrLf

            Dim rsSubCategories As Recordset, sSQL As String
            sSQL = "select * from SUBCATEGORIES where _
                CategoryCode="
            sSQL = sSQL + .ReadParam("Category")
            Set rsSubCategories = db.OpenRecordset(sSQL)
            Dim iPos As Integer
            iPos = 0
            Do While Not rsSubCategories.EOF
                If (iPos Mod ITEMS_PER_LINE) = 0 Then
                    If iPos <> 0 Then sOut = sOut + "</TR>"

                    sOut = sOut + "<TR>"
                End If
                sOut = sOut + "<TD WIDTH=" + CStr(100 \ _
                    ITEMS_PER_LINE) + "%>"
                sOut = sOut + "<A HREF=""" + cgi.ReadScriptName
                sOut = sOut + "?ACTION=DOITEMS&SubCategory="
                sOut = sOut + CStr(rsSubCategories _
                    ("SubCategoryCode")) + """>"
                sOut = sOut + CheckNull(rsSubCategories _
                    ("SubCategory"), "")
                sOut = sOut + "</A></TD>"
```

```
            iPos = iPos + 1
            rsSubCategories.MoveNext
        Loop

        sOut = sOut + "</TABLE>" + vbCrLf
        rsSubCategories.Close

        .WriteCGI sOut + "</BODY>" + vbCrLf
        .WriteCGI "</HTML>"
    End With
End Sub

Sub DoItems()
    With cgi
        Dim rs As Recordset, sQuery As String, sOut As String
        sQuery = "select * from DATA where SubCategoryCode="
        sQuery = sQuery + .ReadParam("SubCategory")
        Set rs = db.OpenRecordset(sQuery, dbOpenDynaset)

        sOut = SearchTop
        Dim cKeywords As Collection
        Set cKeywords = New Collection

        Dim iRows As Integer, fNextBunch As Boolean
        iRows = 0
        fNextBunch = False
        If rs.EOF Then
            sOut = sOut + "<H3>Search did not retrieve any _
                rows</H3>" + vbCrLf
        Else
            Dim sTopRow As String, sTopIsInstr As String
            rs.MoveFirst
            sOut = sOut + "<H3>Search resulted in the following _
                items</H3>"

            ' mass ordering
            sOut = sOut + "<FORM METHOD=POST ACTION="""
            sOut = sOut + .ReadScriptName + """>" + vbCrLf
            sOut = sOut + "<INPUT TYPE=HIDDEN NAME=ACTION _
                VALUE=""DOMASSORDER"">"
            sOut = sOut + vbCrLf
```

```
      sOut = sOut + vbCrLf + "<TABLE BORDER=1 WIDTH=100%>" _
         + vbCrLf


      sOut = sOut + SearchRow(rs, cKeywords, True)
      Dim SubCategory As Integer
      SubCategory = rs("SubCategoryCode")


      Do While Not rs.EOF
         ' show category/subcategory codes?
         If (SubCategory <> rs("SubCategoryCode")) Then
            sOut = sOut + SearchRow(rs, cKeywords, True)
            SubCategory = rs("SubCategoryCode")
         End If

         sOut = sOut + SearchRow(rs, cKeywords)
         rs.MoveNext
      Loop
      sOut = sOut + "</TABLE>"


      ' mass order
      sOut = sOut + "<BR><CENTER>"
      sOut = sOut + "<INPUT TYPE=SUBMIT NAME=SUBMIT "
      sOut = sOut + "VALUE=""Order checked items"""
      sOut = sOut + " OnClick=""return _
         AtLeastOneCheckBox();"">"
      sOut = sOut + "<INPUT TYPE=BUTTON NAME=ALLON _
         VALUE=""Select all"""
      sOut = sOut + " OnClick=""return CheckAll(true);"">"
      sOut = sOut + "<INPUT TYPE=BUTTON NAME=ALLOFF _
         VALUE=""Unselect all"""
      sOut = sOut + " OnClick=""return CheckAll(false);"">"
      sOut = sOut + "</CENTER></FORM>" + vbCrLf
      sOut = sOut + JavaAtLeastOneCheckBox
      sOut = sOut + JavaCheckAll

   End If
   Set cKeywords = Nothing

   sOut = sOut + SearchBottom
   cgi.WriteCGI sOut
   rs.Close
```

```
            End With
        End Sub


        Sub DoCheckOut()
            Dim sOut As String, sShoppingBag As String

            ' get the contents of the shopping bag
            sShoppingBag = GetShoppingBag

            sOut = "<HTML>" + vbCrLf
            sOut = sOut + "<HEAD>" + NoCache + "</HEAD>" + vbCrLf

            ' if empty, show err.
            If sShoppingBag <> "" Then
                sOut = sOut + "<BODY BGCOLOR=#ffdd99>" + vbCrLf
                sOut = sOut + "<H2> Shopping bag contents<HR></H2>" + _
                    vbCrLf
                sOut = sOut + sShoppingBag
                sOut = sOut + "</BODY>" + vbCrLf
                sOut = sOut + "</HTML>" + vbCrLf
            Else
                sOut = sOut + "<BODY BGCOLOR=#ffdddd>" + vbCrLf
                sOut = sOut + "<H2> Shopping bag is empty!</H2><HR>" + _
                    vbCrLf
                sOut = sOut + "</BODY>" + vbCrLf
                sOut = sOut + "</HTML>" + vbCrLf
            End If
            cgi.WriteCGI sOut
        End Sub

        Sub DoEmptyShoppingBag()
            ClearShoppingBag

            ' it should be empty so this should show a clear...
            ' — shopping bag.
            DoCheckOut
        End Sub



        Sub DoMassOrder()
```

```
            ' order all of the files first!
        Dim item As Object
        For Each item In cgi.cParameters
          If (InStr(item.Name, "Item") = 1 And item.Value = "ON") _
                Then
            AddShoppingBagItem item.Name, 1
          End If
        Next

    DoCheckOut
End Sub

Sub DoSubmit()
    ' an actual order!
    With cgi
      RefreshShoppingBag

        ' now show a quote for entries in shopping bag
        Dim sOut As String
        sOut = GetShoppingBag("DOVERIFYSUMBIT", False)

        .WriteCGI "<HTML>" + vbCrLf
        .WriteCGI "<HEAD>" + NoCache + "</HEAD>" + vbCrLf

        If (sOut = "") Then
          ' empty shopping bag!
          sOut = sOut + "<BODY BGCOLOR=#ffdddd>" + vbCrLf
          sOut = sOut + "<H2> Shopping bag is empty!</H2><HR>" _
                + vbCrLf
      Else
          ' sOut contains the entire shopping bag

          .WriteCGI "<BODY BGCOLOR=#ffffff>" + vbCrLf
          .WriteCGI "<H2>Shopping bag contents</H2><HR>"
          .WriteCGI sOut
          .WriteCGI "<H2>User Information</H2><HR>"
          .WriteCGI ShowUserInformation
          .WriteCGI ShowCreditCardInformation

          .WriteCGI "</FORM>"
      End If
```

```
        .WriteCGI "</BODY>" + vbCrLf
        .WriteCGI "</HTML>"
    End With
End Sub

Sub DoVerifySubmit()
    Dim sOut As String

    ' update the information in shopping bag.
    RefreshShoppingBag
    ' update the user information (to what was submitted)
    UpdateUserInformation
    ' submit the shopping bag information to database
    SubmitShoppingbag

    sOut = "<HTML>" + vbCrLf
    sOut = sOut + "<HEAD>" + NoCache + "</HEAD>" + vbCrLf
    sOut = sOut + "<BODY BGCOLOR=#ffffff>" + vbCrLf

    sOut = sOut + "<H2>Information has been successfuly _
            submitted </H2>"

    sOut = sOut + "</BODY>" + vbCrLf
    sOut = sOut + "</HTML>"
    cgi.WriteCGI sOut
End Sub


Function GetItemKey(ByVal sName As String) As Integer
    ' look for the number after "Item"
    GetItemKey = CInt(Mid$(sName, Len("Item") + 1))
End Function


Function GetShoppingBag(Optional vSubmitText As Variant,_
            Optional vTerminateForm As Variant) As String

    Dim sOut As String, sSubmitText As String
    If IsMissing(vSubmitText) Then
        ' default submission instruction
        sSubmitText = "DOSUBMIT"
```

```
        Else
           sSubmitText = vSubmitText
        End If

        With cgi
           Dim item As Object, fItems As Boolean
           Dim fItemsExist As Boolean
           fItemsExist = False
           Dim rs As Recordset
           Set rs = db.OpenRecordset("select * from DATA", _
                 dbOpenDynaset, dbReadOnly)
           For Each item In .cCookies
              ' has to be the beginning.
              If (InStr(item.Name, "Item") = 1) Then
                 If Not fItemsExist Then
                    ' start it all out

                    sOut = sOut + "<FORM METHOD=POST ACTION="""
                    sOut = sOut + .ReadScriptName
                    sOut = sOut + """>" + vbCrLf
                    sOut = sOut + "<INPUT TYPE=HIDDEN"
                    sOut = sOut + " NAME=ACTION VALUE=""" + _
                       sSubmitText + """>"
                    sOut = sOut + "<CENTER><TABLE BORDER=1 _
                       WIDTH=80%>" + vbCrLf
                    sOut = sOut + "<TR>" + vbCrLf
                    sOut = sOut + "<TH WIDTH=80% BGCOLOR=#ffffff>"
                    sOut = sOut + "Item name"
                    sOut = sOut + "</TH>" + vbCrLf
                    sOut = sOut + "<TH WIDTH=10% BGCOLOR=#ffffff>"
                    sOut = sOut + "Quantity"
                    sOut = sOut + "</TH>" + vbCrLf
                    sOut = sOut + "<TH WIDTH=10% BGCOLOR=#ffffff>"
                    sOut = sOut + "Cost"
                    sOut = sOut + "</TH>" + vbCrLf
                    sOut = sOut + "</TR>" + vbCrLf
                 End If


                 Dim iItemKey As Integer
                 iItemKey = GetItemKey(item.Name)
```

```
        rs.FindFirst "Key=" + CStr(iItemKey)

sOut = sOut + "<TR>" + vbCrLf
'fatal error!
If Not rs.NoMatch Then
   ' item information.
   sOut = sOut + "<TD WIDTH=80%>"
   sOut = sOut + rs("Title")
   sOut = sOut + "</TD>" + vbCrLf
   sOut = sOut + "<TD WIDTH=10% ALIGN=CENTER>"
   sOut = sOut + "<INPUT TYPE=TEXT SIZE=4 _
      MAXLENGTH=4 NAME="""
   sOut = sOut + CStr(item.Name) + """ "
   sOut = sOut + "Value=""" + item.Value + """ _
      OnChange="""
   sOut = sOut + CStr(item.Name) + _
      ".value=Validate("
   sOut = sOut + CStr(item.Name) + ".value);B"
   sOut = sOut + CStr(item.Name) + ".value=Dollar("
   sOut = sOut + CStr(item.Name) + ".value * "
   sOut = sOut + CStr(rs("Price"))
   sOut = sOut + "); return true"">"
   sOut = sOut + "</TD>" + vbCrLf
   sOut = sOut + "<TD WIDTH=10% ALIGN=CENTER _
      BGCOLOR=#00ffff>"
   sOut = sOut + "<INPUT TYPE=TEXT SIZE=4 _
      MAXLENGTH=1 NAME=""B"
   sOut = sOut + CStr(item.Name) + """ "
   sOut = sOut + "Value="""
   sOut = sOut + Format$(CDbl(item.Value) * _
      CDbl(rs("Price")), "Currency")
   sOut = sOut + """ OnChange="""
   sOut = sOut + CStr(item.Name) + _
      ".value=Validate("
   sOut = sOut + CStr(item.Name) + ".value);B"
   sOut = sOut + CStr(item.Name) + ".value=Dollar("
   sOut = sOut + CStr(item.Name) + ".value * "
   sOut = sOut + CStr(rs("Price")) + "); return _
      true"">"
   sOut = sOut + "</TD>" + vbCrLf
Else
```

```
                          sOut = sOut + "<TD>Error locating Item!</TD>" + _
                              vbCrLf
                  End If
                  sOut = sOut + "</TR>" + vbCrLf

                  fItemsExist = True
              End If
          Next
          rs.Close
      End With


      ' if nothing exists, I don't need to close anything out!
      If fItemsExist Then
          'close it out.
          sOut = sOut + JavaNumberValidate
          sOut = sOut + "</TABLE></CENTER><BR>"
          Dim fTerminateForm As Boolean
          fTerminateForm = True
          If Not IsMissing(vTerminateForm) Then fTerminateForm = _
              vTerminateForm

          If fTerminateForm Then
              sOut = sOut + "<CENTER><INPUT TYPE=SUBMIT NAME=_
                  SUBMIT VALUE="""
              sOut = sOut + "Purchase files"
              sOut = sOut + """">"
              sOut = sOut + "</CENTER></FORM>"
          End If
      Else

      End If
      GetShoppingBag = sOut
  End Function


  Function JavaNumberValidate() As String
      Dim sOut As String

      sOut = "<SCRIPT LANGUAGE=""JavaScript"">" + vbCrLf
      sOut = sOut + "<!—" + vbCrLf
```

```
sOut = sOut + "function Validate(text) {" + vbCrLf
sOut = sOut + "var iOut;" + vbCrLf
sOut = sOut + "iOut= parseInt(text);" + vbCrLf
sOut = sOut + "if (isNaN(iOut))" + vbCrLf
sOut = sOut + "iOut= 1;" + vbCrLf
sOut = sOut + "return iOut;" + vbCrLf
sOut = sOut + "}" + vbCrLf
sOut = sOut + "function Dollar(text) {" + vbCrLf
sOut = sOut + "var dollarOut, dOut;" + vbCrLf
sOut = sOut + "dOut= text* 100;" + vbCrLf
sOut = sOut + "dOut= Math.round(dOut)/100;" + vbCrLf
sOut = sOut + "dollarOut = ""$"" + String(dOut);" + _
        vbCrLf
sOut = sOut + "return dollarOut;" + vbCrLf
sOut = sOut + "}" + vbCrLf
sOut = sOut + "// ->" + vbCrLf
sOut = sOut + "</SCRIPT>" + vbCrLf


JavaNumberValidate = sOut
End Function

Function JavaAtLeastOneCheckBox() As String
   Dim sOut As String

   sOut = sOut + vbCrLf + "<SCRIPT language=""JavaScript""> _
            <!--" + vbCrLf
   sOut = sOut + "function AtLeastOneCheckBox() {" + vbCrLf
   sOut = sOut + " var i, fOneActive" + vbCrLf
   sOut = sOut + " fOneActive=false;" + vbCrLf
   sOut = sOut + " for (i=0;i<document.forms _
            [0].elements.length;i++) {" + vbCrLf
   sOut = sOut + " if _
      (document.forms[0].elements[i].name.indexOf(""Item"",0)> _
            -1) {" + vbCrLf
   sOut = sOut + " if (document.forms[0].elements _
            [i].checked==true) {"
   sOut = sOut + vbCrLf
   sOut = sOut + "fOneActive=true;" + vbCrLf
   sOut = sOut + "break;" + vbCrLf
   sOut = sOut + "} " + vbCrLf
   sOut = sOut + "} " + vbCrLf
```

```
      sOut = sOut + "} " + vbCrLf
      sOut = sOut + "return fOneActive;" + vbCrLf
      sOut = sOut + "} " + vbCrLf
      sOut = sOut + " //--></SCRIPT>" + vbCrLf


   JavaAtLeastOneCheckBox = sOut
End Function


Function JavaCheckAll() As String
   Dim sOut As String

   sOut = sOut + vbCrLf + "<SCRIPT language=""JavaScript""> _
         <!--" + vbCrLf
   sOut = sOut + "function CheckAll(fCheckAll) {" + vbCrLf
   sOut = sOut + " var i" + vbCrLf
   sOut = sOut + " for (i=0;i<document.forms_
            [0].elements.length;i++) {" + vbCrLf
   sOut = sOut + " if _(document.forms[0].elements_
            [i].name.indexOf(""Item"",0)> -1) {" + vbCrLf
   sOut = sOut + "document.forms[0].elements_
            [i].checked=fCheckAll;"
   sOut = sOut + vbCrLf
   sOut = sOut + "} " + vbCrLf
   sOut = sOut + "} " + vbCrLf
   sOut = sOut + "return false;" + vbCrLf
   sOut = sOut + "} " + vbCrLf
   sOut = sOut + " //--></SCRIPT>" + vbCrLf


   JavaCheckAll = sOut
End Function


Sub main()
On Error GoTo RegisterErr ' register oCGI only if having _
            problems!
   Set cgi = New oCGI2
On Error GoTo NormalErr
   cgi.ProcessCGI Command
   cgi.ProcessVirtualCookies COOKIE_TTL
   'Load frmVBCrash
   Set db = Workspaces(0).OpenDatabase(App.Path + _
            "\ShoppingBag2.mdb")
```

```
        ' security is first and foremost, it will delegate _
                authority later on!
        DoUserSecurity

        db.Close
        Set cgi = Nothing
        End
    NormalErr:
        cgi.WriteCGI "<HTML><BODY>Error:" + Error$ + _
                "</BODY></HTML>"
        Set cgi = Nothing ' Just in case
        End
    RegisterErr:
        Resume RegisterOCGI2
    RegisterOCGI2:
        On Error GoTo RegisterOCGI2Err
        oCGI2Register
        Set cgi = New oCGI2

        cgi.WriteCGI "<HTML><HEAD>"
        ' if the user can't wait - refresh it myself!
        cgi.WriteCGI "<META HTTP-EQUIV=""Refresh"" CONTENT=1>"
        cgi.WriteCGI "</HEAD>"
        cgi.WriteCGI "<BODY BGCOLOR=#ffffff>"
        cgi.WriteCGI "Please reload document, the system should _
                work now!"
        cgi.WriteCGI "</BODY></HTML>"

        Set cgi = Nothing
        Set db = Nothing ' this works for uninitialized objects _
                too!
    RegisterOCGI2Err:
        End
    End Sub



    Sub DoShowButtons()
        With cgi
            .WriteCGI "<HTML>" + vbCrLf
            .WriteCGI "<BODY BGCOLOR=#aaaaaa>" + vbCrLf
            .WriteCGI "<H3>"
```

```
          ' change hyperlinks into images by using <IMG SRC=> tag.
          .WriteCGI "<A HREF="""" + .ReadScriptName
          .WriteCGI "?ACTION=DOSHOWSEARCH"" TARGET=MAIN>_
                  [Search]</A> * "

          ' jump to empty shopping bag instruction.
          .WriteCGI "<A HREF="""" + .ReadScriptName
          .WriteCGI "?ACTION=DOEMPTYSHOPPINGBAG"" _
                  TARGET=MAIN>[Empty Shopping"
          .WriteCGI " Bag]</A> * "

          ' view the shopping bag.
          .WriteCGI "<A HREF="""" + .ReadScriptName
          .WriteCGI "?ACTION=DOCHECKOUT"" TARGET=MAIN>[View _
                  shopping bag / Checkout]"
          .WriteCGI "</A> * "

          ' category/subcategory search
          .WriteCGI "<A HREF="""" + .ReadScriptName
          .WriteCGI "?ACTION=DOCATEGORIES"" _
                  TARGET=MAIN>[Category/SubCategory]</A>"

          .WriteCGI "</H3>" + vbCrLf

          .WriteCGI "</BODY>" + vbCrLf
          .WriteCGI "</HTML>"
      End With
  End Sub


  Sub HomePage()
      Select Case cgi.ReadParam("ACTION")
        Case "DOSEARCH":
          DoSearch ' perform a forward search
        Case "DOSEARCHBACK":
          DoSearchBack ' perform a backwards search.
        Case "DOSHOWSEARCH":
          DoShowSearch ' show search HTML screen (could be _
                  done externally!).
        Case "DOSHOWBUTTONS":
          DoShowButtons ' show button frame (could be done _
                  externally!).
```

```
              Case "DOCHECKOUT":
                DoCheckOut ' check out (aka, view shopping bag)
              Case "DOEMPTYSHOPPINGBAG":
                DoEmptyShoppingBag ' empty shopping bag
              Case "DOADDITEM"
                DoAddItem ' add items.
              Case "DOSUBMIT"
                DoSubmit ' submit items (after viewing shopping bag)
              Case "DOVERIFYSUMBIT"
                DoVerifySubmit ' final verification of information _
                    (+credit card)
              Case "DOMASSORDER"
                DoMassOrder ' order lots of items at once!
              Case "DOCATEGORIES"
                DoCategories ' Show all of the categories
              Case "DOSUBCATEGORIES"
                DoSubCategories ' Show all of the SubCategories for _
                    a specific category
              Case "DOITEMS"
                DoItems ' Show all of the items for a specific _
                    SubCategory
              Case Else: ' anything else!
                DoShowFrames ' default home page!
          End Select
      End Sub


      Sub DoShowFrames()
          With cgi
              ' expire everything tomorrow!
              .WriteCGI "<HTML>" + vbCrLf
              .WriteCGI "<HEAD>" + NoCache + vbCrLf
              .WriteCGI "<TITLE>Shopping Bag oCGI sample application _
                    </TITLE>" + vbCrLf
              .WriteCGI "</HEAD>" + vbCrLf
              ' first frame = 20%, the other will take up the rest _
                    of the location
              .WriteCGI "<FRAMESET BORDER=1 ROWS=20%,*>"
              .WriteCGI " <FRAME NAME=""BUTTONS"" SCROLLING=NO SRC="""
              .WriteCGI .ReadScriptName + "?ACTION=DOSHOWBUTTONS"">"
              .WriteCGI " <FRAME NAME=""MAIN"" SRC="""
              .WriteCGI .ReadScriptName + "?ACTION=DOSHOWSEARCH"">"
```

```
                        .WriteCGI "</FRAMESET>"

                        .WriteCGI "</HTML>"
                End With
        End Sub


        Function NoCache() As String
                NoCache = "<META NAME=""Pragma"" CONTENT=""no-cache"">" _
                                + vbCrLf
        End Function


        Sub RefreshShoppingBag()
                ClearShoppingBag

                ' transfer parameters BACK into shopping bag
                Dim item As Object
                For Each item In cgi.cParameters
                        If (InStr(item.Name, "Item") = 1) Then ' has to be the _
                                beginning.
                                If (IsNumeric(item.Value)) Then
                                        If (CInt(item.Value) > 0) Then
                                                AddShoppingBagItem item.Name, CInt(item.Value)
                                        End If
                                End If
                        End If
                Next
        End Sub


        Function ShowCreditCardInformation() As String
                Dim sOut As String
                sOut = "<H3>Credit card information</H3><HR>"

                sOut = sOut + "<TABLE BORDER=1 WIDTH=80% BGCOLOR=#aaffff>"
                sOut = sOut + "<TR><TH WIDTH=30%>Credit Card number _
                                </TH><TD>"
                sOut = sOut + "<INPUT TYPE=TEXT MAXLENGTH=20 NAME= _
                                ""CreditCard"""
                sOut = sOut + " VALUE=""""></TD></TR>"
                sOut = sOut + "<TR><TH>Expiration date</TH><TD>"
                sOut = sOut + "<INPUT TYPE=TEXT MAXLENGTH=5 NAME= _
                                ""ExpirationDate"""
```

```
        sOut = sOut + " VALUE=""""></TD></TR>"
        sOut = sOut + "</TABLE>"
        sOut = sOut + "<BR><CENTER>"
        sOut = sOut + "<INPUT TYPE=SUBMIT NAME=SUBMIT VALUE= _
                ""Purchase files"">"
        sOut = sOut + "</CENTER>"


        ShowCreditCardInformation = sOut
    End Function


    Function ShowUserInformation() As String
        Dim sOut As String, rsUser As Recordset
        Set rsUser = db.OpenRecordset("select * from USERS where _
                UserID=" + sUID)
        If rsUser.EOF Then
          ' fatal error!
            sOut = "<H2><FONT COLOR=RED>"
            sOut = sOut + "Error retrieving information about _
                user!<BR>"
            sOut = sOut + "Please log in and try again!"
            sOut = "</FONT></H2>"
        Else
          ' form should already be set up for us...
            sOut = "<TABLE BORDER=1 WIDTH=80% BGCOLOR=#ffff00>"
            sOut = sOut + "<TR><TH>Full Name</TH><TD WIDTH=30%>"
            sOut = sOut + "<INPUT TYPE=TEXT MAXLENGTH=50 NAME=_
                ""FullName"""
            sOut = sOut + " VALUE=""" + CheckNull _
                (rsUser("FullName"), "")
            sOut = sOut + """></TD></TR>"
            sOut = sOut + "<TR><TH>Address</TH><TD>"
            sOut = sOut + "<INPUT TYPE=TEXT SIZE=50 MAXLENGTH=50 _
                NAME=""Address"""
            sOut = sOut + " VALUE=""" + CheckNull _
                (rsUser("Address"), "")
            sOut = sOut + """></TD></TR>"
            sOut = sOut + "<TR><TH>City/State</TH><TD>"
            sOut = sOut + "<INPUT TYPE=TEXT MAXLENGTH=35 NAME= _
                ""CityState"""
            sOut = sOut + " VALUE=""" + CheckNull(rsUser _
                ("CityState"), "")
```

```
        sOut = sOut + """"></TD></TR>"
        sOut = sOut + "<TR><TH>Zip</TH><TD>"
        sOut = sOut + "<INPUT TYPE=TEXT MAXLENGTH=11 NAME=_
            """Zip"""
        sOut = sOut + " VALUE=""" + CheckNull(rsUser("Zip"), "")
        sOut = sOut + """"></TD></TR>"
        sOut = sOut + "<TR><TH>Email</TH><TD>"
        sOut = sOut + "<INPUT TYPE=TEXT MAXLENGTH=50 NAME=_
            """Email"""
        sOut = sOut + " VALUE=""" + CheckNull(rsUser("Email"), "")
        sOut = sOut + """"></TD></TR>"
        sOut = sOut + "<TR><TH>Phone</TH><TD>"
        sOut = sOut + "<INPUT TYPE=TEXT MAXLENGTH=15 _
            NAME="""Phone"""
        sOut = sOut + " VALUE=""" + CheckNull(rsUser("Phone"), "")
        sOut = sOut + """"></TD></TR>"
        sOut = sOut + "</TABLE>"
    End If

    rsUser.Close
    ShowUserInformation = sOut
End Function

Sub SubmitShoppingbag()
    Dim rsOrder As Recordset, lOrderSession As Long
    Set rsOrder = db.OpenRecordset("ORDER_SESSION")

    rsOrder.AddNew
    rsOrder("UserID") = sUID
    rsOrder("Filled") = False
    rsOrder("PurchaseDate") = Now
    rsOrder("CreditCard") = cgi.ReadParam("CreditCard")
    rsOrder("ExpirationDate") = cgi.ReadParam("ExpirationDate")
    rsOrder.Update

    ' move to the last modified item (so I can pick up _
            OrderSession
    rsOrder.Bookmark = rsOrder.LastModified
    lOrderSession = rsOrder("OrderSession")

    Set rsOrder = db.OpenRecordset("PURCHASE_ITEMS")
```

```
Dim item As Object
For Each item In cgi.cCookies
    If (InStr(item.Name, "Item") = 1) Then ' has to be the _
            beginning.
        rsOrder.AddNew
        rsOrder("OrderSession") = lOrderSession
        rsOrder("ItemKey") = GetItemKey(item.Name)
        rsOrder("Quantity") = item.Value
        rsOrder.Update
    End If
Next
rsOrder.Close
' empty everything out!
ClearShoppingBag
End Sub

Sub UpdateUserInformation()
    Dim rsUser As Recordset
    Set rsUser = db.OpenRecordset("select * from USERS where _
            UserID=" + sUID)
    If Not rsUser.EOF Then
        rsUser.Edit
        rsUser("FullName") = cgi.ReadParam("FullName")
        rsUser("Address") = cgi.ReadParam("Address")
        rsUser("CityState") = cgi.ReadParam("CityState")
        rsUser("Zip") = cgi.ReadParam("Zip")
        rsUser("Email") = cgi.ReadParam("Email")
        rsUser("Phone") = cgi.ReadParam("Phone")
        rsUser.Update
    End If

    rsUser.Close
End Sub
```

Snapshots of Enhanced Shopping Bag

Figure 10.1 shows multiple selections of items as a result of a search. Figure 10.2 shows the category, subcategory search. Figure 10.3 shows the results of a particular subcategory search.

Figure 10.1
Multiple selection pages

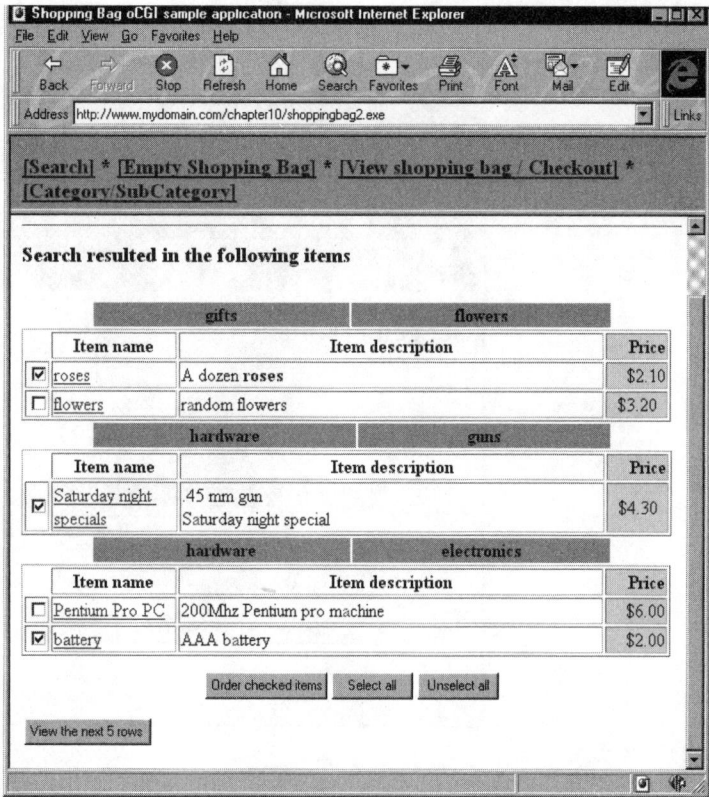

Figure 10.2
Category/subcategory
search

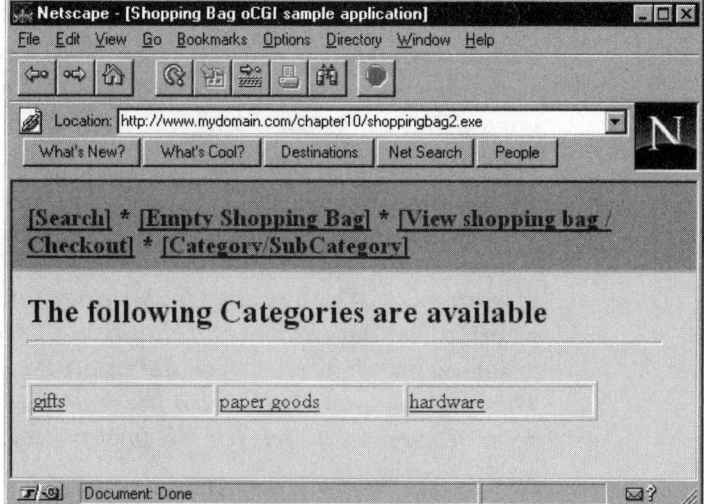

Figure 10.3
Subsequent
category/subcategory
search results

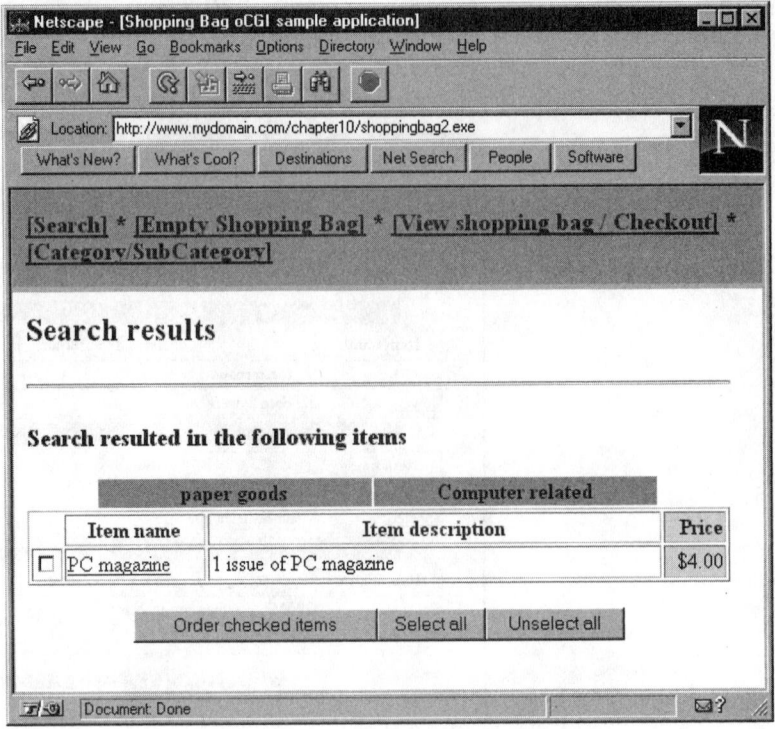

Summary

This chapter has given several examples of where JavaScript code can enhance a standard CGI application, while retaining its portability and thin client "status." The reader can further enhance this or other applications using JavaScript to provide a comprehensive, robust and interactive application.

A well-versed VB programmer has, in all likelihood, adapted a fair amount of debugging techniques for use in standard application development. Debugging CGI applications, however, is somewhat different from debugging a regular VB application. The next chapter deals with these differences, and presents several ways in which the VB programmer can thoroughly debug a CGI application.

THE DEBUGGING PROCESS

- Debugging advantages of static linking to the oCGI library
- Debug output
- Using message boxes
- Using VB5's logging facility
- Attaching a real debugger to the application
- Using Windows NT's command line processor
- Using VB's command line arguments
- Remarks and error messages
- Unattended execution and error event logging
- Debugging cookies
- Last resort: Elimination

Most of these debugging techniques require hands-on interaction with the machine running the CGI process. Often, some of the debugging can take place locally. It is, however, recommended that the CGI application be tested on a real web server (even a local one) before posting it up for public usage.

Debugging in oCGI Code

Instead of referencing the DLL version of oCGI, the programmer can easily add the oCGI source code into the system. Once there, the programmer can debug and even modify it.

Stepping into the oCGI code often helps clarify some bugs that would otherwise be much harder to figure out.

Among other debugging traits, the programmer can utilize a static oCGI link by placing a *Debug.Print* command in the *WriteCGI* function call. This causes the CGI application's output to be printed onto the debug window, which often helps in determining what the application is doing and what is wrong with the HTML output it produces. Figure 11.1 shows the oCGI library (statically linked) using *Debug.Print* to display the HTML in Visual Basic's immediate window.

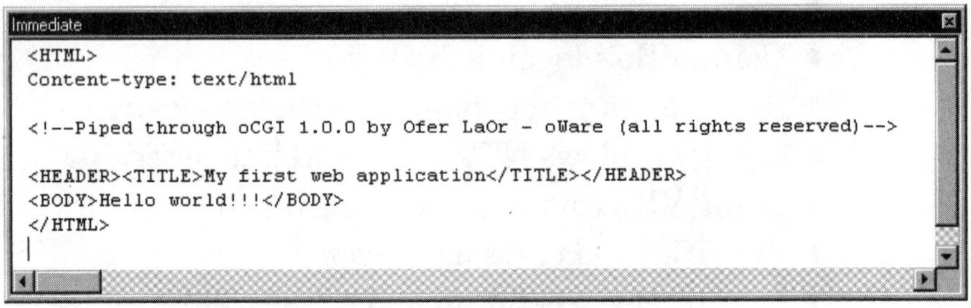

Figure 11.1
HTML information in VB's immediate window

```
Immediate                                                          ×
 <HTML>
 Content-type: text/html

 <!--Piped through oCGI 1.0.0 by Ofer LaOr - oWare (all rights reserved)-->

 <HEADER><TITLE>My first web application</TITLE></HEADER>
 <BODY>Hello world!!!</BODY>
 </HTML>
 |
```

Using MessageBox in a CGI Application

The most useful debugging tool available to the CGI programmer using Visual Basic is the ability to produce Message boxes. Often, there are situations where knowing the actual run-time status of the application can be sufficient in order to determine some of the parameters or hidden causes that may be contributing to the actual bug.

It should be noted that a standard *MsgBox* call is likely to cause many problems, because the application is running under the context of the web server service. Services, as mentioned before, cannot interact with the desktop.

Placing a normal message box in your program, or causing one to be invoked by the program (e.g., errors), causes the application to wait for the user to press the message box buttons before proceeding. The **allow service to interact with Desktop** checkbox is no help either! This application may not even terminate when the web service stops.

One of the flags for the Win32 API call that allows services to interact with the desktop is the MB_SERVICE_NOTIFICATION flag. This allows a message box to be displayed by a service or a process that runs under the context of a service (that's us!). The flags in Windows NT 3.x (where it was introduced) and Windows NT 4.0 are different.

In Windows NT 4.0 the flag is equal to &H200000&.

In Windows NT 3.x the flag is equal to &H40000H. Unless it is previously know that NT 4.0 (or higher) is the target platform, as in cases where IIS is used and the application requires cookies, the programmer must determine the version of Windows NT that the application is being debugged under, and change the flag value accordingly.

Interestingly enough, the standard *MsgBox* function inherent in Visual Basic 4.0x does not accept this number as a valid button flag. If the number is placed as a flag, the *MsgBox* function raises a runtime error for overflow. This is because *MsgBox* expects a normal integer, whereas the Windows MessageBox flags are long integers.

In this case, the Win32 API MessageBox function should be used. This function is declared as follows:

```
Declare Function MessageBox Lib "user32" Alias "MessageBoxA" _
        (ByVal hWnd As Long , ByVal lpText As String, _
         ByVal lpCaption As String, ByVal wType As _
         Long) As Long
```

The *hWnd* parameter must be zero for the message box to be displayed from within a service context. The *lpText* parameter specifies the text that will show up within the message box. The *lpCaption* parameter contains the caption text for the message box. The *wType* parameter should contain the MB_SERVICE_NOTIFICATION flag (&H200000&).

The following code causes the message to appear (even when running as a CGI application):

```
MessageBox 0, "text is a way of life!", "caption", _
        &H200000
```

Other flags can be added to the *wType* parameter that allow the user to stop the process, or continue, as well as make other decisions that may be required in a runtime-debugging environment.

The message box can be invoked when errors occur with specific information about where the error occurred and the error description. This tool can also be used to determine variable contents and system status at specific subroutines.

Although Visual Basic's *MsgBox* function is not effective in the context of a service, it can be made to be using VBA's ability to overload functions. Simply create a working *MsgBox* function to replace the system *MsgBox* function, and it will automatically be used in all places (other than in error handling, since that is not actually handled by *MsgBox*).

The modified *MsgBox* function works as follows:

```
Function MsgBox(prompt$, Optional buttons, Optional title, _
        Optional helpfile, Optional context)
    If IsMissing(buttons) Then buttons = 0
    If IsMissing(title) Then title = ""
    MsgBox = MessageBox(0, CStr(prompt), CStr(title), &H200000 _
        + CLng(buttons))
End Function
```

Any calls made to the standard Visual Basic *MsgBox* function will operate correctly using this overload. This is because your project is given precedence by Visual Basic when it is searching for the appropriate function implementation to be executed. This precedence-setting can be verified by looking through the object browser. Figure 11.2 displays a message box initiated from a CGI application.

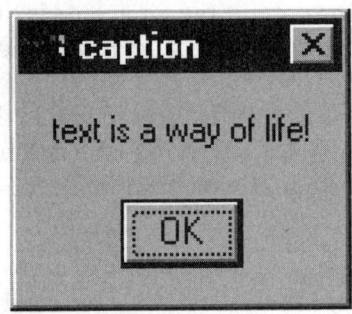

The Visual Basic Logging Facility

As previously mentioned, Visual Basic 5.0 contains a new logging facility. This facility can be used for various applications, such as audit trails.

The programmer can utilize this facility to log errors or event states that will later allow him to determine the reason why the application failed to complete a task. The logging facility can log information to either the Windows NT application log (this can be retrieved remotely by an administrator using another Windows NT event viewer, or in Windows 95 by utilizing the client administration toolkit found in the Windows NT resource kit CD), or a log file.

The *App.StartLogging* method allows the programmer to turn on the logging facility and direct it to either the requested log file (and log file properties) or to the Windows NT application event log. When using the file option, the application is given an opportunity to erase the previous contents of a log file, or append new items to the end of the existing log file (if one is found). The application may also wish to leave a separate file for each instance of the application being executed, denoting the complete flow of execution within that particular instance.

In order to add a log record to the log file/event-log, the *App.LogEvent* method should be called by the application. This method enables you to log a particular event, as well as to assign that event an importance level (Error, Warning or Information).

If logging should occur without a prior call to *App.StartLogging*, a Windows NT machine defaults to the application event log. In Windows

95, the default file for events is **"vbevents"** (this default can be changed by using the *App.LogPath* property).

It is generally recommended that you use the *App.StartLogging* facility instead of relying on system defaults. Figures 11.3 and 11.4 show the two methods of saving events to the log.

Figure 11.3
Windows NT log event with a few logged events

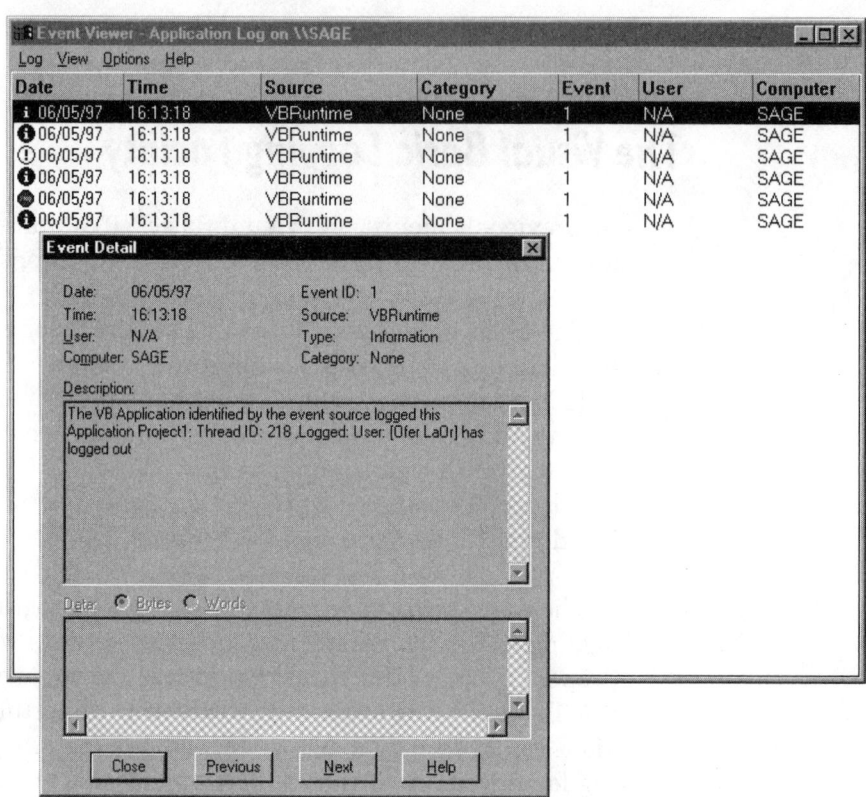

Figure 11.4
Text file containing logged events

Attaching a Real Debugger into the Application

Prior to Visual Basic 5.0, Visual Basic applications could only be debugged within the actual Visual Basic *IDE* (Integrated Development Environment). This often proved problematic in real world situations, where the environment behaves differently than in the outside world.

One of the best debugging additions to Visual Basic 5.0 is the addition of symbolic debugging in compiled applications. This check box (in the make EXE option dialog box) causes the VB compiler to produce debugging information that can be used by any CodeView enabled application (like the Microsoft Developer's Studio, as well as a plethora of other third-party debuggers). Visual C++ 4.x or higher is typically used for debugging such applications.

When an error occurs (i.e., when the application accesses memory outside of its allowed range), the Developer's Studio can be used to debug the Visual basic code from within the actual run-time environment.

In most debugging situations, the developer studio can be activated beforehand. This application creates a message box (using the techniques described before), allowing the debugger to attach to the running application. The debugger attaches using one of many options, the easiest of which is via the debug option in the Windows NT task manager. Simply bring up the task manager (**Control-Shift-Escape**) and right-click on the process you wish to debug. Pressing the debug menu causes the developer studio to start debugging the application. Placing a break point immediately following the message box allows you to stop execution in the right location. At this point, the message box can continue, and a standard debug session can take place.

The DebugBreak and OutputDebugString API functions can be used to assist debugging in the DevStudio environment as well.

Debugging a Visual Basic application within the developer's studio will take some getting used to, because of the different environments. This, however, can give the programmer great insight on how Visual Basic applications work and how Visual Basic maintains variables and compiles code.

Several bugs are quite hard to track without a real debugging environment that allows the user to debug directly within the run-time execution environment. One such example is heavy cookie usage which is extremely hard to simulate within Visual Basic. Figures 11.5 -11.7 show how a debugger can attach to a VB application.

Figure 11.5
VC++ 4.2 debugging a
VB application

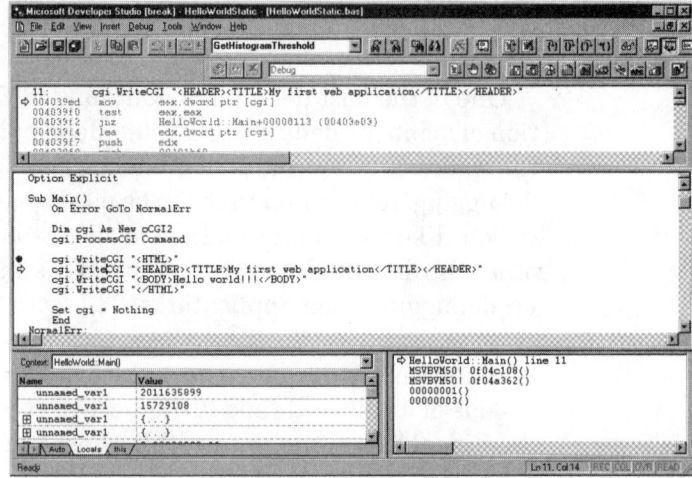

Figure 11.6
Viewing a VB variable
from within VC++

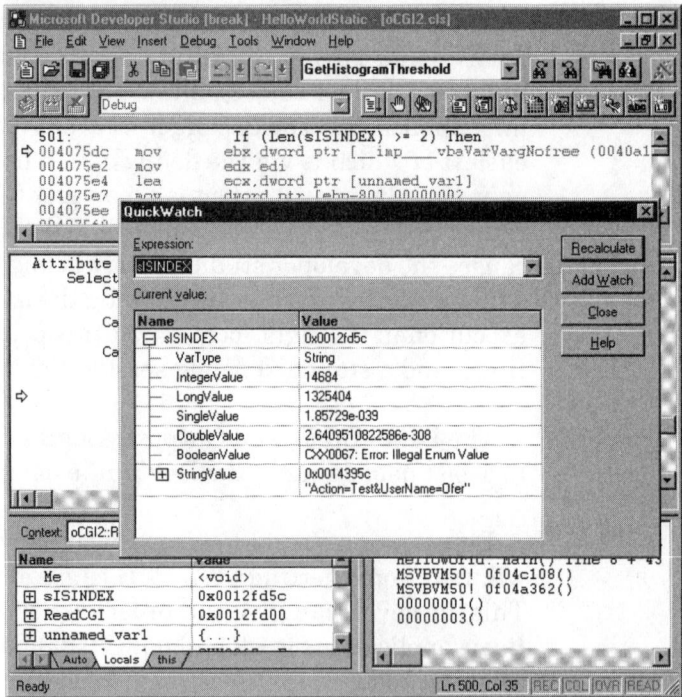

Figure 11.7
Attaching VC++ to VB
source code

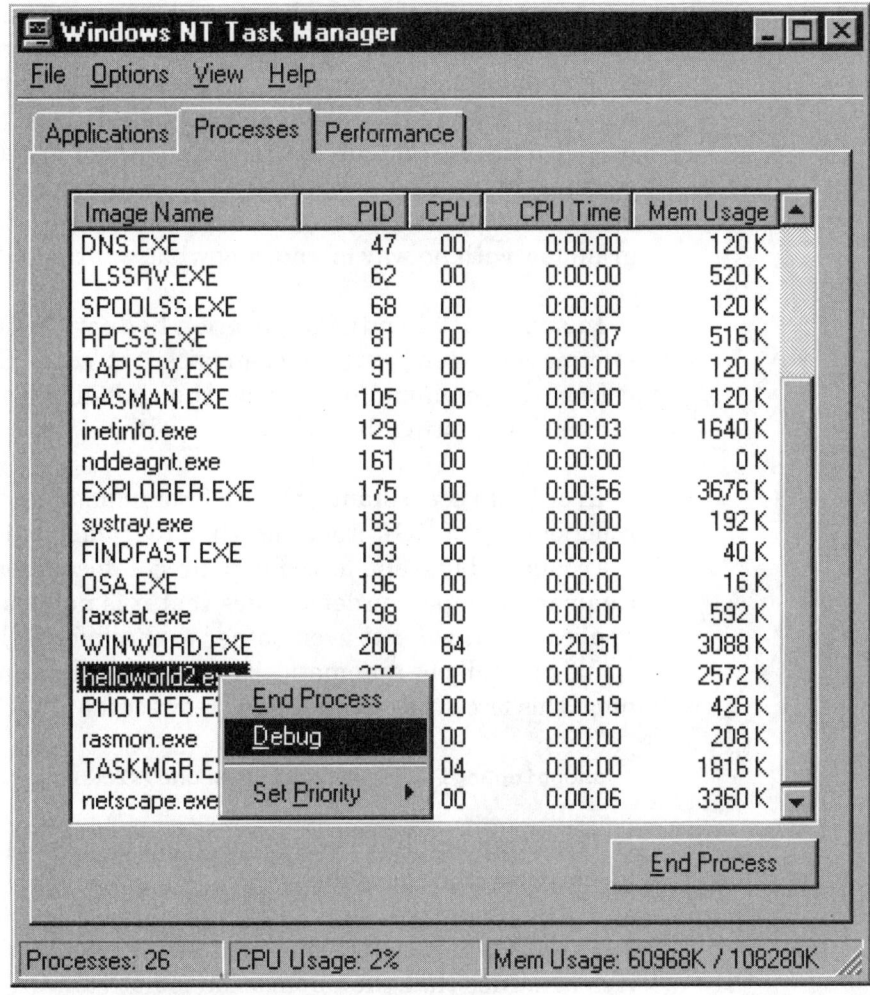

Using the Windows NT Command Line Processor When Debugging

Since CGI applications basically utilize STDIN and STOUT for communication with the server, it is possible to run CGI applications from the command line.

This often proves useful in determining if the error has occurred only in the server's environment, or in other environments as well. It also proves helpful in debugging HTTP headers (e.g., cookies) since these are "swallowed up" by the browser and will not show up when you're viewing the source of the HTML stream. Some browsers, even when they require manual verification of cookie acceptance, will not display all of the information about the cookie (Microsoft Internet Explorer only displays the contents of the cookie without its name (which may also contain interesting information). If the program returns erroneous HTTP headers, the browser will completely reject it, leaving the programmer with no way of knowing what went wrong.

In addition, when the application halts without providing further information (often the result of an uncaught Visual Basic error), running it from the command line causes the offending error to be displayed, rather than halting the CGI process without indicative information.

In order to use a standard "DOS" command line for determining the functionality of CGI programs, the program should be executed from the command line and forced to redirect information to a file. Since the command line parser determines that it is not dealing with a console application, it will not even bother to check for STDOUT activity that would normally be automatically displayed when an application is running. This forces the application to redirect the STDOUT stream to a file.

```
ShoppingBag1.exe "ACTION=DOSHOWBUTTONS" > t.txt
```

This command line causes the shopping bag application to redirect its output to the `t.txt` file.

The oCGI library recognizes enclosing quotes for parameters when it determines that the application is not running under the server's context. These enclosing quotes are ignored, allowing VB to accept any parameters the user passes via command line without the enclosing quotes (which tell the command line parser to pass everything *within* the quotes to the application as a single parameter).

Since the command line parser recognizes that this is a non-console application, it does not wait for the application to terminate before returning to the command prompt. If the programmer monitors the output file carefully, he will notice that it starts out as zero size and suddenly grows larger. As soon as the application truly terminates, the file handle is released and the true size of the file is displayed. Viewing the contents using notepad should only be done *after* the application has completely terminated.

The output file usually looks like this:

```
Content-type: text/html

<!—Piped through oCGI 2.0.50 by Ofer LaOr - oWare (all
          rights reserved)—>
<HTML><HEADER>My first web application</HEADER><BODY>Hello
          world!!!</BODY></HTML>
```

The first part, separated by two CR/LF combinations, is the HTTP header. This header is added by oCGI after all of the cookies and virtual cookies, telling the browser to expect an HTML stream immediately afterwards.

The oCGI revision is stamped as the first HTML stream entry, as a remark, and is not shown on the browser page. The rest is output from the CGI application. When an application statically links to the oCGI code, the version/revision numbers are those of the application, rather than of oCGI. The programmer may wish to modify the initial HTML tag to a more suitable copyright notice, rather than maintaining the standard oCGI notice.

Cookies and other HTTP instructions show up before the Content type HTTP tag. Figures 11.8 and 11.9 show how a console application's output can be redirected, as well as the contents of the redirected output.

Figure 11.8
Redirected console application

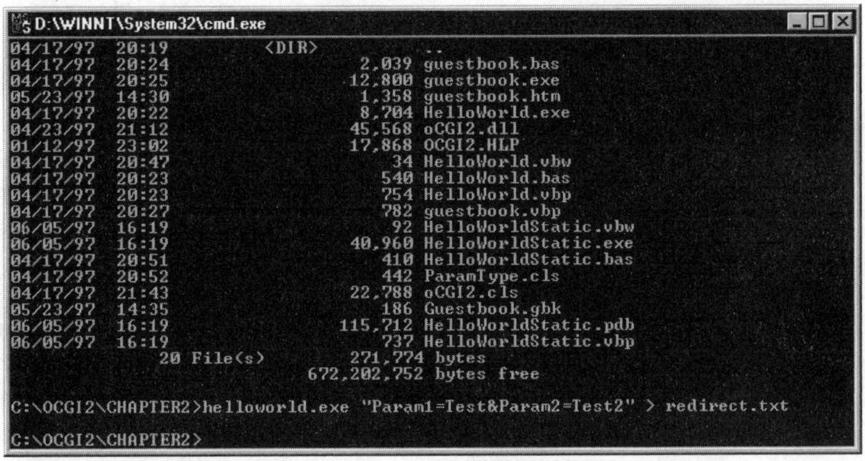

Figure 11.9
Redirected file
contents

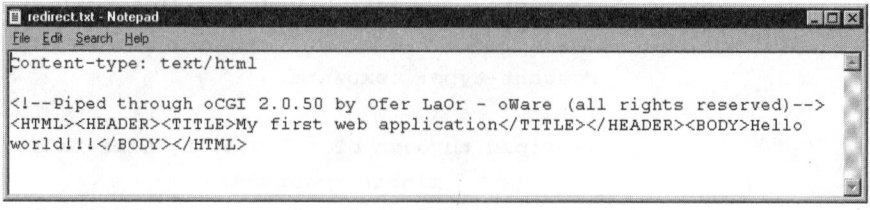

Using the Visual Basic Command Line Arguments

When debugging a CGI application, problems often occur that require the programmer to utilize a real debugging environment. The development environment is often the most suitable solution for debugging. This is because Visual Basic is constantly being interpreted by the development environment, allowing the developer to quickly modify the application, during the debug session, until the application is production-ready.

This bypasses the need to compile and link, stopping the debugging session mid-stream. It can be detrimental in situations where getting to a particular debugging situation is a bit more difficult than simply placing a breakpoint (enabling a breakpoint only after a particular stage in the program has been met). The ability for Visual Basic developers to try a particular code snippet (without having to stop what they are doing) over and over, until the application works correctly, is a great boon for VB.

The Visual Basic development environment is a fairly close facsimile to the web server. The main differences are the parameters, cookies and other environment variables. When a particular page does not work properly, the Visual Basic environment can emulate it by setting the application parameters correctly.

If the form reaches the debugging point by submitting a form (if an A HREF is involved, simply determine what the parameter string that's passed to the CGI application is) using the POST or GET methods, simply modify these forms to submit information via the ISINDEX submission method.

Using the ISINDEX submission method forces the browser to display the full URL of the parameters that it passes to the application. This will show up in the URL location of the browser. The parameters (everything following the ? character in the URL) should be copied to the clipboard and placed in the command line argument section of the Visual Basic development environment (this can be found under the Project | properties menu).

Once there, the application should behave exactly as it does when the server executes the same parameters. The oCGI library senses that it is not running under the server's context, and utilizes the command line arguments as valid server-passed parameters.

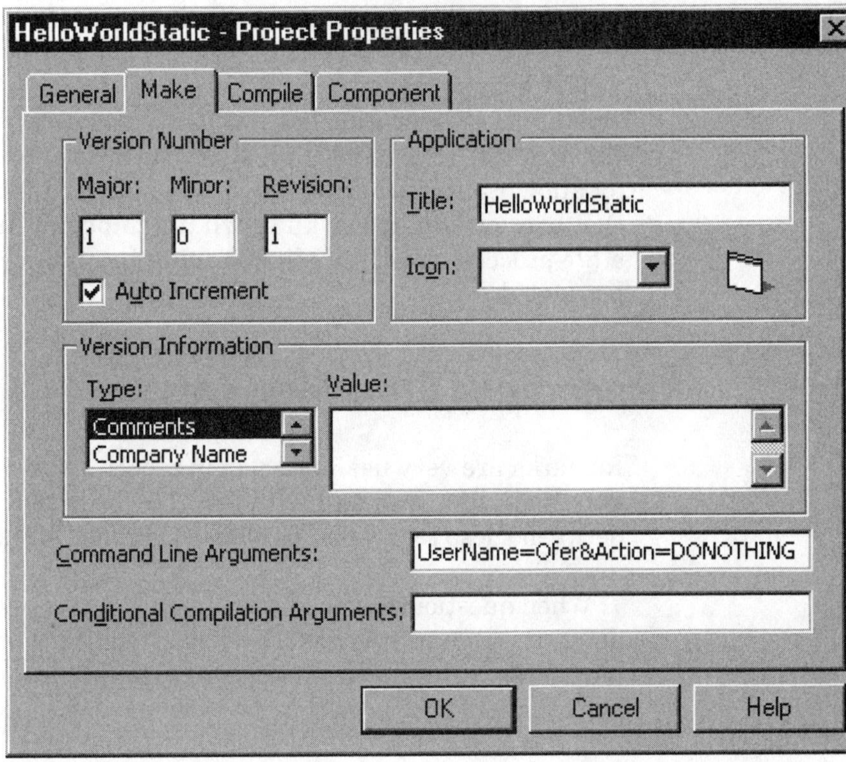

Figure 11.10
VB command line arguments dialog box

Cookies are much harder to debug. When debugging cookies, a routine must be added that appends new items to the *cCookies* collection, right after *cgi.ProcessCGI* subroutine is executed.

Often, Cookie-based applications require interaction with a true debugger (like the Microsoft Developer's studio), as previously noted.

When debugging from within Visual Basic, it is often useful to turn on the "Break on all errors" check box. This allows the programmer to view potential errors, "double-faults" (errors *within* error handlers).

There are various other tools that will catch Visual Basic bugs. These normally act like Microsoft's Developer's studio does when utilizing the "Create Symbolic debug info" check box.

It is beyond the scope of this book to cover standard debugging techniques when using an environment such as Visual Basic. The ability to quickly debug applications, as well as the art of writing code with fewer bugs, is a skill that improves with experience.

The Visual Basic *Beep* function is also useful in determining whether the application has reached a particular section or not. Using the *MessageBeep* Win32 API function further enhances this feature by allowing the programmer to select any number of audio "codes" that can let him or her know what's going on. An example of this is a file processing CGI application that beeps once for every file it has processed.

Remarks and Error Messages

Remarks are very useful debugging tools. These are HTML tags that start with <!— and end with —>. The browser ignores anything in between these tags when parsing the HTML stream.

When questioning specific parameters or values of parameters/variables, the remark tag functions as a type of "watch" following up on parameter values or function calls. This technique can help identify bugs that only occur on the live system (or with live data).

Since error messages must be caught by the application, a smart error message handling system helps resolve bugs quickly. A global error handler in main catches any uncaught errors, but a localized error handling section in each function helps isolate the exact problem. This is done by having the error handling code do a call *WriteCGI* with the actual error message (*Error$*), as well as the name of the function where the error occurred. This helps isolate nasty bugs that occur infrequently or intermittently (for instance, a type mismatch in a particular function can often be detected by reviewing the function's code carefully in instances where the error is hard to debug, using a debugging environment).

```
<!—DoMyBidding: Invalid Use of Null. [91]—>
```

In sensitive systems, such as credit card processing applications, errors should be logged into a dedicated log file. This allows the developer to note errors without resorting to asking users for exact error messages.

Often, leaving an error message in a remark allows the programmer to inspect and debug the error (or add additional conditions to prevent the error from reoccurring). One option is to place an error message asking the user to attach the entire erroneous document and send it to the programmer. Since this causes the HTML for the web page to be attached, the programmer can inspect the hidden message quite easily. Figure 11.11 shows the standard oCGI version remark embedded in HTML source.

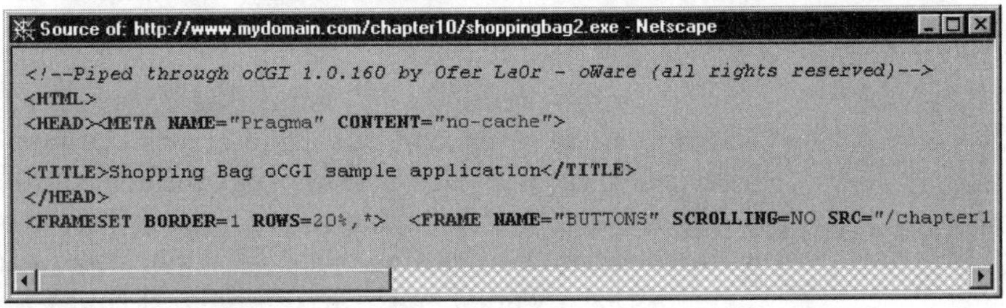

Figure 11.11
Netscape browser displaying a remark stamp in HTML source

Unattended Execution and Event Logging

Among the new offerings in Visual Basic version 5.0 is multithreaded ActiveX EXE servers. These are applications that serve (either locally or remotely via DCOM or via Remote OLE automation) one or more ActiveX enabled clients. Since Visual Basic now targets server applications in addition to client applications, it must be much more fault-tolerant than ever before. Figure 11.12 shows the unattended execution dialog box.

Figure 11.12

The unattended
execution dialog box

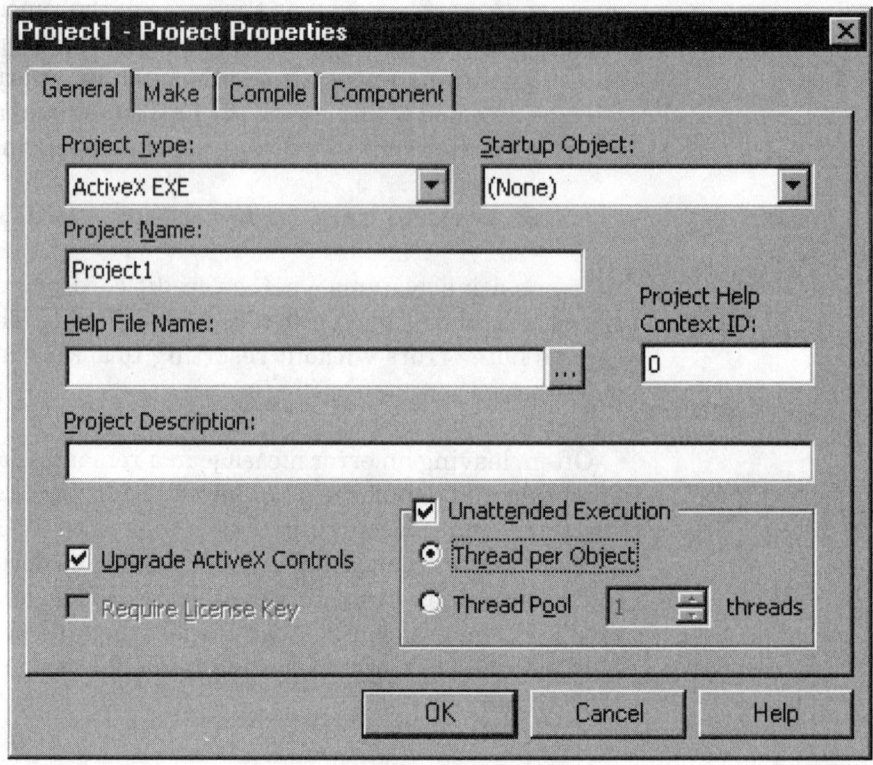

Previous versions of Visual Basic were far from fault-tolerant. Frequently, uncaught run-time errors brought an application to a screeching halt. But a safe programmer could easily implement a higher degree of fault tolerance simply by using **on error** statements in each function calling "path." This enabled each function to catch errors locally and behave accordingly. At times, though, an application could still trigger an error in a location not protected by an **on error** handler.

In CGI applications, the situation is much better than in standard applications. This is because a CGI application lives and dies within the context of one parent function call: **Sub Main**. It allows the programmer to handle errors centrally by placing an **on error** statement in the beginning of **Sub Main**.

The unattended execution feature provides an interesting alternative to this solution. It is primarily oriented towards providing an ActiveX server (be it an In Process DLL or a standard ActiveX executable) with more fault-tolerance. Standard Visual Basic library calls (sitting in MSVBVM50.DLL for both P-code applications, as well as compiled VB 5.0 applications) are now aware of this feature and can log a message to a log file when functions requiring user-interface occur.

Unfortunately, this functionality only supports built-in functions (i.e., not WINAPI calls) that are aware of the Unattended execution option. An application or library can test for this via the *App.UnattendedApp* variable, which is true if the application is unattended.

There are a few perks to being an unattended application. Multithreading, unfortunately, only influences multiuse-classes which are likely to be irrelevant to CGI applications (unless they double as ActiveX servers too). Error handling, on the other hand, is very much a relevant perk. Any errors that the application creates (yes, even double fault) are recorded into the log file and subsequently cause the application to end promptly. Message boxes and other VB features automatically log but will not terminate the application. This allows the user to utilize Message boxes that cannot effect the Web server.

Unattended applications are far from perfect for CGI applications. Because they cannot have user interfaces, Visual Basic will not permit an unattended application to utilize forms (if a form already exists). This prevents an unattended CGI application from utilizing OCXs within them. While most of the applications presented in this book do not utilize OCXs, they are still bad candidates for unattended execution.

Because unattended execution applications are oriented towards ActiveX applications/libraries, the project they live in must contain at least one class. The registration process for this class will be tested upon every entry to the application (since CGI applications must be Executables which, when containing ActiveX components, check for valid registration every time they are executed). This causes a performance hit and also pollutes the registry (which is polluted enough as it is...) and exposes useless classes to the system.

When using the unattended execution feature, Visual Basic needs to know *where* to log the information to. Various options can be selected via the *App.StartLogging* function:

- **VbLogAuto** — When running under Windows 95, the information is logged to a file (specified as a parameter to *App.StartLogging*). When running under Windows NT (which the CGI application is most likely to run under), the information is logged to the application event log (with the application's title used as the application source for each event). This is the most appropriate option for CGI applications.

- **VbLogOff** — No logging takes place. Log events simply go to nowhere (with no way to trace what happened).

- **VbLogToFile** — Always logs to a file (this works in both Windows 95 and Windows NT). The file name is specified as a parameter to *App.StartLogging*.

- **VbLogToNT** — Forces an application running under windows NT to log events to the application event log. When running under Windows 95, the errors are simply discarded.

- **VbLogOverwrite** —This specifies that event logging takes place in a log file (it is Or-ed with the log file options). When used in conjunction with a Windows NT event log flag, this flag has no meaning. The log file will be recreated every time the application is executed. The file name is specified as a parameter to *App.StartLogging*. This is the least appropriate option when running as a CGI application.

The application can utilize these in the following manner:

```
App.StartLogging App.Path + "\errlog.txt", vbLogToFile
```

In order to work properly, this statement should be placed at the beginning of the Sub Main subroutine.

When creating unattended applications, the user may be tempted to create an ActiveX executable (in the application wizard) rather than the standard executable. Figure 11.13 shows the ActiveX tab with unattended execution turned on.

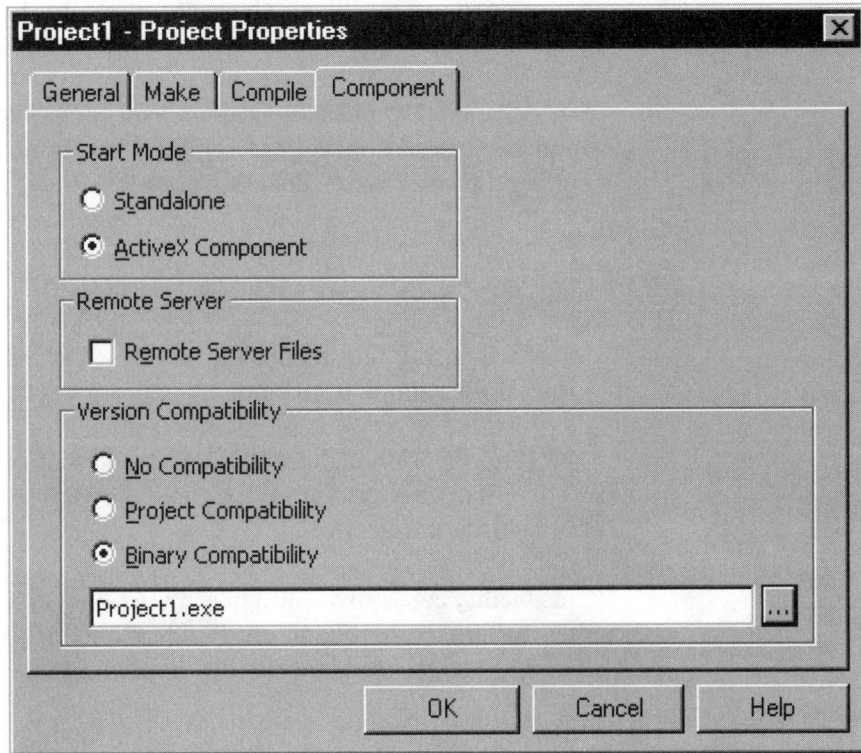

This creates a situation where the application does not execute Sub Main. Rather, the default behavior for such a project dictates that the application execute with no code, until the last reference to it is destroyed.

In order to make Sub Main run (otherwise, the CGI application will not work), turn to the project properties dialog box. First, the Startup object should be selected as **Sub Main** (rather than nothing, which is the default for ActiveX executables). Next, the component tab should have the **Standalone** option selected, rather than the default "ActiveX component" behavior. This forces the application to remain running in the background, *without* executing Main, until the last reference to all of the objects in the executable is released.

It should be noted that standard executables (with no forms) can be unattended applications just the same. Standard applications have a disabled component tab. This is because no classes in the project can be exposed to the outside (the only conceptual difference between ActiveX and standard executables). These standard applications, however, can use forms in just the same way as ActiveX applications.

Since standard applications cannot expose class to the outside, the performance hit (and subsequent registry "white-noise") associated with registering these classes does not occur.

Event Logging Without Unattended Execution

The event-logging feature in Visual Basic can be utilized whether or not the application is unattended.

A CGI application utilizes this to log relevant information (e.g., login statistics, etc.) that can later be compiled by another application, or collected by an administrator.

This facility can also be used in conjunction with standard Visual Basic error handlers to produce an unattended "like" application, without some of the rough edges that unattended application development implies.

To utilize the event-logging facilities in Visual Basic, an application calls the *App.LogEvent* method. This allows the application to log events onto the NT event log or standard log file (the default is a function of the hosting operating system). It should be noted that a normal, non-unattended execution application with an uncaught error will still cause a message box to appear, possibly halting the web server that had executed the application. This will occur regardless of whether the *App.StartLogging* method has been used or not.

P-Code applications (non-compiled applications) cannot use the explicit *App.LogEvent* facility, regardless of whether or not they have called *App.StartLogging*.

Debugging Cookies

Cookies are much harder to debug than regular parameters. The first problem with cookie debugging is that sample cookies are often placed to test the application out within the debugging environment. A better approach is to create a debug routine that will place the test cookies in the *cCookies* collection.

Once the application is tested with a real browser, the programmer can turn on the cookie verification option, which displays the name (not all of the browsers display this information), value and expiration date of each cookie. This lets the programmer knows whether or not the application has received the cookies correctly.

Another approach is to place a simple *WriteCGI* call that causes subsequent HTTP requests (e.g., cookie strings) to be displayed in the browser window. Unfortunately, this type of approach is fatal for Virtual cookies, is hard to debug, and is very difficult to use for debugging.

An alternative approach is to iterate through the cookies in the *cCookies* collection and print them all to an HTML remark. Once found, these cookies can be placed in the cookie debugging function for more detailed debugging.

Most often, bugs in virtual cookies, as well as in regular cookie applications, require the intervention of a real debugger. Figure 11.14 shows a debugged cookie application.

Figure 11.14
Debugging cookies

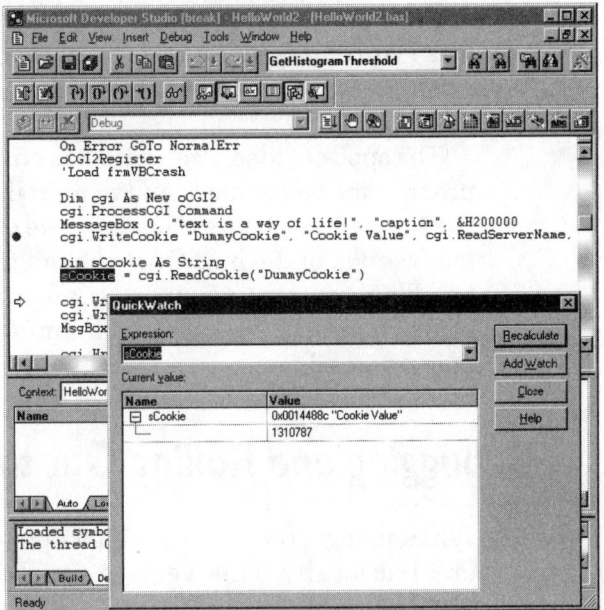

Elimination as a Last Resort

With modern development techniques that try to encapsulate and isolate functionality into subroutines, "side effect" bugs occur less frequently than before.

Still, a programmer may encounter a bug after a big change. This bug does not go away regardless of what the programmer changes. In a difficult-to-debug environment such as CGI, elimination should be used only as a last resort.

This technique, in addition to its little brother — inverse elimination — can often determine where the problem code is located, in a fairly quick manner.

The idea is that the error is somewhere in the code. If we can eliminate the section of code where the problem resides, we should be able to slowly localize the elimination area until we track down the section of code that is responsible for the bug or error. When using this technique, the programmer often suspects a large amount of code of containing the bug/error. If the programmer determines that the bug is still there, he or she should proceed to remark more code. Once the bug is gone, the programmer needs to determine the section of code that was last remarked, and works his way back by removing some of the remarks until the bug reappears.

The opposite idea also works effectively: a new project is created. The programmer adds more and more code from the previous project until the bug/error appears. This time, he or she attempts to isolate a minimal version of the bug. Once the programmer isolates the bug, he may be able to determine what is causing it to occur, and make serious changes to the test code (with minimal changes to the actual project being worked on).

Debugging and Rolling Out the Application

When using FrontPage 97, a complete version of the web site can be created locally. This version can be employed for debugging and verification.

Once the application is reasonably stable locally, the entire web site (including any associated HTML pages and CGI applications) can be rolled out to the actual web server. The connection to the server can be secured with Windows NT user security, as well as SSL, in order to prevent unwanted eyes from taking a peek at the information.

The user can utilize the CGI-bin directory, or create new directories for executables via the easy-to-use FrontPage interface. FrontPage 97 is ideal for such interactions with the server, and gives the programmer endless flexibility in rolling out applications.

Figure 11.15
FrontPage explorer screen

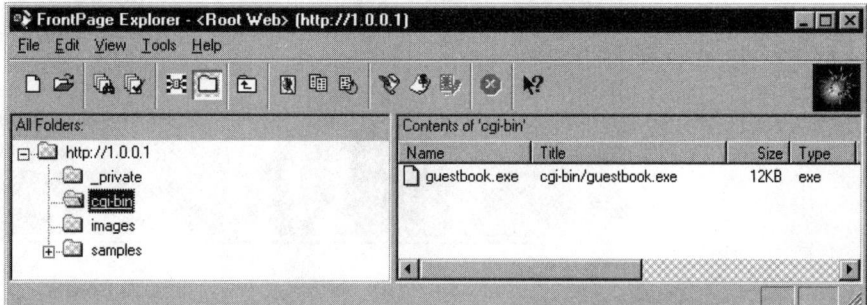

Testing the application locally requires that the personal web server support cookies. Most such servers (including the Microsoft personal web server) do not support these advanced features. This usually means that Windows NT server is used for development of the site. Microsoft's Personal Web Server (PWS) that comes with Frontpage 97 (it can be downloaded separately now from Microsoft's web site, and comes with Windows 95 OSR2 and the upcoming Memphis as a standard component) supports cookies, and will work with oCGI out of the box. Note the video example on the CD-ROM accompanying this book.

Once the local web server looks about right, the entire web site can be transported "magically" onto the production web server using FrontPage's publishing facility. FrontPage also enables the programmer to interact directly with the web server, allowing him to roll out new versions of the application effortlessly.

Before FrontPage 97 extensions were rolled out, FrontPage (Windows 95 edition) had a web-publishing wizard that performed any FTP actions needed to upload software. This wizard can be downloaded and used to roll out the application to the production web server.

Alternatively, the programmer can do this quite easily using Windows NT/95 built-in FTP application. Figure 11.16 demonstrates this.

Figure 11.16
Uploading an application using command line FTP

```
D:\WINNT\System32\cmd.exe
01/12/97  22:02                17,868 OCGI2.HLP
01/11/97  17:09                   573 UBcrash.frm
              12 File(s)         72,154 bytes
                         1,407,615,488 bytes free

D:\oCGI book\Chapter2>ftp 1.0.0.1
Connected to 1.0.0.1.
220 sage Microsoft FTP Service (Version 3.0).
User (1.0.0.1:(none)): laor
331 Password required for laor.
Password:
230 User laor logged in.
ftp> cd scripts
250 CWD command successful.
ftp> bin
200 Type set to I.
ftp> put guestbook.exe
200 PORT command successful.
150 Opening BINARY mode data connection for guestbook.exe.
226 Transfer complete.
11776 bytes sent in 0.01 seconds (1177.60 Kbytes/sec)
ftp> quit
221

D:\oCGI book\Chapter2>
```

Summary

An important thing to remember about debugging is that one can only reduce, not eradicate the number of bugs in one's code. This means that no amount of debugging can make any (typical) project "bug-proof." Therefore, the ability of the programmer to locate as many bugs (or make the program as fault-aware) as possible will decide how well the application will operate.

As previously shown, the main thing missing from traditional CGI programming is interactivity with the user. Users are typically computer literate and have used several applications other than CGI. They are aware of how simple and interactive native applications can be, and they will demand the same interactivity from your application.

This includes simple validation, shortcuts (as shown in Chapter 10, with the check box selection routines), and even interactive online help. Our next chapter discusses and demonstrates such techniques.

PART III

OCGI AND CLIENT SIDE CONSTRUCTS/ADVANCED ISSUES

ADDING JAVASCRIPT TO THE MIX

- Mandatory field validation
- Verifying that at least one check box has been selected
- Making sure the user changes the default value
- Verifying numeric edit boxes
- Verifying password verifications
- Verifying a user submission
- Navigation with JavaScript
- JavaScript-based online help for web applications

Chapter 10 has already shown us some preliminary JavaScript code that is effective in inducing client functionality, as well as in minimal validation. These ideas, however, must be extended in order for us to utilize more of the great features that JavaScript introduces.

In addition to simple validation, JavaScript can create new windows, retrieve information, manipulate HTML, and interact with the user.

JavaScript is more useful than VB script in these types of interactions with a client, because it is implemented in the two most popular browsers.

Validation

Validation is simply another form of interaction with the user. Without live validation on the client side, the application must validate information on the server, and resubmit the form with the appropriate changes.

This method of server side validation was prevalent prior to the advent of client side scripting. The complexity factor of such validation drops significantly when the client is allowed to perform the validation locally. This enables the server to forgo some of the validation code, as well as reentry of information into the data fields' values. In addition, the error message is presented in a better (more eye catching) way and performance improves dramatically — because the form does not need to be submitted, no program is executed on the server, and the HTML stream need not be sent down to the browser again.

Primary uses for validation interactions are:

- Making sure that mandatory fields are filled
- Making sure that at least one check box has been selected
- Making sure that the user has changed a default value
- Making sure that numeric edit boxes are actually numeric
- Making sure that invalid selections have not been made
- Making sure that a password field verification has been entered correctly
- Verifying that the user wants to submit the information

Validating Mandatory Fields

When verifying that the user has filled the mandatory fields, it is recommended that these fields be marked differently (i.e., by coloring the textual description of what the field contains using a different color, or bolding it).

The form's *OnSubmit* event is used to validate mandatory fields, because these are required regardless of the submission button pressed.

The value of the edit box can be determined using the following script segment:

```
if (window.document.forms[0].T1.value=="") {
   alert("T1 must be filled out!");
   return false;
}
return true;
```

This source code tests the value of the text box T1. If it is empty, a message box pops up with "T1 must be filled out!" In this case, the return value is false and the form cannot be submitted.

This source code can exist either in the event declaration or in a dedicated JavaScript environment (either separate .JS file or inside the HTML stream). When this code segment is declared in a dedicated JavaScript code segment, the code is completely self contained.

When the code is enclosed in quotes (because it exists directly within the event) it should appear as follows:

```
<form method="POST" ACTION="/scripts/test.exe"
onsubmit=
"if (window.document.forms[0].T1.value==&quot;&quot;) {
   alert(&quot;testing 1234&quot;);
   return false;
}
return true;">
```

The quotes within the JavaScript code segment use the **"** instead of standard quotes. This prevents the JavaScript parser in the browser from mistaking them for the end of the JavaScript code segment.

The long notation:

```
Window.document.forms[0].T1.value
```

Some browsers do not require this long notation. Rather, the following, shorter, notation can be implemented in Netscape browsers:

```
forms[0].T1.value
```

Microsoft browsers, however, only accept the long notation as valid. For full compatibility, this book will utilize only the long notation guaranteed to work in both Internet Explorer and Netscape Navigator.

In order for the CGI application to generate this segment, the following code can be used:

```
sOut = sOut + "<form method=""POST"""
sOut = sOut + "ACTION=""" + cgi.ReadScriptName
sOut = sOut + """ onSubmit=""" + vbCrLf
sOut = sOut + "if (window.document.forms[0].T1.value== _
        &quot;&quot;) {" + vbCrLf
sOut = sOut + "alert(&quot;testing 1234&quot;);" + vbCrLf
sOut = sOut + "    return false;" + vbCrLf
sOut = sOut + "}" + vbCrLf
sOut = sOut + " return true;"">" + vbCrLf

cgi.WriteCGI sOut
```

Figures 12.1 and 12.2 demonstrate the differences between Netscape and Microsoft browsers' alerts.

Figure 12.1
Netscape browser
JavaScript alert

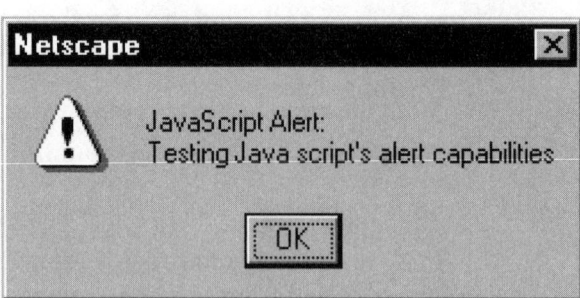

Figure 12.2
Microsoft browser
identical JavaScript alert

Making Sure at Least One Check Box Has Been Selected

In some scenarios, the user is presented with a number of selection check-boxes. Often, he or she must choose at least one check box in the given selection. In Chapter 10, the application utilized a check box detection function: *AtLeastOneCheckBox*. This script, however, can be changed to prompt users with an alert, so that they know **why** the form would not submit.

```
function AtLeastOneCheckBox() {
  var i, fOneActive
  fOneActive=false;
  for (i=0;i<document.forms[0].elements.length;i++) {"
  if (document.forms[0].elements[i].name.indexOf("Item",0)> _
         -1) {
    if (document.forms[0].elements[i].checked==true) {
      fOneActive=true;
      break;
    }
  }
  if (!fOneActive) {
    alert("at least one Item check box should be _
         selected!");
  }
  return fOneActive;
}
```

Making Sure that the User Has Changed the Default Value

Combo boxes often include a special default entry that tells the user what to do with it. A cleaner alternative is to simply add some header text that describes the functionality of the check box. In either case, the system should validate the combo box prior to submission, in order to prevent the submission of an invalid or empty combo box entry.

This is implemented in much the same way as previous validations. The following is the portable way of finding out if a specific choice has been selected:

```
if (document.forms[0].cmbSelection.options[0].selected) {
    alert("Please choose a valid entry in the checkbox _
            before submitting the form!");
}
```

Listboxes do not usually require validation. They *can* be validated, however, in much the same way as selections (combo boxes).

Making Sure that Numeric Edit Boxes are Actually Numeric

There are two ways of validating numeric numbers. One — forcing the edit box to become numeric as it changes — has already been demonstrated in Chapter 10.

An alternative also permits the application to validate the numeric values (making sure that they are higher than zero, or that "Maximum" is higher than "Minimum"). Utilizing the *parseInt* JavaScript routine performs the numeric evaluation. An equivalent function is *parseFloat* (which evaluates double precision real numbers). The *isNaN* JavaScript function returns a true value *if* the numeric parsing has not succeeded.

The following code snippet should be placed in the *onSubmit* event or the *onClick* event for the submitting button:

```
var iMin, iMax
iMin= parseInt(document.forms[0].minField.value);
if (isNaN(iMin)) { // isNaN= is Not a Number!
   alert("Please enter a valid mimimum value!");
   return false;
}
iMax= parseInt(document.forms[0].maxField.value);
if (isNaN(iMax)) {
   alert("Please enter a valid maximum value!");
   return false;
}
if (iMin<= 0) {
   alert("The minimum field must contain a valid value");
   return false;
}
if (iMax<= 0) {
   alert("The maximum field must contain a valid value");
   return false;
}
if (iMin>= iMax) {
   alert("The minimum field must contain a smaller value _
         than the maximum");
   return false;
}
return true;
```

Making Sure that Invalid Selections Have Not Been Chosen

When radio buttons are used in a few distinct groups, some combinations may not be valid. For example, if the user wants to download a file, one group of radio-buttons might specify the file type, and a second might specify compression algorithms. It is likely that some file formats will not compress very well — so the validation should prevent the user from selecting a specific compression technique for the given file format.

In order to do something like this, the value of the offending radio buttons should be ascertained:

```
function CheckData() {
    if (document.forms[0].optionFormat[0].checked) {" +
        if (document.forms[0].optionCompression[0].checked) {
        alert("This format cannot be compressed!");
        ocument.forms[0].optionCompression[0].checked=false;
        return false;
            }

    }
```

Making Sure that a Password Verification Has Been Entered Correctly

When doing password validation, it is important that the secondary validated password be identical to the password field. The following JavaScript code snippet ensures that the form fields are identical:

```
function CheckPasswords()
{
    if (document.forms[0].password.value=="") {
        alert("the password must be entered in order to proceed!");
        return false;
    }

    if (document.forms[0].password.value!=
            document.forms[0].passwordValidation.value) {
        alert("password must be verified exactly!");
        return false;
    }
}
```

The submission can be validated using the following validation code:

```
<form method="POST" ACTION="/scripts/test.exe" _
            onsubmit="return ValidateCombo()">
```

Placing validation code within the button's *onClick* event only works in Netscape Navigator versions 3.x or higher. The validation code *will* fire off, but the event cannot stop the form from being submitted (at least, not with a standard return value). The *onClick* event handler, however, can still manipulate the browser by modifying the window's state, submitting the window to another location, and modifying the window's URL location.

Verifying that the User is Ready to Submit the Information

When performing delicate operations, it is often wise to ask the user if he is definitely ready to proceed. One example of such an operation is the shopping bag application and the "empty shopping bag" function. We certainly do not want this function to complete if the user jumps there by mistake.

```
<A onClick="return window.confirm(&quot;are you sure you _
        want to proceed?&quot;)"
HREF="/chapter10/shoppingbag2.exe?ACTION=DOEMPTYSHOPPINGBAG" _
        TARGET=MAIN>[Empty Shopping Bag]
</A>
```

This, unfortunately, only works from Netscape browsers. For Microsoft browsers, non-anchor events should be used:

```
<FORM METHOD=POST ACTION="/chapter10/shoppingbag2.exe"
  onSubmit="return window.confirm(&quot;are you sure you _
        want to proceed?&quot;)"
TARGET=MAIN>
<input name="ACTION" value="DOEMPTYSHOPPINGBAG">
<input type="image" name="image1" src="/myimage.gif" _
        align="bottom"
  border="0" width="119" height="520">
</FORM>
```

This can be placed in a small, borderless table that allows the buttons to be laid out side by side.

Additional events (e.g., the *onMouseOver* in anchor tags) that are available in the Netscape browsers permit simple validation, intelligent interaction (e.g., highlighting an image when the mouse is over the image). Microsoft's browser does not support some of these extensions, and tends to support fewer events. IE4 promises to change this situation.

Navigation with JavaScript

This feature allows JavaScript functions to navigate windows to other locations, including navigating backwards and forwards in the window history. This is useful when the programmer needs two or more distinct frames or windows to change location, or when he or she needs a backward button (for instance, to do a kludgy backward search with forward only record-sets).

The `window.document.location.href` variable allows the JavaScript code to modify the URL for a particular window's document (this also works with frames).

The `window.document.back` and `forward` functions allow the programmer to place such buttons or move to these positions at will.

Online Help for CGI Applications

This is perhaps the most innovative of the JavaScript "ideas" presented in this book. Just like any other application, the user wants context sensitive help for the form he or she is currently working on.

This is especially effective when dealing with a frame-based system. Once submitted, the JavaScript function can figure out where the user is on the frame that contains online-help. This is done with the aid of a hidden input that is not used by the program, and contains help information context as the value. This serves the application in the same way that the *HelpContextID* works with Window's help files.

When triggered, the JavaScript code accesses the frame it is presenting help on, and attempts to retrieve the help context. Once found, a new window is created that contains the referenced help context.

Online help information can be retrieved from a variety of places, including predefined HTML scripts or relevant text from a database. This is useful in producing searchable help. Additionally, the help can be merged from a variety of locations. A single help page may contain information about each of its components; the text for which can be referenced in the database individually.

The Source Code for OnlineHelp.bas:

```
Option Explicit

Declare Function oCGI2Register Lib "oCGI2.dll" Alias _
        "DllRegisterServer" () As Long
Dim cgi As oCGI2
Sub DoDataFrame1()
   With cgi
      .WriteCGI "<HTML>" + vbCrLf
      .WriteCGI "<HEADER></HEADER>" + vbCrLf
      .WriteCGI "<BODY BGCOLOR=#ffffff>" + vbCrLf
      .WriteCGI "<FORM>" + vbCrLf
      .WriteCGI "<INPUT TYPE=HIDDEN NAME=""HelpContextID"""
      .WriteCGI "Value = ""DATAFRAME1"" > " + vbCrLf
      .WriteCGI "</FORM> " + vbCrLf
      .WriteCGI "<H2> Frame 1</H2>" + vbCrLf
      .WriteCGI "<A HREF=""" + .ReadScriptName
      .WriteCGI "?ACTION=DATAFRAME2"">" + vbCrLf
      .WriteCGI "<H3> press here to go to frame 2</H3>" + _
            vbCrLf
      .WriteCGI "</A>" + vbCrLf
      .WriteCGI "</HTML>" + vbCrLf
   End With
End Sub

Sub DoDataFrame2()
   With cgi
      .WriteCGI "<HTML>" + vbCrLf
      .WriteCGI "<HEADER></HEADER>" + vbCrLf
      .WriteCGI "<BODY BGCOLOR=#ffffff>" + vbCrLf
      .WriteCGI "<FORM>" + vbCrLf
      .WriteCGI "<INPUT TYPE=HIDDEN NAME=""HelpContextID"""
      .WriteCGI "Value = ""DATAFRAME2"" > " + vbCrLf
      .WriteCGI "</FORM> " + vbCrLf
      .WriteCGI "<H2> Frame 2</H2>" + vbCrLf
      .WriteCGI "<A HREF=""" + .ReadScriptName
```

```
         .WriteCGI "?ACTION=DATAFRAME3"">" + vbCrLf
         .WriteCGI "<H3> press here to go to frame 3</H3>" + _
               vbCrLf
         .WriteCGI "</A>" + vbCrLf
         .WriteCGI "</HTML>" + vbCrLf
      End With
End Sub


Sub DoDataFrame3()
   With cgi
      .WriteCGI "<HTML>" + vbCrLf
      .WriteCGI "<HEADER></HEADER>" + vbCrLf
      .WriteCGI "<BODY BGCOLOR=#ffffff>" + vbCrLf
      .WriteCGI "<FORM>" + vbCrLf
      .WriteCGI "<INPUT TYPE=HIDDEN NAME=""HelpContextID"""
      .WriteCGI "Value = ""DATAFRAME3"" > " + vbCrLf
      .WriteCGI "</FORM> " + vbCrLf
      .WriteCGI "<H2> Frame 3</H2>" + vbCrLf
      .WriteCGI "<A HREF=""" + .ReadScriptName
      .WriteCGI "?ACTION=DATAFRAME1"">" + vbCrLf
      .WriteCGI "<H3> press here to go to frame 1</H3>" + _
               vbCrLf
      .WriteCGI "</A>" + vbCrLf
      .WriteCGI "</HTML>" + vbCrLf
   End With
End Sub

Sub DoHelp()
   With cgi
      .WriteCGI "<HTML>" + vbCrLf
      .WriteCGI "<HEAD><TITLE>Sample online Help _
            </TITLE></HEAD>" + vbCrLf
      .WriteCGI "<BODY BGCOLOR=#aabbcc>" + vbCrLf
      Select Case .ReadParam("HelpContextID")
        Case "DATAFRAME1"
           .WriteCGI "<H1>online help for First frame!</H1>"
           .WriteCGI "<HR WIDTH=80%>" + vbCrLf
           .WriteCGI "This is <I>sample</I> help for <B>data _
             frame 1</B>"
           .WriteCGI vbCrLf
        Case "DATAFRAME2"
```

```
                .WriteCGI "<H1>online help for second frame!</H1>"
                .WriteCGI "<HR WIDTH=80%>" + vbCrLf
                .WriteCGI "This is <I>sample</I> help for <B>data _
                    frame 2</B>"
                .WriteCGI vbCrLf
            Case Else
                .WriteCGI "<H1>topic was not found!</H1>"
                .WriteCGI "<HR WIDTH=80%>" + vbCrLf
                .WriteCGI "This is <I>sample</I> help for _
                    <B>unknown topic!</B>"
                .WriteCGI vbCrLf
        End Select
        .WriteCGI "</BODY></HTML>" + vbCrLf
    End With
End Sub

Sub DoHelpFrame()
    With cgi
        .WriteCGI "<HTML>" + vbCrLf
        .WriteCGI "<HEADER></HEADER>" + vbCrLf
        .WriteCGI "<BODY BGCOLOR=#aaaaaa>" + vbCrLf
        .WriteCGI "<FORM>" + vbCrLf
        .WriteCGI "<INPUT TYPE=BUTTON NAME=""HelpMe"" "
        .WriteCGI "Value=""Help!"" "
        .WriteCGI "onClick=""DoHelp()"""
        .WriteCGI "> " + vbCrLf
        .WriteCGI "</FORM> " + vbCrLf
        .WriteCGI JavaDoHelp
        .WriteCGI "</HTML>" + vbCrLf
    End With
End Sub

Sub HomePage()
    With cgi
        Select Case .ReadParam("ACTION")
        Case "HELPFRAME"
            DoHelpFrame
        Case "HELP"
            DoHelp
        Case "DATAFRAME1"
            DoDataFrame1
```

```
        Case "DATAFRAME2"
          DoDataFrame2
        Case "DATAFRAME3"
          DoDataFrame3
        Case Else
          .WriteCGI "<HTML>" + vbCrLf
          .WriteCGI "<HEADER><TITLE> Welcome to the online _
              help application"
          .WriteCGI "</TITLE></HEADER>" + vbCrLf
          .WriteCGI "<FRAMESET ROWS=50,* BORDER=0>"
          .WriteCGI " <FRAME BORDER=0 FRAMEBORDER=0 NORESIZE _
              SCROLLING=NO"
          .WriteCGI " SRC="""
          .WriteCGI .ReadScriptName + "?ACTION=HELPFRAME"" _
              NAME=""HELP"">"
          .WriteCGI " <FRAME BORDER=1 SCROLLING=YES _
              FRAMEBORDER=0 SRC="""
          .WriteCGI .ReadScriptName + "?ACTION=DATAFRAME1"" _
              NAME=""CONTENT"">"
          .WriteCGI "</FRAMESET>"

          .WriteCGI "</HTML>"
      End Select
    End With
End Sub



Function JavaDoHelp() As String
  Dim sOut As String
  sOut = "<SCRIPT LANGUAGE=""JavaScript"">" + vbCrLf
  sOut = sOut + "<!—" + vbCrLf
  sOut = sOut + " function DoHelp() {" + vbCrLf
  sOut = sOut + " var sHelpContext, helpWindow, sScript;" _
          + vbCrLf
  sOut = sOut + " if (typeof(parent.CONTENT.document.forms_
          [0].HelpContextID)"
  sOut = sOut + " ==""undefined"") {" + vbCrLf
  sOut = sOut + " alert ("" no online help for this _
          form "");" + vbCrLf
  sOut = sOut + " return false;" + vbCrLf
  sOut = sOut + " }" + vbCrLf
```

```vb
    sOut = sOut + " sHelpContext= _
            parent.CONTENT.document.forms[0]."
    sOut = sOut + "HelpContextID.value;" + vbCrLf
    sOut = sOut + " sScript=""" + cgi.ReadScriptName
    sOut = sOut + "?ACTION=HELP&HelpContextID="""
    sOut = sOut + "+ sHelpContext;" + vbCrLf
    sOut = sOut + " helpWindow=window.open(sScript"
    sOut = sOut + ",""helpWindow"","
    sOut = sOut + """toolbar=no,scrollbars=yes,_
            width=500,height=200"");"
    sOut = sOut + vbCrLf + "return false;" + vbCrLf
    sOut = sOut + "}" + vbCrLf
    sOut = sOut + "//-->" + vbCrLf
    sOut = sOut + "</SCRIPT>" + vbCrLf


    JavaDoHelp = sOut
End Function

Sub main()
On Error GoTo RegisterErr ' register oCGI only if having _
            problems!
    Set cgi = New oCGI2
On Error GoTo NormalErr
    cgi.ProcessCGI Command
    'Load frmVBCrash

    HomePage


    Set cgi = Nothing
    End
NormalErr:
    cgi.WriteCGI "<HTML><BODY>Error:" + Error$ + _
            "</BODY></HTML>"
    Set cgi = Nothing ' never hurts!
    End
RegisterErr:
    oCGI2Register
    End
End Sub
```

Online Help Screen Shots

Figures 12.3 and 12.4 show two distinct help file pages.

Figure 12.3
Online help page for
the first screen

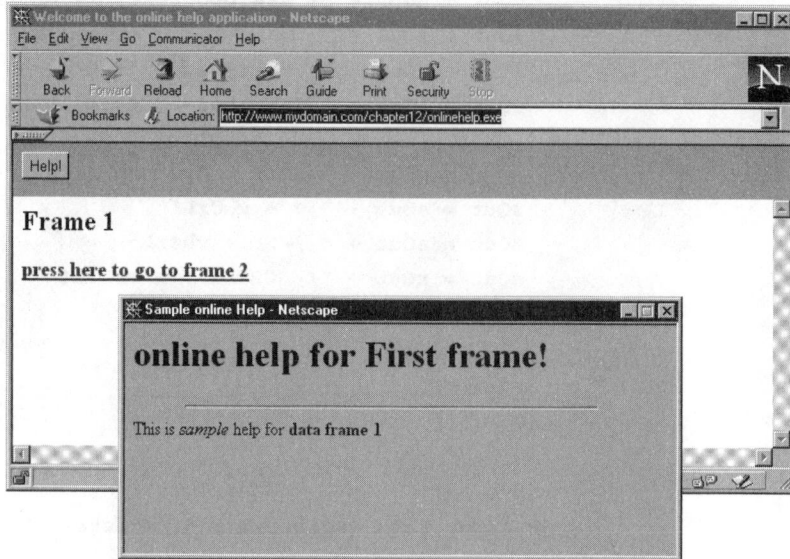

Figure 12.4
Online help page for
the second screen

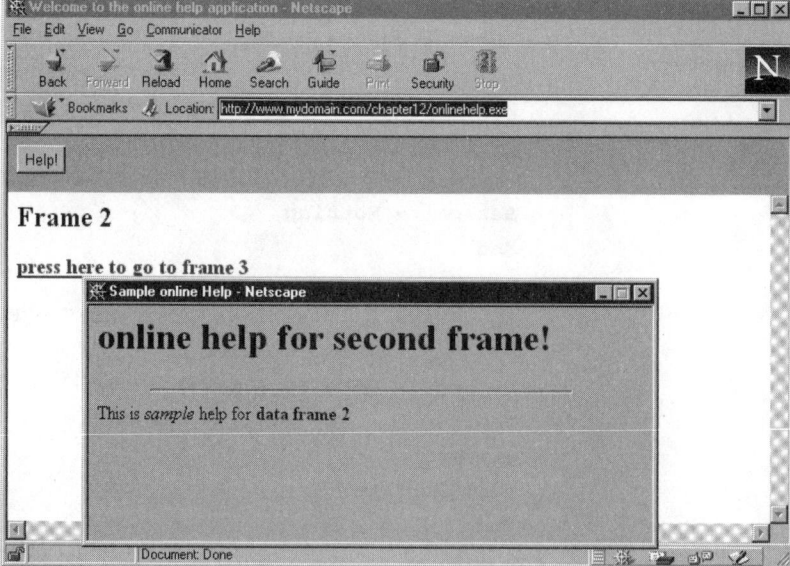

Notes

Netscape 2.0 browsers do not support the typeof JavaScript function. In situations where Netscape 2.0 compatibility is crucial, the check for the existence of the HelpContextID input should be removed. A try/catch block should be placed around the contents of the DoHelp JavaScript function that will help determine whether the HelpContextID element exists or not.

Figure 12.5 demonstrates the online help screens in Internet Explorer 4.0.

Figure 12.5
Online help in Internet Explorer

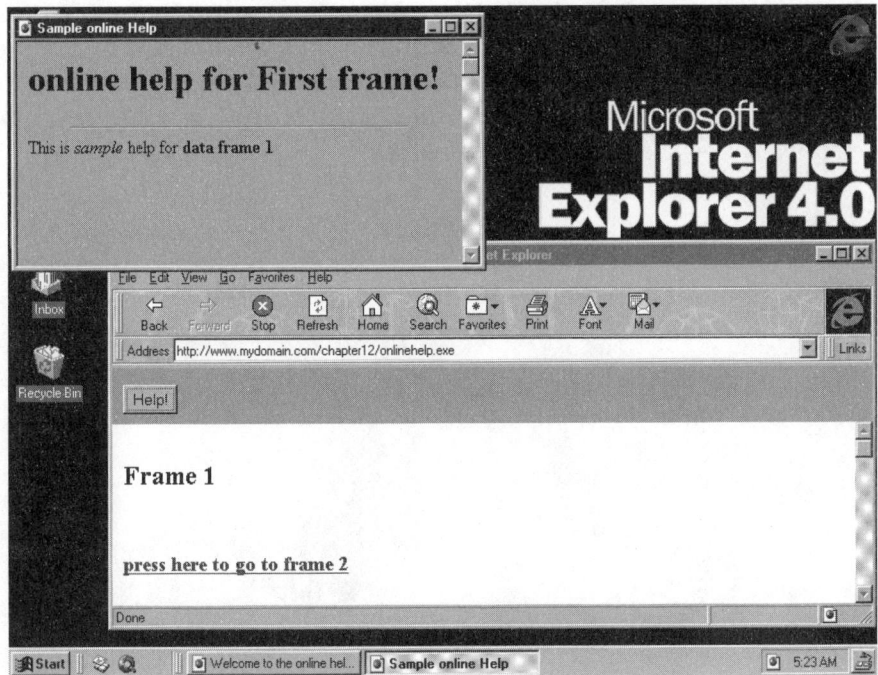

Summary

Interaction with the user is critical to an application's success. An end user wants the most interactive application possible. The portability of the application from one system to another, or from one browser to another, does not make a difference to the user — who typically uses either Microsoft's or Netscape's browsers (some prefer to have both on their systems). JavaScript gives CGI applications the ability to interact with the user on a limited basis.

In order for the user to receive native level interactivity from the application, localized components can be used. Our next chapter will contrast the differences between competing localized components (namely, Java applets, Plug-Ins, ActiveX controls and ActiveX documents).

13

LOCALIZED VB COMPONENTS

- Client Side VB constructs
- ActiveX controls embedded in web pages
- ActiveX documents
- Java applets vs. ActiveX documents
- Sample C/S ActiveX document with a standard CGI application server

CLIENT-SIDE VB CONSTRUCTS

When creating complete client/server applications on the Internet, the programmer is faced with quite a few options. Some of these have already been demonstrated in previous chapters.

A good client/server solution requires at least minimal client side cooperation. Standard CGI applications utilize a thin client with minimal intelligence and power. JavaScript enhances this, allowing the client side to create minimalistic applications, but is primarily used for validation and simple client interaction. Browser technology is essentially static, which means that a decent client side solution requires more than the minimal interaction facilities that HTML can provide.

Java applets were created for this particular purpose. These offer a stand-alone application, hosted in a Java-enabled browser. Java applets can communicate with each other using JavaScript glue logic. An essentially static web page can contain interactive components, glued together with JavaScript, to give the user a more interactive application.

True interactive applications are usually created using a single dedicated Java applet rather than this distributed technology. In some instances, JavaScript has been used to enhance and improve the communication between browser and applet.

Java is a powerful tool and language. It is not, however, without faults. Performance for the Java virtual machine have been greatly improved in recent years, but it is still sluggish. Large-scale applications have not yet been written for Java, and there aren't that many ready-to-use components that the Java programmer can employ to create quick applications. Furthermore, the Java language is quite different than C++ and necessitates retraining on the part of C++ programmers. Development tools for Java are improving, but are still nowhere near the advanced level the Visual C++ or Visual Basic development platforms presently offer.

Microsoft's Strategy on the Client Side

While fully supporting Java and JavaScript, Microsoft's strategy is somewhat different. By focusing on their prevailing software constructs, Microsoft has been able to produce a great Internet strategy while maintaining control of the desktop. Similar to the JavaScript's original functionality (which is to be used as glue logic for Java applets), VB-Script can also be used in Microsoft browsers as glue logic for ActiveX controls.

ActiveX controls enable this concept to be event-driven. These components are easily created with a host of development tools (such as Visual Basic 5, Visual C++ 4 or 5, Delphi and others).

All ActiveX documents and components are embedded in HTML utilizing the OBJECT tag. The object tag defines basic ActiveX component details. The ID defines the object's name. The object tag also defines the width and height of the object in the document. The CLAS-SID is the identifier that defines the ActiveX component. Each ActiveX component has a singular CLASSID (a.k.a. CLSID) that uniquely defines that component to the world. Finally, the codebase for the component is defined — informing the browser where that component can be found on the Internet (if it has not already been installed on the client machine).

Additionally, parameters can be defined between the <OBJECT> and </OBJECT> tags. These determine the default settings for the object's parameters, allowing the object to initialize correctly right from the start.

Following is sample code utilizing the marquee custom control, using VBScript as glue logic:

```
<OBJECT ID="Marquee" WIDTH=500 HEIGHT=47
   classid="clsid:27B5DFD5-2E4B-11D0-9D52-00AA00A74E07"
   codebase="/vbasic/controls/samples/AxMrquee.CAB#_
              version=1,0,0,0">
<PARAM Name="Text" Value="Testing 1234">
</OBJECT>

<SCRIPT LANGUAGE="VBScript">
<!—
Sub Window_onLoad
   Marquee.Text = "Marquee text"
   Marquee.Scrolling = True
End Sub
—>
</SCRIPT>
```

Figure 13.1 shows how the Marquee control can be used on a page.

Figure 13.2 demonstrates how the page would look in FrontPage 97.

Figure 13.1
Use of Marquee
ActiveX control

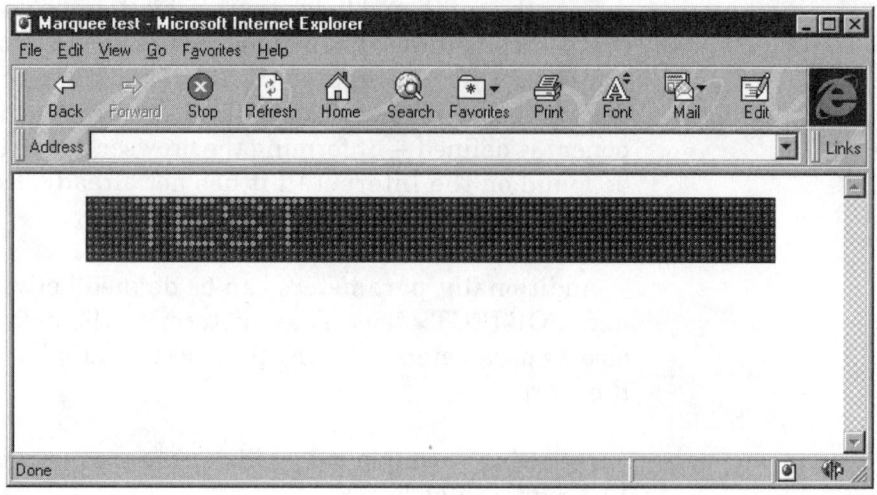

Figure 13.2
The same page
when designed in
FrontPage 97

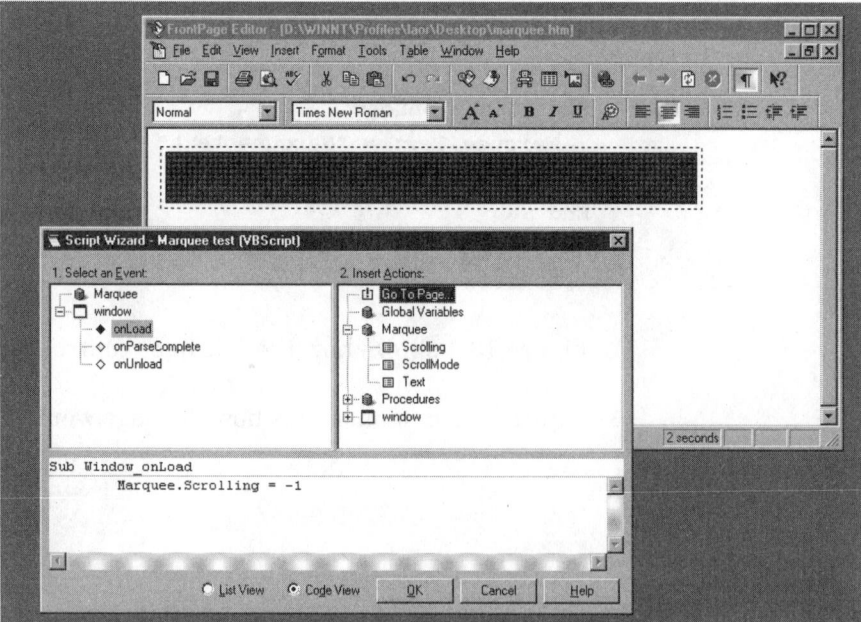

This code intentionally defines a default text message, and later reloads it during window load. It shows how information can be sent to the object statically as well as dynamically, using standard VBScript.

Again, the concept of employing components that utilize browser scripting to tie everything together is somewhat constrictive. VBScript is an interpreted language (in much the same way as JavaScript). This concept essentially relies on the fact that most of the application's intelligence lies in its components. But, this hypothesis has simply not proven itself in the real world. Most real-world Visual Basic applications utilize a large number of ActiveX controls; yet Visual Basic is far from being just simple glue logic for these controls. In real world applications, most of the "interesting" application code would actually reside in this glue logic. In other words, VB code is not normally considered an after-thought after the ActiveX components are put into place.

One way to resolve this is to create an ActiveX control that could encompass the entire application. The only deficiency in this is that additional glue logic (to initialize and populate the control's properties) would still be required. Additionally, ActiveX controls have little or no power over the hosting application. An ActiveX control cannot cause the browser to move forward or back or navigate to another URL. An ActiveX control cannot determine how it is displayed, cannot add menu items to its host, control scrolling, or even provide more than one form. In short, this concept is quite limiting to a programmer, and does not provide the facilities needed to create a comprehensive application.

Object-Oriented Clients

Microsoft realized long ago that an object-oriented file system was the way to go. This was one of the main targets in creating Cairo, Microsoft's first truly object-oriented operating system (whether or not this technology will end up in NT 5.0 is still unclear). The idea is to blur the lines between applications and documents. System folders can be, in reality, an application; a document can contain more documents, as well as other applications.

This concept has gotten a slow start, but provides many benefits. The first step that Microsoft took with the concept was the Office Binder in

Microsoft Office 95. It provided a clue as to how future applications could contain true object-oriented documents. In Microsoft's future super-environment, an ActiveX document can contain any number of underlying objects and/or documents.

ActiveX documents can be created using Visual Basic, and are much more capable than simple controls of interacting with the host container. An ActiveX document can instruct its host to save parameters, and can expose methods and properties to other objects hosted in the container. An ActiveX document controls how it is viewed in its container, and controls user-interface elements (scroll bars, viewport and even menus) for the container. An ActiveX document may request its container to move to another document, or to navigate to another URL (if it is an Internet-enabled ActiveX document container).

Visual Basic ActiveX documents are actually embedded onto a web page by simply referencing a VBD file. This file acts as a "go-between" between the DLL or EXE containing the actual ActiveX document. The container utilizes this file to communicate with the ActiveX document directly. The DLL or EXE containing the forms is, in actuality, a simple ActiveX application (or library) capable of containing standard VB forms and other components (these can be activated by the ActiveX documents as needed — e.g., when filling parameters). A programmer can essentially create an application that runs as either an ActiveX document or a standard application, depending on how it was activated.

Because of this technology implementation, parameters cannot be passed onto documents off the bat. The concept behind ActiveX documents dictates that they utilize the standard provided methods in order to save and retrieve information from their containers. This method uses a property bag, which is a universal tool for containers to save client information, without the clients knowing how or where this information is stored.

There are so many great features about ActiveX documents that the subject obviously surpasses this book's scope. Rather than focusing on placements of ActiveX controls in web pages and implementing the glue logic around them (this topic would grow stale soon from over-exposure, with not enough users), this chapter will focus on interactions between ActiveX documents and CGI server side applications.

Security, Security! (And Reliability Too!)

On the reliability front, ActiveX documents are significantly more prone to nasty system bugs that could alter something on the machine (either intentionally or incidentally). Java applets, on the other hand, are oriented *towards* security and are designed to be much safer. It should be noted that Microsoft's implementation of Java opens up the WIN32 API, rendering it as "unsafe" as any other application or tool on one's system (this is known as JActive).

Again, Java applets have their faults too (for instance, performance). ActiveX documents, however, are generally in the same game-field as Netscape plug-ins, rather than Java applets. Like plug-ins, ActiveX documents are oriented towards performance and ease of use (i.e., the ability to access local resources seamlessly), rather than security.

In order to prevent unwanted intrusion on the part of an enticing but dangerous web page, ActiveX documents (as well as other ActiveX components) can be digitally signed. This procedure does not actually validate that the application does what it claims (or doesn't do what it claims not to do). Plug-ins, or any downloaded application, for that matter, cannot make a different claim (a user should always be wary of downloaded applications). Instead, this procedure enables the user to validate that a reputable, trackable company or programmer has created the application or component.

ActiveX Document Containers

There are presently two major containers for ActiveX documents. The first is the Office Binder for Microsoft Office 95. The present Office Binder implementation (for Office 97) is much more able-bodied, and provides the user with a host of great features.

The most important ActiveX document container is the Microsoft Internet Explorer. There are many versions of this browser, the most significant of which is version 4.0. This version merges with the operating system in order to blur the distinction between local folders, remote folders, URLs and ActiveX documents, and even ActiveX components. The concept is of great value and provides the developer with infinite possibilities on the application end. Older Microsoft browsers, such as Internet Explorer 3.0x, fully support ActiveX documents as well.

The future third host for ActiveX containers will be Microsoft operating systems such as Memphis and Cairo (planning to merge in the early 21st century). These will slowly add object-oriented file system capabilities to provide more complex functionality than Internet Explorer 4.0. The ability to handle more complex compound ActiveX documents will be integrated into the operating system. This means that a user can browse in an ActiveX document directly from the explorer, without giving notice to the hosting location (e.g., a folder, an application, another compound document).

There are less intuitive ActiveX document containers out there. One example is the Visual Basic IDE itself. It allows you to create ActiveX documents which can be used by Visual Basic as an Add-In. This is quite useful in certain situations. In most cases, however, building a Visual Basic Add-In as a standard application is simply easier to handle.

Standard applications can also host ActiveX documents by hosting the Microsoft WebBrowser control. This control works in conjunction with Internet Explorer 3.0x's SHDOCVW.DLL (Show Document View) and permits an application to host any Internet-Explorer enabled application. Since WebBrowser can host an ActiveX document, as we will demonstrate in this chapter, a Visual Basic application can contain any number of ActiveX documents, as needed.

Additionally, since WebBrowser supports frames, these documents can be on the same level *or* in a hierarchical format. Interaction between documents, however, is somewhat limited. The WebBrowser control does not provide a means for communication between controls. This, however, can be overcome by utilizing a non-inproc ActiveX component (i.e., ActiveX Executable) which can be referenced in the base HTML document via the object HTML tag. This component acts as a communications gateway between the other components.

Netscape browsers have some changes built in to recent versions that acknowledge the popularity of the *COM* (Common Object Model, the basis of OLE and ActiveX). Not only have Netscape browsers assumed an ActiveX interface, Netscape Navigator version 4.0x also adds the ability to edit OLE enabled documents (not ActiveX documents) such as Word documents in place. The next step, bureaucracy willing, is to add native ActiveX document support — enabling ActiveX documents to run transparently regardless of the hosting browser. Given the browser race to accumulate as many features as possible (often stealing good ideas from your competitor), this would seem like a sure bet if this technology takes off the way Microsoft plans. Currently, this is partially supported with the aid of a Netscape plug-in.

Alternate Routes

There are several advantages to using ActiveX documents over regular Visual Basic applications. An ActiveX document does not need to communicate with a file system in order to save properties, and it can be integrated into a more compound application. Using frames, ActiveX documents and regular HTML documents and objects coexist, and provide an attractive, seamless web application. The ActiveX document is downloaded and installed by the browser with no user interaction. An ActiveX document improves on standard ActiveX controls in many ways, the most significant of which is the ability to load multiple forms and to request the hosting environment to move from one such form (or document) onto another.

A browser-centric ActiveX document can interact with CGI applications easily by asking the hosting browser to request the appropriate application with the correct parameters. The browser then shows the results, with minimal effort. This type of concept provides the programmer with a simple way to create smart browser applications, making no change to the back-end (or with support to various types of Internet clients). These applications provide a smarter was in which to submit information to the CGI application.

ActiveX documents can utilize ActiveX controls and more importantly, can contact and utilize local databases. This is a great boon for client/server applications that require local databases as well as server-based databases. Applications can utilize this feature in order to create comprehensive solutions, and provide caching, or even local information databases that periodically update themselves (virus scanners, magazines, ads, press releases and more) without requiring the application to contact the server every time it needs information.

Presently, Visual Basic can create fully functional ActiveX documents that work under all of the ActiveX-document hosting environments mentioned previously.

Designing the Mapping C/S Application

First, let us lay out the requirements for the upcoming application. Its purpose is to allow clients to perform searches on a graphical map. These searches should include a category and a search area. After searching an area, the user sees the list of items residing in the selected area that are covered in one of the selected category criteria.

This type of map application allows users to view purely relevant information (like clothing stores in a particular search area) without having to download a large database containing many categories completely useless to them. A company might also use this type of application to provide context-sensitive help on forms, or to give users a way to view the location for local distributors for their products.

An application like this has many *types* of clients. The simplest client would be a browser. A standard HTML browser can be used to browse the map database and, with a small JavaScript application, interact with the application in much the same way a more functional application could. This, however, does not provide the user with the full range of possibilities that a totally functional client application could.

Alternatively, an ActiveX control can be created (or various ones can be integrated, using VB Script). Better yet, a fully functional client application that would be better integrated and truly compiled, rather than interpreted, can be created.

On the server end, the standard client/server way of implementing such an application requires the server to interact with client using DCOM or even TCP/IP. This, however, is limiting on the client front, and requires a full-blown client application in order to work. A standard CGI application works better in this case by allowing any client to work with the same server application. This is the reason web-servers have been such an explosive force in the marketplace — they allow several types of clients to access the same information easily.

An ActiveX client for the mapping application can read and interpret output from the CGI *MapServer* application and simply display it in an alternative manner. Additionally, the ActiveX client can create an enhanced mapping client. This way, everyone has the capability of accessing the server, and more enhanced clients (like a Java-enabled client, or an ActiveX document-enabled client) can provide more information to the server, better user interface, and can display the information in a more comprehensive manner.

The MapServer CGI Application

In order to provide many types of clients with the same level of service, the server application utilizes the standard CGI style. The server accepts an area to search, and a list of categories. The server then returns the items it finds, in the requested area, that are of the selected category type.

In order to provide smart clients with smarter content, some of the fields in the HTML stream contain hidden clues that a smart client can easily pick up. Standard browsers will ignore these tags as remarks.

The map server's function is to receive a list of items, and an area in which to search. The server then searches a local database (which could be quite big) for compliant items. Once these are found, the server returns the retrieved rows onto the client. The client, in turn, displays this information using the capabilities at its disposal.

A smart client, for example, could provide the user with a scrollable map to search through, and could display the results so that the client can view all of the selected items [in the view window].

The client shown here is not as smart as the one described above. It does, however, demonstrate how standard ActiveX documents can be created to take over the browser, interact with a CGI server, and display information in a comprehensive manner. The Map client provides the user with a display of the map, allowing him to select an area. The user can also select any number of items in the Item checkbox list. Once the user is ready, he can press the search button (or alternatively, use the provided menu that integrates with Internet Explorer's own menus). The client then contacts the *MapServer* and retrieves information in much the same manner as any other client. This information is then parsed and displayed directly on the map. To the user, it looks like a local operation; but, in effect, this is a full-blown client/server application.

The *MapServer*'s database is simple, containing the following fields:

Table 13.1

The MapInformation table layout

Table: MAPINFORMATION Field Name	Field Type	Remark
LocationID	Autonumber (long integer)	Primary key- identifies record.
X	Integer	The horizontal position of the item on the map.
Y	Integer	The vertical position of the item on the map.
Type	Long Integer	A lookup to the type of Items that exist in the system ("foreign key" to the Types table).
Description	Text(50)	A textual description of the item or location.

Table 13.2

The Types table layout

Table: TYPES Field Name	Field Type	Remark
Type	Autonumber (long integer)	Primary key- identifies record.
Description	Text(50)	A textual description of the location type.

The Types table identifies the possible types of locations that can be searched for on the map. Each such type contains an identifying code and a textual description.

The MapInformation table contains the actual points on the map. Each point has a unique identifier used as a key. Each point has a vertical and horizontal position, a type and a text description.

When searching for something on the map, the server needs to look for items that have a horizontal and vertical position corresponding to the search area. Additionally, the type field should match one of the user-selected types. A user may want to search for *just* Malls — this idea allows the server to do away with unwanted information on the map.

ProcessMap Subroutine

The *MapServer* application contains one noteworthy subroutine: *ProcessMap*. This subroutine starts the web page and determines its parameters. The Left, Top, Right, Bottom parameters should contain information about the search area. The parameters starting with Item, followed by the Type codes that the user selected, will be submitted as parameters, signifying the checkboxes the user had selected when he submitted the original form.

The *ProcessMap* function goes through all of the possible types. Items that are identified as selected (i.e., that are not empty strings) are incorporated into the SQL query.

The query utilizes the BETWEEN SQL clause. This clause enables SQL statements to search for items in a selected range. There are two independent ranges that need to be tested for in this situation: the horizontal range and vertical range. The BETWEEN clause only tests for areas within a *bounding range*. This means items that exist on the border will not be selected. For this purpose, the *ProcessMap* function subtracts one from the left (or top) ranges and adds one to the right (or bottom) ranges. This permits items that are actually *on* the borderline to be included in the query as well.

The query tests for both horizontal and vertical positioning, then proceeds to test for item types. If no item types are included, the query will include them all (by simply *not* referencing the type field in the WHERE clause).

The query looks something like this:

```
select * from MapInformation, Types where Types.Type= _
       MapInformation.Type and (x between 5 and 19) and _
          (y between -1 and 100) AND (MapInformation.Type= _
          0 or MapInformation.Type=2)
```

This SQL statement lists all of the items in the *MapInformation* and *Types* tables. The first WHERE clause allows the join to work correctly (by only showing the items in the *Types* table that correspond to the correct type in each *MapInformation* row). The x and y ranges are tested for and verified. The types shown will be either type 0 or type 2 (whatever these types may be).

Once the query is initiated, the *ProcessMap* subroutine determines whether any items were returned by the query. If so, the subroutine iterates through the returned rows and places each in a separate table row. The first table column contains the description for the returned map item, as well as the hidden information for smarter clients. The next table column contains the X and Y coordinates of the returned item. The final column contains the text description of the item's type. (This information was retrieved by performing the join in the select statement.) Alternatively, the query could utilize a subselect to retrieve this information, an outer join (if items are suspected not to contain any type, but they still need to show up on the map) or by performing a separate, additional query for each of the returned items.

The MapServer Source Code

Following is the source code for the *MapServer* CGI application.

Notes

Since this project cannot be used in Visual Basic 4.0, the standard Load frmVBCrash statement was not included in this application.

```
Option Explicit

Declare Function oCGI2Register Lib "oCGI2.dll" Alias _
        "DllRegisterServer" () As Long

Dim cgi As New oCGI2
' this creates the HTML serving as the response to client _
        requests
Sub ProcessMap()
  'start the HTML going
  cgi.WriteCGI "<HTML><HEAD><TITLE>" + vbCrLf
  cgi.WriteCGI "Map Server</TITLE></HEAD><BODY _
        BGCOLOR=#ffffff>" + vbCrLf

  Dim sQuery As String, MaxItems As Integer
  Dim db As Database, rs As Recordset
```

```
' open the database
Set db = Workspaces(0).OpenDatabase(App.Path + _
         "\MapServer.Mdb", False, False)


' find out how many types we currently support.
' — the client should have no more check-boxes than this _
         number.
sQuery = "select MAX(Type) as MAX_TYPE from Types"
Set rs = db.OpenRecordset(sQuery)
MaxItems = rs("MAX_TYPE")
rs.Close


sQuery = "select * from MapInformation, Types where "
sQuery = sQuery + " Types.Type=MapInformation.Type "
sQuery = sQuery + " and (x between "
Dim sLeft As String, sRight As String
sLeft = cgi.ReadParam("Left")
' between only catches items that are MORE than this _
         amount
sQuery = sQuery + CStr(CInt(sLeft) - 1)


sRight = cgi.ReadParam("Right")
' between only catches items that are LESS than this _
         amount
sQuery = sQuery + " and " + CStr(CInt(sRight) + 1) + ") "


Dim iTop As Integer, iBottom As Integer
' between only catches items that are MORE than this _
         amount
iTop = CInt(cgi.ReadParam("Top")) - 1
sQuery = sQuery + " and (y between " + CStr(iTop)


' between only catches items that are LESS than this _
         amount
iBottom = CInt(cgi.ReadParam("Bottom")) + 1
sQuery = sQuery + " and " + CStr(iBottom) + ") "


' get the items and build them into the query.
Dim nItems As Integer, iItem As Integer
nItems = 0
For iItem = 0 To MaxItems
```

```
   Dim sParam As String
   sParam = cgi.ReadParam("Item" + CStr(iItem))
   If (sParam <> "") Then
      sQuery = sQuery + IIf(nItems = 0, " AND (", " OR ")
      sQuery = sQuery + "MapInformation.Type=" + _
         CStr(iItem)
      nItems = nItems + 1
   End If
Next
' if there are any items, there are parenthesis to close.
sQuery = sQuery + IIf(nItems = 0, "", ")")

' run the query.
Set rs = db.OpenRecordset(sQuery, dbOpenDynaset)
If (rs.EOF) Then
   ' no items found.
   cgi.WriteCGI "<H2>Could not find any items on the _
         map.</H2>" + vbCrLf
Else
   ' enclose each item in its own table.
   cgi.WriteCGI "<TABLE WIDTH=100% BORDER=1>" + vbCrLf
   Do While Not rs.EOF
      cgi.WriteCGI "<TR><TD>"

      ' information for SMART clients (e.g., MapClient)
      cgi.WriteCGI "<!--XYINFO=" + CStr(rs("x")) + "," + _
         CStr(rs("y"))
      cgi.WriteCGI "," + CStr(rs("MapInformation.Type")) + _
         "-->"
      ' information for standard clients (e.g., Netscape _
         browser).
      cgi.WriteCGI rs("MapInformation.Description")
      cgi.WriteCGI "</TD><TD>" + vbCrLf
      cgi.WriteCGI CStr(rs("x")) + "," + CStr(rs("y"))
      cgi.WriteCGI "</TD><TD>" + vbCrLf
      cgi.WriteCGI rs("Types.Description")
      cgi.WriteCGI "</TD></TR>" + vbCrLf
      rs.MoveNext
   Loop
   cgi.WriteCGI "</TABLE>" + vbCrLf
End If
```

```
        rs.Close
        db.Close
        cgi.WriteCGI "</BODY></HTML>" + vbCrLf
End Sub

Sub Main()
    On Error GoTo NormalErr
    oCGI2Register
    cgi.ProcessCGI Command

    ' handle the request
    ProcessMap

    Set cgi = Nothing
    End
NormalErr:
    Beep
    cgi.WriteCGI "error:" + Error$
End Sub
```

Figure 13.3 demonstrates how a standard browser client sees a reply from the Map server using standard HTML.

Figure 13.3
Browser client
displaying HTML reply
from Map server

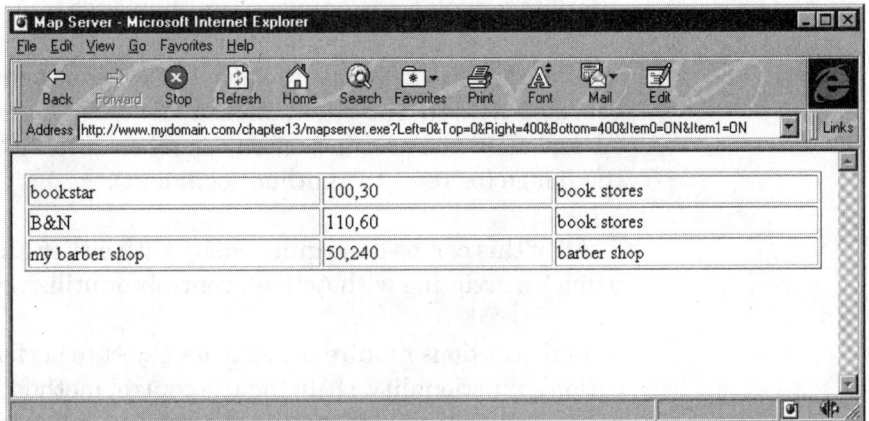

The MapClient

The mapping application was selected for this chapter because of its high demand on graphics. The graphics in themselves are simple at best. They do demonstrate, however, the primitive nature of the HTML technology.

The best user interface that a similar mapping application could utilize would be similar to MapIt! This is an HTML mapping tool that simply creates on the fly GIFs as requested by the user. All of the buttons and actions the user can perform (i.e., focusing on an area, performing searches) yield a complete rewrite of the entire screen. Since graphic operations incur a high bandwidth cost on the web, this concept is completely unsuitable for Internet-based systems. Because of the low bandwidth capability, the map information should be transferred in a non-graphical manner and drawn locally.

This is also costly on the client side. In overall performance, a good client side application (written in Java or Visual Basic using ActiveX controls or documents) is likely to improve on this concept, performance-wise, on all but the fastest Internet bandwidths.

Most Internet surfers don't actually sit on multiple T1s. Rather, the typical connection speed is often 28.8 K baud. This type of user cannot afford to download an image more than once.

Starting with this assumption, the concept behind the smart client becomes clearer. The client should download the map image as needed, and allow the user to perform searches on it without having to reload the image (or refer to another document).

All of this can be done quite easily with either Microsoft Technique — using VB scripting with ActiveX controls or utilizing ActiveX documents.

Both solutions require the ActiveX object to perform most of the application's functionality. Utilizing the control method, the application may require the browser to submit a form and move to another page. This means that map searches require a dedicated map server CGI application and that searches could be expensive.

The browser needs to verify the control every time the web page is reloaded and significant processing occurs on both control and browser. Additionally, the control is likely to require additional scripting support in order to truly integrate with the browser.

To create such a simple application, an ActiveX document-based application is a simpler, better choice. In other situations, however, a component-based web page may well be more appropriate.

Creating the ActiveX Document-Based Application

The *MapClient* actually has a *UserDocument* that takes care of all of the functionality in the client application.

In this particular situation, there is no need to have more than one ActiveX document. It should be noted, however, that a single application can contain multiple pages. This improves the overall performance of the local application by having the user download the complete (or semi-complete) application as needed.

ActiveX documents contained in a browser such as Internet Explorer can utilize the Hyperlink object to make the browser jump, or refer to another URL or ActiveX document (by referring to its VBD file).

Each ActiveX document in the office binder is called a *section*. When hosted in a binder, the document must utilize the container's parent and add a section:

```
Set objX = UserDocument.Parent.Parent.Sections
```

The sections object allows the document to reference other ActiveX documents in the same binder (and communicate with them, using exposed public properties and methods), or even add or remove additional sections.

```
UserDocument.Parent.Parent.Sections.Add , _
        "c:\myapplication\SecondDoc.vbd"
```

An ActiveX document container capable of Internet access actually utilizes the navigation capabilities of the container to display a secondary document:

```
UserDocument.HyperLink.NavigateTo _
          "file://c:\myapplication\SecondDoc.vbd"
```

In order to determine the type of container (to navigate onto another document), a document should test the type name for the container hosting it:

```
TypeName(UserDocument.Parent)
```

This statement yields the results "WebBrowser" for Internet explorer and "Section" for the Office Binder. Since the result of the Internet Explorer TypeName could be unpredictable, it is better to test for the binder value — which is predefined.

For an icon to show up correctly for an ActiveX document, the icon should be assigned to the actual document. In Section-based containers (like Binder) each document of a particular type is assigned that icon, making the document easily recognizable.

ActiveX Documents DLLs vs. EXEs

ActiveX documents are, in essence, another form of a standard ActiveX application or library. The major difference is the VBD file that defines the object's interfaces, and the actual ActiveX documents that comply to the ActiveX document interface standard.

There is some confusion as to when DLLs and EXEs should be used to create ActiveX documents. The decision as to whether to utilize a DLL or EXEs is similar to that of standard ActiveX applications. DLLs are in-process libraries. This means they will execute under the same context as the hosting environment (in this case, the browser). While providing faster response, the in-process component is able to access some task-specific information. At times, this makes for a healthy relationship between host and library (for instance, oCGI and a hosting

Visual Basic CGI application). At other times, it can be intrusive, and may allow an ActiveX document to access some of the inner workings of the host, or even cause it to crash.

ActiveX components run as an Executable function somewhat differently than identical code placed in an ActiveX DLL. Because there is a single running application, it serves all concurrently-running clients. When running several concurrent instances of ActiveX components embedded in an ActiveX EXE, these all run off of the same Executable in memory. All of these can share information via their global variables. (In some instances, this can produce unwanted side effects).

In this case, we would like to maximize performance with no interaction between the different instances of the ActiveX document. For this reason, the *MapClient* ActiveX document will be implemented using an In-process ActiveX document DLL.

Figure 13.4
VB Compile dialog box

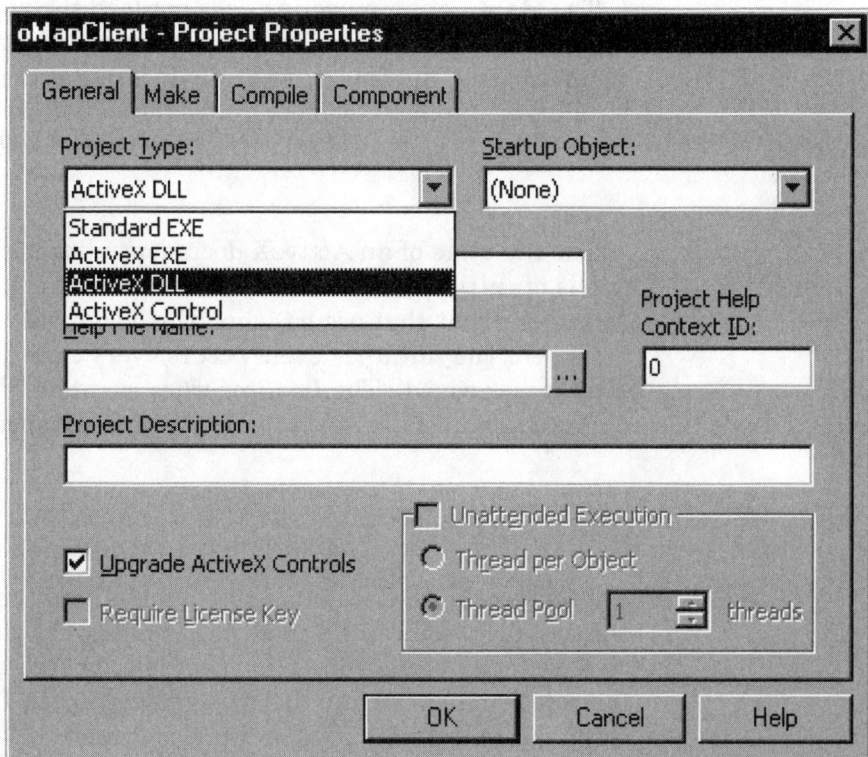

MapClient

In this scenario, only a single ActiveX document is required. The MapClient ActiveX document first loads the map image. The map image is not embedded directly into the application, in order to minimize download time. When the image is preloaded into the application, Visual Basic places it there as a standard bitmap image. This causes the application's size to increase significantly (causing slower download times for it). Since Visual Basic 5 can now read GIF images, the map image is loaded asynchronously from the server when it is first initialized. This also enables system operators to modify the actual map as needed. One improvement that can be made in this simple application is to resize the map so that the document allows scrolling through it if it is too big for the present view-port.

The MapClient application does not load the map location types on the fly. Rather, these are embedded into the system to prevent overcomplication. This feature is easily incorporated into the application by allowing the client to query the server for possible types (and descriptions of these types) and selecting color codes for these at run time.

The life cycle of an ActiveX document allows it to perform several levels of initialization. The ActiveX document first starts with the *Initialize* event that occurs when the document object is loaded and activated. The *Initialize* event occurs every time a control loads (even after it was saved). The *InitProperties* event, on the other hand, only occurs when initializing a completely new instance of an object.

WriteProperties Event

Persistent objects are saved through the *WriteProperties* event. When the container determines that the document has changed and needs to be saved, the *WriteProperties* event is triggered and the document's information is saved into the *PropertyBag* object. This object is provided by the container and allows the container to save the information in an undefined format or file.

When a persistent document needs its information loaded, the container triggers the *ReadProperties* event, allowing the document to retrieve information utilizing the provided *PropertyBag* object.

In order to let the container know whether some document properties have been changed (in order for the container to know that a *WriteProperties* event is required to save the document) the *PropertyChanged* function is called. This function can be called with a specific parameter noting the exact property that has changed (this requires the *WriteProperties* implementation to be smart enough to only commit those items declared as changed), or without any parameters — declare that the entire document must be committed.

AsyncRead

In order for the document to retrieve the map graphic at run-time, the new *AsyncRead* Visual Basic facility has been incorporated into the application. This function causes the application to download a requested file in the background. It is quite useful for a variety of options. In this scenario, the *MapClient* application utilizes this facility to download the map graphic onto the picture box control.

When initiating an asynchronic request, the URL, or file location, of where the graphic is located is specified. Additionally, the type of information transferred by the request is determined. There are three categories of information that can be downloaded utilizing the *AnsycRead* function call. These are:

1. Picture (demonstrated in the map client application)

2. Binary stream (which is simply a stream of binary information)

3. A file

Information such as HTML documents can also be retrieved with this system. However, these require the use of the file Async type. When retrieving standard HTML information (incidentally, such information can easily be retrieved from a CGI application) a temporary file containing it is created and referenced. This makes downloading from web servers quite inconvenient. An optional property name can also be added, providing the application with a way to identify the object when it is finished downloading. Alternatively, the HTML can be retrieved as a binary stream and later converted into a string.

When an asynchronous request is complete, the *AsyncReadComplete* event is triggered. The parameter it passes allows the event handling routine to determine what object has completed its download, as well as to ascertain ability to retrieve its contents.

The *AnsyncProp.PropertyName* contains the name of the object once retrieval has completed. Since the application currently only retrieves one object (the map graphic), any other property name will cause an error to be displayed. Since the object requested is a graphic, it can be directly assigned to the *pictMap* picture box control.

AsyncProp.Value

When retrieving binary information, the *AsyncProp.Value* object contains the appropriate binary information. When accessing a standard HTML file (or other types of files) a temporary file is created. The *AsyncProp.Value* contains the name of the temporary file with the downloaded information.

Should the asynchronous operation encounter an error, the *AsyncReadComplete* event will still be triggered. This time, however, the *AsyncProp.Value* contains an erroneous state. This triggers the appropriate error when the value is accessed. This requires the presence of some error handling code inside the *AsyncReadComplete* event.

The ActiveX document contains a rectangle with a dashed border. The rectangle can be dynamically stretched as the mouse drags. This is done using standard Visual Basic events (*MouseDown* and *MouseMove*).

PerformSearch

When the search is initiated (after the rectangle is positioned correctly), either by pressing the search button or via a menu option (which is added through the standard menu editor for the document), the *PerformSearch* subroutine is called.

The picture graphic is host to a label and a circle. These are used to dynamically allocate and position the returned map items. The *PerformSearch* subroutine first unloads any residual traces of these objects created during the previous search. The search facilities (button and menu option) are disabled to allow the search to take place, without interruptions or a search resubmission.

Next, the parameters for the *MapServer* application are prepared for submission. There are several ways in which the *MapClient* could actually communicate with the server. The simplest communication method has already been described previously: the *AsyncRead* facility. This facility however, requires the application to retrieve the information from a file *after* the information is completely transferred over (after which the temporary file should be removed). This solution lacks elegance, and is sure to produce significant numbers of temporary files when the application is interrupted before removing them.

An additional way to produce a viable result is to use the hosting browser to navigate to the target URL. This method results in a good application for providing a user interface to the querying portion of the application. In order to provide a complete solution, on the other hand, the application should also handle the incoming results of the URL request.

The new Microsoft Internet transfer control was integrated into the application in order to communicate with the server. This control provides a fully functional connection control to FTP and HTTP sites. There are various ways it can be used to transfer information.

The *Execute* method has been chosen because of its versatility. This method can be used to fill in details as they arrive, and it can submit the information in all of the standard CGI submission methods (POST, ISINDEX or GET). The GET submission method has been used for reasons which will become clear toward the end of the chapter.

The *StateChanged* event is triggered for the Internet transfer control as the state changes. The state for this control changes when the control resolves the URL, when it contacts the server, when it transfers the parameters to the server, as information is retrieved from the server, and when the information is completely transferred over (or when an error occurs instead). Information can be retrieved via the *GetChunk* method in sections. When no more information exists, the *GetChunk* method returns an empty string. At this point, the combined information retrieved via the *GetChunk* method is the output HTML stream submitted by the Map server.

OpenURL

Alternatively the *OpenURL* method could be used with the URL of the server and parameters. The *OpenURL* method returns with the output HTML string and is subsequently synchronous in nature (rather than asynchronous, as the application had been implemented). If an error occurs, an error will be triggered around the statement.

The *OpenURL* method acts internally like a synchronous version of *Execute* and subsequent *GetChunk* function calls until the entire document is in place. Interestingly, the *OpenURL* method can retrieve FTP and HTTP documents that are either text or binary. For binary calls, a binary array with no predetermined size should be created and set to the value of the *OpenURL* call:

```
Dim bArr() As Byte
bArr() = iNetConnection.OpenURL("http://www.myDomain.com/_
            myGif.GIF", icByteArray)
```

An *Execute* request can end up as one of two conditions: a successful download, or an error. When an error occurs, an error message is initiated and the search facilities enabled (search button and search menu).

ProcessResponse

When the URL request is returned successfully, information is gathered via consecutive *GetChunk* calls, and submitted to the *ProcessResponse* subroutine for display. The search facilities are later enabled for subsequent searches.

The *ProcessResponse* subroutine takes care of parsing the HTML response from the Map server, and displays that information on the actual map graphic. Each row of the search output has a special code, embedded into each row, containing search information for the smart map clients (that's us!). This information always starts with the "XYIN-FO=" string. Of course, a more complex string that cannot also occur in the data stream can (and should) be used instead.

The subroutine will continue to loop as long as it locates more XYIN-FO strings. For each such string, the subroutine parses the subsequent information following the XYINFO. This information contains the X and Y coordinates of the item on the screen, the color code for the item (which correlates to the Type of item it is) and the description of the map item.

Next, the subroutine creates and points a new circle object that will be placed around the target Item. A new label containing the text for the item's description is created and placed next to the item location. The color code for both the circle and text forecolor is set to the same as that of the appropriate checkbox color code for the item type.

Once this subroutine terminates, the application is ready to submit a new search, as needed.

The Source Code for the MapClient

```
Option Explicit
Dim originX As Integer, originY As Integer
Dim sURLImage As String
Private Sub PerformSearch()
   Dim sTarget As String, sParameters As String
   Dim iPoint As Integer

   ' disable a "re-search".
   cmdSearch.Enabled = False
   'mnuSearch.Enabled = False

   ' kill any residue circles and points from the previous _
         searches
   For iPoint = 1 To lblMapText.UBound
     Unload lblMapText(iPoint)
     Unload circlePoint(iPoint)
   Next
   ' point to the target map server.
```

```
        sTarget = txtTarget + "\MapServer.exe"

    ' if nothing's selected, choose everything!
    If Not rect1.Visible Then
      rect1.Left = 0
      rect1.Top = 0
      rect1.Width = UserDocument.ScaleWidth
      rect1.Height = UserDocument.ScaleHeight
    End If

    sParameters = "Left=" + CStr(rect1.Left)
    sParameters = sParameters + "&Top=" + CStr(rect1.Top)
    sParameters = sParameters + "&Right=" + CStr(rect1.Left _
          + rect1.Width)
    sParameters = sParameters + "&Bottom=" + CStr(rect1.Top _
          + rect1.Height)

    ' make sure that our container saves the information for _
          later use!
    Dim i As Integer
    For i = 0 To chkItems.Count - 1
      If (chkItems.Item(i).Value = 1) Then
        sParameters = sParameters + "&Item" + CStr(i) + "=" _
          + CStr(chkItems.Item(0).Value)
      End If
    Next


    ' lets go- submit the request to the server.
    ' GET is the easiest submission method.
    inetConnection.Execute sTarget + "?" + sParameters, "GET"
    PropertyChanged
End Sub
Private Sub cmdSearch_Click()
  PerformSearch
End Sub

Private Sub mnuSearch_Click()
  PerformSearch
End Sub
```

```vb
Private Sub inetConnection_StateChanged(ByVal State As _
        Integer)
Select Case State
  Case icResponseCompleted: ' our information is here!
    Dim vData As Variant, sOutData As String

    ' shouldn't be more than 1024, but who knows.
    vData = inetConnection.GetChunk(1024, icString)
    Do While LenB(vData) > 0
      sOutData = sOutData + CStr(vData)
      vData = inetConnection.GetChunk(1024, icString)
    Loop

    ' process the HTML that we got back.
    ' NOTE: server can basically send anything that we _
        want,
    ' — not JUST HTML, even binary information...
    ProcessResponse sOutData
    ' enable a new search
    cmdSearch.Enabled = True
    'mnuSearch.Enabled = True
  Case icError:
    ' an error occured.
    MsgBox "unable to contact target"
    ' enable a new search
    cmdSearch.Enabled = True
    'mnuSearch.Enabled = True
End Select
End Sub

Sub ProcessResponse(ByVal sHTML As String)
  ' make rectangle invisible
  rect1.Visible = False

  ' search for XYPOS in sHTML, that's my spot
  Const XYINFO = "XYINFO="

  Dim iPoint As Integer
  iPoint = 1

  Dim iPos As Integer
```

```
Do While True
    iPos = InStr(sHTML, XYINFO)
    If (iPos <= 0) Then Exit Do
    ' XYINFO=X,Y,INDEX
    sHTML = Mid$(sHTML, iPos + Len(XYINFO))
    iPos = InStr(sHTML, ",")
    Dim x As Integer, y As Integer, iIndex As Integer
    Dim sText As String

    ' get X
    x = CInt(Left(sHTML, iPos - 1))
    ' trim the rest.
    sHTML = Mid$(sHTML, iPos + 1)

    ' get Y
    iPos = InStr(sHTML, ",")
    y = CInt(Left$(sHTML, iPos - 1))
    ' trim the rest.
    sHTML = Mid$(sHTML, iPos + 1)

    ' get the end for index.
    iPos = InStr(sHTML, "->")
    iIndex = CInt(Left$(sHTML, iPos - 1))

    iPos = InStr(sHTML, ">")
    ' trim the rest.
    sHTML = Mid$(sHTML, iPos + 1)

    iPos = InStr(sHTML, "</")
    sText = Left$(sHTML, iPos - 1)

    ' create a circle, point it to the right spot.
    Load circlePoint(iPoint)
    circlePoint(iPoint).Top = y - _
        (circlePoint(iPoint).Height / 2)
    circlePoint(iPoint).Left = x - _
        (circlePoint(iPoint).Width / 2)
    circlePoint(iPoint).BorderColor = _
        CLng(chkItems(iIndex).ForeColor)

    Load lblMapText(iPoint)
```

```vb
        lblMapText(iPoint).Caption = sText
        lblMapText(iPoint).ForeColor = _
              chkItems(iIndex).ForeColor
        lblMapText(iPoint).Top = y + 4
        lblMapText(iPoint).Left = x + 4
        lblMapText(iPoint).Visible = True
        circlePoint(iPoint).Visible = True

        iPoint = iPoint + 1
    Loop
End Sub


Private Sub pictMap_MouseDown(Button As Integer, Shift As _
          Integer, x As Single, y As Single)

    ' start the drag process
    rect1.Visible = True
    originX = x
    originY = y
    rect1.Top = y
    rect1.Left = x
    rect1.Width = 0
    rect1.Height = 0
End Sub


Private Sub pictMap_MouseMove(Button As Integer, Shift As _
          Integer, x As Single, y As Single)

    ' drag the mouse
    If (Button And vbLeftButton) > 0 Then
      Dim sx As Integer, sy As Integer
      Dim ex As Integer, ey As Integer
      If (x < originX) Then
        sx = x
        ex = originX
      Else
        sx = originX
        ex = x
      End If
      If (y < originY) Then
        sy = y
```

```
          ey = originY
      Else
          sy = originY
          ey = y
      End If
      If (sx < 0) Then
          sx = 0
      End If
      If (sy < 0) Then
          sy = 0
      End If


      If (ex > pictMap.ScaleWidth) Then
          ex = pictMap.ScaleWidth - 1
      End If
      If (ey > pictMap.ScaleHeight) Then
          ey = pictMap.ScaleHeight - 1
      End If
      rect1.Left = sx
      rect1.Top = sy
      rect1.Width = ex - sx
      rect1.Height = ey - sy
    End If
End Sub


Private Sub UserDocument_AsyncReadComplete(AsyncProp As _
        AsyncProperty)
On Error GoTo ExitAsyncComplete
    ' finished reading the image.
    Select Case AsyncProp.PropertyName
      Case "Image":
        ' the value should contain the image I was waiting for.
        pictMap.Picture = AsyncProp.Value
      Case Else:
        MsgBox "Error, unknow async info."
    End Select
    Exit Sub
ExitAsyncComplete:
    ' couldn't get to the information.
    MsgBox "error accessing " + AsyncProp.PropertyName
    Exit Sub
```

```vb
End Sub

Private Sub UserDocument_InitProperties()
  'default!
  sURLImage = "http://1.0.0.1/chapter13/map.gif"

  ' start the process going for the async image retrieval
  AsyncRead sURLImage, vbAsyncTypePicture, _
          PropertyName:="Image"
End Sub

Private Sub UserDocument_ReadProperties(PropBag As PropertyBag)
  ' read all of the properties
  rect1.Left = PropBag.ReadProperty("Left", 0)
  rect1.Top = PropBag.ReadProperty("Top", 0)
  rect1.Width = PropBag.ReadProperty("Width", 0)
  rect1.Height = PropBag.ReadProperty("Height", 0)
  sURLImage = PropBag.ReadProperty("Image", "map.gif")

  ' start (another?!) image transfer for the image.
  pictMap.Picture = LoadPicture()
  AsyncRead sURLImage, vbAsyncTypePicture, _
          PropertyName:="Image"

  txtTarget = PropBag.ReadProperty("Target", _
          "http://1.0.0.1/chapter13")
  Dim i As Integer
  For i = 0 To chkItems.Count - 1
    chkItems.Item(i).Value = PropBag.ReadProperty("Item" + _
          CStr(i), 0)
  Next
End Sub

Private Sub UserDocument_WriteProperties(PropBag As _
          PropertyBag)
  ' write the properties to my container for saving.

  PropBag.WriteProperty "Left", rect1.Left
  PropBag.WriteProperty "Top", rect1.Top
  PropBag.WriteProperty "Width", rect1.Width
  PropBag.WriteProperty "Height", rect1.Height
```

```
      PropBag.WriteProperty "Image", sURLImage
      PropBag.WriteProperty "Target", txtTarget.Text
      Dim i As Integer
      For i = 0 To chkItems.Count - 1
        PropBag.WriteProperty ("Item" + CStr(i)), _
                chkItems.Item(i).Value
      Next
    End Sub


    Public Property Get Image() As Variant
        ' get the image value from the outside.
        Image = sURLImage
    End Property


    Public Property Let Image(ByVal vNewValue As Variant)
        ' set the image value from the outside
        sURLImage = vNewValue
        PropertyChanged "Image"

        ' clear the image so that the user knows something's _
                going on.
        pictMap.Picture = LoadPicture()
        ' start reading the image.
        AsyncRead sURLImage, vbAsyncTypePicture, _
                PropertyName:="Image"
    End Property
```

The Internet Transfer Control

You may be wondering why the GET submission technique was utilized this time, rather than POST — which I've been using throughout the book. The POST request simply does not work with the Internet Transfer Control as released with Visual Basic.

This recognized bug in the Internet Transfer control is described in article Q167706 in Microsoft's Knowledge base.

Microsoft's solution was the WININET APIs, which are included with the ActiveX SDK to resolve this issue. Browsing through this simple example of posting information to a web server, it is easy to understand why the GET technique was more adaptable to this application.

In situations where a web application simply does not recognize requests other than POST, the WININET technique of posting information to the server can be used.

Embedding the Client and Rolling it Out

In order to roll out the application correctly, the document can simply be referenced. In order for this to work, though, the appropriate application (the MapClient.Exe application containing the ActiveX document) must already have been registered.

Since it is likely that this application is not yet installed, the Setup Wizard that comes with Visual Basic 5.0 can be used to provide a CAB file and installation HTML file. The HTML file contains an object declaration that enables the browser to download the component, if it has not already been installed on the machine. A simple VBScript code is used to enable the document to turn into a single frame containing the application. This is done after the browser downloads the component (in this case, the Visual Basic ActiveX document). To the user, it seems completely transparent — as if the document is taking over the entire browser area.

In order to utilize the object correctly, the target HTML contains both a frame with the Visual Basic document in it *and* the object declaration that allows the browser to automatically download the document as needed.

The following HTML demonstrates how a standard HTML script hosts an ActiveX component such as MapClient. The first portion references the object, in order to cause the browser to fetch it if it is not already installed on the client's machine. The second portion uses VB Script to create a single frame, which will cover the entire browser window. Obviously, additional frames can be incorporated here to make a nicer looking web page or provide additional features, such as online help. Additional HTML can be employed in order to support non-Microsoft browsers for this applicaiton.

```
<HTML>
<OBJECT ID="MapClient1"
CLASSID="CLSID:B9D8E52D-BEDD-11D0-B788-204C4F4F5020"
CODEBASE="MapClient.CAB#version=1,0,0,0">
```

```
</OBJECT>

<SCRIPT LANGUAGE="VBScript">
Sub Window_OnLoad
  Document.Open
  Document.Write "<FRAMESET>"
  Document.Write "<FRAME SRC=""MapClient1.VBD"">"
  Document.Write "</FRAMESET>"
  Document.Close
End Sub
</SCRIPT>
</HTML>
```

The setup program creates a CAB file using several support files (these are left behind by the MakCab utility that compresses the information into the CAB file). The INF file in the support directory can be modified by hand to include or change some of the features offered by the CAB facility. This can be utilized to modify the default behavior of a standard CAB file.

Figures 13.5-13.7 demonstrate how the ActiveX document appears when embedded within the different document hosts.

Figure 13.5
Document embedded
in Internet explorer

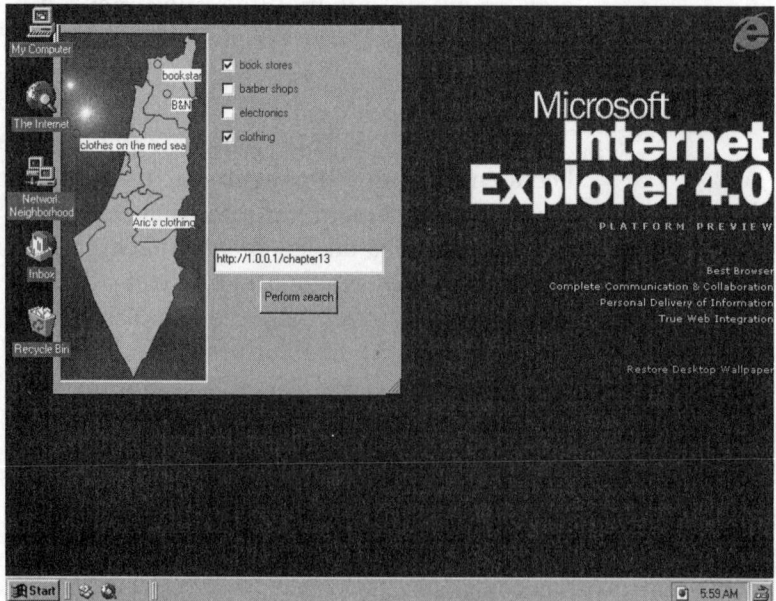

Figure 13.6
Document embedded
in Microsoft Office
Binder

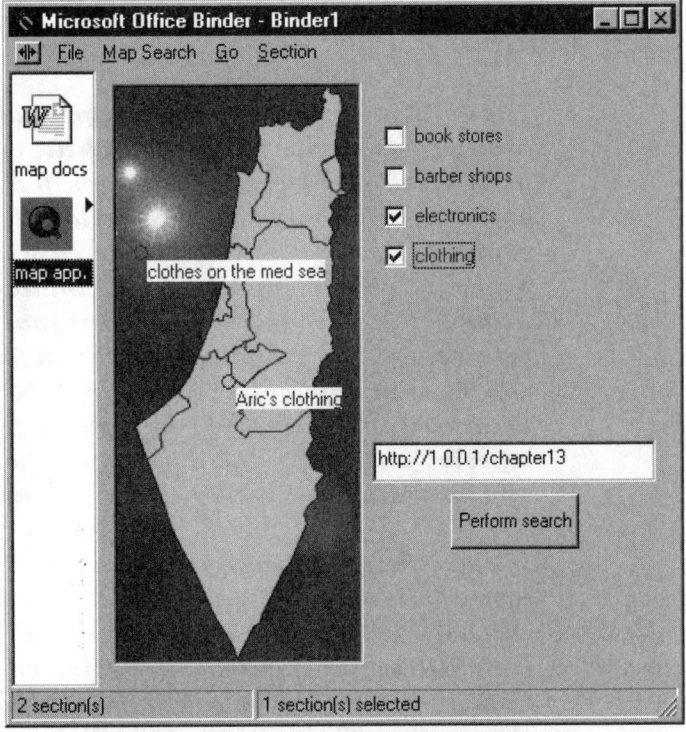

Figure 13.6
Document embedded
in Microsoft Office
Binder

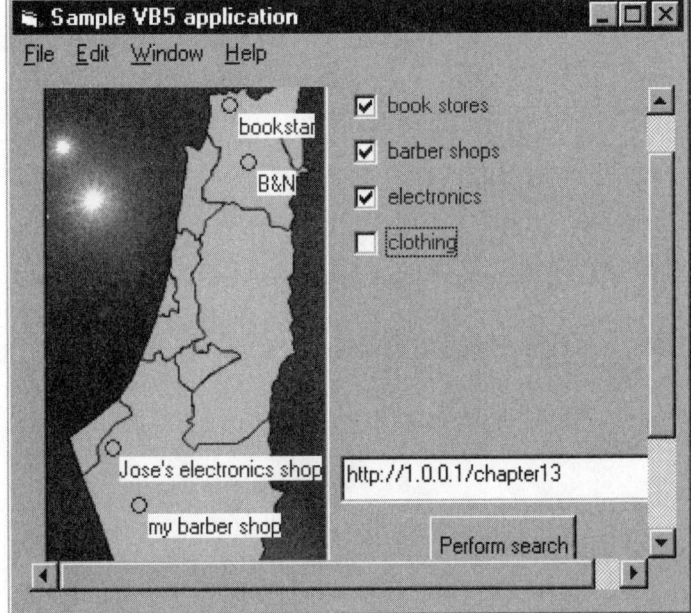

Figure 13.7
Document embedded
in a standalone
application

Summary

The ability to produce complete applications from within the browser has merits, but provides little or no portability between browsers. It is rumored that Microsoft will come out with a Java operation code-enabled VB compiler. This and Intel's future Java-enabled processors will likely increase the viability of native performance VB/Java applications running in a browser. Until then, using ActiveX documents is my personal preference for writing Internet-deployed applications to run from within the browser. Of course, most applications can simply be Internet-enabled without necessarily running within a browser. ActiveX documents are especially useful for Intranet applications where both browser and operating systems for clients are mandatorily Microsoft's.

In order for us to deploy enterprise level applications, however, several pieces of information are still missing. Our next chapter will outline these pieces of information, including connectivity with SQL server, and load balancing between servers. In addition, the reader may require piping of non-HTML data from the application. The next chapter will demonstrate piping of sound and graphics through a CGI program.

CHAPTER 14

ADVANCED ISSUES

- Using Access or SQL server for the web application
- Using ODBC to connect to remote SQL servers
- Load balancing techniques
- Sending out binary information from the CGI application (sound, graphics)
- Multimedia enhanced hello world application
- Piping atypical formats to the web browser
- The hit counter application
- Communicating with the outside world
- Live image and document scans
- Distributed applications
- Scheduled activation

When dealing with smaller sites where fewer concurrent customers interface with the application, it is often easier to utilize a LAN based database such as Microsoft Access. Access 97 (interfaced via ODBC, or DAO 3.5) is a much more robust database than previous releases. It does, however, limit the realistic number of effective, *concurrent* connections to a rather small number: around 5-10 users.

Figure 14.1
Building a query using
Access 97

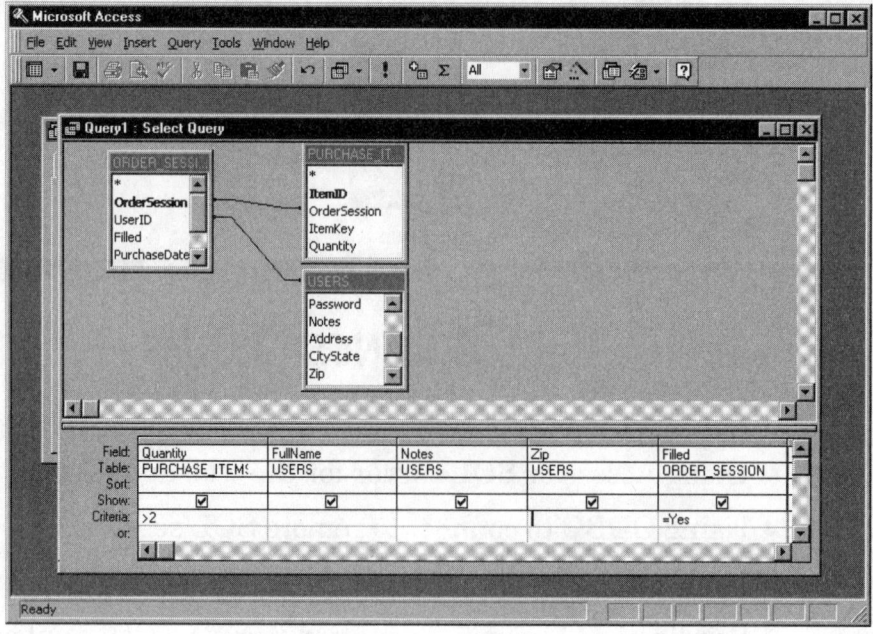

When dealing with a site that may require more than this number of concurrent users, it is recommended that a true Client/Server system, such as Microsoft SQL server, be used. This type of solution, albeit expensive, often yields significant improvements in speed when a larger number of concurrent connections are utilized.

To further improve performance, complete "mirroring" can be utilized by separating the web application from the database. Mirroring of the application can be done on several levels. The simplest method is to set up an ODBC connection in several web servers — all connected to the same backend SQL server. Each web server executes the application locally, but utilizes the backend database server in order to communicate the information back to the browser clients.

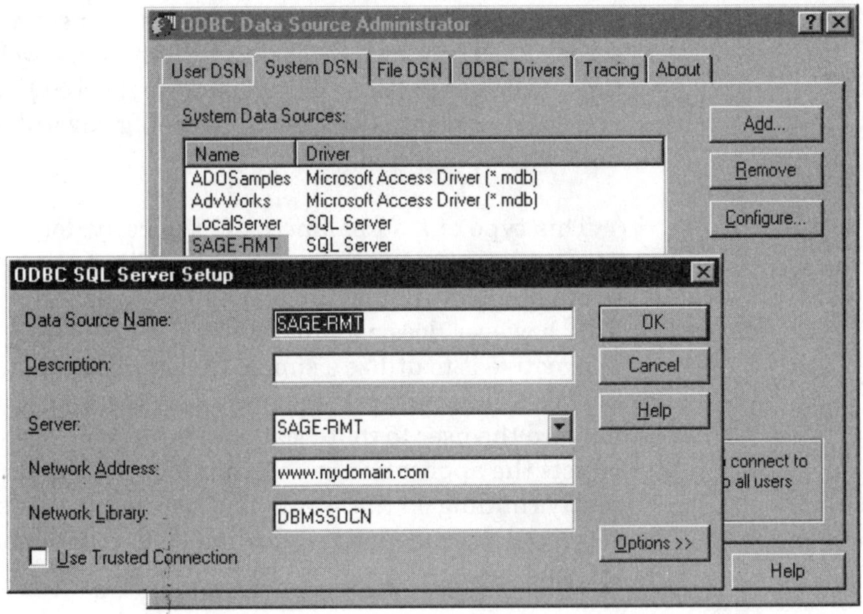

Figure 14.2
ODBC admin dialog
box setting a remote
SQL connection

This scenario often proves sufficient in most high end situations. A good web server can handle a large number of transactions, whereas a web browser is often required to perform more menial tasks which can slow down the application significantly. By separating the application functionality from the database, a high performance n-tier application can be created quite easily, and with minimal additional cost.

A more complex scenario requires several SQL servers, synchronizing with each other, with the help of the replication facilities in SQL server. Static information and non-redundant information (items to be purchased, or user information that must be immediately available to all of the web servers) can be placed on one central server, or else copied from one central server to all of the replicated ones. Dynamic information (i.e., tables containing the user orders) can be placed on a local, distributed server, which replicates back to the main server on a timely basis. Tables should all utilize timestamps in order to aid the synchronization process.

In order to utilize several servers for load balancing, a few changes must be made in the system. One approach is to have the original HTML form forward the browser to a particular server.

This type of load balancing forwards the user over to a different web server. Each user keeps working with the same web server for the duration of the connection. When using several SQL servers, this type of approach prevents the user from seeing several versions of the same data while connected.

This type of load balancing is typically done on the referring web page, utilizing a simple JavaScript code that randomly picks a web server out of the available range, then forwards the browser to that server. This, however, does not provide a real sense of load balancing. A smarter alternative is to utilize a simple CGI application that determines which SQL server is currently occupied with the fewest number of users, and forward the user to that location. The *sp_who* system stored-procedure assists the application in determining what kinds of processes are currently running on the server, and how many users are currently being serviced. Executing the following select statement will retrieve this information:

```
EXECUTE SP_WHO
```

Which will return the current tasks running on the server, in the following format:

spid	status	loginame	hostname	blk	dbname	cmd
1	sleeping	sa		0	master	MIRROR HANDLER
2	sleeping	sa		0	master	LAZY WRITER
3	sleeping	sa		0	master	CHECKPOINT SLEEP
4	sleeping	sa		0	master	RA MANAGER
10	sleeping	ocgiuser	OCGI	0	OCGI2	AWAITING COMMAND
11	runnable	ocgiuser	OCGI	0	OCGI2	SELECT

```
(1 row(s) affected)
```

When writing SQL server-based applications, it is recommended that these applications use their own login name. This login name can be used to limit the applications security rights in the database.

When using the *sp_who* stored procedure, a parameter can be passed which narrows down the items returned, based on login name. When this feature is used with a valid login name, it looks like this:

```
EXECUTE SP_WHO ocgiuser
```

With the following results:

spid	status	loginame	hostname	blk	dbname	cmd
10	sleeping	ocgiuser	OCGI	0	OCGI2	AWAITING COMMAND
11	runnable	ocgiuser	OCGI	0	OCGI2	SELECT

```
(1 row(s) affected)
```

By counting the number of rows that are not "sleeping," the system can determine how busy a particular SQL server currently is.

A simpler load-balancing system relies on DNS records. The browser uses DNS to convert an URL into an IP address. Normally, an address DNS record looks like:

```
www IN A 1.0.0.1
```

which lets the browser know that www (in whichever domain the DNS file refers to) is in address 1.0.0.1. (This is a bogus IP address; a real DNS record would have a real IP address.)

DNS-based load-balancing uses more than one IP address for a particular URL. For example:

```
www IN A 1.0.0.1
www IN A 1.0.0.2
www IN A 1.0.0.3
www IN A 1.0.0.4
```

The DNS server distributes each of these IP addresses evenly to requesting browsers. The first browser gets the first IP address; the next receives the next one, and so forth.

This approach assumes that most users will create about the same amount of load. Since the browsers only query for an IP address when the URL is first decoded, the IP address will persist throughout a particular session.

Several web sites use this technique for load balancing inside of their standard web content, not just in the web applications. While Netscape generally load-balances using distinct servers — each running the same applications (by having them replicate the script directories, in addition to the content directories), the Microsoft web-sites primarily use DNS load-balancing. This can be demonstrated by pinging **www.microsoft.com** more than once:

```
D:\>ping www.microsoft.com

Pinging www.microsoft.com [207.68.137.59] with 32 bytes of _
            data:

Reply from 207.68.137.59: bytes=32 time=300ms TTL=52
Reply from 207.68.137.59: bytes=32 time=772ms TTL=52
Reply from 207.68.137.59: bytes=32 time=771ms TTL=52
Reply from 207.68.137.59: bytes=32 time=1382ms TTL=52

D:\>ping www.microsoft.com

Pinging www.microsoft.com [207.68.156.52] with 32 bytes of _
            data:

Reply from 207.68.156.52: bytes=32 time=580ms TTL=53
Reply from 207.68.156.52: bytes=32 time=180ms TTL=53
Reply from 207.68.156.52: bytes=32 time=161ms TTL=53
Reply from 207.68.156.52: bytes=32 time=160ms TTL=53
```

Note that the IP address changed between consecutive pings.

Database Access

When accessing an ODBC-based database or a LAN-based database (like Access), you can utilize DAO. It is often beneficial to use *read only* dynasets (or keysets) instead of snapshots, with regard to memory requirements and speed.

If ODBC is being used for select statements, the direct SQL option should be used for optimum performance. Adding, removing and updating items via direct SQL execute commands is significantly faster than doing so via Visual Basic native methods.

When using Access 97, the DAO 3.5 library can be referenced and used for quicker, more efficient Access database access. Reportedly, DAO 3.5 is significantly faster than previous Jet engine releases.

When using SQL server, the programmer should utilize RDO or ADO whenever possible. This library can significantly improve performance when used correctly. The syntax difference between RDO and DAO is minimal. RDO and ADO are only available in the Visual Basic Enterprise edition (they are available through various other Microsoft products as well). COM enabled distributed applications can utilize the Microsoft transation server for load balancing.

MIME Types — Sending Out Binary Information from an Application

Occasionally, an application is required to stream binary data other than HTML text for the browser. This can include images, sounds and any other mime data types.

The raw data for this information can come from any source: database, an actual file or from the application itself. This is a great tool for securely transmitting images or other binary files. The data for the file never leaves the source, and no duplicates are required.

Using the application to stream information can be useful because it has the ability to terminate the connection mid-stream, or to transmit information that is up-to-date or even interactive.

Fully controlling the actual transmission of binary data to the user allows the system to enforce security, and prevents the user from directly accessing the binary files.

When dealing with an application that transmits images, most browsers are prepared to accept an image from a CGI source. On the other hand, not all browsers are well-equipped to handle all MIME types.

For example, Netscape browsers have great difficulty reading audio files directly from a CGI application. The reason for this is found in both the browser and the browser's audio plug-in. The browser downloads the audio stream and saves it with an erroneous extension: .EXE. The browser assumes that this is the extension, since it is the extension of the CGI application file it has just used for downloading. The audio plug-in (which is, incidentally, a utility made by Netscape, and bundled with the Navigator browser) cannot recognize the extension as a valid audio file, and thus sends out an error without ascertaining whether the file is really valid or not. Non-basic audio files (i.e., AU and AIFF audio files) may or may not have this problem, depending on their particular plug-in traits.

Microsoft's browser, on the other hand, uses a smarter audio plug-in (the ActiveMovie application, which is a general purpose-multimedia player with drivers for practically any mainstream multimedia format in existence). Microsoft's plug-in does not automatically assume the file type based on extension, but verifies this — consequently causing the user to hear actual sounds correctly.

The following application demonstrates how binary data can be "piped" into the browser. The actual piping is done through the *PipeMIME* subroutine. This subroutine sends any file source to the browser (it first sends the MIME type, which is transmitted to it as a parameter).

This application utilizes the **audio/basic** (covering AIFF and AU formats) as well as **image/jpeg** (covering JPEG) files.

Source Code for HelloWorld3

```
Option Explicit

Declare Function oCGI2Register Lib "oCGI2.dll" Alias _
        "DllRegisterServer" () As Long

Dim cgi As New oCGI2
Sub HelloWorld()
  Select Case (cgi.ReadParam("type"))
    Case "au"
```

```
            Open App.Path + "\helloworld.au" For Binary Access _
                Read As #1
            PipeMIME "audio/basic", 1
            Close #1
        Case "jpeg"
            Open App.Path + "\helloworld.jpg" For Binary Access _
                Read As #1
            PipeMIME "image/jpeg", 1
            Close #1
        Case ""
            cgi.WriteCGI "<HTML><HEAD>"
            cgi.WriteCGI "<TITLE>Hello World </TITLE></HEAD>"
            cgi.WriteCGI "<BODY BGCOLOR=#aabbcc><CENTER>"
            cgi.WriteCGI "<H1>Hello World!</H1>"
            cgi.WriteCGI "<IMG SRC="""" + cgi.ReadScriptName
            cgi.WriteCGI "?type=jpeg""> <BR>"
            cgi.WriteCGI "<A HREF="""" + cgi.ReadScriptName
            cgi.WriteCGI "?type=au""> Hear ME! </A>"
            cgi.WriteCGI "</CENTER></BODY></HTML>"
      End Select
End Sub

Sub PipeMIME(sMime As String, iFile As Integer)
    cgi.WriteCGI "Content-type: " + sMime, False
    cgi.WriteCGI vbCrLf, False
    cgi.WriteCGI vbCrLf, False
    Dim sOut As String
    On Error GoTo FILEEOF
    Do While Not EOF(1)
        sOut = Input(1, iFile)
        cgi.WriteCGI sOut, False
    Loop
FILEEOF:
    Exit Sub
End Sub

Sub Main()
    On Error GoTo NormalErr
    'Load frmVBCrash

    cgi.ProcessCGI Command
```

```
        HelloWorld
        End
    NormalErr:
        Beep
        oCGI2Register
        End
    End Sub
```

Figure 14.3 demonstrates the results of the hello world CGI application.

Figure 14.3
The hello world
application output

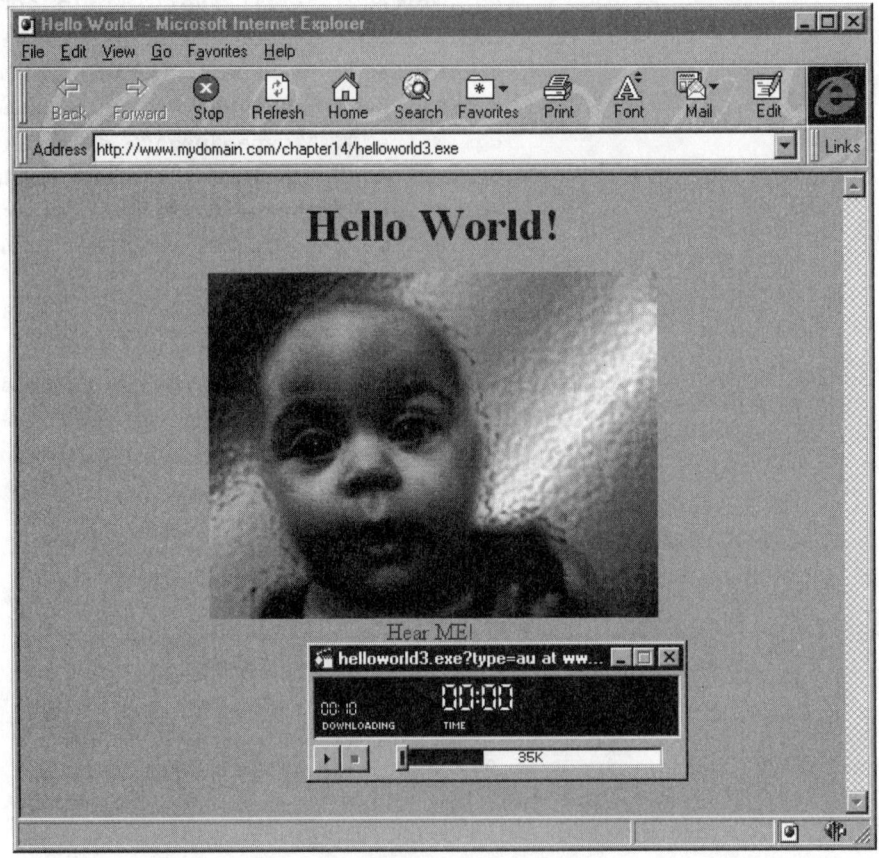

A similar function can be created to pipe any binary information from a database using an OLE field. With a bound form and OLE container object, you can do this. Data is inserted into the object using the

ReadFromFile function, and saved to a file using the *SaveToFile* function. A temporary file is created which, in turn, will be streamed via the CGI interface, and deleted when the application terminates. It should be noted that retrieving *BLOBs* (Binary Large Objects) from databases such as Access and SQL server is a time-consuming process and should be used in only marginal situations. Often, you can simply employ the database to locate the actual file path, rather than the content of the file itself. The file can then be retrieved via standard Operating System interfaces.

Piping Atypical Formats

As previously mentioned, the Netscape audio application will not accept the piped audio that the HelloWorld3 application sends it. Nothing is actually wrong with this data or content type. But the Netscape browser saves the output of `Helloworld3.exe` in a temporary file with an EXE extension. Then the browser executes the audio application, using that temporary file as a parameter. This application relies on a valid extension to determine and audition the file type. Since EXE is by no means a valid sound file extension, the audio application simply displays an error. Since Macintoshes use a resource fork (rather than a simple file extension) to associate with an application, Macs audition the audio correctly (provided a helper application was correctly set up for the particular audio mime type in question). Windows and UNIX Netscape browsers, however, rely on file extensions, and consequently are not "smart" enough to audition the file.

Microsoft's audio application parses the content of the file to determine its type. This allows it to play the audio file correctly.

Since this problem is inherent in the way that Windows (traditionally, DOS and UNIX too) uses files, the workaround for it is a bit complex.

It should be noted that this problem will recur with any application that relies on file extensions and is listed as a Netscape (or Microsoft) help application. Either system will have a problem getting file types when it receives the information from a "piping" application.

The only workaround for this (while still retaining the concept of a piping application, which is crucial for "pay as you go" type services) is to make the browser think it is reading a standard file extension, while at the same time causing the server to think that the piping application is being executed.

Other techniques are riskier: saving a temporary file, and having the piping application save the information onto that file while placing a simple meta refresh tag. Once the file is saved, the piping application terminates, and the browser switches onto the refreshed page (which can be the piped file). Problems? When do you remove this temporary file from the system?

In order to resolve this (and other problems I've encountered), I've created the oRedirector ISAPI filter. This filter (including source code) can be found on the CD that comes with this book. The redirector uses a simple INI file to allow a server to redirect any file to any other file.

The following oRedirector INI file section redirects a standard AU URL into a piping application. Note that cookies still apply (allowing the application to review information about the user — such as account balance, etc.):

```
[www.mydomain.com]
Commit=1
/chapter14/redirected.au=/chapter14/helloworld3.exe?type=au
```

Parameters can also be applied. The oRedirector filter does not work across servers (it will only redirect one URL in the server to another URL on the same server) but virtual paths onto another server *will* work, since they operate like a standard URL file path within the current server.

Every time that the virtual web server **www.mydomain.com** sees the URL **/chapter14/redirected.au,** it actually executes **/chapter14/HelloWorld3.exe** with the parameter **type=au**. While HelloWorld3 retrieves the information, the browser thinks that a standard AU file (**redirected.au**) is being fetched, and saves the cached files with the AU file extension. Since the file extension is correct, the associated helper application has no trouble working!

This technique can be used for applications piping any MIME type, allowing the MIME helper application to work correctly, regardless of file extensions.

The oRedirector application can do much more than this. However, its uses are outside of the scope of this book. For more information about oRedirector, how to install it, or how it works, please refer to the documentation on the CD.

The Hit-Counter Application

The hit counter application does not differ much from the previous example. This application simply exercises more intelligence regarding which files should be piped, and in what order.

The application uses the Windows registry in order to save the hit count for every reference it receives. Each time the application is executed, it displays a single digit of the hit counter (based on the parameters it receives). On the last digit, it increments the hit count for the referenced page.

The hit counter itself is a simple client for its counting abilities — this can be demonstrated by running the counter application without any parameters. Any web page now references the counter application in order to view each digit. Because of the complexity involved in building a GIF image at run-time, this application simply breaks down the task by requiring that each digit be a separate call to counter.

The counter uses "Ref" as a parameter specifying the name of the document at hand. The "Digit" parameter determines which digit is currently being displayed. (The least significant digit is "digit" zero.)

Counter maintains an array of 10 GIFs — one per digit, which it pipes as needed. These files are found in the same directory as the hit-counter application. There are several ActiveX controls that would enable the CGI programmer to build applications that generate and pipe GIFs "on the fly."

Source Code for Counter

```
Option Explicit

Declare Function oCGI2Register Lib "oCGI2.dll" Alias _
        "DllRegisterServer" () As Long


Dim cgi As New oCGI2

Public Const HKEY_CURRENT_USER = &H80000001
Public Const HKEY_LOCAL_MACHINE = &H80000002

Public Const REG_DWORD = 4
Public Const REG_SZ = 1
Public Const KEY_SET_VALUE = &H2
Public Const KEY_CREATE_SUB_KEY = &H4
Public Const KEY_CREATE_LINK = &H20
Public Const KEY_QUERY_VALUE = &H1
Public Const KEY_NOTIFY = &H10
Public Const KEY_EVENT = &H1
Public Const KEY_ENUMERATE_SUB_KEYS = &H8


Declare Function RegQueryValueEx Lib "advapi32.dll" Alias _
        "RegQueryValueExA" (ByVal hKey As Long, ByVal _
        lpValueName As String, ByVal lpReserved As _
        Long, lpType As Long, ByVal lpData As Any, _
        lpcbData As Long) As Long
Declare Function RegSetValueEx Lib "advapi32.dll" Alias _
        "RegSetValueExA" (ByVal hKey As Long, ByVal _
        lpValueName As String, ByVal Reserved As _
        Long, ByVal dwType As Long, ByVal lpData _
        As Any, ByVal cbData As Long) As Long
Declare Function RegCloseKey Lib "advapi32.dll" (ByVal hKey _
        As Long) As Long
Declare Function RegOpenKeyEx Lib "advapi32.dll" Alias _
        "RegOpenKeyExA" (ByVal hKey As Long, ByVal _
        lpSubKey As String, ByVal ulOptions As Long, _
        ByVal samDesired As Long, phkResult As Long) _
        As Long
```

```
Declare Function RegCreateKey Lib "advapi32.dll" Alias _
        "RegCreateKeyA" (ByVal hKey As Long, ByVal _
            lpSubKey As String, phkResult As Long) As Long

Declare Sub Sleep Lib "kernel32" (ByVal dwMilliseconds As _
        Long)

Sub DoCounter()
  If IsNumeric(cgi.ReadParam("Digit")) Then
    ' this part spits out a single digit.
    ' only increment the counterif this is the last digit _
            and ' it was already piped out!
    Dim power As Integer
    power = CInt(cgi.ReadParam("Digit"))

    Dim sNumber As Integer
    sNumber = CStr(ReadNumber(False))

    Dim iDigit As Integer
    iDigit = ((sNumber \ (10 ^ power)) Mod 10)

    Open App.Path + "\digit" + CStr(iDigit) + ".gif" _
            For Binary Access Read As #1

    PipeMIME "image/gif", 1
    Close #1
    ' increment image if this was the last digit.
    If (power = 0) Then
      ' wait a while for the others to get the right _
            number!
      Sleep 300
      ReadNumber True
    End If

  Else
    cgi.WriteCGI "<HTML><HEAD><TITLE>"
    cgi.WriteCGI "Sample counter screen</TITLE></HEAD>"
    cgi.WriteCGI "<BODY BGCOLOR=#fffccc>"
    cgi.WriteCGI "<H2> This page has been accessed:"

    ' 4 digits (3-2-1-0)
```

```vb
        Dim i As Integer
        For i = 3 To 0 Step -1
          cgi.WriteCGI "<IMG SRC=""" + cgi.ReadScriptName
          cgi.WriteCGI "?Ref=" + cgi.ReadScriptName + "&Digit="
          cgi.WriteCGI CStr(i) + """>"
        Next

        cgi.WriteCGI " times!</H2><BODY>"
        cgi.WriteCGI "</HTML>"
    End If
End Sub


Sub main()
    On Error GoTo NormalErr
    oCGI2Register
    'Load frmVBCrash

    cgi.ProcessCGI Command

    DoCounter

    End
NormalErr:
    Beep
    End
End Sub



Sub PipeMIME(sMime As String, iFile As Integer)
    cgi.WriteCGI "Content-type: " + sMime, False
    cgi.WriteCGI vbCrLf, False
    cgi.WriteCGI vbCrLf, False
    Dim sOut As String
    On Error GoTo FILEEOF
    Do While Not EOF(1)
      sOut = Input(1, iFile)
      cgi.WriteCGI sOut, False
    Loop
FILEEOF:
    Exit Sub
End Sub
```

```
Function ReadNumber(fIncrement As Boolean) As Integer
  With cgi
    Dim iNumber As Integer

    Dim lResult As Long, lKey As Long, sParam As String
    RegCreateKey HKEY_LOCAL_MACHINE, "Software\oWare _
        \Counter", sParam = Space(300)
    lResult = RegQueryValueEx(lKey, .ReadParam("Ref"), 0, _
        REG_SZ, sParam, Len(sParam))
    If (lResult = 0) Then
      iNumber = CInt(Left(sParam, InStr(sParam, Chr(0)) - _
        1))
    Else
      iNumber = 1
    End If
    ReadNumber = iNumber
    If (fIncrement) Then
      iNumber = iNumber + 1
      RegSetValueEx lKey, .ReadParam("ref"), 0, REG_SZ, _
        CStr(iNumber), Len(CStr(iNumber))
    End If
    RegCloseKey lKey
  End With
End Function
```

Figures 14.4 and 14.5 demonstrate the output from the Hit counter CGI application.

Figure 14.4
Hit counter output

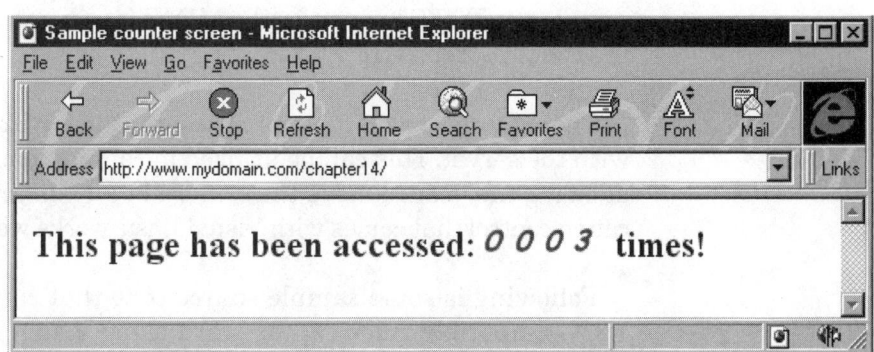

Figure 14.5
Hit counter output,
incremental view

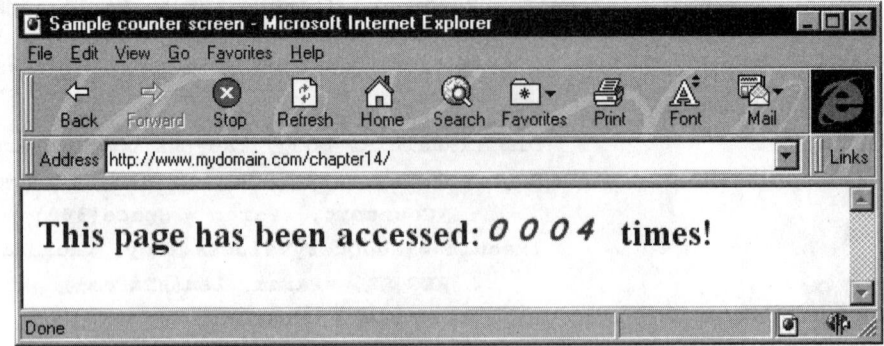

Live Images

Video capture cards are cheap commodities today.

It is quite easy to interface with Video for Windows in order to get an updated "capture" (this is simply by importing the cap Win32 API functions and messages). Most capture functions are actually macros that send WM messages to the capture window. This is easily ported into Visual Basic.

The capture can be converted into a GIF image using 3rd party OCX controls (unfortunately, VB5 PictureBox control supports reading GIFs and JPG files natively, but the *SavePicture* function does *not* support these formats). The file is fed directly into the HTTP stream by using *WriteCGI* with *fStartCGI* as false. The WriteCGI function must first contain the HTTP header for the MIME type being sent (image/gif) and the content of the GIF file.

There are several step-motor kits that use RS232 to communicate with the server. This can be utilized in conjunction with the system — allowing the user to move the camera in any direction. The communication control that comes with Visual Basic works well with such devices.

Following is some sample source code that captures video from a VFW-compatible video capture card using Visual Basic, and places it in an image-compatible picture control. A control with GIF compatibility (for instance, LEAD tool's image control) enables such source code to save a full "live" GIF image:

```
hWndC = capCreateCaptureWindow("VFW", WS_CHILD Or _
        WS_VISIBLE, x, y, w, h, hParentWnd, 1)
SendMessage(hWndC, WM_CAP_DRIVER_CONNECT, 0, 0)
SendMessage hWndC, WM_CAP_SET_SCALE, -1, 0
SetWindowPos hWndC, 0, x, y, w, h, SWP_NOZORDER Or _
        SWP_NOACTIVATE
SendMessage hWndC, WM_CAP_EDIT_COPY, 0, 0
SendMessage hWndC, WM_CAP_DRIVER_DISCONNECT, 0, 0
DestroyWindow hWndC
imgMyImage.Picture = Clipboard.GetData
```

Now, the image control contains a valid Bitmap with the live image captured. Convert this bitmap into a GIF or JPG and reference it in order for the outside world to view it correctly. This conversion process can be done using a graphic library (in the form of an OCX or a DLL) such as LEADTools.

To save this information to a bitmap file use:

```
SavePicture imgMyImage.Picture, "c:\currentimage.bmp"
```

Following is simple OLE automation code that will convert graphic files from any PhotoShop-compatible format to any other PhotoShop-compatible format. This code requires a complete installation of PhotoShop on the web server, and also requires that the application reference the Adobe PhotoShop Type library.

```
Dim o As PhotoshopApplication
Dim oAction As IAutoPSDoc
Set o = New PhotoshopApplication
Set oAction = o.Open("c:\currentimage.bmp")
oAction.SaveTo App.Path + "\currentimage.gif"
oAction.Close
o.Quit
Set o = Nothing
```

Figure 14.6
Object browser view
of Adobe's ActiveX
objects

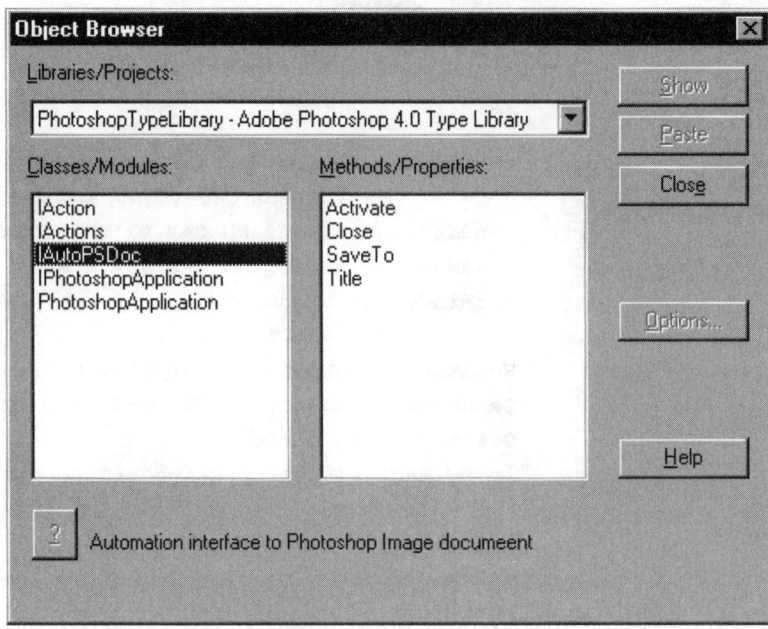

A live video ActiveX document using VFW can be found on the CD
along with its Visual Basic 5 source code.

Figure 14.7
Live image view in
browser

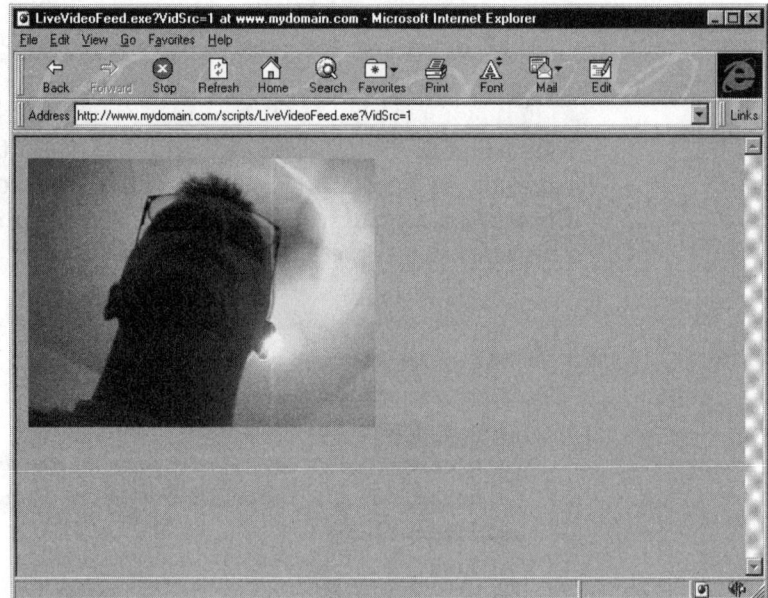

Live Document Scan

An HP scanner uses very simple OLE automation codes which can easily be imported into the application, providing Web clients with a "scan at will" CGI application.

There are several OCX controls that support scanning and TWAIN. Most of these can save the files to a GIF format (e.g., LEADTools). When using an HP-ScanJet scanner, software for the scan is automatically installed. The only problem is converting this file to a GIF format (the scanner uses a bitmap for this purpose).

The DeskScan software that comes with ScanJet 2 and up provides an OLE-document that allows the placement of a scanned document into any OLE-compatible tool. (The PictureScan software that comes with some ScanJet scanners should also work.) Simply create an OLE container control on a form, and embed a DeskScan object in it. The following code will activate the scanner:

```
scan1.DoVerb -2 'Start scanning!
Do While scan1.AppIsRunning 'wait until it's done _
          scanning!
   DoEvents
Loop
If scan1.LpOleObject = 0 then exit sub 'cancelled or _
          another error
scan1.AppIsRunning = True 'activate the scanning software
SavePicture scan1.Image, "c:\currentimage.bmp"
Scan1.AppIsRunning = False
```

When using this code in conjunction with the previous image conversion example, the application either streams this information to the user (reads the contents and pipes them back as an image/gif MIME type), or simply references the GIF image file.

When a Non-Database Central Entity Exists

When there is one or more central entity serving as a "backend" to the application, a non-SQL server solution is required.

This type of entity might be an external resource or sensor, such as a temperature gauge or speed sensor. Another backend might be a host connection, or a credit card processing system.

If a single backend connection is needed, a separate server application should be created to service it. When this application needs to be independent of the CGI application (such as a sensor) — the application must be executed as a service on the system (using Windows NT resource kit's SRVANY application). The application communicates with the CGI applications via a database interface, files or via DCOM (or Microsoft Transaction Server).

When the backend application has to be triggered on the fly, DCOM (or Visual Basic's remote OLE automation) should be used for communication between applications.

DCOM is used to interface between running applications supporting OLE automation on different machines. The syntax is like calling a local object function, but the function is actually executed on a different machine. This can be useful when a Windows NT CGI application needs to interact with a device that can only be interfaced under Windows 95 (e.g., video capture cards that do not support Windows NT).

When a single credit card transaction system has to handle several applications (or several servers), a single application can be created on a dedicated server. The application is executed as a service, and exports a multi-creatable Visual Basic class. This class can be exported via DCOM or remote OLE automation to other machines.

Since the class is multi-creatable and the application runs constantly, each new instance of it uses the existing application instead of creating a new one. This allows the application to employ global variables for synchronization among the various clients — enabling a single client to take hold of the resource at any given time. A collection can be used as a queue for clients. Once a client takes hold of it, that client can interface with the resource using the Class's API.

When live response is not required, a database can be used as a scheduling or synchronization device. Each client seeking to create a credit card transaction places a request in a dedicated table. The credit card application will constantly query this table for new requests that are yet to be filled. Once this application completes the request, it will update the record accordingly (as well as add any auditing records that may be required) and look for the next record in the recordset. Once the recordset is clear, the application can "sleep" for a while, and re-query the database for more records later.

Using DCOM in both directions is also possible — by having objects send each other messages like "events" in standard OCX controls. This is particularly important when the user needs to be updated in a live manner (for instance, when a response could take a while — by which time the user may be required to have other important information available on the screen).

It should be noted that the application on the other side will not specify which instance of the CGI application it wants to talk to. This means that the CGI application does not terminate as well as a synchronization object on this machine (e.g., saving the information to a file with a pre-agreed name).

Notes

DCOM (and DCOM for Windows 95) may require some security rights for both OLE automation classes and the registry to be enabled for interacting applications.

Figure 14.8
DCOM configuration

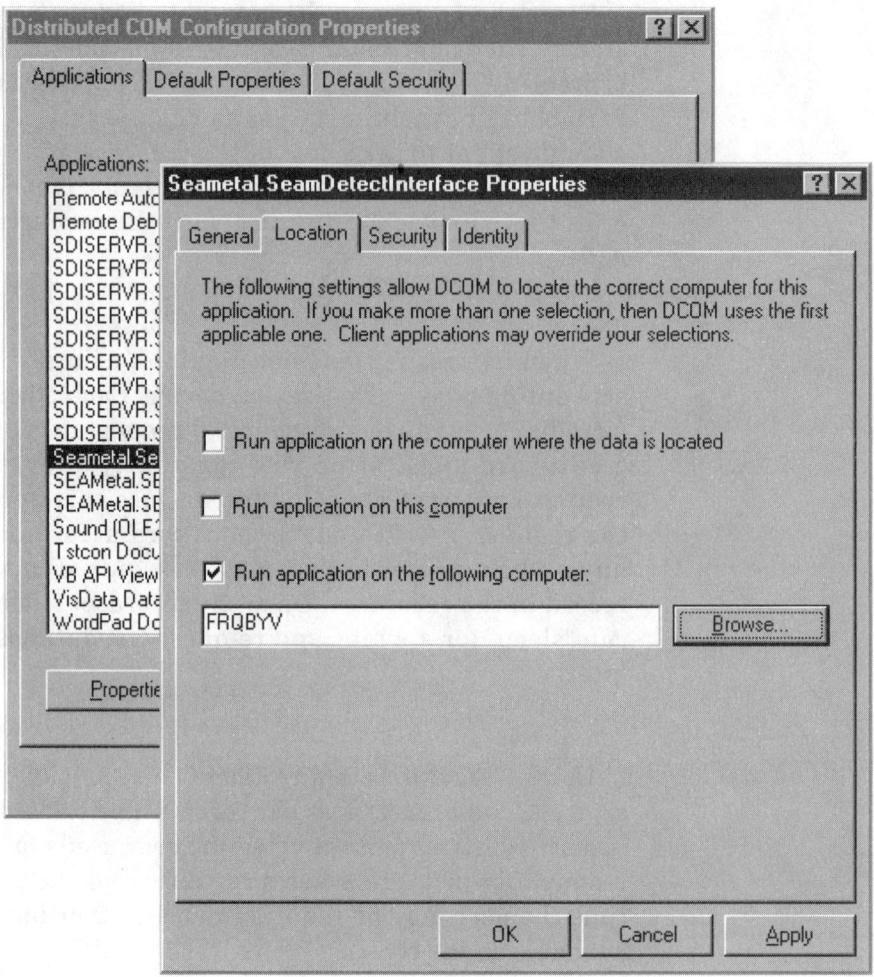

Monitoring the state of a distributed application can be quite complex. Microsoft's Transaction Server is a great tool for monitoring and distributing DCOM-ActiveX components. Transaction Server can also monitor how active each component is, and verify that the distributed system is not being bogged down by a particular component on a particular server. This is a great complementary tool for managing and even debugging distributed component applications.

Transaction Server is used primarily for load-balancing and tracking/controlling transactions in a distributed ActiveX environment. This is quite useful in the cases of a heavily distributed application. Several equivalent SQL servers interact with several equivalent ActiveX servers. A number of web servers (most likely using the DNS method of load-balancing) utilize these ActiveX components. The Microsoft Transaction Server determines which server each ActiveX component is actually created in, and performs load-balancing on the SQL servers. Each layer is monitored and controlled by Transaction Server — giving the manager a "bird's eye view" of the entire system. The forthcoming IIS 4.0 will be integrated with transaction server, to allow complete tracking of particular web page hits.

Transaction Server enables a distributed application to transparently add more servers to the particular area that needs most help: the database layer, the application layer, or the web server layer. The addition of a new server requires only an adjustment on the part of Transaction Server in order to permit DCOM to forward ActiveX component requests to the new load-balancing servers. This type of monitoring over ActiveX components also allows the system to track and manage components, such as credit card controls, to determine how many credit card transactions are actually taking place at any given time.

Scheduled Activation

Often a system needs periodic processing, such as closing credit-card batches or cleaning up old files. This can be done by writing a plain application to handle single instances of this timed action (such as closing the current credit-card batch) in conjunction with Windows NT's scheduler service.

The scheduler service already comes with Windows NT. It starts up, by default, to manual activation. This is easily modified via the control panel | services | startup dialog box. Modifying the setting to automatic ensures that the schedule service activates as Windows NT starts up.

Commands are scheduled with the aid of the "AT" command. A graphical interface which is bundled in the Windows NT resource kit has been created for this command. Figure 14.9 demonstrates how easy it is to manage the command line interface.

Figure 14.9
Scheduler information

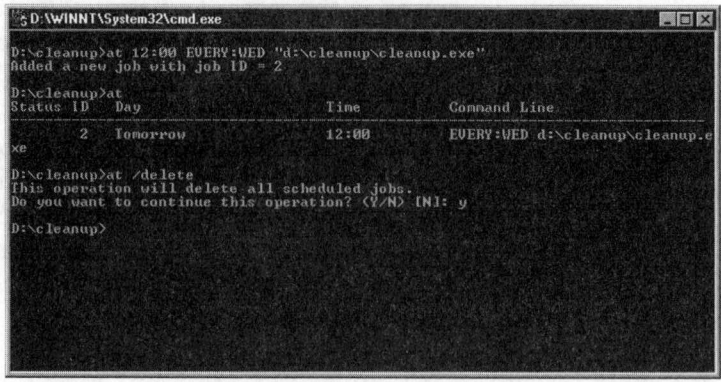

This demonstrates the creation of new scheduled tasks, views the existing scheduled tasks and deletion of said tasks. Figure 14.10 shows the scheduler service in the control panel services dialog box.

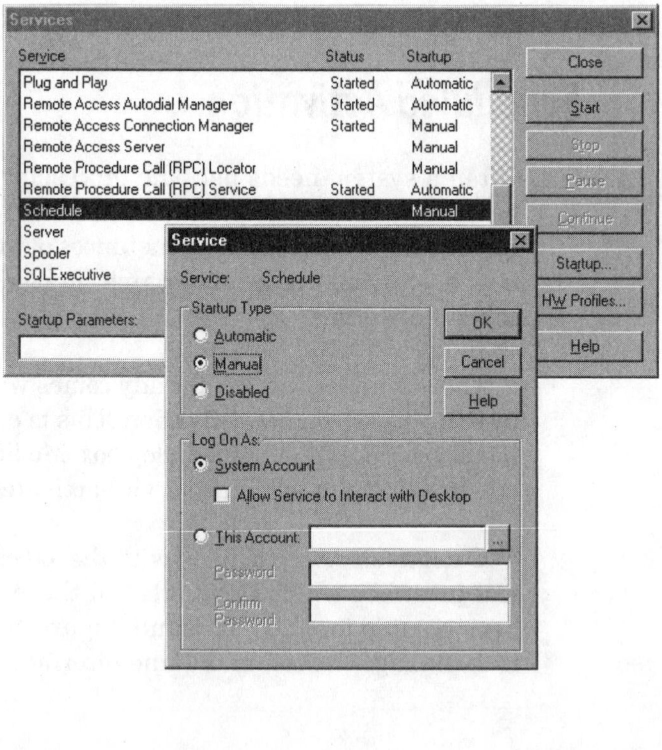

Figure 14.10
Control panel with Scheduler service being displayed

SQL Server Issues

Porting a CGI application to SQL server is quite different than moving it to an upscaled version of Access. SQL server is a much more complex beast, and requires careful implementation.

SQL server operates by managing its disk space locally, instead of using the operating system. This is achieved by pre-allocating database devices, each of which is a big file, capable of any number of actual databases. Each database can be placed in one or more such database devices.

This technique, however, precludes SQL server from being able to expand these files, should the database device become full. The stored procedure SP_SPACEUSED allows the system to verify that there is enough disk space, and sends a warning to the system administrator *before* space runs out:

database_name	database_size	unallocated space
VIS	40.50 MB	37.78 MB

reserved	data	index_size	unused
2788 KB	1006 KB	140 KB	1642 KB

Log space is also crucial. Should that run out, SQL server will not allow the system to proceed. The **tempdb** database is a constant source of problems. This is the database used by SQL server to keep transaction information, rollback information, and other temporary pieces of data for the server. This database defaults to 2M of hard drive for logging. It should be expanded significantly in order to prevent the server from continually halting after a large number of operations (e.g., lots of consecutive inserts) have been made.

An easily implemented option is to utilize the following stored procedure:

```
USE MYDATABASE
DUMP TRANSACTION MYDATABASE WITH NO_LOG
```

This tells the SQL server to erase the log portion of the MYDATA-BASE database. A similar command can be done with tempdb:

```
USE tempdb
DUMP TRANSACTION tempdb WITH NO_LOG
```

after some inserts have been made. This prevents the log section of tempdb from filling up.

Executing this type of stored procedure is often not enabled by simple *db.Execute,* and requires an RDO connection to the server:

```
Dim sConnect as string

sConnect = "DSN=SD;UID=username; PWD=password"

Dim Cn as rdoConnection

Set Cn = rdoWorkspaces(0).OpenConnection("", _
            rdDriverNoPrompt, false, sConnect)

Dim sSQL as string
sSQL = "USE tempdb" + vbCrlf
sSQL = sSQL + "DUMP TRANSACTION tempdb WITH NO_LOG"
Cn.Execute sSQL
Cn.Close
```

Security is also an issue with SQL server. It is a good idea to use a SQL server account for the CGI application that has as few rights as possible, in order for the application to operate correctly. This further protects the system, since hackers can only access the same information as the application. They cannot delete, modify or access secured information in this manner.

SQL server's SQL syntax is different from Access. The most noticeable differences are:

- Renaming a result field: `Select testField as MYFIELD from myTable` will work under Access, but not SQL server. The "AS" keyword should be removed to make this work under SQL server.

- Access uses non-standard inner-join and outer-join syntax. This syntax works transparently on SQL server when utilizing ODBC. When using a direct SQL connection, DBLIB or RDO, the native syntax prevails. ADO also requires a native syntax interface. The Access style query is:

```
SELECT Table1.test1 AS myTest FROM Table1 LEFT JOIN Table2 _
    ON Table1.ID = Table2.ID;
```

This query will only work on Access databases (or ODBC databases) Translating it into SQL server style requires the use of outer joins (standard join with the *= equality operator).

Due to a horrible bug in SQL Server 6.5, the deletion or modification of rows when using an ODBC often fails, with the infamous "Data has changed, operation stopped" error. This is quickly resolved by adding a *timestamp column* to each of the tables. Note that until the timestamp value is valid, the old values in the database could still cause the ODBC error (allowing the application and user to modify or delete only *new* rows). A simple update statement can resolve this:

```
Update Orders SET OrderAmount = OrderAmount
```

This type of statement updates each and every field; by doing so, the timestamp fields are filled and the rows can now be easily modified.

SQL server-supported protocols can affect security between client and server. Having the server simply deny service to the TCP/IP protocol is an easily applicable security measure. This requires that the local network run an additional protocol (e.g., NWLink IPX or the NetBEUI protocol) but provides a foolproof blockade to the outside world.

Other methods for preventing direct access to the server are blocking the specific IP address from the outside, blocking the TCP/UDP ports by which the server communicates with the outside, and utilizing a true firewall solution.

Often, however, a real ODBC connection to the outside must be made. There are a number of encryption solutions that ride on top of ODBC to protect the SQL server data and secure the user validation. In any case, the database administrator should take special care to modify the default password for the system administrator (the SA user defaults to an empty password, giving easy access to SQL server databases in cases where this fact was overlooked).

IIS and ASP

Several good things have been added to IIS 3.0 and the Active Server Pages (ASP). Among the more noticeable features, such as the addition of SSL 2.0 and 3.0 support (client side certificates), there were quite a few other new things brewing under the hood.

IIS 3.0 supports multiple default documents. This allows the administrator to specify a virtual directory containing **default.htm** will be used, and that, if the server can't find that document, it will go to the next in line. This dialog box does not prevent the administrator from using CGI scripts as default documents for a web server. Figure 14.11 shows the virtual directory properties dialog box for IIS.

Figure 14.11
IIS virtual directory
properties

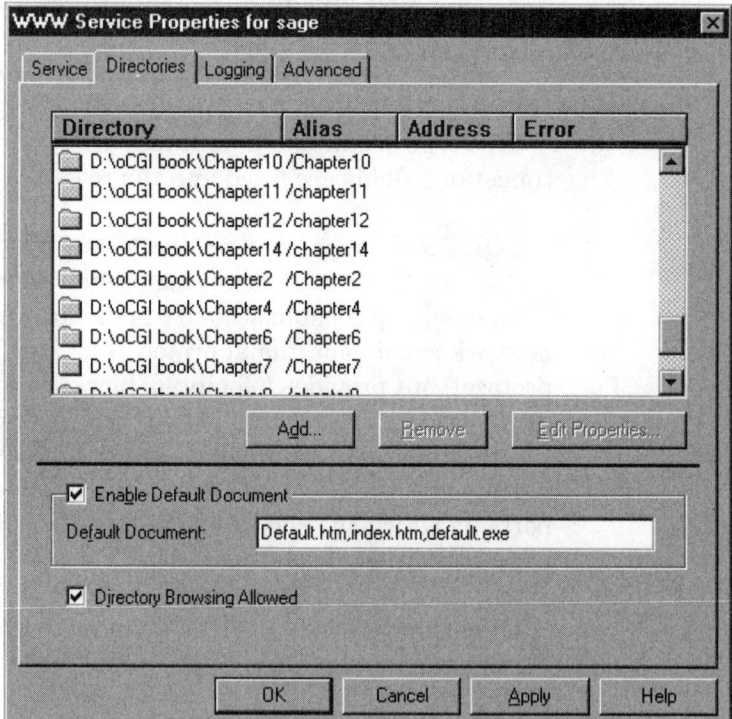

This enables a virtual directory to contain a default application (`default.exe`) that runs without letting the user know it is actually being executed. With the POST submission technique, this effectively hides the fact that a dynamic process is being executed, or bypasses the need for an otherwise-unnecessary web page.

This is especially effective when the home page for a web site uses a dynamic application such as this. Microsoft often uses this trick in its own web sites for presenting dynamic content on home (or root) pages.

Figure 14.12 shows additional features enabling the administrator to directly manage virtual directories from the directories themselves.

Figure 14.12
The virtual directory
dialog box/tab

IIS 4 adds further functionality by integrating IIS with the Microsoft Transaction Server (MTS) allowing web transaction to be closely monitored and controlled. This release also adds to the ability to crash-proof components running under the IIS environment, transaction-based control and resource pool management on the server end. These features further push IIS to the forefront of the web serve arena.

Summary

In this chapter we have demonstrated how enterprise-level applications are deployed and balanced. Piping binary data to the browser has several advantages over referencing public files accessible by anyone who knows the URL for those files.

CGI is not the only method in which VB applications can be used to deploy web applications for the server side (the client side has been discussed thoroughly in Chapter 13). Microsoft Active Server Pages has been Microsoft's recommended method of deploying web server applications. Our next chapter describes how ASP applications are written, and how server side VB-Script and VB ActiveX applications interact with the web server.

15

ACTIVE SERVER PAGES

- The historical background on ASP
- Sessions in ASP
- Session-wide objects
- Internet URL search engines
- Automated investigation of URLs
- ASP document primer — server side scripts
- Cookies and parameters in ASP documents

HISTORICAL BACKGROUND

As we've seen in the first few chapters, the market is currently booming with countless solutions to creating web-based applications. Most of these are mediocre (the author predicts that stronger words are likely to be used by readers who've tried out some of these solutions).

Microsoft's offerings in this arena aren't spotless either. Microsoft's first attempt at a developmental strategy was in the form of an API that could be used to process DLLs created with C++. This API, called *ISAPI*, covered everything from Internet filtering applications to full-blown web-based applications. The pros and cons of ISAPI are described in the beginning of this book.

The industry failed to support ISAPI due to its complex and proprietary nature. A few loyal Microsoft followers did add ISAPI support to their web servers, enabling Microsoft to quickly take over their market share.

Microsoft released a buggy solution for less sophisticated developers. This unsupported utility enabled any OLE automation-producing language or development tool (e.g., Visual Basic 4.0) to produce Internet server applications.

The product proved extremely unreliable. Nevertheless, it was the only solution available to many programmers (apart from WINCGI, which was far from ideal). OLEISAPI version 1.0 was not multithreaded, so any process could slow or shut down the running web server. A runaway query could halt all access to a web-based database.

In addition, debugging these applications was extremely difficult. OLEISAPI did not work well with ActiveX executables; it "preferred" in-process DLLs.

Microsoft recognized early on that a good client/server solution was desperately needed. This is why *Active Server Pages* was created.

Active Server Pages (ASP) is integrated into Microsoft's third release of their web server (IIS version 3.0). ASP is actually one of IIS's strongest points.

OLEISAPI is still supported somewhat through Microsoft. The second release of this library showed great promise and improved most of the deficiencies in the previous release. However, it is not a supported library, and lacks most of the heavy functionality required by serious developers.

Active Server Pages — What is it, Anyway?

The concept behind ASP is simple. ASP is an extremely smart ISAPI "plug in." It is smart enough to know VB Script; this allows ASP to produce HTML on the fly. VB Script is identical to Visual Basic in syntax, but lacks most of the advanced features found in Visual Basic for Applications (VBA) 5.0.

The problem is that ASP is orientated towards HTML rather than the programming aspect of the applications. Most web applications, however, can be developed in ASP without external support.

ASP provides the programmer with various ways to communicate with the outside world. The most important feature of ASP is its ability to utilize server-based in-process DLLs in order to complete complicated tasks that are not appropriately implemented in VB Script.

These outside components interact with ASP to create a comprehensive solution that is invisible to the user. ASP also utilizes standard ActiveX executables (even remote ones), but for security and performance reasons, the default settings for ASP prohibit this without modification to some registry settings. Figure 15.1 shows the registry setting prohibiting or enabling out-of-process ActiveX applications from executing within ASP. Figure 15.2 shows the response from ASP when asked for execution of a prohibited out-of-process object.

Figure 15.1

Registry setting enabling ASP to run out-of-process ActiveX applications

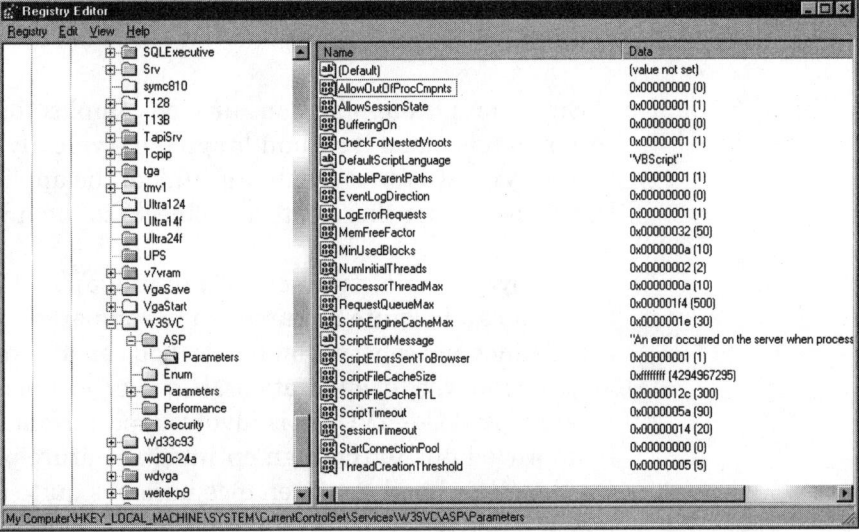

Figure 15.2
ASP not allowing an
ActiveX EXE to
execute

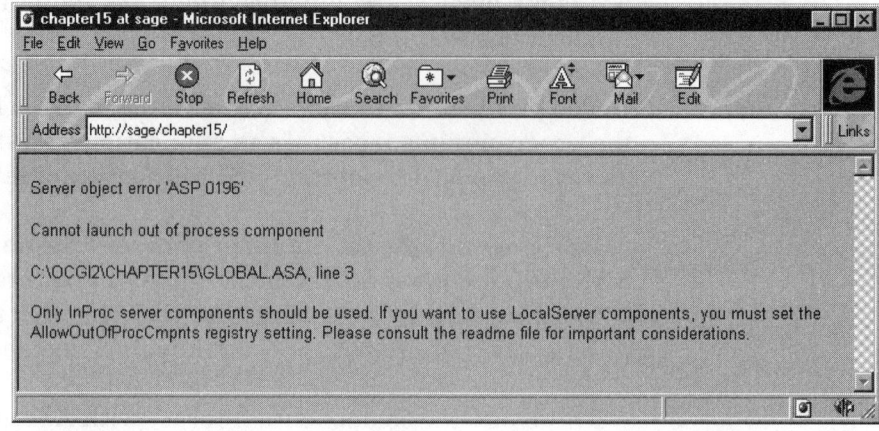

Active Server Pages Sessions

ASP does not handle sessions the same way CGI applications do. CGI applications complete a page and terminate, thereby taking a performance hit due to reinitialization of various objects (queries and database connections), and the time it takes to actually execute the application.

ASP, on the other hand, tracks sessions and keeps the main scripting engine (which is embedded into ASP itself) running at all times. When executing simple applications, this technique often proves faster than standard CGI applications.

Since complex applications are too complex for VBScript, Microsoft recommends using a second language (typically Visual Basic, Visual C++, or Visual J++) to create the bulk of the application. OLE automation is used to tie these external objects to the ASP system.

The overhead of two sets of languages and OLE automation in between can be quite a crutch when compared to systems with a single, distinct and cohesive language, and can also present a performance loss in some types of applications. However, in other types of applications, where Visual C++ (VC++) is involved, performance can be significantly improved due to the high optimizing nature of the VC++ compiler. On the other hand, maintenance becomes quite a chore when a large mix of languages is used in a project with more than one programmer.

ASP's ability to track user sessions allows the programmer to create ActiveX components that accompany the user throughout his session. Each such object can perform most of the functions the user requests, and maintains the user information without keeping it on the client end or in a database. Each object also maintains items that relate to the user, such as recordsets, so that these do not have to be recreated every time the user interacts with the application. It should be noted, however, that this type of programming also requires substantially *more* memory from the server than alternative methods.

ASP maintains the session utilizing a single cookie that accompanies the user from the beginning of the session to the end. This cookie is sent over to the user the first time an Active Server Pages document is requested by a browser. These documents contain server-based Visual Basic script code, HTML for the user, and any additional client-side scripts the user may need (i.e., VB script or Java Script).

Figure 15.3
ASPSESSIONID cookie verification dialog box in Netscape browser

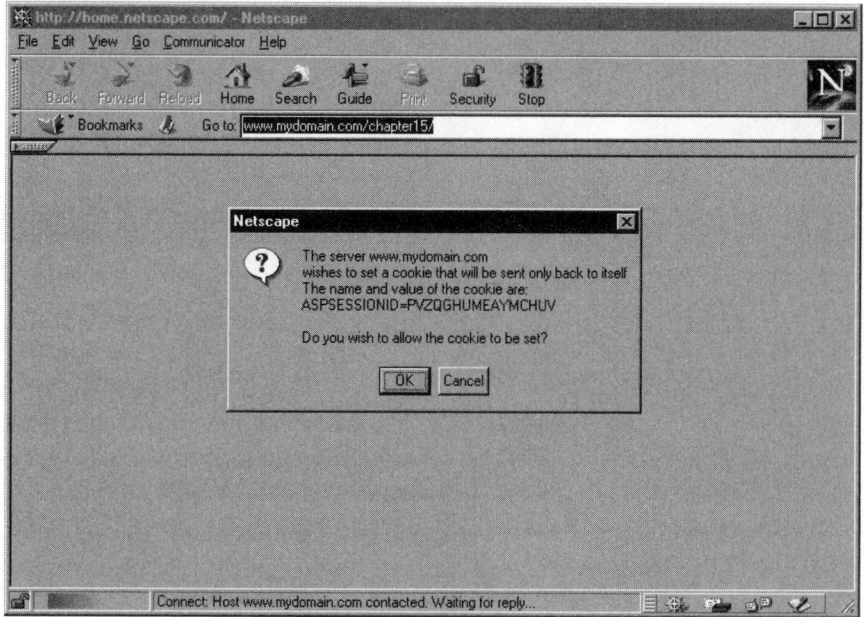

In order to maintain cookies, ASP requires any client browser that interacts with it to support them.

The session manager in ASP determines whether a session is completed by keeping track (in memory) of all current session cookies. If a particular session has not interacted with the server for more than a predetermined period of time, that session is considered terminated. ASP then shuts down all associated interfaces and concludes the session. The typical "timeout" for an ASP server is 20 minutes (this can be modified in ASP's registry settings):

```
HKEY_LOCAL_MACHINE\SYSTEM\CurrentControlSet\Services\W3SVC_
          \ASP\Parameters\
```

AllowSessionState — Enables/disables the session state system using the *ASPSessionID* cookie.

SessionTimeout — The number of minutes a session does not interact with the server before a particular session is terminated.

Figure 15.4
ASP timeout registry setting

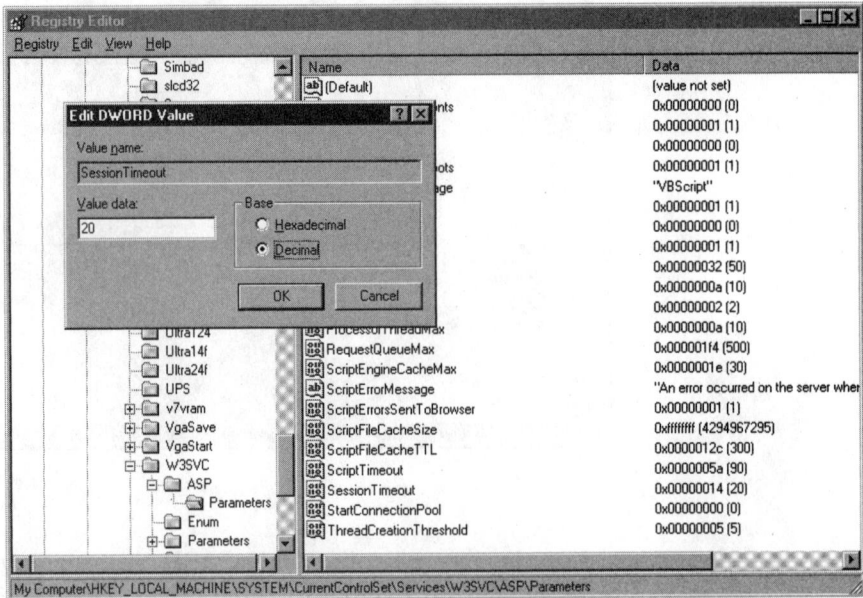

ASP Scripts also have a timeout period, at the end of which they must conclude. Otherwise, the server terminates them after the time-out has passed. This timeout period can be controlled via the registry:

ScriptTimeout — The time, in seconds, that an ASP script "times out" after.

A CGI application might emulate the session concept by interfacing with an ActiveX executable class possessing a single, publicly creatable interface that provides for session management. Implementation of this type of solution is beyond the scope of this book.

Session-Wide Objects

ASP gives the programmer two ways to create session-based variables. Each virtual directory contains a **GLOBAL.ASA** file. ASP reads this file when the user requests an ASP document in a directory that contains a **GLOBAL.ASA** file for the first time. This file contains VB script code to initialize global variables that are either session-based, or that can "live" until the server is shut down.

By utilizing server-based global variables that initialize with the server and terminate with it, the user can provide an accurate user count, or create global objects that do not require any additional over-head to initialize with each session.

ASP documents can also create session-based objects/variables that are accessible by any other ASP document, in the same virtual directory, during the same particular session. This enables ASP documents to interact with each other, without the need for parameter-passing or cookies.

In effect, the **GLOBAL.ASA** file can be viewed as the class constructor and destructor, and ASP documents can be viewed as the methods and properties of a particular web-application "class."

The Holy-Diver Internet Search Engine

The Holy-Diver search engine was created to demonstrate ASP's ability to communicate with the outside world. This application is ASP-based and provides the most basic of Internet search engines.

The server uses the simplest search engine (the INSTR SQL statement) to enable users to search for web sites within its database. This functionality can be developed with a typical ASP solution: utilizing ADO to create a session-wide Recordset that allows the user to move forwards and backwards.

In order to demonstrate ASP's ability to communicate with other ActiveX objects, this functionality has been implemented using standard Visual Basic objects.

The *oINetSearch* application exposes a single class: *searchClass*. An object of this class accompanies each browser session, and provides most of the functionality the Holy-Diver Internet search engine needs. An object of this type is automatically created at the beginning of each session, and destroyed when that session is terminated by ASP.

The *searchClass* class maintains an open Recordset with the user's currently selected keywords. This permits the application to maintain the current position of the user and proceed to the next set of rows upon request. By keeping the Recordset open in this way, the class saves initialization time for populating the Recordset, each time the user requests it. On the down side, this might greatly complicate things should the user navigate back in the browser and press *refresh* — since it would cause the application to proceed to the *next* set of rows, rather than providing the user with the correct rows.

In order to fix this, the programmer must do what most CGI applications already do — keep the positioning information on the client rather than the server. The bookmark object can be parsed and saved as a cookie (or a parameter) to be retrieved by the application, in order to implement this feature correctly.

The Holy-Diver application, however, does not employ such constructs. These are left for the programmer to implement, should he choose to do so. Rather, the Holy-Diver application focuses on the URL submission portion of the application since the search portion has already been covered in this book.

Investigating URLs

Most Internet search engines provide their users with more than the ability to submit URLs and descriptions in their databases; these applications "go out" and investigate the submitted web sites. Often, they not only analyze keywords (using meta tags) and information on the actual page, but they may fan out to investigate referenced web pages as well. This need to recursively investigate hyperlinked document is why most Internet search engines use the spider metaphor.

In order for the Holy-Diver search engine to provide this functionality, it must first have the ability to request and retrieve HTML documents for a submitted URL. Prior to Visual Basic 5.0 this had to be done with third-party browser controls (e.g., Webber or Netmanage's Internet development suite).

Due to Microsoft's heavy focus on web-based development, Visual Basic 5.0 contains several web-enabled controls which can be used to construct a full-fledged web browser. These utilize a local implementation of the "Sweeper SDK" that is currently being used to construct Internet Explorer 4.0, thus finally completely integrating the web with the operating system.

The Internet search must be able to perform certain functions in order to handle URL submission. It must be able to retrieve documents for any particular URL. It must parse the HTML for the particular URL to analyze the contents of the web page. Finally, the application must be able to locate subsequent hyperlinks and proceed to investigate them.

To prevent substantial performance and recursion problems, this application only investigates up to 8 levels beneath, including the originally submitted URL.

The application implements only a relatively simple parsing mechanism to locate both hyperlinks and relevant information (i.e., not HTML) in the retrieved documents. It attempts to locate text which is outside of any tags (this identifies normal text). The first such text which the search engine finds (usually the title of the application) is indexed for use in user searches.

Hyperlinks are referenced in two major ways (other than forms, which will not be investigated here): through the anchor tag (**A HREF**) and through the source tag (**SRC**). The anchor tag usually depicts standard hyperlinked text or graphics, whereas the SRC tag usually references frames and images. This program does not analyze images or other binary information (although an interesting addition to the application would be to reference each encountered GIF or JPEG file and provide an index for them). Frames, however, will definitely be investigated. Figure 15.5 shows a typical web page. Figure 15.6 shows the HTML representation with HREF and SRC references highlighted.

Figure 15.5

A typical web page

```
: View or Edit HTML                                                    _ □ X

</head>

<table border="0" cellpadding="0" cellspacing="0">
    <tr>
        <td><a href="RGrieve/sf_robgrieve.htm" target="right"><img
        src="iconBob2.gif" border="0" width="72" height="100"></a></td>
    </tr>
    <tr>
        <td><a href="GKing/sf_gregking.htm" target="right"><img
        src="iconGreg2.gif" border="0" width="72" height="100"></a></td>
    </tr>
    <tr>
        <td><a href="RNokes/sf_robnokes.htm" target="right"><img
        src="iconRob2.gif" border="0" width="72" height="100"></a></td>
    </tr>
    <tr>
        <td><a href="YDelpuech/sf_yann.htm" target="right"><img
        src="iconYann2.gif" border="0" width="72" height="100"></a></td>
    </tr>
</table>

<p> </p>
</body>
</html>
```

```
C Original   ⊙ Current    ☑ Show Color Coding         OK      Cancel      Help
View or edit the current HTML
```

General Application Considerations

This application retrieves the URL information synchronously (rather than asynchronously, as in previous chapters) to prevent reentrancy. Recursion levels, however, should be monitored for various reasons.

The most important consideration in an Internet search engine is performance. Tying down the server for significant processing associated with a vast hyperlinked network is not beneficial to the search engine. Additionally, the memory and processing requirements incurred by more than 8 levels of recursion are substantial, and can cause various problems on the server resulting from overuse of system resources.

To prevent recursion of more than 8 levels, the main recursion function must be able to count the levels of recursion. This can be done with a single static integer variable. This variable automatically starts out as zero when the function is first called. The function tests the value of this variable in order to verify that the recursion limit has not been encountered. If this limit has been reached, the function simply terminates. Next, the function increments this variable. When the function finishes its processing, it decrements the variable. By doing this, every recursion level causes this variable to increment until a limit is reached, in which case the function stops executing any further down the particular track. This feature also precludes pollution of the search database with a hyperlink-intensive web site (as often occurs in most commercial-grade Internet search engines).

This particular application requires the use of an OCX to do URL retrieval. Whereas standard ActiveX documents/controls already have the ability to retrieve Internet documents via the asynchronous read functionality, standard DLLs must use the Internet transfer control in order to retrieve documents.

Because of this, the application cannot be set to unattended execution (which would not permit it to include a form).

Interestingly, ASP bypasses the standard CGI problem of what happens when the application crashes. Rather than halting indefinitely, the ASP server catches any Visual Basic errors and displays them on the requesting browser. The detail level for these errors is minimal, however.

This is the default behavior for ASP, controlled via the following registry setting:

ScriptErrorsSentToBrowser — This flag determines whether ASP errors are sent to the user or not.

Figure 15.7
An error in VB class
running under ASP
context

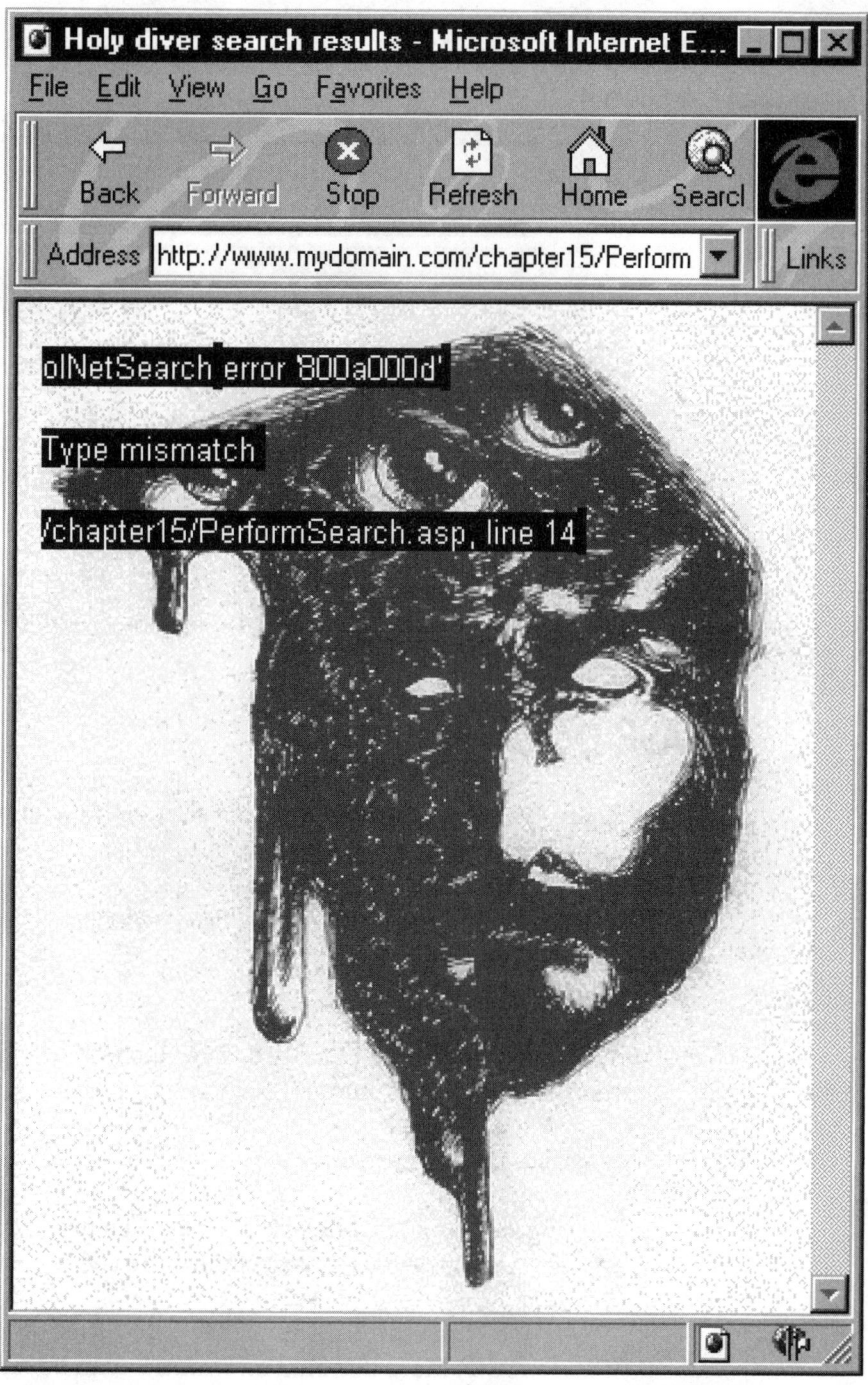

Figure 15.7
An error in VB class running under ASP context

ASP provides significantly more detail for errors in actual ASP documents since the VB Script processor is embedded within ASP.

Figure 15.8

ASP script errors in an ASP document

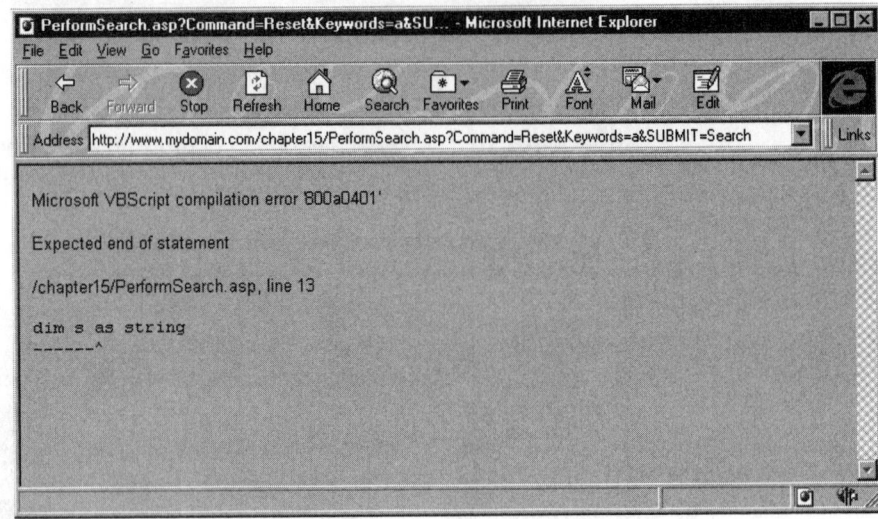

ASP Document Primer

There are two types of server side scripts that can be included in a standard ASP document:

```
<SCRIPT LANGUAGE=VBScript RUNAT=Server>
... SCRIPT TEXT ...
</SCRIPT>
```

This type of script usually defines global functions and variables for the rest of the document.

```
<% SCRIPT CONTENTS %>
```

Scripts within the enclosing `<% %>` tags are processed by the server, rather than passed on to the client browser.

Many of the standard methods and functions of Visual Basic are found in ASP. More detailed information can be located in the ASP documentation (which is included with ASP).

Returning information from an ASP/outside function is done via the `<%=` tag:

```
<H2> Hello Mr. <%=Session("UserName")%> </H2>
```

Of special note is variable declaration. Variables can only be declared as variant in ASP's server-side VB Script. When communicating with foreign objects, the string and integer conversion functions are often required in order to successfully call outside methods.

When submitting information to another ASP document, parameters are passed to it as in a standard CGI application.

Following is a typical call to a secondary ASP document:

```
<form action="SecondDocument.asp" method=ISINDEX>
<input type="text"
        size="20"
        name="Keywords"
        value="<%=Session("CurrentKeywords")%>">
<input type="submit"
        name="SUBMIT"
        value="Search"></p>
</form>
```

Session-based objects can be saved and retrieved using the *Session* keyword, as shown above. These variables are created the first time they are assigned a value.

Local variables can be created using the standard *Dim* keyword:

```
Dim t
t = Request.QueryString("Command")
```

The *Request* object contains all the submitted information from the client's browser, including parameters and cookies. The *QueryString* function returns a portion of the entire query string containing the parameters in question. The code statements above return the value contained in the input control *Command* in the referring form/hyperlink.

Alternatively, in the case of forms submitted using the POST method, the Form function will help resolve these:

```
The command you selected was <%= Request.Form("Command") %>
```

The *Request* object can also be used to retrieve the values of cookies. Cookies are retrieved using the *Cookies* function/collection:

```
Request.Cookies("CookieName)("CookieKey")
```

where *CookieName* is the actual name of the cookie being retrieved. A secondary key can be used which resembles virtual cookies somewhat. This idea allows the programmer to put more than one cookie (using different keys under the same cookie name) together into a single "virtual cookie." Apart from its inability to produce a single large cookie string, this provides the same functionality as oCGI's virtual cookies.

Cookies are set using the *Response* object and *Cookies* function/collection:

```
Response.Cookies("myCookie")="my Value"
```

This enables subsequent calls to retrieve the cookie through:

```
Request.Cookies("myCookie) — containing "my Value"
```

The key concept can be exercised by the following statement:

```
Response.Cookies("myCookie")("myKey")="my Value"
```

resulting in subsequent calls to

```
Request.Cookies("myCookie")("myKey")
```

containing "my Value"

Additional Considerations

Since ASP provides the ability to interact with ActiveX executables (albeit after a slight registry modification), this may tempt the programmer to try developing the application in this manner — so that Visual Basic can then debug the application.

Sadly, ASP prevents this by simply "timing out" the ASP document, if Visual Basic attempts to debug a referred object.

In addition, ActiveX executables behave differently than their DLL counterparts (e.g., in process vs. out of process) which can cause differences with regard to how an application behaves in each case. The programmer should be aware of these. In addition, performance for ActiveX executables is likely to be dramatically reduced in comparison with an in-process DLL.

There are additional techniques to interface Visual Basic and ASP (using referenced objects from ASP, as well as two-way communication between the object and ASP) but these are beyond the scope of this book.

The Holy-Diver Database Layout

The database from the standard search engine, included in the beginning of the book, has been adapted to this project. Modifications have been kept to a minimum, in order to allow the reader to concentrate on the application:

Table 15.1

The holy diver DATA table layout

Table: DATA Field Name	Field Type	Remark
Key	Autonumber (long integer)	Primary key- identifies record.
Title	Text(50)	Title of the URL.
Data	Text(250), Indexed	The URL.

The Global.ASA File

The global ASA file takes care of the allocation and removal of the *searchForMe* object. This is the Visual Basic ActiveX DLL object that manages searches and new URL submissions.

The script tag notifies ASP that this is a VB script code segment that is meant to run on the server. The *Session_OnStart* event occurs when a new user/browser references an ASP document in the current directory. In such a scenario, a new instance of the *oINetSearch.SearchClass* is created and assigned to the session-wide variable "*searchForMe*." This variable is later referenced for search and submit purposes.

The *Session_OnEnd* has been included here for completeness. All session wide-variables are removed from the system implicitly as the session terminates, because they go out of scope. In certain instances, however, additional functionalities are required (such as writing to a local file, or updating an application-wide object) that must occur explicitly *upon* session termination.

```
<SCRIPT LANGUAGE=VBScript RUNAT=Server>
SUB Session_OnStart
  set Session("searchForMe")= Server.CreateObject_
          ("oINetSearch.SearchClass")
END SUB

</SCRIPT>

<SCRIPT LANGUAGE=VBScript RUNAT=Server>
SUB Session_OnEnd
  set Session("searchForMe")= nothing
END SUB
</SCRIPT>
```

The Default.ASP File

This is the first file referenced by the user. Using the multiple default home-page specification in IIS 3.0, **default.asp** can be made into a default home page. This allows the user to specify a directory and immediately get a response, rather than utilizing a redirector or a `default.htm` file that would refer the browser (perhaps automatically using the meta refresh tag) to the `default.asp` document.

Figure 15.9
IIS 3 enabling several
default web pages (with
DEFAULT.ASP
highlighted)

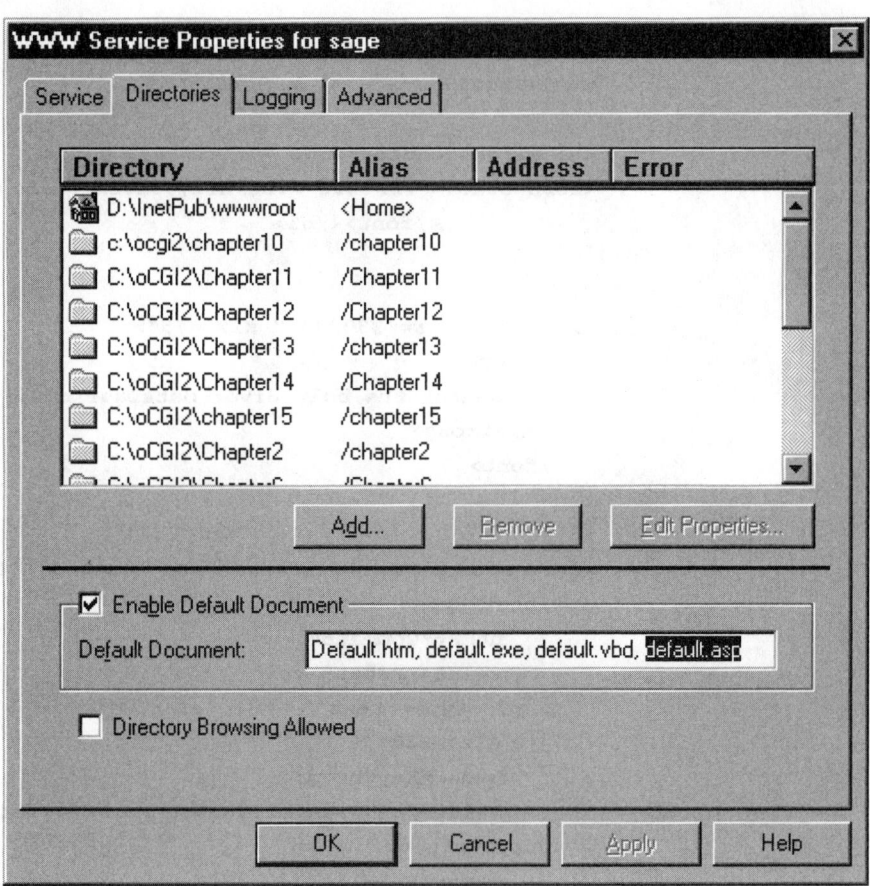

The default ASP file's primary function is to display the main screen. Aside from a few minor features, it could very well be a standard HTML file. It basically creates two forms: one for searching the database and one for submitting URLs into it.

The first form, used for searching the database, contains the only script in the file. This retrieves the existing keywords, automatically filling the last search results into the contents of the search edit box.

```
<html>
<head>
  <meta http-equiv="Content-Type"
  content="text/html; charset=iso-8859-1">
  <title>The holy diver search engine</title>
</head>

<body background="holy-diver.gif" bgcolor="#000000"
text="#000000">

<h1 align="center">
<font color="#FF0000">The Holy diver search engine _
          </font></h1>

<p>
  <font color="#800000" size="5">
    <strong>
      Search the holy diver database now:
    </strong>
  </font>
</p>

<form action="PerformSearch.asp" method=ISINDEX>
  <input type="hidden"
      name="Command"
      value="Reset"><p>
  <input type="text"
      size="20"
      name="Keywords"
      value="<%=Session("searchForMe").GetKeywords()%>">
  <input type="submit"
      name="SUBMIT"
      value="Search"></p>
</form>

<form action="SubmitURL.asp" method=ISINDEX>
  <p> </p>
  <p><font color="#800000" size="5">
  <strong>Insert new URLs
  into the holy-diver search engine!
  </strong></font></p><p>
```

```
    <input type="text"
          size="20"
          name="URL">
    <input type="submit"
        name="SUBMIT"
        value="SUBMIT URL"> </p>
</form>
</body>
</html>
```

The PerformSearch ASP File

This file utilizes the search object's *PerformSearch* function. This function receives a command (currently either **Reset** or **Next**) that tells it how to proceed with the next few rows. If the command is **Reset**, the function restarts the search. If the command is **Next**, the subsequent rows are transmitted back.

The *PerformSearch* ASP file determines if there are any rows to begin with and, if so, displays the appropriate message (the same HTML code used to display the search form in the default ASP file).

If information is available, it is retrieved and displayed. Next, the script determines if more information is available. If so, the **Next** button is added, allowing the user to proceed to the next search page.

```
<html>
<head>
<meta http-equiv="Content-Type"
content="text/html; charset=iso-8859-1">
<title>Holy diver search results</title>
</head>
<body background="holy-diver.gif"
    bgcolor="#000000"
    link="#FF0000">
<%
    dim vCommand, sKeywords
    function DoSearch()
        vCommand= Request.QueryString("Command")
        DoSearch=Session("searchForMe").PerformSearch(vCommand)
```

```
        end function
%>
<%
  sKeywords= Request.QueryString("Keywords")
  Session("searchForMe").SetKeywords CStr(sKeywords)
%>


<%If (Session("searchForMe").MoreToCome) or
(Request.QueryString("Command") = "Reset") then %>


<%
  dim vOut
  vOut=DoSearch()
%>


  <%If vOut="" then %>
  <h2><font color="#800000">
  No items have been found for this search
  </font></h2>
  <p><font color="#800000">try again?!
  </font></p>

  <form action="PerformSearch.asp"
      method=ISINDEX>
    <input type="hidden"
      name="Command"
      value="Reset"><p>
    <input type="text"
      size="20"
      name="Keywords"
      value="<%=sKeywords%>">
    <input type="submit"
      name="SUBMIT"
      value="Search"> </p>
  </form>
<%Else%>
<%=vOut%>
<%If Session("searchForMe").MoreToCome then%>
  <form action="PerformSearch.asp" method=ISINDEX>
    <input type="hidden"
      name="Keywords"
```

```
                value="<%=sKeywords%>">
        <input type="hidden"
          name="Command"
          value="Next">
        <p><font color="#004000">
        <input type="submit"
          name="SUBMIT"
          value="Next">
        </font></p>
        </form>
    <%End If%>
    <%End If%>
    <%End If%>
  </body>
  </html>
```

The *DoSearch* server-side function is the first referenced function. A page-wide variable is declared, holding the current command. The *DoSearch* function then fills this variable with the command parameter (**Reset** or **Next**). Next, the function calls the *PerformSearch* method in the *searchForMe* object with the retrieved command parameter. This initiates the search. Once completed, information gathered in the search is placed as the return value for *DoSearch*.

The ASP script starts out the first real command by retrieving keywords from the request parameters. These are passed on to the *searchForMe* object via the *SetKeywords* method. If the keywords are new, the object requeries the database to retrieve the new recordset. If the keywords are the same as in previous attempts, the command variable determines if the current rows are to be retrieved, or whether or not the search engine should requery the database (requerying refreshes the recordset, and is especially relevant in forward-only supporting databases, or servers such as SQL).

The script next determines if there are more items to come. If this is a new query (i.e., the command is **Reset**), it is ignored.

Next, the *DoSearch* server function is initiated to determine the results. If there were no items to start with, the *vOut* variable will be empty. In this case, a form is shown on the screen that allows the user to modify the keywords and search again. The original keywords are displayed as the default value for the next search, helping the user in case a typo had caused the empty result set.

If there was information in *vOut*, the script then displays that information on the screen. The script next determines if there are more items by using the *MoreToCome* method. If there are additional items, a form is created, allowing the user to proceed onto the next search screen.

The SubmitURL ASP File

This file simply calls the *searchForMe* object and asks it to investigate a particular URL. It determines the URL about to be sent, and makes sure that an URL has been selected. If no URL has been selected, an error message appears.

```
<html>
<head>
<meta http-equiv="Content-Type"
content="text/html; charset=iso-8859-1">
<title>Done investigating submitted Holy Diver URL</title>
</head>

<body background="holy-diver.gif"
   bgcolor="#000000">
<%
   dim sURL
   sURL= Request.QueryString("URL")
%>

<%If sURL="" then%>
   <h2><font color="#800000" size="6">
   an empty URL won't work!
   </font></h2>

<%else%>
   <h2><font color="#000080">
   Done processing [<%=sURL%>]...
   </font></h2>
   <%Session("searchForMe").Investigate sURL%>
```

```
<%End If%>

</body>
</html>
```

The searchClass File

The searchClass focuses on searching for, submitting, and parsing submitted URLs.

The class initializes by opening the search database and clearing some local variables out.

It terminates by closing the database and recordset (unnecessary, but it maintains good housekeeping habits).

The *SetKeywords* subroutine creates a new recordset if one is needed, and sets the session-specific recordset to the appropriate SQL statement. This could obviously be improved to include more substantial search capabilities (such as keyword parsing or reordering of results, based on the number of keywords found).

The *GetKeywords* function simply retrieves existing keywords for the ASP scripts.

The *PerformSearch* function first determines if the **Reset** command is in place. If it is, the Recordset is requeried. If no items have been retrieved, the function exists with an empty string. This subsequently causes the *PerformSearch* ASP script to display a new search form.

Next, an HTML table is generated and each item in the recordset placed into that table. Since the Data field is a hyperlink, it is placed twice: once as a hyperlink and the second time as the text the hyperlink encapsulates. This allows the user to see where he is jumping, and to jump there with a click of the mouse. The function closes out the HTML table tag, and returns the HTML to the calling ASP script.

This function shows how the recordset accompanies a user session, so that if the user retrieves more rows from the recordset, very little actual processing needs to be done. Of course, this may not be the best idea when there are huge numbers of rows where a large chunk of memory could be assigned to a particular session. In such cases, a maximum number of rows can be implemented using the TOP SQL statement. Additional options include maintaining a row position (using *AbsolutePosition*), and requerying the database and repositioning to the previous row, thus continuing the search where the user left off.

The *MoreToCome* function determines if the recordset contains more records. This function also tests for BOF in order to enable future use of backward search.

The *NumSteps* function determines the number of maximum rows returned by each search call. A small modification to the code can make this a read/write property, allowing you to modify the number of rows returned in each search page.

Investigate Function

The *Investigate* function is a recursive routine used to investigate particular URLs. This function begins by making sure that the maximum number of recursive steps has not been reached. The URL is then tested for known, unsupported protocols and formats (Mailto, FTP, gopher, GIF and JPG files). If these are encountered, the subroutine terminates and returns to the caller.

If this is a root call (a call initiated from the outside), the *frmINetInvestigate* form is loaded. This form holds the Internet control used to retrieve the URL contents. The only thing worth noting is that the INet control settings have been modified on the form so that it times out within 20 seconds, rather than the default 60 seconds. This speeds things up on a non-responsive web server.

Next, the URL is fixed up. In many cases, hyperlinks and other references to HTML documents do not contain the entire directory path for the HTML. This function simply makes sure that an URL is complete, not just based on the existing URL (like a file name in the same virtual directory as the linking file). The linking file is also sent to *RearrangeURL* in case the URL *references* it.

There are two forms of hyperlink references. The first simply states a file name. The browser, in this case, has to assume this file is in the same directory as the referring URL. The second option starts with a slash (or often a backslash, so both are supported) and assumes the same server, only with a completely different path. Of course, many URLs contain the full path, including server name and protocol. In such a case the *RearrangeURL* will not modify the URL.

Next, the URL contents are retrieved via the *OpenURL* function in object *inetInvestigate*, which is located in *frmINetInvestigate*. The returned HTML string is passed to the *ParseHTML* function, which takes care of subsequent parsing and recursive calls as needed. The *frmINetInvestigate* form is unloaded, if necessary, and the recursion level decreased.

ParseHTML Subroutine

The *ParseHTML* subroutine is at the heart of the simple HTML parsing that takes place in this application. It first attempts to locate a portion of the HTML string not enclosed by any HTML tags. The first such string found is typically the title of the URL. When this string is located, it is used in a call to the *InsertURLInfo* function. This function then inserts the URL information into the database. If that URL is already in the database, however, a *false return* code is displayed and the function terminates. Otherwise, the subroutine proceeds to parse the rest of the URL.

The *ParseHTML* subroutine continues to search where the first search left off. This time, however, it does so with the aid of the *FollowHyperlink* subroutine. This subroutine attempts to locate a particular hyperlink or reference in the remainder of the HTML string, and subsequently parses a portion of it for investigation. Two calls are made. The first follows the more traditional A HREF (or "anchor") hyperlinks. The next call follows SRC links that usually refer to images and frames (which is what we're actually looking for).

The *FollowHyperlink* utilizes the Visual Basic *InStr* function to locate the searched tag in the HTML string. If it is found, this function next determines whether the hyperlink is enclosed in quotes (it usually is). In either case, a delimiter is determined, and a second *InStr* call used to find the end of the hyperlink. If the search is fruitful, the *Investigate* subroutine is called (recursively, this time) to investigate the URL.

The *RearrangeURL* subroutine first determines if an URL already contains an HTTP header. If it does, the subroutine has nothing more to do and terminates. If it does not, the subroutine determines whether the URL refers to just the server or to the entire path of the original referring URL. If the new URL *does* start with a slash, then the function proceeds to search for just the web server's location.

The subroutine proceeds to locate the HTTP:// portion (by searching for the colon and two subsequent slashes). The next subsequent slash or backslash denotes that this is the web server's name. If none is found, then the entire string is the web server's name, which is appended to the beginning of the new URL.

It is simpler to locate an entire path. The subroutine simply transverses the string from end to beginning until it reaches a slash/backslash. Everything before that point is the path of the original document, and is appended to the beginning of the new URL. If no slashes are found, the entire original string is added. The subroutine next determines if the HTTP:// protocol header needs to be added as well (this occurs when the referring URL, for some reason, does not contain the HTTP:// header). If so, the subroutine inserts it to the beginning of the new URL. Because the URL is passed by reference (which is the default variable passing technique in Visual Basic), the information is reflected back in the calling subroutine.

The SearchClass Source Code

```
Option Explicit

Private sKeywords As String
Private fKeywords As Boolean
Private rsConnection As Recordset
Private dbConnection As Database
Dim sQuery As String

Private Sub Class_Initialize()
    Set dbConnection = Workspaces(0).OpenDatabase(App.Path + _
```

```
                              "\search2.mdb")
        sKeywords = ""
        fKeywords = False
    End Sub


    Private Sub Class_Terminate()
        Set rsConnection = Nothing
        dbConnection.Close
    End Sub


    Public Sub SetKeywords(newSKeywords As String)
        If (sKeywords <> newSKeywords Or Not fKeywords) Then
            fKeywords = True
            sKeywords = newSKeywords
            sQuery = "select * from DATA where INSTR(TITLE,'" + _
                    sKeywords + "')> 0"
            Set rsConnection = dbConnection.OpenRecordset(sQuery)
        End If
    End Sub


    Public Function GetKeywords() As String
        GetKeywords = sKeywords
    End Function


    Public Function PerformSearch(vCommand As Variant) As String
        If (InStr(vCommand, "Reset")) Then
            fKeywords = False
            SetKeywords sKeywords
        End If

        If (rsConnection.EOF Or rsConnection.BOF) Then
            PerformSearch = ""
            Exit Function
        End If

        Dim sOut As String
        sOut = "<CENTER><TABLE WIDTH=80% BORDER=1>" + vbCrLf
        Dim iPos As Integer
        For iPos = 1 To NumSteps
            If (rsConnection.EOF Or rsConnection.BOF) Then
                Exit For
```

```
        End If

        sOut = sOut + "<TR><TH WIDTH=40% BGCOLOR=#ffffff>" + _
            vbCrLf
        sOut = sOut + rsConnection("Title")
        sOut = sOut + "</TH><TD WIDTH=60% BGCOLOR=#ffffff>" + _
            vbCrLf
        sOut = sOut + "<A HREF="""""
        sOut = sOut + rsConnection("Data") + """">"
        sOut = sOut + rsConnection("Data") + "</A>" + vbCrLf

        sOut = sOut + "</TD></TR>" + vbCrLf
        rsConnection.MoveNext
    Next
    Out = sOut + "</TABLE></CENTER>"
    PerformSearch = sOut
End Function


Public Function MoreToCome() As Boolean
On Error GoTo MoreToComeErr
    If (rsConnection.EOF Or rsConnection.BOF) Then
        MoreToCome = False
    Else
        MoreToCome = True
    End If
    Exit Function
MoreToComeErr:
    MoreToCome = False
    Exit Function
End Function


Public Function CurPosition() As Variant
    CurPosition = rsConnection.Bookmark
End Function


Public Function NumSteps() As Long
    NumSteps = 10
End Functio


Private Sub ParseHTML(ByVal sURL As String, ByVal sHTML As _
            String)
```

```
        If (sHTML = "") Then Exit Sub

'look for the first string that's not within <>
Dim iPos As Integer, iLevel As Integer
For iPos = 1 To Len(sHTML)
  Dim sText As String
  Select Case Mid$(sHTML, iPos, 1)
    Case "<":
      iLevel = iLevel + 1
    Case ">"
      iLevel = iLevel - 1
    Case Chr$(10), Chr$(13):
    Case " ":
  Case Else
    If iLevel = 0 Then
      sHTML = Mid$(sHTML, iPos)
      iPos = InStr(sHTML, "<")
      If (iPos = 0) Then iPos = Len(sHTML) - iPos
      If (Not InsertURLInfo( _
            sURL, Mid$(sHTML, 1, iPos - 1))) Then
        'already parsed this one!
        Exit Sub
      End If
      Exit For
    End If
  End Select
Next
If (iPos < Len(sHTML)) Then
  FollowHyperlink "<A HREF=", iPos, sHTML, sURL
  FollowHyperlink "SRC=", iPos, sHTML, sURL
End If
End Sub

Sub FollowHyperlink(sHyperlink As String, ByVal iPos As _
          Integer, sHTML As String, ByVal sURL As String)

  Dim sLocalHTML As String
  sLocalHTML = sHTML
  Do While (1)
    iPos = InStr(iPos, UCase(sLocalHTML), sHyperlink)
    If (iPos = 0) Then Exit Do
```

```
      sLocalHTML = Mid$(sLocalHTML, iPos + Len(sHyperlink))
      Dim sDelimiter As String
      Select Case Left$(sLocalHTML, 1)
        Case """":
          sDelimiter = """"
          sLocalHTML = Mid$(sLocalHTML, 2)
        Case "'":
          sLocalHTML = Mid$(sLocalHTML, 2)
          sDelimiter = "'"
        Case Else
          sDelimiter = "<"
      End Select

      iPos = InStr(sLocalHTML, sDelimiter)
      If (iPos > 1) Then
        Investigate Left$(sLocalHTML, iPos - 1), True, sURL
        sLocalHTML = Mid$(sLocalHTML, iPos)
      End If
    Loop
End Sub



Function InsertURLInfo(sData As String, sTitle As String) _
        As Boolean
On Error GoTo InsertURLInfoErr
  Dim rsInsert As Recordset, sSQL As String
  sSQL = "select * from DATA where Data='" + sData + "'"
  Set rsInsert = dbConnection.OpenRecordset(sSQL)
  If (rsInsert.EOF) Then
    rsInsert.AddNew
    rsInsert("Title") = sTitle
    rsInsert("Data") = sData
    rsInsert.Update
    InsertURLInfo = True
  Else
    InsertURLInfo = False
  End If
  rsInsert.Close
  Exit Function
InsertURLInfoErr:
  InsertURLInfo = False
```

```
        Exit Function
    End Function


    Private Sub RearrangeURL(sURL As String, ByVal sOriginalURL _
            As String)
        'already fixed up!
        If (InStr(UCase$(sURL), "HTTP:") = 1) Then Exit Sub

        Dim iPos As Integer
        If (Left$(sURL, 1) = "/") Then
            'find the first colon if it's there.
            iPos = InStr(sOriginalURL, ":")
            If (iPos > 0) Then
                If (Mid$(sOriginalURL, iPos, 1) = "\" Or _
                    Mid$(sOriginalURL, iPos, 1) = "/") Then

                    iPos = iPos + 1
                    If (Mid$(sOriginalURL, iPos, 1) = "\" Or _
                        Mid$(sOriginalURL, iPos, 1) = "/") Then

                        iPos = iPos + 1
                    End If
                End If
                Dim iPosSlash1 As Integer, iPosSlash2 As Integer
                iPosSlash1 = InStr(iPos, sOriginalURL, "\")
                If (iPosSlash1 = 0) Then iPosSlash1 = _
                    Len(sOriginalURL)
                iPosSlash2 = InStr(iPos, sOriginalURL, "/")
                If (iPosSlash2 = 0) Then iPosSlash2 = _
                    Len(sOriginalURL)
                iPos = IIf(iPosSlash2 < iPosSlash1, iPosSlash2, _
                    iPosSlash1)

                sURL = Left$(sURL, iPos) + sURL
            Else
                Exit Sub
            End If
        Else 'need to find the last slash/backslash in _
                sOriginalURL
            For iPos = Len(sOriginalURL) To 1 Step -1
                If (Mid$(sOriginalURL, iPos, 1) = "\" Or _
```

```vb
                Mid$(sOriginalURL, iPos, 1) = "/") Then
            Exit For
        End If
    Next
    Dim iHTTP As Integer
    iHTTP = InStr(UCase$(sOriginalURL), "HTTP:")
    If ((iHTTP > 0) And (iPos - (iHTTP + Len("HTTP:")) _
            < 2)) Then
        iPos = Len(sOriginalURL) ' found the slashes after _
            the HTTP
    ElseIf (iPos = 0) Then
        iPos = Len(sOriginalURL)
    End If
    If (Right$(Left$(sOriginalURL, iPos), 1) = "\" Or _
            Right$(Left$(sOriginalURL, iPos), 1) = "/") Then
        sURL = Left$(sOriginalURL, iPos) + sURL
    Else
        sURL = Left$(sOriginalURL, iPos) + "/" + sURL
    End If
    If (InStr(UCase$(sURL), "HTTP:") <> 1) Then
        sURL = "HTTP://" + sURL
    End If

  End If
End Sub


Public Sub Investigate(ByVal sURL As String, Optional _
            fIgnoreForm As Boolean, Optional sOriginalURL _
            As String)

' make sure I don't go too far down or I'll drown!
Static iRecursionLevel As Integer
    If (iRecursionLevel > 8) Then Exit Sub
    iRecursionLevel = iRecursionLevel + 1

    ' get rid of all the things I know I don't handle!
    If (InStr(UCase$(sURL), "MAILTO:") > 0) Then Exit Sub
    If (InStr(UCase$(sURL), "FTP:") > 0) Then Exit Sub
    If (InStr(UCase$(sURL), ".GIF") > 0) Then Exit Sub
    If (InStr(UCase$(sURL), ".JPG") > 0) Then Exit Sub
    If (InStr(UCase$(sURL), "GOPHER:") > 0) Then Exit Sub
```

```
' recursively call myself with this function until I _
        run out of URLs!
If (Not fIgnoreForm) Then
   Load frmINetInvestigate
End If
Dim sHTML As String

If (sOriginalURL <> "") Then
   RearrangeURL sURL, sOriginalURL
End If
On Error GoTo errHTML
   sHTML = frmINetInvestigate.inetInvestigate.OpenURL(sURL, _
        icString)
   ParseHTML sURL, sHTML
errHTML:
   If (Not fIgnoreForm) Then
      Unload frmINetInvestigate
   End If

   iRecursionLevel = iRecursionLevel - 1
   Exit Sub
End Sub
```

Snapshots of the Search Application

Figure 15.10 shows the initial search page. Figure 15.11 shows the snapshot of subsequent search results from the Holy Diver Internet search engine. Figure 15.12 shows how to submit a new page into the system. Figure 15.13 shows the contents of the Access database after submission of a new web page.

Figure 15.10
Snapshot of initial
search page

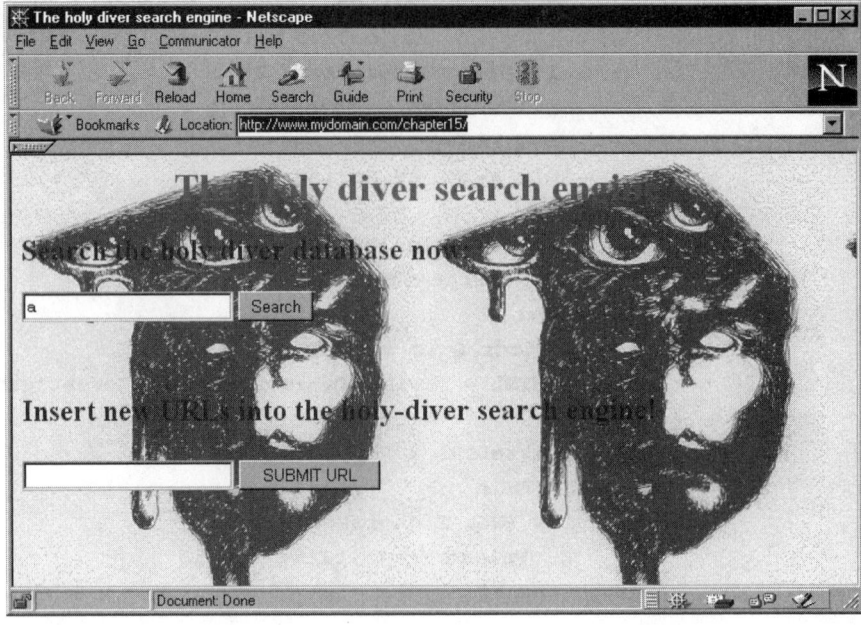

Figure 15.11
Snapshot of search
results

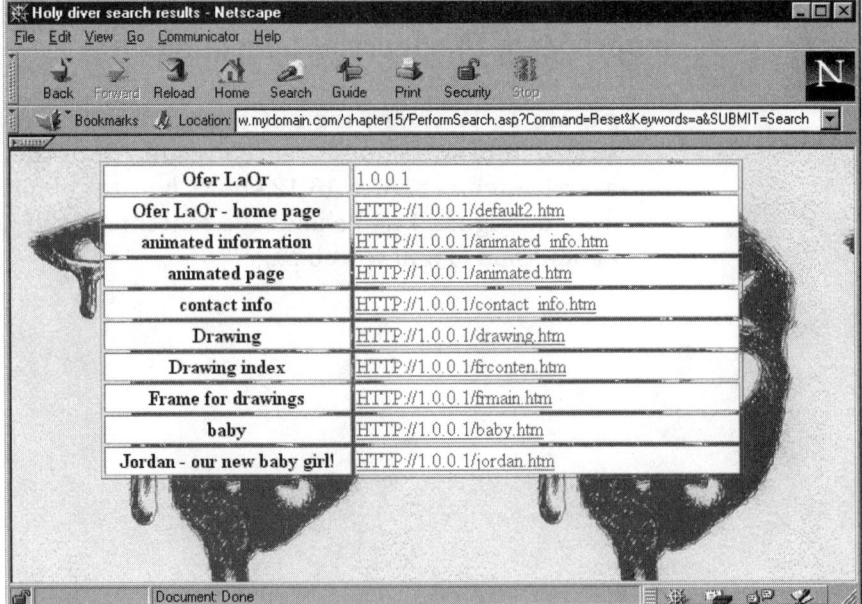

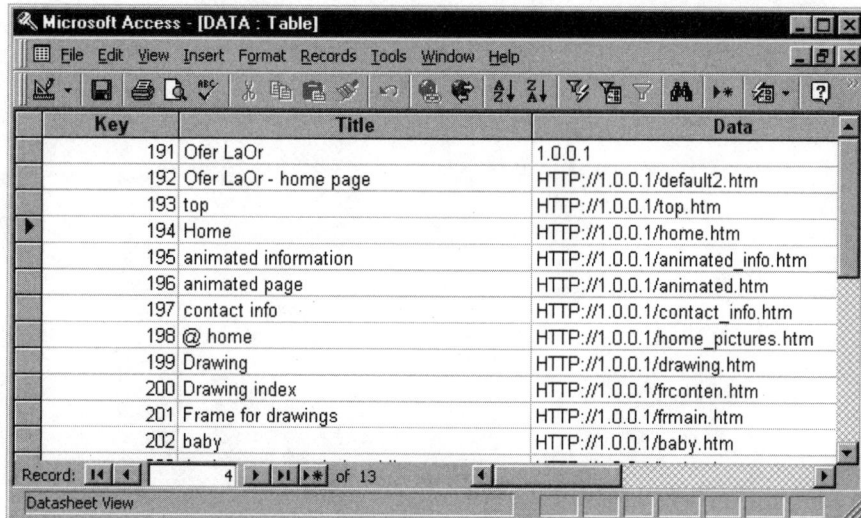

Summary

This chapter has demonstrated how ASP interacts with server side Visual Basic applications. Several other alternatives enable VB to interact with a web server. The Active Server Pages method is certainly not this author's favorite method of communicating with the server.

Our next chapter deals with the future, and with my views on recent, as well as upcoming technology trends.

16

WHAT'S NEXT?

- HTTP/1.1
- HTTP/NG
- The future of CGI
- Graphic formats
- HTML
- Plug-ins
- Push technology
- Java
- Script languages

HTTP/1.1

HTTP has been undergoing a slow revolution of late. Several initiatives are currently underway to resolve the biggest flaws in the HTTP protocol.

This protocol was created for the purpose of transferring small quantities of text without compression or graphics. HTTP is connectionless, and does not handle simultaneous loads very well. Overall, the current HTTP protocol (version 1.0) has been outgrown by the content it has been transferring in recent years.

Growing as quickly as it has, HTTP's creators have not had a chance to correct its primary deficiencies. Low performance, loss of packets, connectionlessness, lack of persistence of data and lack of support for compression are some problems that HTTP needs to quickly fix. Since it is the most popular protocol on the Internet, its deficiencies are slowing everyone down significantly.

A recent benchmark concluded that an optimal HTTP protocol, in conjunction with some new compression techniques, could produce more reliable communication and increase performance by a factor of up to 8 times.

HTTP version 1.1 is somewhat of an improvement. It should not be viewed as a panacea, though, since it is still missing some necessary pieces. But HTTP/1.1 does provide a significant shot in the arm for the Internet and the web. Some of the issues that have been resolved are the question of connection persistence, and the integration of cookies into the protocol (up until now this was a separate entity). By fixing the connection persistence problem, the major problems that have plagued the Internet can be alleviated or resolved altogether.

Another issue HTTP/1.0 raised concerned the multitude of IP addresses that are currently required in order to give each domain its own home page. This has been one of the major reasons for the the vast IP number shortage problem. (The problem was festering just around the corner, since IPv6 [a.k.a., IP/NG] has been slow in implementation.) One way or another, the problem had to be resolved — either IP addresses were going to be available in sparse quantity, all the routers and servers on the Internet had to be modified for IPv6, or the biggest IP hog around (HTTP, that is) had to be revised.

The modification in HTTP allows a single IP address to host any number of web pages. This alleviates the need for multihoming web servers (a single web server uses up lots of IP addresses, each of which is connected to a virtual web directory and initial home page), serving lots of IP addresses, so that each IP has its own dedicated home page.

One nice feature brought about by the addition of persistent connections is that portions of files (ranges) can be sent over the connection — allowing a browser to request a portion it may be missing. Imagine a standard browser implementation that would allow you to continue to download after being cut off after downloading 11Megs out of 12Megs of your favorite game, and then resume the transfer instantaneously. (This feature is already present in some non-standard TCP/IP protocols and Netscape's newest browser to some degree.)

Persistence, however, was designed into the protocol to lessen the high number of lost packets resulting from the connectionless state of HTTP. The server or browser can still cut off the connection midstream, in which case the protocol requires a reconnection in order to resume. This prevents a situation where each server is overloaded by a high number of open connections — each requiring its own local resources — while most of these connections are not active.

HTTP/1.1 support in upcoming browsers is definite. Since both Netscape and Microsoft are providing support on the client side, the majority of browsers will be HTTP/1.1 enabled by mid-1998.

On the server side, however, migration may be slower. Since new server software would need to be installed, an expensive and even risky task, most existing servers are slow to migrate. Since all of the major vendors will provide HTTP/1.1 in their next releases, it is my hope that, within 2 or 3 years, the majority of web browsers will be interacting with HTTP/1.1 servers.

Since HTTP/1.1 is only downward-compatible in some respects, the high number of IP addresses that are currently in use for the purpose of multihoming may go down somewhat slowly.

CGI

It's hard to foresee the changes CGI may undertake. Many proprietary interfaces such as ISAPI and NSAPI previously threatened to take over the interface arena, but have yet to do so.

There are many deficiencies in the way CGI applications are currently being utilized. First, the performance and resources factor, which is the result of a key problem in CGI applications: the re-execution of the application for each instance of a running client script. Moreover, these scripts are required to continue, regardless of whether the originating browser/client is still connected or not.

CGI is fashioned after HTTP. Considering the pending modifications in the HTTP protocol, it is very likely that CGI will undergo significant modifications of its own.

CGI applications will simply work transparently when HTTP/1.1 is implemented into all popular servers (this should take place before the end of 1997). The great new features embedded in HTTP/1.1 cannot not be directly utilized via the current CGI technology.

One of these new features — which, when used properly, will greatly improve performance — is persistent connections. One example of how CGI can tackle such issues is FAST-CGI, a non-standard which demonstrates how standard CGI technology can be greatly improved. FAST-CGI works on a complete session, minimizing the instancing performance problem. Once a session is broken, a FAST-CGI application immediately stops utilizing expensive system resources. Since HTTP/1.1 sessions can "time out" and resume using a new connection, FAST-CGI applications still need to use cookies to achieve complete persistence.

HTTPING

This protocol may eventually replace HTTP/1.1 in a few years. It is still too early to tell what features will be included. Performance, however, is a major concern — so it is likely that compression will be integrated natively into this protocol.

HTML

HTML was, from the beginning, a moving duck in a world full of slow turtles. The HTML specs could change overnight, after which one more browser implementation would fail to comply with it correctly. The Internet world has simply preferred to go with quick solutions, rather than wait for the standards to come in. This has caused a market with beta de-facto standards and lots of ad-hoc solutions.

Some upcoming technologies threaten to set aside HTML as the primary means of transferring documents to the desktop.

Cascading style sheets is a significant topic that has probably run its course. It was promoted heavily as a quick way to overcome some of HTML's shortcomings. But the fact that there is no way to dictate to the browser how the end document will look is the main problem of many such technologies.

This feature, originally listed as a feature of HTML, is now being viewed as a deficiency. The original thought behind it was that each machine would display the HTML document based on the capabilities of the local machine. If heavy processing was involved, Windows CE palmtops could never have had their own Internet explorer.

Dynamic HTML

The latest of these offerings, and probably the most interesting, is *Dynamic HTML* (DHTML). This format has been created by Microsoft and will only be supported by Internet Explorer 4. DHTML supports ActiveX plug-ins in many interactive variations and provides a new level of interactivity with web servers and on the desktop as a whole. A quick glance at IE4 is enough to demonstrate that this is the way to the future.

Interestingly, Netscape's implementation of DHTML could not be more different than Microsoft's own. Netscape's focus was primarily on cross platform support, whereas Microsoft's goal was clearly the "Windows everywhere" theme (i.e., Microsoft's DHTML only works for Windows platforms).

Unfortunately, there's no way of knowing if this technology will be embraced by the industry. Since it is proprietary (and it is, after all, Microsoft's own), and will only work on Windows operating systems (at least to begin with) this technology cannot be embraced by the entire industry. Anyone on USENET can see the number of Microsoft bashers on the Internet. With Microsoft's recent embrace of Apple, IE4 and Microsoft's DHTML may be a standard in 90% of desktop machines, creating a force to be reckoned with.

There are also several DHTML push technologies which are worth exploring.

Transitions and other effects can be integrated into DHTML by vendors. This allows the customization level to grow exponentially as software vendors target more components for this technology.

Netscape's offerings for their next browser seem to be an attempt to circumvent the operating system's native interface, providing their communicator interface instead. Unfortunately, push technology, even though it is very hot today, will probably not be enough to convince people to trade in their reliable operating system interfaces. Microsoft's IE4 initiative is unique, since it builds on the current implementation. This type of solution has a greater chance of succeeding because Windows 97 will likely use the exact same user interface — allowing users a single user interface in three distinct operating systems (Windows 95, Windows 97, Windows NT). This is not counting Cairo, the next version of Windows NT, which could have a newer interface.

One terrific thing about DHTML is its ability to modify the appearance of browser and page before the browser has time to completely download the entire script.

Netscape's browser, while supporting cascading style sheets, is only compatible with Microsoft's version of CSS1 in a minimal fashion. Previously, when Netscape controlled about 90% of the browser market share, Netscape was able to create de-facto standards that were adopted by the rest of the industry. With Microsoft's current Internet Explorer market share, this may no longer be the case.

Which standard will prevail? It's hard to tell. With Microsoft's huge desktop operating system market share, it is easy to see Internet explorer on every desktop in a few years. This does not, by any means, mean that Navigator/Communicator is doomed for failure. It does mean, however, that Netscape must stay innovative to maintain a winning hand.

On the developmental platform, Netscape has a long way to go in order to reach Microsoft's current position. Programmers and content providers will decide the future standards. Whichever standard is easiest and most comfortable for programmers to work in (and boasts the most supported desktops) will likely triumph.

This book has demonstrated the ease in which a client/server application can be developed using Visual Basic 5 and ActiveX documents.

Client/server VB5 ActiveX document applications can also be created utilizing DCOM or standard TCP/IP protocols. Since these components are easily integrated into a web browser (or, in the case of IE4, as a desktop component) — this technology seems like a genuine winner.

HTML 4.0

The present reigning standard, HTML 3.2, will soon be superceded by the HTML 4.0 specification, as recently announced by the World Wide Web Consortium (W3C). The W3C has made it their policy to take the most recent advances in local HTML implementation, and improve them so that they are completely standard among browsers. Since this is binding on the browser end, most web designers try to meet the latest W3C standards.

This latest version of HTML improves on previous versions by:

1. Enhancing forms — Adding the ability for rich HTML to appear in any button, read-only controls, grouped controls and keyboard shortcuts for controls and other titles.

2. Inline frames — These are similar to those implemented in Microsoft browsers.

3. Enhancing tables — Columns can now be grouped and more control exerted over borders and other design factors.

4. Enhancing objects — Further improvements integrating objects, fonts, and other objects and style sheets into web pages.

5. New entities — New entities for symbols and glyphs have been added for use in mathematics, markup and internationalization purposes.

Both Microsoft browsers and Netscape browsers are committed to supporting these standards — allowing CGI and other web applications to further flourish with ever more advanced content.

Graphics Formats

GIF files are certainly not the ultimate graphic format. But they are perfect for small animations and partially realistic images. For more realistic images, JPEGs provide a better compression. Progressive JPEGS and interlaced GIFs are an attempt to let the user download *and* see what he's downloading at the same time.

Some new technologies should improve on these formats. The Portable Network Graphics (PNG) format will provide better compression with better graphics.

Recent new technologies involving wavelet compression seem to provide compression rates of up to five times more than JPEG files currently do. Since most of the traffic on the Net involves binary images, this could greatly improve the Net's performance.

Video formats are also improving. The next MPEG standard targets the inclusion of hyperlinks and other types of multimedia into the MPEG video stream. Apple's plans for Quicktime are less definite, but — with their concept of breaking up the Mac operating system into interoperable components — this may yet become a winning technology.

When progressive JPEG files were first introduced, they were designed to give the user a preview of what was coming. This, however, was not widely adopted by the industry and, like interlaced GIFs, initially provided slower performance with fairly blurry graphics.

One innovative idea that's become popular has been to utilize animated GIFs to provide a similar effect. The first GIF in the animation is a low-resolution graphics format (which can contain fewer colors, or even be black and white).

It is more than likely that browser makers will try to bypass UNISYS's hold on the industry (they hold the patent for the GIF graphic file format and the compression technology it is based on) by embracing a similarly featured format without the royalty down-side of GIF.

Plug-ins

Netscape originated this idea with Navigator 2. Plug-ins interact with the browser on a component level as a client-side application running within the browser. Microsoft's technology, the ActiveX document/component, provides a more cohesive solution. The integration between browser, operating system and component is simply more complete here. Its ability to sign components (vs. plug-ins, which cannot be signed) and for component makers to mark their product as "script safe" and "initialization safe" allows several levels of security to take place.

Push Technology

Push technology has been around for a relatively short time. PointCast originated this concept as a smart screen saver, capable of displaying smarter live content. Both Microsoft and Netscape recently went all out trying to integrate push technology into their respective products. Netscape actually integrated a new PointCast client into their browser, as well as provided native Netcast support.

Microsoft's concept is a bit more complex, and supports many types of push technology concepts. First, Internet Explorer 4 provides the user with the ability to sign up for a particular "push service" (or channel). This comes in the form of a simple web page that can be automatically downloaded, offline or online, by the browser on a regular basis. Additionally, the service can be provided by an offline/online ActiveX component that is integrated into the desktop. This component communicates with the server side (the way that *MapClient* contacts *MapServer*) in order to provide the user with new information (i.e., the news). Since these components can actually run as miniature applications, using local or remote databases and other operating system capabilities and interfaces, this feature offers virtually unlimited possibilities for content providers and programmers, as well as for the end-user market.

Java

Java has been touted as the next C++. There was massive hype by the media concerning this language, which has been adopted by virtually every big player in the industry. But a few problems have prevented it from being used in large scale application development.

First, Java integrates the best features of C++ with the worst of Visual Basic. This makes it fairly difficult to deal with Java components (as is the case with VBX/OCX vendors). There are not many mainstream library vendors; hence, programming is still a major chore in which every minor GUI task must be created by the programmer, rather than the library vendor. Development platforms are not nearly as advanced as those in Visual Basic, Delphi or C++. Finally, Java performance, while getting faster all the time, still lags behind that of its competitors; it is a slow, slow language.

Most of these problems are completely resolvable. Developmental platforms, APIs (for interacting with server components, DCOM, MAPI, ODBC and other outside components) are partially complete. With every Java release, vast improvements on the language and component side are made. Finally, Java virtual machines and Java op-codes (integrated right into Intel CPU chips, for example) will make Java applications perform as well as native applications.

Since the Java micro-code instructions are publicly known, it should be noted that other languages will also be able to compile to native Java environments. Once performance of the universal Java virtual machine is improved, it can act as a universal client for applications. It is more than likely that Java Virtual machine (VM) compilers will be created for the major development languages such as Delphi and Visual Basic.

This is already happening; the W3C standards committee is working with vendors to produce a Modula-3 version that would run under the Java Virtual Machine. While Modula-3 is not a mainstream development language, it has definite merits as an object-oriented language (with Pascal style syntax) and will likely gain more followers with its move to the Java VM platform.

As a long-time C++ programmer, I know the average level of most of the C++ programmers out there. Most of them are struggling along because of the complexity and design concepts brought upon them by this language. Don't get me wrong; I still think there's absolutely nothing you cannot do with C++ (whereas Visual Basic may need an occasional ActiveX control or library to do something). C++, however, is simply too complex a language for the average programmer.

Similarly, the actual Java language is fairly complex. Granted, most of the biggest hurdles in C++ have been removed, but the overall concept may be just too much. Visual Basic, on the other hand, is just right on the complexity scale for most programmers. This means that the work force is more readily available, and applications are less expensive to develop. Also, it is a much easier language to maintain and extend. Given a good Java compiler for VB (Visual Basic for the Java VM?) with good DCOM/COM support, Microsoft can raise VB to a cross platform development system for the entire enterprise. On the down side, this will allow many Windows-only programmers to shift to other potential platforms (which would be a bad thing, from Microsoft's perspective). Given that it is likely that some company is presently working on such a compiler, it is equally as likely that Microsoft will buy out that company and present the programmer with a new generic Visual Basic target platform.

Script Languages

As you may have noticed, I am not a big scripting language fan. VBA has been integrated into everything but microwaves. Mostly, this allows for a clean integration between several applications. A clean ActiveX interface to an application and a good scripting language enables a Microsoft Word VBA script to interact with any other application and perform complex tasks from within the word processor.

The downsizing of VBA to VB-Script has me confused. This language does *not* support the leading features in Visual Basic, nor does it provide interaction with *real* external ActiveX components. It has been targeted as glue logic for ActiveX components residing in web pages. While interesting on the programming end, this concept is not likely to be widely accepted. First, any real application shies away from such glue logic technology. It is likely that this will be used for small-time component interaction, such as banners and special effects on web pages. More complex applications will probably utilize more integrated solutions, such as ActiveX documents, Java applications, etc.

JavaScript, on the other hand, provides a truly useful scripting language that is more or less universal. It can be used for validation, simple web interaction and more complex HTML manipulations. Used with a smart server side component, a smart HTML application is easily created.

It should be noted, however, that this language desperately needs an established standard. The standard will allow it to work transparently in any browser. Given that such standards take considerable time to become popular and that technologies on the web are moving so quickly, it may be that by the time a standards committee is finished discussing this language, the web will have changed so much that there is no longer any use for JavaScript.

Currently the only standards committee working on a JavaScript standard is ECMA (the European Computer Manufacturers Association). The ECMA-262 standard attempts to standardize the language and is backed up by both Microsoft and Netscape. The standard is based on Netscape's own de facto standard. Microsoft's implementation of JScript 3.0 promises to adhere to this standard. This is definitely a step in the right direction on part of all the companies involved.

APPENDIXES

APPENDIX A

oCGI REFERENCE

- Public methods
- Public collections
- Public variables
- Private methods, variables, constants

PUBLIC DECLARATIONS

```
Const STD_INPUT_HANDLE = -10&
Const STD_OUTPUT_HANDLE = -11&
```

These are the standard input and output handles that are sent as parameters to the *GetStdHandle* Win 32 API function. The *WriteFile* and *ReadFile* API functions are used with the retrieved handle, in order to read or write the CGI streams.

The STDIN stream is read-only when detecting that a POST submission method has been used. Otherwise, the input parameters are retrieved via command line or environment variables. Output is always sent via STDOUT.

```
Const NBlock = 3800
```

This is the maximum block size for a virtual cookie. Netscape browsers support 4000 bytes per cookie. *NBlock* supports less because some characters may require expansion (e.g., illegal ASCII characters), which could cause the cookie string to expand.

```
Const DEFAULT_MAX_POST = 10000
```

This is the default maximum size allowed as the input parameter string.

```
Public MaxPost As Long
```

This number is equal by default to DEFAULT_MAX_POST. It can, however, be modified by the application immediately following the initialization of the oCGI library. In scenarios where it is possible that more items would be sent as parameters (this should not surpass 32,000 since some browsers will not support such a big buffer — especially under 16-bit Windows).

```
Public cParameters As New Collection
```

This collection is automatically allocated as needed and contains objects of type *ParamType*. Each item contains a single parameter. This collection can be accessed directly or via the *ReadParam* function.

Cookies

```
Public cCookies As New Collection
```

This collection contains the cookies. Cookies can be accessed directly via the cookie collection or via the *ReadCookie* function.

```
' have we started writing HTTP yet?
Dim fStartedCGI As Boolean
```

This variable is local to the oCGI library and allows the oCGI library to determine if the content type has already been declared. This helps the library determine if that tag is needed yet or not. When the tag is finally produced (during the first *WriteCGI* call with an unspecified or true *fStartCGI*), virtual cookies are placed in the STDOUT stream *before* the content type HTTP tag.

```
' value of compressed cookies
Dim VirtualTTL As Integer
```

This maintains the time virtual cookies will "live" (in units of days).

```
Dim fModifiedVirtual As Boolean, fCommittedVirtual As Boolean
```

The *fModifiedVirtual* helps determine if virtual cookies have been changed during a session. If not, there is no need to commit the virtual cookie string to the outside. The *fCommittedVirtual* flag helps the oCGI library determine whether the virtual cookies have already been committed to the STDOUT stream.

```
Dim nVirtualCookies As Integer, sVirtualCookies As String
```

The *nVirtualCookies* holds the original number of actual cookies where the virtual cookie string resides. This is useful in deleting surplus cookies if some virtual cookies are removed from the system. The *sVirtualCookies* holds the entire virtual cookie string. This can be broken up (if needed) into standard cookies when the virtual cookies are committed.

```
Const NMaxVirtualCookies = 19
```

This constant holds the maximum number of cookies the virtual cookie system can support. Netscape browsers allow for a total of 20 cookies per site/application. Since it is often useful to have an additional, standard cookie, the system only supports up to 19 virtual cookies by default. This number can be modified to allow for more room on the virtual cookie stream. Note that each real cookie may hold up to 4000 bytes, whereas the system limits this number to *NBlock* (which is a slightly lower number). To get the maximum capacity out of the cookie space in the browser, modify *NBlock* to 4000 and *NMaxVirtualCookies* to 20.

```
Private Sub ClearCollection(cCollection As Collection)
   Dim iPos As Integer
   For iPos = 1 To cCollection.Count
     cCollection.Remove 1
   Next
End Sub
```

The *ClearCollection* subroutine simply goes through a collection and removes all of the elements in it. The private subroutines: *SetCookies* and *SetParams* use this function for the *cCookies* and *cParameters* collections, respectively.

```
Private Sub CommitVirtualCookies()
    If Not fModifiedVirtual Then Exit Sub ' not needed, _
            nothing's changed
    ' break it down into any number of blocks and save them.
    Dim sTotal As String, sCurrent As String
    sTotal = sVirtualCookies

    Dim i As Integer
    For i = 1 To NMaxVirtualCookies
        sCurrent = Left$(sTotal, NBlock)
        sTotal = Mid$(sTotal, NBlock)

        If (sCurrent <> "") Then
            If VirtualTTL > 0 Then
                WriteCookie "_" + CStr(i), sCurrent, ReadServerName, _
                    ReadScriptName, CDate(Now + VirtualTTL)
            Else
                WriteCookie "_" + CStr(i), sCurrent, _
                    ReadServerName, ReadScriptName
            End If
        Else
            ' if less than or equal to compressed cookies, _
                delete the extra cookie!
            If (i <= nVirtualCookies) Then
                If VirtualTTL > 0 Then
                    WriteCookie "_" + CStr(i), "", ReadServerName, _
                        ReadScriptName, CDate(Now - VirtualTTL)
                Else
                    WriteCookie "_" + CStr(i), "", ReadServerName, _
                        ReadScriptName
                End If
            End If
        End If
    Next
    fCommittedVirtual = True
    fModifiedVirtual = False
End Sub
```

The *CommitVirtualCookies* subroutine goes through the *sVirtualCookies* string and breaks it into segments of *NBlock* size. Each block is placed in a real cookie and written out (virtual cookies are kept as an underscore and number identifying their relative position in the cookie string). If there are fewer cookie strings now than there were before, those cookies are removed by using an expiration date that has already passed (defaults to 14 days before today = `Now` - `VirtualTTL`). When the *VirtualTTL* value is less than or equal to zero, the cookie will not have an expiration date (*it will not be persistent*) and will contain an empty value. This subroutine uses the current server and current script for virtual cookies. Once the iteration through the cookie string is done, the *fCommittedVirtual* flag is turned on to prevent the system from committing the cookie string more than once.

```
Public Sub DeleteVirtualCookie(sName As String, Optional _
        sValue As Variant)
    Dim iPos As Integer, iEnd As Integer, sNewValue As _
        String, sNewCookies As String
    sNewValue = sName + IIf(IsMissing(sValue), "=", "=" + _
        CStr(sValue))

    ' surgically remove the value from the virtual cookie _
        string.
    sNewCookies = RecursiveDelete(sVirtualCookies, sNewValue, _
        IsMissing(sValue))
    If (sVirtualCookies <> sNewCookies) Then fModifiedVirtual _
        = True
    sVirtualCookies = sNewCookies
End Sub
```

The *DeleteVirtualCookie* subroutine removes a virtual cookie from the virtual cookie string. If the optional value is not specified, the subroutine searches for the name of the cookie with an equal sign. If the value is specified, it is also part of the search string. The *RecursiveDelete* function is used to remove the string from the virtual cookie string. If the virtual cookie string has been modified, the *fModifiedVirtual* flag is turned on.

```
Public Function ReadServerSecured() As Boolean
    ReadServerSecured = IIf(Environ("SERVER_PORT_SECURE") = _
        "0", False, True)
End Function
```

The *ReadServerSecured* function is used to determine if the current script is running securely under SSL. If the communication between server and browser is secured, this function returns a true value.

```
Public Function ReadUserAgent() As String
    Dim iPos As Integer, sUserAgent As String

    sUserAgent = Environ("HTTP_USER_AGENT")
    iPos = InStr(sUserAgent, "MSIE")
    If (iPos > 0) Then
        sUserAgent = "Microsoft Internet Explorer (" + _
                Mid$(sUserAgent, iPos + 5)
    Else
        iPos = InStr(sUserAgent, "Mozilla")
        If iPos >= 0 Then
            sUserAgent = "Netscape or compatible " + _
                Mid$(sUserAgent, iPos + 8)
        End If
    End If
    ReadUserAgent = sUserAgent
End Function
```

The *ReadUserAgent* function attempts to identify the user's browser type and version. It identifies Microsoft Internet explorer and Netscape browsers. These browsers employ notation that is less than readable.

```
Public Function ReadServerName() As String
    ReadServerName = Environ("SERVER_NAME")
End Function
```

The *ReadServerName* function returns the name of the server. This function returns a value in the following form: **www.mydomain.com**

```
Public Function ReadGatewayInterface() As String
    ReadGatewayInterface = Environ("GATEWAY_INTERFACE") ' _
            CGI/1.1
End Function
```

The *ReadGatewayInterface* function returns the current gateway interface. CGI/1.0 does not offer support for cookies. CGI/1.1 is the implementation used by most current web servers.

```
Public Function ReadServerPort() As String
  ReadServerPort = Environ("SERVER_PORT") ' 80
End Function
```

The *ReadServerPort* function returns the port number currently being used for communication between server and browser. The default port number for standard HTTP communication is port "80". Secure communication typically uses port "443".

```
Public Function ReadScriptName() As String
  ReadScriptName = Environ("SCRIPT_NAME")
End Function
```

The *ReadScriptName* function returns the currently executing script's name. This is often useful in conjunction with the *ReadServerName* function in producing the URL that makes the CGI application execute. Returns a value in the following form: /myscript.exe. Merged with ReadServerName yields: `cgi.ReadServerName + cgi.ReadScriptName` = **http://www.mydomain.com/myPath/myScript.exe**

```
Public Sub ProcessVirtualCookies(Optional NewVirtualTTL As _
          Variant)
  If (Not IsMissing(NewVirtualTTL)) Then
    VirtualTTL = NewVirtualTTL
  End If

  nVirtualCookies = 0
  sVirtualCookies = ""
  Dim i As Integer, sCookie As String
  For i = 1 To NMaxVirtualCookies
    sCookie = ReadCookie("_" + CStr(i))
    If (sCookie <> "") Then
      sVirtualCookies = sVirtualCookies + sCookie
      nVirtualCookies = i

      'remove this cookie from the cookie list.
      cCookies.Remove ("_" + CStr(i))
    End If
  Next

  If (sVirtualCookies = "") Then Exit Sub
```

```
Dim request As String
request = sVirtualCookies
' now, untangle the mess...
Dim iPos As Integer
Do
    ' look for the first appearance of the= sign.
    iPos = InStr(request, "=")
    If (IsNull(iPos) Or iPos = 0) Then
      Exit Do
    End If

    Dim sName As String, sVal As String
    sName = Left$(request, iPos - 1)
    sVal = Mid$(request, iPos + 1)

    iPos = InStr(sVal, "&")
    If (IsNull(iPos) Or iPos = 0) Then
      request = ""
    Else
      sVal = Left$(sVal, iPos - 1)
      request = Trim$(Mid$(request, Len(sVal) + Len(sName) _
          + 3))
    End If

    Dim entry As ParamType
    Set entry = New ParamType
    entry.Name = sName
    entry.Value = sVal

    On Error GoTo DuplicateKeyErr
    cCookies.Add Item:=entry, Key:=sName
    On Error GoTo 0

  Loop
  Exit Sub
DuplicateKeyErr:
  If Err.Number <> 457 Then Exit Sub ' serious error!
  cCookies.Add Item:=entry ' no key!
  Resume Next
End Sub
```

The *ProcessVirtualCookie* subroutine processes virtual cookie strings into standard cookies, allowing the user to access them via the standard *ReadCookie* function. If the *NewVirtualTTL* parameter is specified, the system copies that value to the VirtualTTL global variable. This is later used in the *CommitVirtualCookies* subroutine.

The subroutine starts by clearing the virtual cookie string and the number of virtual cookies. The routine iterates through the possible virtual cookie values and appends each virtual cookie to the virtual cookie string. As each virtual cookie is located, it is removed from the *cCookies* collection. The nVirtualCookies variable is set to the maximum number of virtual cookie strings found in this search.

At this point, if no cookies are found, the subroutine terminates. The subroutine parses the virtual cookie string for equality signs. Each item is split into name and value. A new *ParamType* object is allocated and the name and value inserted into it. The object is added into the *cCookies* collection, with its name being used as the collection's key. Unfortunately, if there are two identical entries with the same name, an error will occur. In that case, the *DuplicateKeyErr* error will be triggered. If the function determines that the error wasn't number 457 (duplicate key) — the function exits with an error. When the duplicate error occurs, the item is added into the collection without a key.

```
Public Function ReadParam(sName As String) As String
On Error GoTo EndReadParam ' parameter that hasn't shown
    ReadParam = ""
    ReadParam = cParameters(sName).Value
EndReadParam:
    Exit Function
End Function
```

The *ReadParam* function ascertains the name of a parameter and retrieves the value for it. This function operates by using the collection's key (which is the name of the parameter) to quickly retrieve the parameter. This only works after the *SetParams* subroutine, which parses the parameter string and places the parameters into the *cParameters* collection. If the item is not found in the collection, an error occurs and a blank string is returned from the function. When using multiple items with the same name, the first is always retrieved via this function (identical names require the application to iterate through the items in *cParameters*).

```
Public Function ReadRemoteAddress() As String
   ReadRemoteAddress = Environ("REMOTE_ADDR")
End Function
```

The *ReadRemoteAddress* function returns the IP address of the browser. It returns a value in the following form: "127.0.0.1".

```
Public Function ReadRemoteHost() As String
   ReadRemoteHost = Environ("REMOTE_HOST")
End Function
```

The *ReadRemoteHost* function returns the host name for the remote client (browser). If the client has a reverse DNS value it will return it: **ppp12.Interline.net**. If there is no reverse DNS value and the remote machine has a local machine name (this is the computer name in Microsoft WFW, Windows 95 and Windows NT), it will take the form: **SAGE**.

```
Public Function ReadRemoteFrom() As String
   ReadRemoteFrom = Environ("HTTP_FROM")
End Function
```

The *ReadRemoteFrom* function uses a non-standard extension in Netscape servers and browsers. It returns the remote client's e-mail address if the client chooses to make that visible. This function should not be used in systems that may need to be ported to non-Netscape environments. It returns a value in the following form: **myname@mydomain.com**.

```
Private Sub ClearJunk(param As String)
   Dim iPos As Integer, i As Integer
   Dim newParam As String

   ' first clear all + signs.
   Do
      iPos = InStr(param, "+")
      If (IsNull(iPos) Or iPos = 0) Then
         Exit Do
      End If
      param = Left$(param, iPos - 1) & " " & Mid$(param, iPos + 1)
   Loop
```

```
' clear all %.
Do
   iPos = InStr(param, "%")
   If (IsNull(iPos) Or iPos = 0) Then
     Exit Do
   End If

   newParam = "&H" + Mid$(param, iPos + 1, 2)
   param = Left$(param, iPos - 1) & Chr$(CInt(newParam)) & _
         Mid$(param, iPos + 3)
Loop
End Sub
```

The *ClearJunk* subroutine decodes the CGI syntax back into normal ASCII text. This subroutine first iterates to find all + signs and converts them into spaces. Next, it searches for %XX where XX is the hexadecimal code for the ASCII value. The value is retrieved and converted from its hex value back into ASCII, using the *Chr$* Visual Basic function.

```
Public Sub ProcessCGI(Optional sCommand As Variant)
   SetParams ReadCGI(sCommand)
   SetCookies ReadCookieString()
End Sub
```

The *ProcessCGI* routine is used to process and decode the parameters and cookies and place them into the *cParameters* and *cCookies* collections, respectively. The *SetParams* routine is used to decode the parameters. It uses the command string if it determines the parameters by the server via the ISINDEX submission method (or when the system is being debugged using a command line interface). *ReadCGI* determines the submission method and returns the parameter string for parsing by the *SetParams* subroutine. Similarly, the *ReadCookieString* function returns the cookie string for parsing by the *SetCookies* subroutine.

```
Private Function RecursiveDelete(sVirtualCookies As String, _
sMatch As String, fPartialMatch As Boolean) As String

   If sMatch = sVirtualCookies Then
     RecursiveDelete = ""
     Exit Function
   End If
```

```
If fPartialMatch Then
  Select Case InStr(sVirtualCookies, sMatch)
    Case 0 ' partial match - couldn't find the string, _
        just exit!
      RecursiveDelete = sVirtualCookies
      Exit Function
    Case 1 ' found it at the beginning!
      If (InStr(sVirtualCookies, "&") < 1) Then ' no end,_
          i.e., this is it!
        RecursiveDelete = ""
        Exit Function
      End If
  End Select
Else ' should at least find the beginning of it, _
        otherwise, why waste the time?
  If InStr(sVirtualCookies, sMatch) = 0 Then
    RecursiveDelete = sVirtualCookies
  End If
End If

Dim iPos As Integer, sLeft As String, sRight As String
iPos = InStr(sVirtualCookies, "&")

' if here, must be a full match (case 1 handles this _
        otherwise!).
If (iPos < 1) Then
  RecursiveDelete = sVirtualCookies
  Exit Function
End If
sLeft = RecursiveDelete(Left$(sVirtualCookies, iPos - 1), _
        sMatch, fPartialMatch)
sRight = RecursiveDelete(Mid$(sVirtualCookies, iPos + 1), _
        sMatch, fPartialMatch)
If (sLeft = "") Then
  RecursiveDelete = sRight
ElseIf (sRight = "") Then
  RecursiveDelete = sLeft
Else
  RecursiveDelete = sLeft + "&" + sRight
End If
End Function
```

The *RecursiveDelete* function recursively searches for the *sMatch* string inside of *sVirtualCookies,* and removes it. If the routine can't locate the matched string, it returns the original string. If it finds the string at the beginning and there are no more parameters after that item, it returns an empty string.

This function then splits the string into two sections, each of which is searched recursively for the item. More accurately, the left side is either the item or another parameter, which will be returned; whereas the right side is recursively evaluated.

```
Private Sub SetCookies(ByVal request As String, Optional _
        fDeleteCookies As Variant)
  If (IsMissing(fDeleteCookies)) Then
    ClearCollection cCookies
  ElseIf fDeleteCookies Then
    ClearCollection cCookies
  End If


  ' skip trailing CR/LF (if there is one...)
  Do While (Len(request) > 0)
    If ((Right$(request, 1) = Chr$(13)) Or (Right$(request,_
          1) = Chr$(10))) Then
      request = Mid$(request, 1, Len(request) - 1)
    Else
      Exit Do
    End If
  Loop

  Dim iPos As Integer
  Do
    ' look for the first appearance of the= sign.
    iPos = InStr(request, "=")
    If (IsNull(iPos) Or iPos = 0) Then
      Exit Do
    End If

    Dim sName As String, sVal As String
    sName = Left$(request, iPos - 1)
    sVal = Mid$(request, iPos + 1)
```

```
    iPos = InStr(sVal, ";")
    If (IsNull(iPos) Or iPos = 0) Then
      request = ""
    Else
      sVal = Left$(sVal, iPos - 1)
      request = Trim$(Mid$(request, Len(sVal) + Len(sName) _
        + 3))
    End If

    ClearJunk sName
    ClearJunk sVal

    Dim entry As ParamType
    Set entry = New ParamType
    entry.Name = Trim$(sName)
    entry.Value = Trim$(sVal)

    On Error GoTo DuplicateKeyErr
    cCookies.Add Item:=entry, Key:=sName
    On Error GoTo 0

  Loop
  Exit Sub
DuplicateKeyErr:
  If Err.Number <> 457 Then Exit Sub ' serious error!
  cCookies.Add Item:=entry ' no key!
  Resume Next

End Sub
```

The *SetCookies* subroutine processes the cookie string and places
each entry into the *cCookies* collection. This subroutine first clears the
cCookies collection *if* the *fDeleteCookies* flag is true or missing. Next, it
removes any trailing carriage returns. The subroutine looks for the
equal sign, the left side of which is the name of the current cookie. A
semicolon or the end of the cookie string binds the value for the cookie. A new *ParamType* object is allocated, and the cookie is inserted into
the *cCookies* collection, using the name as the collection key. The
Microsoft and Netscape browsers are not supposed to support identically named cookies, but other browsers may support them — crash-
ing the application. Also, the cookie specification does not elaborate on

how identically named cookies for different, valid, domains should be handled. For this purpose, the duplicate key error is managed by inserting the cookie, with no key information, into the *cCookies* collection.

```
Private Sub SetParams(ByVal request As String, Optional _
              fDeleteParameters As Variant)
   ' delete params if they are missing
   If (IsMissing(fDeleteParameters)) Then
      ClearCollection cParameters
   ElseIf fDeleteParameters Then
      ClearCollection cParameters
   End If


   ' skip trailing CR/LF
   Do While (Len(request) > 0)
      If ((Right$(request, 1) = Chr$(13)) Or (Right$(request, _
             1) = Chr$(10))) Then
         request = Mid$(request, 1, Len(request) - 1)
      Else
         Exit Do
      End If
   Loop


   Dim iPos As Integer
   Do
      ' look for the first appearance of the= sign.
      iPos = InStr(request, "=")
      If (IsNull(iPos) Or iPos = 0) Then
         Exit Do
      End If

      Dim sName As String, sVal As String
      sName = Left$(request, iPos - 1)
      sVal = Mid$(request, iPos + 1)

      iPos = InStr(sVal, "&")
      If (IsNull(iPos) Or iPos = 0) Then
         request = ""
      Else
         sVal = Left$(sVal, iPos - 1)
         request = Mid$(request, Len(sVal) + Len(sName) + 3)
```

```
        End If

        ClearJunk sName
        ClearJunk sVal
        Dim entry As ParamType
        Set entry = New ParamType
        entry.Name = sName
        entry.Value = sVal
        ' ok duplicate names can reoccur, bypass them this way:
        On Error GoTo DuplicateKeyErr
        cParameters.Add Item:=entry, Key:=sName
        On Error GoTo 0

    Loop
    Exit Sub
DuplicateKeyErr:
    If Err.Number <> 457 Then Exit Sub ' serious error!
    cParameters.Add Item:=entry ' no key!
    Resume Next
End Sub
```

The *SetParams* subroutine handles and decodes parameters into the
cParameters collection. This subroutine first clears the *cParameters* collection *if* the *fDeleteParameters* flag is true or missing. Next, the trailing carriage return is removed. The browser adds this carriage return
when the user submits the form using the Enter button.

The subroutine looks for the equal sign, the left side of which is the
name of the current parameter. An ampersand or the end of the cookie string bounds the value for the parameter. A new *ParamType* object
is allocated, and the parameter is inserted into the *cParameters* collection, using the name as the collection key. Parameters can have identical
names, so the duplicate key error is managed by adding the parameter into the *cParameters* collection with no key value. The *ReadParam*
function uses the collection's key value, and will only retrieve the first
parameter with a given name. In order to read identically named parameters, the program must iterate through the *cParameters* collection.

```
Public Function ReadCookie(sCookie As String) As String
On Error GoTo ExitReadCookie ' probably wrong cookie
    ReadCookie = ""
```

```
    ReadCookie = cCookies(sCookie).Value
ExitReadCookie:
  Exit Function
End Function
```

The *ReadCookie* function locates the name of a cookie and retrieves the value for it. Since virtual cookies are converted into real cookies by the *ProcessVirtualCookies* subroutine, this function can also be used to retrieve virtual cookies. The function operates by using the collection's key (which is the name of the cookie) to quickly retrieve the cookie. This will only work *after* the *SetCookies* subroutine, which parses the cookie string and places the cookies into the *cCookies* collection. If the item is not found in the collection, an error occurs and a blank string is returned from the function. When using multiple items with the same name, the first is always retrieved with this function (identical names require the application to iterate through the items in *cCookies*).

```
Public Function ReadCookieString() As String
  ReadCookieString = Environ("HTTP_COOKIE")
End Function
```

The *ReadCookieString* returns the raw, unparsed cookie string.

```
Public Function ReadCGI(Optional sISINDEX As Variant) As _
          String
  Select Case Environ("REQUEST_METHOD")
    Case "GET", "PUT", "HEAD":
      ReadCGI = Environ("QUERY_STRING")
    Case "POST":
      ReadCGI = ReadPOST()
    Case Else: ' when everything else - debugging or ISINDEX!
      ' check if surrounded by quote marks (=run manually _
        from command line!).
      If (Not IsMissing(sISINDEX)) Then
        If (Len(sISINDEX) >= 2) Then
          sISINDEX = Trim$(sISINDEX)
          If (Left$(sISINDEX, 1) = """") And _
            (Right$(sISINDEX, 1) = """") Then
            sISINDEX = Mid$(sISINDEX, 2, Len(sISINDEX) - 2)
          End If
        End If
```

```
        End If

        ReadCGI = sISINDEX
    End Select
End Function
```

The *ReadCGI* function returns the raw parameter string. This function first determines the submission method, after which it retrieves the parameter list from the appropriate source.

The GET, PUT, and HEAD submission methods submit the parameter string via the QUERY_STRING environment variable.

The POST submission method utilizes the *ReadPost* method to retrieve parameters via the STDIN stream.

In all other cases, especially the ISINDEX submission method and when debugging, the function retrieves the information via the sISINDEX parameter (which is the command line passed on to the application). When running the application via command line, the parameters are enclosed in quotes. For that reason, these quotes are removed if detected.

```
Private Sub startCGI()
    If Not (fStartedCGI) Then
        If (Not fCommittedVirtual And (Len(sVirtualCookies) > _
                0) Or fModifiedVirtual) Then

            CommitVirtualCookies
        End If
        fStartedCGI = True
        WriteCGI "Content-type: text/html" + vbCrLf + vbCrLf + _
                + "<!-Piped through oCGI " + CStr(App.Major) + _
                "." + CStr(App.Minor) + "." + CStr(App.Revision)_
                + " by Ofer LaOr - oWare (all rights _
                reserved)->" + vbCrLf, False
    End If
End Sub
```

The *StartCGI* subroutine is called internally by the *WriteCGI* subroutine in order to place the initial HTTP tags and commit the virtual cookie strings. This subroutine first ascertains that it has not previously been executed. Next, it determines if the virtual cookies need to be committed. If so, the *CommitVirtualCookies* subroutine is called. The *fStartCGI* flag is turned on for future use. The HTTP content-type tag is sent, and the version information for the oCGI library imprinted into the STDOUT stream.

```
Public Sub WriteCookie(sName As String, sValue As String, _
          sDomain As String, Optional sPath As Variant, _
          Optional expires As Variant)

   Dim sCookie As String
   sCookie = "Set-Cookie: " + sName + "=" + sValue + ";"

   If Not IsMissing(sDomain) Then
     If (sDomain <> "") Then
       sCookie = sCookie + " domain=" + sDomain + ";"
     End If
   End If
   If Not IsMissing(sPath) Then
     If (sPath <> "") Then
       sCookie = sCookie + " path=" + sPath + ";"
     End If
   Else
     sCookie = sCookie + " path=/" + ";"
   End If
   If Not IsMissing(expires) Then
     sCookie = sCookie + " expires=" + Format(expires, _
           "dddd, dd-mmm-yyyy hh:mm:ss")
   End If
   WriteCGI sCookie + Chr$(10), False
End Sub
```

The *WriteCookie* subroutine writes a standard cookie out to the STDOUT stream. The routine should be called prior to any *WriteCGI* calls that cause the *StartCGI* to send the content-type HTTP tag out.

The subroutine sends out the cookie by using the Set-Cookie HTTP tag with the name and value of the cookie. Next, the domain for which the cookie will be sent is optionally specified. This can be the following:

the name of the current server (most popular) or a more general domain specification (for instance, ***.mydomain.com** will cause the cookie to be sent to all servers that match this domain specification).

The optional *sPath* parameter specifies the path underneath the domain for which the cookie will be sent. This can be the following: the name of the current script (most popular) or a more general path specification (/ will specify any application under the root, /scripts/ specifies all of the CGI application in the scripts directory).

The expiration date for the cookie is determined next, if it is specified in the function call, using the standard cookie date format.

Notes

When it is not specified, the cookie will persist for as long as the user is connected in a particular session (non-persistent cookies will not be saved to the user's disk drive)

```
Public Sub WriteVirtualCookie(sName As String, sValue As _
           String, Optional fNotUnique As Variant)

  ' first, find out if the cookie is already out there!
  Dim iPos As Integer, iEnd As Integer

  If (IsMissing(fNotUnique)) Then
    DeleteVirtualCookie sName
  ElseIf (Not fNotUnique) Then
    DeleteVirtualCookie sName
  Else
    DeleteVirtualCookie sName, sValue
  End If
  sVirtualCookies = sVirtualCookies + _
          IIf(Len(sVirtualCookies) = 0, "", "&") _
            + sName + "=" + sValue

  fModifiedVirtual = True
End Sub
```

The *WriteVirtualCookie* subroutine writes out a virtual cookie onto the virtual cookie string. If the cookie has a unique name, the *DeleteVirtualCookie* is used to make sure that there isn't another instance of it with another value somewhere else on the cookie string. The cookie name and value is appended to the end of the virtual cookie string. The *fModifiedVirtual* flag is turned on to make sure the virtual cookie string is committed.

```
Public Sub WriteCGI(sText As String, Optional fStartCGI As _
          Variant)
  Dim lWritten As Long, lReserved As Long
  Static hConsole As Long

  If (IsMissing(fStartCGI)) Then
    startCGI
  ElseIf (fStartCGI = True) Then
    startCGI
  End If

  lReserved = 0
  If hConsole = 0 Then
    hConsole = GetStdHandle(STD_OUTPUT_HANDLE)
  End If
  WriteFile hConsole, (sText), Len(sText), lWritten, _
          lReserved
End Sub
```

The *WriteCGI* subroutine allows the application to send information to the browser. This subroutine first determines if the StartCGI subroutine needs to be called to let the browser know what type of information it will be receiving (via the Content-type HTTP tag). Next, the standard handle for STDOUT is retrieved (unless it was retrieved successfully by a previous WriteCGI call). The *WriteFile* Win32 API function is used to send the *sText* parameter contents to the STDOUT stream.

```
Private Function ReadPOST() As String
  ' only works with POST!!!
  Static sText As String
  If (sText <> "") Then
    ReadPOST = sText
    Exit Function
  End If
```

```
      Dim lWritten As Long, lReserved As Long
      Dim hConsole As Long

      sText = Space(MaxPost)
      lReserved = 0
      If (hConsole = 0) Then
        hConsole = GetStdHandle(STD_INPUT_HANDLE)
      End If
      ReadFile hConsole, sText, Len(sText) - 1, lWritten, _
               lReserved
      sText = Trim$(sText)
      sText = Left$(sText, Len(sText) - 1) ` kill \0
      ReadPOST = sText
    End Function
```

The *ReadPOST* function is used by the system to retrieve the parameter string when the POST submission method is used. This is the most popular submission method and retrieves the information from the STDIN stream.

The function first determines if it was previously called, and returns the last string if it was. This prevents it from stalling if the ReadPost function is called more than once in an application utilizing the POST submission method.

The function next allocates space for sText (using *MaxPost* as the amount of pre-allocated space for the function) for the *ReadFile* API function call. The file handle for STDIN is retrieved and the input stream is read via the *ReadFile* Win32 API function. The returned string is trimmed and the trailing NULL character removed (because *ReadFile* is oriented towards C/C++ function calls, there will always be a trailing NULL character at the end of the string).

```
    Private Sub Class_Initialize()
      MaxPost = DEFAULT_MAX_POST
    End Sub
```

The oCGI class initializes the MaxPost parameter with the default maximum post value. This value can be modified at run time in order to allow bigger parameter strings to be passed on. This should be used in situations where a large number of parameters exist on the form, or where a particular edit box is expected to contain large amounts of text. Some browsers limit the parameters to 32,768 (32K) bytes.

Allocating large amounts of memory may slow the overall system performance significantly. This is especially true when many instances of the application are executed and the operating system must juggle large amounts of virtual memory.

Windows NT tends to slow to a crawl when doing this type of juggling, mostly at the expense of new processes (CGI applications fall under that category).

PERFORMANCE TUNING CGI APPLICATIONS

- Techniques of improving application speed
- Improving connection speed with SQL server
- SQL statement performance tuning

VISUAL BASIC DLLs

The first factor slowing down Visual Basic-based CGI applications is the Visual Basic DLLs. A compiled version of the CGI applications should always be rolled out. This will reduce the memory footprint for the application dramatically and so will improve the overall performance. In cases where the VB runtime is known to be running, p-code will actually load faster.

The application itself usually does not slow down the system if database access is optimal or minimal. The Visual Basic code profiler is a great tool in performance tuning the Visual Basic application. Since this profiler works best on non-user interface modules, it works from within the development environment and lets you determine which functions in the application take longer to execute. These can be optimized locally.

When doing processor-intensive operations that are not ideally performed by Visual Basic, it is generally a good idea to write those in other tools (e.g., Visual C++) and link to the CGI application via an OLE automation interface, or by declared external functions in the C++ DLL.

When accessing databases, database optimization on the queries is often a good idea. RDO, ADO, DBLIB and ODBC pass-through are all instrumental in greatly improving the performance of most queries.

These tools improve on standard DAO speeds when accessing client/server-based servers because they are closer, communication wise, to the server than standard DAO. The improvements can be drastic if queries are reused (e.g., static record-sets or global record-sets) or are prepared.

BLOBS should be avoided as much as possible due to their strain on network and memory resources.

SQL Server

When using client/server databases, stored procedures (utilizing Transact SQL or another form of server-based SQL-related language, depending on the type of server the application may be accessing) will dramatically improve performance if executed correctly.

It should be noted that most heavy queries are likely to run faster after an SQL specific optimization. It has been the author's experience that some queries that could take 30 hours to run can often be reduced, when optimized by a professional, to run in under 30 minutes. This, however, requires an experienced individual with an incredible knowledge of how the code optimizer on the server operates, and how to make it run faster. To date, I have only met just one such high-level professional.

SQL server is slowest when both client and server are running off of the same machine. When they are split up, the SQL server is dedicated to database activity and the web server(s) contains the CGI application that queries it.

Separating these two functions (n-tier system) can dramatically improve performance. A real data-intensive application can be optimized using a high-performance machine for the SQL server and a mid-level server for the web server. This often yields better results than does the highest-performance machine running both applications.

When using more than one machine for this task, the protocol between client and server is of paramount importance, directly affecting the ability of client and server to communicate with one another.

The protocol by which the SQL server and VB application work is often critical of the overall speed of the queries. Under different network topologies, different protocols may apply. When installing SQL server, the types of network protocols supported by SQL server can be specified (this can also be modified by executing SQL server's setup program). The TCP/IP network protocol, especially when communicating over routed network topologies, is often much slower than IPX. IPX, however, requires a more complex setup on both routers and database clients. Named pipes and multi-protocol communication tools are also somewhat slower than direct IPX connections.

IPX connections most often require a mediator to hold the service's name and MAC address. The "MAC address" is a unique number assigned to each network card and cannot (under normal circumstances) be duplicated. MAC addresses are used to uniquely identify a particular Network Interface Card (NIC).

Because of the existence of the mediator (typically a Novell server, but it can also be a Windows NT server with the appropriate service running), standard installations of the IPX connection method are not likely to work unless a Novell compatible server is on the network. The best way to overcome this problem, as well as improve the performance of the system, is to use a direct IPX connection. In this type of connection, the SQL client already knows the exact location of the SQL server on the network. This permits the application to forgo a mediator, which converts between server name and MAC address. Since the need for this mediator is gone, the effort involved in locating the server every time an SQL transaction executes is removed.

Both client and server must have the appropriate IPX protocol installed. The server must be able to answer IPX-based requests (via the supported network protocols dialog box). The client must specify that this particular server utilizes IPX, and the address for the server must also be specified. This is done via the SQL-Server Client

Configuration utility program. Figure B.1 shows the SQL-Server client configuration utility when setting up an IPX-based direct connection to a SQL server.

Figure B.1

SQL server client
configuration
dialog box

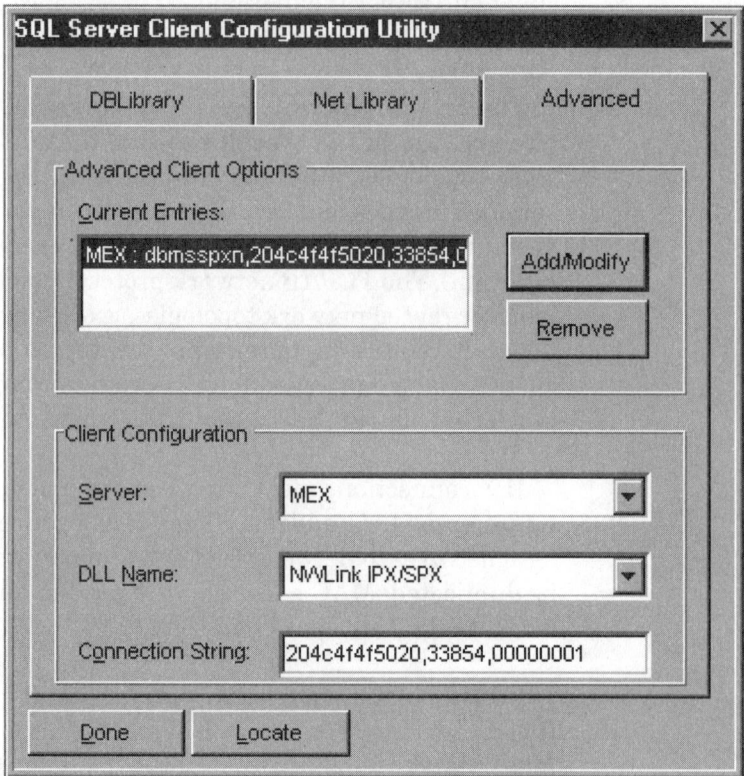

This utility allows every SQL server to be connected to the client in a different manner. The Server-Name is the same server name specified in the ODBC dialog box. The DLL name is the name of the protocol (this is only true for SQL server connections) by which the client communicates with the server. The connection string consists of three parts, separated by commas:

1. The first part is the MAC address for the SQL server being used. This number can be retrieved by executing the **IPXROUTE /CONFIG** command on the actual server.

2. The next part is the IPX socket number with which the client communicates with the server.

3. The last portion is the IPX network number for the server. The **IPXROUTE /CONFIG** command also retrieves this information. The number retrieved by IPXROUTE is, however, in hexadecimal form and must be typed in decimal form in the edit box (the Windows calculator utility can assist in the hexadecimal to decimal conversion). Windows NT often uses a clear (all zeros) IPX network and attempts to detect the network number on the fly. If no other entity on the network specifies the network number, all of the IPX clients will assume the IPX network 0. This will not work in this case, since the SQL server client configuration utility requires a valid IPX network. In such a scenario, the IPX network on the server should be changed to another number (1 is good, because it translates well between decimal and hexadecimal...). Figure B.2 shows how the Microsoft loopback adapter can be configured to test for a direct IPX connection locally.

Figure B.2

The Microsoft loopback adapter

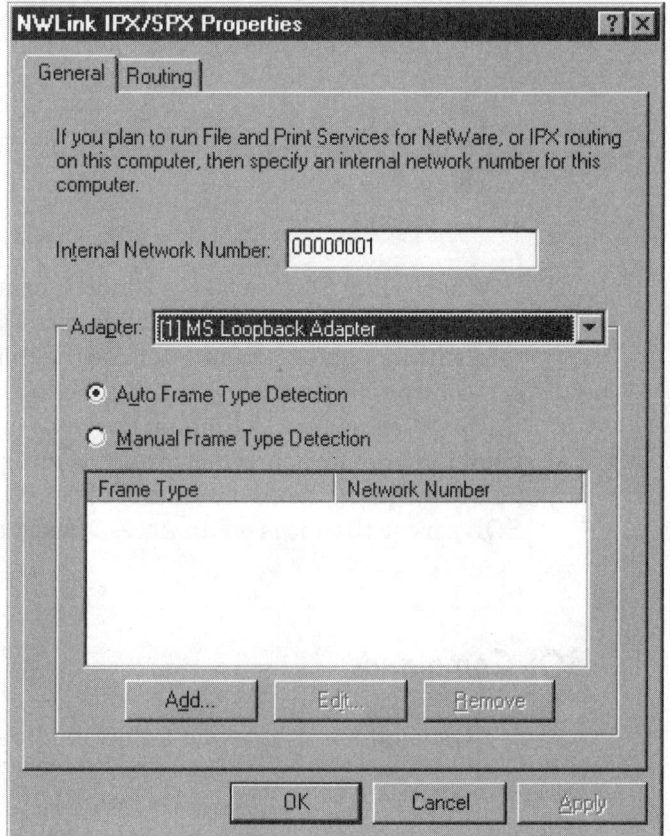

Utilizing transactions correctly also optimizes performance when inserting a massive number of records into the database, since disk access only occurs when the transaction is committed.

The application should limit the concurrent number of open queries to the absolute minimum needed. Each such connection requires some memory allocation on both the SQL client and SQL server (these are both the same if the SQL server runs on the same machine as the web server), resulting in a significant slow-down when the server starts to run out of memory. The server can slow down to a crawl if large amounts of memory are used, requiring it to utilize the swap file.

Long-running queries can kill server performance. When using Access databases, this often requires significant amounts of memory, leading to a complete machine slowdown due to disk swapping.

When running heavy queries on both LAN databases (e.g., Access) and database servers (e.g., SQL server), it is often a good idea to set a limit on the number of results that may be returned. This prevents a large database or an error in the where clause or in a join query causing thousands of rows to be returned — which would slow down the machine, due to memory usage and the CPU requirements of executing such a query.

When using SQL server, a timeout or an asynchronic query can be utilized, with a timeout that will insure the safe return to the application within a given amount of time. Keep in mind that the application can continue executing to infinity, while the user has already cancelled the browser request. A limit on the rows (via the TOP command) is also useful in stopping the query from running forever on an SQL server. A runaway query, however, is much less harmful when executed on an SQL server than it is on an Access-based database.

SQL Commands

SQL Commands to avoid for optimal performance:

- **OR** — The OR keyword often requires the server to forgo using indexes for some operations. The UNION keyword can often be used in place of OR to yield the same results, although they will be sorted differently. The UNION keyword uses two distinct, select statements to yield results — each of which can utilize indexes as needed.

- **LIKE** — The like keyword often requires the SQL optimizer to work hard determining if a row matches the condition or not. This can significantly slow down the query's results.

- **Complex WHERE clause** — Complex where clauses can usually be simplified or made to utilize other filtering techniques (e.g., sorting and dropping unneeded rows), which can improve performance.

- **Complex ORDER BY** — These types of clauses are often expensive with regard to the duration that the optimizer needs to lag on any particular row.

The memory footprint of query results can be minimized (thus optimizing performance) by selecting just the fields that are needed. Granted, select * is easier to create, but is often expensive memory-wise, particularly in inner/outer join queries.

Dynamic and Keyset type recordsets are usually significantly faster than snapshots. Snapshots actually read every single row in the result set, and require memory to maintain this information. Keysets maintain just the record's keys, querying the rest of the information on the fly. In addition, the entire query must take place *when* it is triggered, in order to prevent any changes. Large query results *all* have to be transmitted to the client *before* the query is complete; then the application can proceed. Keysets and Dyansets, on the other hand, can query a number of rows from the database, and when the application requests rows that haven't been reached yet, the query continues.

The complete recordset is committed to memory (i.e., the entire query runs to completion) if the application moves to the last row via the *MoveLast* function. For this reason, the number of rows returned by a query and maintained in a Dynaset or Keyset recordset cannot be determined until the last row has been reached. The query figures that not all of the items may be required, so it optimizes the output. Since this is not usually the case in *CGI applications* where all of the information usually needs to be determined, it is sometimes useful to commit the entire recordset to memory outright by using *MoveLast*.

Forward only recordsets tend to be faster than standard recordsets. They do, however, prevent the application from traversing the database backwards (as in the backward search application).

This type of recordset is usually the default for client/server systems. This is important to note, since the user may depend on the recordset's ability to go backwards, but may not be aware of this feature.

Whenever possible, long integer keys should be used, rather than text. Utilizing indexes on both keys and non-keys also dramatically improves search time in most scenarios. When working with integer keys, use these rather than textual descriptions to reference objects in the database.

For example, the long integer key for an item — rather than the item name — should be maintained on web forms. This lessens the amount of information required between browser and application, and optimizes later queries — when the application requires more information about the item (e.g., price).

The programmer should be aware of how inner- and outer-joins work under both "LAN" databases (Access) and client/server databases (Oracle, Microsoft SQL server, DB2, etc.). Sub-selects, in some situations, can produce the same results as joins, but significantly faster.

LAN-based databases often run more quickly on prepared SQL statements (by embedding them into the database and using the *QueryDef* objects to access a query's parameters).

SENDING OUT E-MAIL

- The SMTP protocol
- Creating a control in Visual Basic
- Using the WinSock control
- Low level Internet protocol with Visual Basic
- UDP and TCP sockets

CREATING AN SMTP-ENABLED PROGRAM

Among Microsoft's original plans for Visual Basic 5 were Netmanage's Internet control pack, containing support for all of the major Internet Protocols.

Microsoft finally backed away from this pack, which never lived passed beta. But Netmanage turned it into a considerable package, and is selling it as a third party add-on to Visual Basic.

Most of the Internet support left in Visual Basic was oriented towards the web, as well as towards support for FTP servers. Microsoft introduced the generic WinSock control, allowing Visual Basic applications to interact with any Internet protocol.

By doing this, Microsoft left the market wide open for Internet control packages from third party vendors. This market, in fact, has boomed in recent years and will continue to do so until Microsoft decides to integrate full Internet protocol support into Visual Basic.

Most of these control packages provide support for a variety of Internet protocols and specifications, including controls that perform telnet sessions, e-mail controls (both incoming – POP/IMAP, and outgoing SMTP), chat (IRC), newsgroup support (NNTP) and more.

Interestingly, I performed a search throughout the Internet and found it difficult to locate free e-mail sending solution for Visual Basic.

An *SMTP* (Simple Mail Transfer Protocol) control is important, because it allows applications to send e-mail to the outside world. Of course, this is the case for normal applications as well as CGI applications. Both types may require information to be sent to to a target user or a system manager.

In addition to providing some insight on how direct Internet protocols work in the real world, writing the SMTP control and support application provides some insight on how Visual Basic 5 can be used to write low-level Internet socket applications. The techniques are applicable to VB ActiveX controls as well as to documents and even standard VB applications.

While a commercial grade SMTP control would likely include support for file attachments (typically using MIME and/or UUECODING binary mail attachment specifications), this SMTP example will only demonstrate simple text transmission onto a mail server.

What are Sockets, Anyway?

The Internet utilizes TCP/IP as its basic communication protocol. This protocol defines two distinct types of packets (a "packet" being a small piece of data, transmitted from one computer on a network and received by another).

- **TCP** — This type of packet defines a direct connection between two points. Information sent via TCP is transmitted reliably. TCP is slower because it requires the sender to wait (albeit asynchronously, upon request) for an acknowledgment packet to arrive. A TCP packet will be sent over again if the Ack package is not received within a predetermined period of time.

- **UDP** — This type of packet may or may not arrive at the destination point. Packets sent out using UDP usually arrive much more quickly than TCP packets. The sender, however, cannot know whether the sent packet ever got to the destination point or not. Packets may not arrive in the order they were sent out. UDP packets are harder to track (sometimes impossible) behind firewalls and are avoided by most Internet applications. They are generally used to broadcast information to multiple recipients (as in video broadcast, multicasting or, most commonly — for *streaming* applications).

When using TCP packets, each Internet application employs *sockets*. A socket connects to other sockets across the Internet to transfer and receive information. Each socket has a numerical port value defined by the application it is used for. While the IP address is usually compared to a phone number, the port number can be compared to the extension, where the person you are calling is located.

The HTTP protocol typically uses port 80 for non-secure communication. This means that, in order for a browser to communicate with an HTTP server, it should use that socket port to initiate the protocol. After connecting with the server, both server and client can move to alternate sockets, if they wish to, allowing new sessions to be established with new partners on the original port.

The SMTP protocol takes place in socket port **25** (also known as the SMTP port).

Once a socket is connected on both ends, a virtual circuit forms between the two sides, at which point a protocol can take place. The protocol is usually based on the port and application being used.

The simplest Internet application, Telnet, merely places a user interface on top of the socket connection — allowing a user to directly communicate with the server on the other end. The Telnet server, on the other hand, can be very versatile, and provides the full functionality of the target server.

Telnet clients usually allow the user to specify a port other than the default (TELNET) port. This allows the user to communicate with other types of servers at will. A user can even retrieve information from the web (using the **GET HTTP** command) with a simple Telnet connection to port 80 of a target web server.

The SMTP Protocol

The *Simple Mail Transfer Protocol* (SMTP) is one of the simpler protocols on the Internet. The *RFC* (Request For Proposal – the document describing the entire breadth of a particular Internet protocol or format) for SMTP, number 821, defines several important commands:

HELO	Used to initiate a session
MAIL FROM	Used to define the properties of the user sending out the information
RCPT TO **RCPT CC**	Used to define the recipient(s) of the particular mail message
DATA	Used to initiate the flow of headers and, subsequently, the data
QUIT	Used to terminate the session

Every such command is followed by an appropriate response from the SMTP server receiving the information. The first portion of each such response is a three-digit number, followed by a text explanation of that number. This method of replying to each server command is typical in most Internet protocols (notably FTP and HTTP).

The most popular return value is **250**, which signifies that the last operation has completed and succeeded. For a complete list of return codes and SMTP commands, please refer to the RFC document, which can be found at:

`http://ds.internic.net/rfc/rfc821.txt`

SMTP Sessions

A typical SMTP session looks like this:

```
HELO MyDomain.com ↵
```

250 SMTP SERVER returns its own name, ID and version...

```
MAIL FROM:Me@myDomain.com ↵
```

250 OK...

```
RCPT TO:Him@hisDomain.com ↵
```

250 OK...

```
DATA ↵
```

354 Server instructions (typically: type CRLF.CRLF when you are done...).

```
From:My Real Name <Me@myDomain.com> ↵
Subject: This is a typical email ↵
Date: Sat, 1 April 2010 06:00:00 -0400 (EDT) ↵
Reply-To:Me@myDomain.com ↵
To: His Real Name <Him@hisDomain.com> ↵
X-Mailer:myOwnSMTP [version 1.1abc] ↵
↵
Dear Mr. Him, ↵
It has come to our attention that you would like to ↵
send out an email. By this time, you should be able to ↵
understand how this works. ↵
Signed, ↵
Me. ↵
↵
. ↵
```

250 Mail server confirms that the email is being sent out ...

```
QUIT ↵
```

-Session terminated-

The process starts with the application trying to send out an e-mail message. That application must first identify itself to the SMTP host. A domain must be used to identify which domain the sending computer belongs to. (This is rarely verified, so a dummy domain name may be used here.)

Next, the e-mail address for the user sending out the e-mail is identified in the MAIL command. This is not verified by the receiving SMTP server either (a "valid looking" e-mail address can be used here).

Next, a list of RCPT commands should be sent to identify the list of target e-mail addresses.

The DATA command identifies that the content of the e-mail message follows. The body of the message also contains some of the headers associated with the message. There have been vast improvements in e-mail clients since SMTP was first designed. Headers have been designed that allow the user to send out ever-more-enhanced information. This includes the e-mail subject, the real name and e-mail address of the sender and recipients (which is not allowed in the MAIL or RCPT commands). Additional information can be placed in headers, including the date the e-mail was sent, the type of mail application the sender is using, the format of the e-mail message (enhanced, MIME enabled, containing file attachments, or even using HTML for a rich text format), the priority for the e-mail, the need for a receipt, and so forth.

More Information about SMTP

SMTP is used by both servers and end-users to deliver messages. When an SMTP server encounters an e-mail message for a local user, it simply places it into that user's mailbox. When the mail server encounters an e-mail message meant for another server, it caches the message and subsequently contacts the real target server, using SMTP to deliver that message.

That being the case, the name of the mail server being used for the SMTP transaction should preferably be a local one. Since the connection between client and server is slow, whereas server-server communication is much quicker, utilizing a local e-mail server to send messages is the most efficient method. This is because both mail server and client are on the same local network, that of the ISP. Information from the e-mail session does not need to go through the entire Internet to get the appropriate mail server. The local mail server typically used for such transactions is named something like: `mail.myISP.com`.

It should be noted that the server receiving the e-mail message cannot verify the actual address specified in the "from header" or the "MAIL

FROM" section. This allows rogue applications to send mass mailings with no return address (the E-Junk we are all familiar with). Such e-mail messages *can* be tracked, however, through the IP trail left by the participating SMTP servers – which enables one to backtrack to the originator's IP address at the time he or she sent the message (in which case the ISP for that IP address can locate the person responsible for the "spam"). Sending spam is a big no-no in the Internet community, and this author particularly hates and denounces it.

Designing the oSMTP Control

The first stage in creating a Visual Basic control is to create a project. Once that's been done, the WinSock control must be added to the list of controls being used by the project.

This enables the oSMTP control to communicate with the SMTP server utilizing WinSock (Window's own version of Brekley sockets, the basic communication mechanism used to communicate over TCP networks).

The oSMTP control should have the following properties:

1. The source e-mail address;

2. A list of target e-mail addresses;

3. The e-mail subject;

4. The content of the message;

5. The name of the mail server used to deliver the e-mail message.

Since there may be a number of target e-mail addresses (both CC and TO), a collection can be used to remember all of those addresses. Any number of headers can also be added, and an additional collection will be used to hold the header entries.

These collections are cleared after every mail send in order to make way for new information (i.e., the next message). The data and subject entries are cleared after an e-mail is sent out, thus preventing old details from seeping into new e-mail messages.

The **target server** and **from address** are unlikely to change from one session to another. In fact, it is more than likely that the programmer will prefer to set these at design time. In order for this to work properly, the UserControl's *WriteProperties* and *ReadProperties* events must be used to save and load the settings for these two entries into the *sTargetHost* and *sFromAddress* variables.

The *TargetHost* and *FromAddress* property functions are simple "wrappers" around corresponding private variables. The LET property subroutines (LET routines permit the user to assign values to property via a function interface) for these two properties utilize the *PropertyChanged* function to notify the hosting environment (Visual Basic) that these properties should subsequently be saved.

The *AddCC* and *AddTo* functions simply insert their parameters into the *cCC* and *cTo* collections, respectively. This enables the control to retrieve each of the To and CC entries as needed.

The *AddHeader* function collects header information and places it into the *cHeader* collection. The name of the header and its content are concatenated and separated by a colon – just as they will be transmitted to the SMTP server.

The *SendMail* function begins by closing any existing sessions that may have previously been left open. Next, this function attempts to connect to the target host. Once a session has been verified, it sends the HELLO command and initiates the SMTP session.

The *CatchErr* function identifies incoming SMTP return codes and determines whether or not the remote host has sent an error message. This function is used after each command that causes the server to respond with a return code.

The **MAIL** command identifies the sending e-mail address (this address is used to send return e-mails, unless alternate **Reply-To** or **From** headers are used).

The **RCPT** command identifies the destination mailbox(es) for the server. The information for **RCPT** is retrieved from the *cTo* and *cCC* collections. Each entry in *cTo* and *cCC* causes a distinct RCPT command to be issued to the server.

The **DATA** command issues next, at which point the application sends out the headers, followed by the actual content of the e-mail message.

First, headers are retrieved from the *cHeaders* collection and sent out to the server. Once they have all been transmitted, a single CRLF (carriage-return character, followed by a line-feed character) separates the header from the actual contents of its e-mail message.

Next, the text content of the e-mail message is transmitted. The end of the message is marked by a CRLF, then a single dot and a final CRLF. This signifies to the server that the message has been sent out to it, in full. At this point, the message is cached and handled by the server. If the message is for a local mailbox, the e-mail is forwarded there; otherwise the server forwards the message to the target servers specified in the e-mail message.

Finally, the **QUIT** command is used to terminate the connection to the SMTP server. At this point, the socket connection is typically broken by the SMTP server, and a new connection must be established for new e-mail messages to be sent out. If a number of consecutive messages are to be sent out, the **QUIT** command should be used only *after* the final e-mail message has completed (this does not apply to this application).

The *CatchError* subroutine simply parses the number preceding the return codes from the remote host. In order to do so, it retrieves the first 3 characters from the return string and checks for one of the reconfigured numerical values. An empty string usually indicates a slow or overwhelmed server, or means that an erroneous command is still being processed by the server. When encountering an empty return string, the *CatchError* subroutine waits longer — allowing the previous transaction more time to complete.

The *Timing* subroutine is used by CatchError and allows the WinSock control some breathing room, the remote host time enough to process the information sent to it. In cases where incoming data should be handled, timing will stop before it times out when incoming data is encountered.

Error Handling

This sample of the oSMTP control uses a very primitive error handling routine. The *CatchErr* subroutine simply retrieves the left 3 characters from information retrieved by the WinSock control. Those characters are parsed and checked.

Valid return codes are 250, 354, 220. Other return-codes are rejected and generate an error. The *Err.Raise* call causes the error to be transferred back to the application using the oSMTP controls. Similarly, socket errors generate an error that is sent to the hosting application. Errors generated after the **QUIT** command is issued are ignored since the socket connection is likely to be broken.

The hosting application traps these errors using the **On Error** Visual Basic error trapping technique.

Source Code

Following is the source code for the SMTP control:

```
Option Explicit

Private Const ErrSource = "Ofer LaOr's SMTP control"
Private sLastSockErr As String
Private lLastSockErr As Long

Public Timeout As Integer

Private sTargetHost As String
Private sFromAddress As String

Private cTo As Collection
Private cCC As Collection

Private sData As String
Private sSubject As String

Private cHeaders As Collection
```

```
Private Declare Function GetTickCount Lib "kernel32" _
            () As Long

Private Sub ClearAll()
   ' initialize everything.

   Set cTo = New Collection
   Set cCC = New Collection
   Set cHeaders = New Collection
   sSubject = ""
   sData = ""
End Sub

Private Sub UserControl_Initialize()
   Timeout = 1000
   ClearAll
End Sub

Private Sub UserControl_Terminate()
   Set cTo = Nothing
   Set cCC = Nothing
   Set cHeaders = Nothing
End Sub


Public Property Get TargetHost() As Variant
   TargetHost = sTargetHost
End Property

Public Property Let TargetHost(ByVal vNewValue As Variant)
   sTargetHost = vNewValue
   PropertyChanged
End Property

' the control should be 25 pixels by 25 pixels wide.
Private Sub UserControl_Resize()
   If (UserControl.Width<> (25 * Screen.TwipsPerPixelX))_
            Then

      UserControl.Width = 25 * Screen.TwipsPerPixelX
   End If
```

```vb
        If (UserControl.Height <> (25 * _
                Screen.TwipsPerPixelY)) Then

            UserControl.Height = 25 * Screen.TwipsPerPixelY
        End If
End Sub

Private Sub UserControl_ReadProperties(PropBag As _
                PropertyBag)

    sTargetHost = PropBag.ReadProperty("TargetHost", "")
    sFromAddress = PropBag.ReadProperty("FromAddress", "")
End Sub

Private Sub UserControl_WriteProperties(PropBag As _
                PropertyBag)

    PropBag.WriteProperty "TargetHost", sTargetHost, ""
    PropBag.WriteProperty "FromAddress", sFromAddress, ""
End Sub

Public Property Get FromAddress() As Variant
    FromAddress = sFromAddress
End Property

Public Property Let FromAddress(ByVal vNewValue As Variant)

    sFromAddress = vNewValue
    PropertyChanged
End Property

Public Property Get Subject() As Variant
    Subject = sSubject
End Property

Public Property Let Subject(ByVal vNewValue As Variant)
    sSubject = vNewValue
End Property

Public Property Get Data() As Variant
    Data = sData
```

```
            End Property

            Public Property Let Data(ByVal vNewValue As Variant)
              sData = vNewValue
            End Property

            Public Sub AddTo(ByVal sTo As String)
              cTo.Add sTo
            End Sub
            Public Sub AddCC(ByVal sCC As String)
              cCC.Add sCC
            End Sub

            Public Sub AddHeader(ByVal sSubject As String, _
                    ByVal sContent As String)

              cHeaders.Add CStr(sSubject + ": " + sContent)
            End Sub

            ' initiate the SMTP protocol.
            Public Sub SendMail()
              With winSockMail
                If (.State <> sckOpen And .State <> sckConnected)_
                    Then
                  .Close
                End If

                If (.RemoteHost <> sTargetHost Or .State = _
                    sckClosed) Then

                  .RemoteHost = sTargetHost
                  .RemotePort = 25
                  .LocalPort = 0
                  .Connect
                End If

                Do While True
                  DoEvents
                  Select Case .State
                    Case 9:
                        Err.Raise lLastSockErr, "WinSock", _
```

```
            sLastSockErr
            Exit Sub
         Case 7:
            Exit Do
   End Select
Loop


.SendData "HELO MyDomain.com" + vbCrLf
Timing
CatchErr
.SendData "MAIL FROM:" + sFromAddress + vbCrLf
CatchErr

Dim vItem As Variant
For Each vItem In cTo
   .SendData "RCPT TO:" + CStr(vItem) + vbCrLf
   CatchErr
Next
For Each vItem In cCC
   .SendData "RCPT CC:" + CStr(vItem) + vbCrLf
   CatchErr
Next
Timing True
.SendData "DATA" + vbCrLf
CatchErr True
.SendData "Subject: " + sSubject + vbCrLf
For Each vItem In cHeaders
   .SendData CStr(vItem) + vbCrLf
Next

' separate between headers and DATA!
.SendData vbCrLf
.SendData sData

' second dot is precautionary.
.SendData vbCrLf + "." + vbCrLf + "." + vbCrLf
CatchErr True
.SendData "QUIT" + vbCrLf
Timing True
Dim sClosingConnectionMessage As String
On Error Resume Next
```

```
            .GetData sClosingConnectionMessage

        End With
        ClearAll
    End Sub

' check for return errors.
Private Sub CatchErr(Optional fIgnoreInput As Boolean)
    Dim strData As String, nTries As Integer
    nTries = 0

    Timing fIgnoreInput
    winSockMail.GetData strData, vbString
    Debug.Print strData
    Do
        Select Case Left$(strData, 3)
            Case "250", "354", "220"
                ' no problems
                Exit Do
            Case ""
                ' no response, perform two more timing.
                ' if this was an error, let the next
                ' CatchErr call catch it.

                Timing fIgnoreInput
                If (fIgnoreInput) Then Exit Do
                If (nTries > 5) Then Exit Do
            Case Else:
                ClearAll
                winSockMail.SendData "QUIT" + vbCrLf
                winSockMail.Close
                Err.Raise CInt(Left$(strData, 3)), _
                    ErrSource, strData
        End Select
        nTries = nTries + 1
    Loop
End Sub

' delay the system for a while.
Private Sub Timing(Optional fIgnoreInput As Boolean)
    Dim lTimer As Long
```

```
            lTimer = GetTickCount()
            Do While (1)
              DoEvents
              If (GetTickCount() - lTimer) > Timeout Then _
                    Exit Sub

              If Not fIgnoreInput Then
                Dim strData As String
                winSockMail.PeekData strData
                If Len(strData) > 0 Then Exit Do
              End If
            Loop
         End Sub

         Private Sub winSockMail_Error(ByVal Number As Integer, _
                 Description As String, ByVal Scode As Long, _
                    ByVal Source As String, ByVal HelpFile As _
                       String, ByVal HelpContext As Long, _
                          CancelDisplay As Boolean)

            lLastSockErr = Number
            sLastSockErr = Description
         End Sub
```

Samples

Figure C.1
E-mail received using
oSMTP control

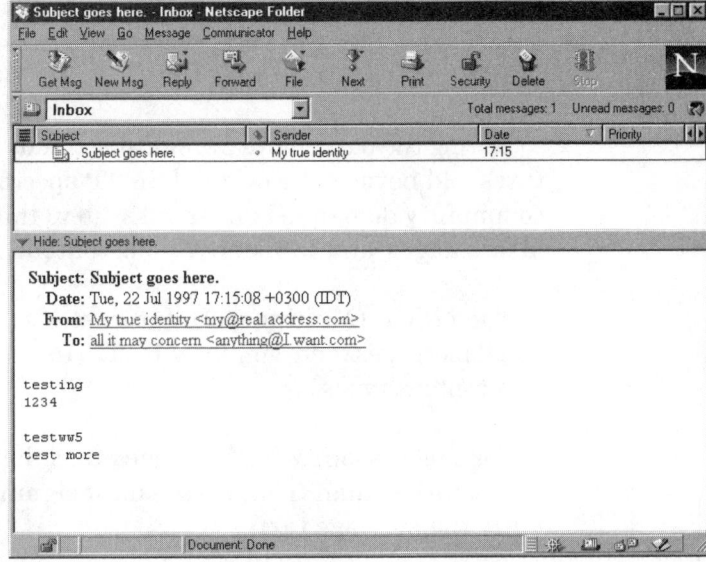

Figure C.2
The application that
sent the e-mail
message with
parameters

File Attachments, MIME and UUencoding

SMTP servers were originally used to transfer pure ASCII text content only. Some older SMTP servers still transfer mail content as 7-bits (ASCII text requires just 7 bits).

During the past few years, industry trends had raised the requirement threshold beyond the original SMTP specifications. The new Internet community demanded an e-mail system that could work across several languages, and transfer various content types in a flexible manner.

The *MIME* (Multipurpose Internet Mail Extension) format allows email messages (and, similarly, HTTP) to transfer multimedia and other rich content types.

For this reason, MIME assumes that the mail server will maintain 8-bits, rather than truncate the most significant bit from each character in the message text.

In most cases, SMTP servers do not truncate the most significant bit any more, and most mail clients today fully support MIME.

The MIME extension for e-mail identifies MIME types (e.g., image/GIF) and also separates the e-mail message into several sections, each containing its own distinct MIME type.

Each such section can contain content such as zip files, rich text or any other file attachments. The **MIME-Version** SMTP-header identifies to the e-mail client that the message contains MIME content.

A simple text usually contains the following MIME content header:

```
Content-Type: text/plain; charset="us-ascii"
Content-Transfer-Encoding: 7bit
```

A zip file attached to an e-mail will have the following MIME content header:

```
Content-Type: application/x-zip-compressed; name="myfile.zip"
Content-Transfer-Encoding: base64
```

Base64 is one method of sending out binary information through MIME. Standard 8-bits are not always valid for entering directly into the SMTP stream for several reasons. Most importantly, the normal flow of binary information might contain a CR/LF combination with a single dot, and another CR/LF. This would cause the server to assume that the mail message had completed, and the server would terminate the session prematurely, effectively cutting off a significant portion of the information.

Most e-mail packages use MIME as the default method of sending e-mail, along with support of other, similar techniques for sending file attachments — such as UUencoding.

MIME content can also specify a character-set, providing full internationalization of characters within e-mail messages. For example, an e-mail written in Greek will show up in Greek in a target e-mail client, if both e-mail applications supported MIME *and* the Greek character set.

UUencoding is a technique for sending and receiving binary information over a 7-bit encoding scheme. UUencoding is the name of a technique for converting 8-bit information into 7-bits. This information is easily transferrable over all SMTP servers and platforms.

Once information reaches its target, the end user receives the UUencoded information, and can use the UUdecoding technique to convert it back into its original form. This technique usually adds 13% more data (1/8 of the data) to the e-mail message.

UUencoding has an added bonus: since the message is pure text, any e-mail package — even one that does not support file attachments — can be used to retrieve the email. After retrieving it, an external UUdecoding utility can transfer the text back into binary format. Similarly, a UUencoding utility can transmit file information using a 7-bit, text only, e-mail package that does not support file attachments.

FILES AND LIBRARIES REQUIRED BY VISUAL BASIC

Files to Watch Out For (Should be Present in all Situations)

- MSVCRT20.DLL
- MSVCRT40.DLL

VB4 — No Database Access

- * OCGI2.DLL
- * OLEPRO32.DLL — note Office 97/VB5 version difference §
- VB40032.DLL

VB4 — Using DAO 3.0 Database Access

- * DAO3032.DLL
- MSJINT32.DLL
- MSJT3032.DLL
- MSJTER32.DLL
- * OCGI2.DLL
- * OLEPRO32.DLL — note Office 97/VB5 version difference §
- VB40032.DLL

VB5 — No Database Access (compiled or using PCode)

- OCGI2.DLL
- OLEPRO32.DLL — note Office 97/VB5 version difference
- MSVBVM50.DLL

VB5 — Using DAO 3.5 Database Access

- * OCGI2.DLL
- * OLEPRO32.DLL — note Office 97/VB5 version difference
- MSVBVM50.DLL
- MSJET35.DLL
- * DAO350.DLL

* Files marked with an asterisk contain ActiveX objects and must be registered (by running regsvr32.exe).

The MSVCRT.DLL file may also be needed as well as MFC42.DLL should some VC++S OLE objects be included in the project.

In situations where an application fails due to a "429 error" (ActiveX library or object missing or cannot be initialized), it is probably the result of a version problem in one of these files or some of these files could be missing altogether.

In cases where other OCXs are used, registration errors could occur **during** the show or load methods for the form containing these OCXs.

When using external ActiveX libraries contained in DLLs and EXEs, the programmer should be aware that these must be registered prior to first use, or a 429 error will occur. In executables, the out-of-process application must be run at least once-in-order to register the ActiveX objects embedded in it. In DLLs, objects should be registered by running RegSvr32 or an equivalent operation (for instance, calling the *OLERegisterServer* function).

Microsoft's RegClean utility is also handy. It clears out invalid entries from the registry, allowing it to maintain validity.

§ Note: Office 97 and Visual Basic 5.0 come with a new OLEPRO32.DLL file that overwrites previous versions. This new file, holding version 5.X, requires different support mechanisms than the original file which comes with Visual Basic 4.0 (OLEPRO32.DLL version 4.X). A 5.X file will not work if it does not have the correct support files and will not register either — resulting in a complete application failure. If you encounter a situation like this, simply remove the offending file and replace it with the original that comes on the Visual Basic 4.0 CD.

APPENDIX **E**

RESOURCES

Web Resources

Http://www.cgi-resources.com

Excellent resource for CGI related information.

Http://www.w3.org
Contains general information about upcoming technologies, specifications for all network protocols and information about HTTP, HTML, CGI, graphic formats, as well as other important information.

Http://hoohoo.ncsa.uiuc.edu/cgi/env.html
Information about CGI environment variables

Http://www.w3.org/pub/WWW/Protocols/HTTP/Forum/
Forums for CGI/HTTP related subjects

Http://www.apache.org/
The best free public web server in existence

Http://www.w3.org/pub/WWW/OOP
Objects on the web, distributed object technology

Http://www.fastcgi.com/
The next generation of CGI? Possibly! Hopefully!

`Http://www.w3.org/pub/WWW/CGI`

CGI related documents from the World Wide Web Consortium

`Http://www.ecma.ch`

A European standards committee involved in the standardization of JavaScript

Visual Basic Resources

`Http://www.microsoft.com/Vbasic`

Most recent information concerning the language, from the people who created it

`Http://www.inquiry.com/Thevbpro`

Contains excellent information and updates; also a great forum for communicating with others

`Http://www.adviser.com`

The Visual Basic / Access advisor web site

`Http://www.vbonline.com/vb-mag`

Great online articles about Visual Basic.

Index

About the Author

Ofer LaOr (K. Bialik, Israel) has been a computer professional for over 12 years. He currently holds degrees in both Electronics and computer science. Ofer has been a C/C++ programmer for over nine years.

Ofer has been working primarily with Visual Basic during the past three years as a software consultant and technical director for Sophtech, a Los Angeles based consulting firm. During that period Ofer had been a driving force in the creation of several web sites including doing the majority of programming for the acclaimed *www.sounddogs.com* web site.

Ofer specializes in Client/Server development, real-time communication and image processing. He is participating in the creation of a new startup company, specializing in image processing for industrial vertical applications.

SOFTWARE AND INFORMATION LICENSE

The software and information on this diskette (collectively referred to as the "Product") are the property of The McGraw-Hill Companies, Inc. ("McGraw-Hill") and are protected by both United States copyright law and international copyright treaty provision. You must treat this Product just like a book, except that you may copy it into a computer to be used and you may make archival copies of the Products for the sole purpose of backing up our software and protecting your investment from loss.

By saying "just like a book," McGraw-Hill means, for example, that the Product may be used by any number of people and may be freely moved from one computer location to another, so long as there is no possibility of the Product (or any part of the Product) being used at one location or on one computer while it is being used at another. Just as a book cannot be read by two different people in two different places at the same time, neither can the Product be used by two different people in two different places at the same time (unless, of course, McGraw-Hill's rights are being violated).

McGraw-Hill reserves the right to alter or modify the contents of the Product at any time.

This agreement is effective until terminated. The Agreement will terminate automatically without notice if you fail to comply with any provisions of this Agreement. In the event of termination by reason of your breach, you will destroy or erase all copies of the Product installed on any computer system or made for backup purposes and shall expunge the Product from your data storage facilities.

LIMITED WARRANTY

McGraw-Hill warrants the physical diskette(s) enclosed herein to be free of defects in materials and workmanship for a period of sixty days from the purchase date. If McGraw-Hill receives written notification within the warranty period of defects in materials or workmanship, and such notification is determined by McGraw-Hill to be correct, McGraw-Hill will replace the defective diskette(s). Send request to:

Customer Service
McGraw-Hill
Gahanna Industrial Park
860 Taylor Station Road
Blacklick, OH 43004-9615

The entire and exclusive liability and remedy for breach of this Limited Warranty shall be limited to replacement of defective diskette(s) and shall not include or extend to any claim for or right to cover any other damages, including but not limited to, loss of profit, data, or use of the software, or special, incidental, or consequential damages or other similar claims, even if McGraw-Hill has been specifically advised as to the possibility of such damages. In no event will McGraw-Hill's liability for any damages to you or any other person ever exceed the lower of suggested list price or actual price paid for the license to use the Product, regardless of any form of the claim.

THE McGRAW-HILL COMPANIES, INC. SPECIFICALLY DISCLAIMS ALL OTHER WARRANTIES, EXPRESS OR IMPLIED, INCLUDING BUT NOT LIMITED TO, ANY IMPLIED WARRANTY OF MERCHANTABILITY OR FITNESS FOR A PARTICULAR PURPOSE. Specifically, McGraw-Hill makes no representation or warranty that the Product is fit for any particular purpose and any implied warranty of merchantability is limited to the sixty day duration of the Limited Warranty covering the physical diskette(s) only (and not the software or information) and is otherwise expressly and specifically disclaimed.

This Limited Warranty gives you specific legal rights; you may have others which may vary from state to state. Some states do not allow the exclusion of incidental or consequential damages, or the limitation on how long an implied warranty lasts, so some of the above may not apply to you.

This Agreement constitutes the entire agreement between the parties relating to use of the Product. The terms of any purchase order shall have no effect on the terms of this Agreement. Failure of McGraw-Hill to insist at any time on strict compliance with this Agreement shall not constitute a waiver of any rights under this Agreement. This Agreement shall be construed and governed in accordance with the laws of New York. If any provision of this Agreement is held to be contrary to law, that provision will be enforced to the maximum extent permissible and the remaining provisions will remain in force and effect.